THE MYSTICAL ELEMENT IN
HEIDEGGER'S THOUGHT

THE MYSTICAL ELEMENT IN HEIDEGGER'S THOUGHT

Jᴏʜɴ **D.** Cᴀᴘᴜᴛᴏ

New York
Fordham University Press
1986

Printed in the United States of America

To Kathy, who knows that
love is without why.

My heart could receive God
if only it chose
to turn toward the Light
as does the rose.

— Angelus Silesius

CONTENTS

ACKNOWLEDGMENTS

THIS book is an outgrowth of an article entitled "Meister Eckhart and the Later Heidegger: The Mystical Element in Heidegger's Thought," published in two parts, copyright 1974 and 1975 by *The Journal of the History of Philosophy*, Vol. XII, No. 4, October, 1974, 479-94, and Vol. XIII, No. 1, January, 1975, 61-80, sections of which were used here by permission of the Editor, Richard Popkin. I would also like to thank Fr. Robert Lechner, Editor of *Philosophy Today*, for permission to use an excerpt from my "The Rose Is Without Why," which was published in Vol. 15, Spring, 1971, 3-15. Finally I thank Ms. Nancy Simco of the *Southern Journal of Philosophy* for permission to include a part of my "The Principle of Sufficient Reason: A Study of a Heideggerian Self-Criticism," which first appeared in Vol. XIII, Winter, 1975, 419-26, of that journal.

I wish to thank Harper & Row, Publishers, for permission to quote from the English translations of the works of Martin Heidegger which they have published.

The verse from Angelus Silesius which appears at the beginning of this book is translated by Frederick Franck, *The Book of Angelus Silesius* (New York: Knopf, 1976).

I am indebted to the American Council of Learned Societies for a Summer, 1972, Grant-in-Aid which made it possible for me to make a beginning in researching the present book.

My almost daily dialogue with my colleague Thomas Busch has been of substantial help to me in giving sharpness and definition to my ideas about Heidegger.

For the typing of the original version of this manuscript I am very grateful to Barbara Ann Zeoli, and for the typing of the revisions to Mrs. Susan Cody and Mrs. Sandy Shupard. I wish to thank, too, the Reverend Richard Breslin, O.S.A., Dean of our college, for deferring the costs associated with the typing.

ACKNOWLEDGMENTS

It is a great pleasure to publicly acknowledge the help of Professor J. Glenn Gray of Colorado College in the writing of this book. He has been a source of encouragement and good advice from the beginning of this project. His confidence in the merits of my approach to Heidegger gave me the courage to believe my own ideas. I heartily thank too Professor J. L. Mehta, Visiting Professor at the School of Divinity of Harvard University, himself the author of one of the truly outstanding books on Heidegger in any language, for the warm support he has lent the present undertaking. I am also grateful to Professor James Collins of St. Louis University who early on took an interest in this project and who has also helped it see the light of day. While the responsibility for this interpretation of Heidegger must rest with me, I am deeply grateful for the help these gracious and distinguished scholars have given me, without which this book would not have been possible.

Finally, I most of all am indebted to my wife, Kathy, whose support of and patience with my work has made a "clearing" in which it was possible for me to work many uninterrupted hours. And I am very grateful to her, too, for the illustration on the cover of the Fordham edition, and for her calligraphy of the verse from Angelus Silesius.

Drexel Hill, Pennsylvania

LIST OF ABBREVIATIONS OF WORKS
USED IN THIS STUDY

Note: References to the works of Heidegger and Eckhart will use the following abbreviations. All references will include a cross reference to the English translation, where such exists. Thus HB, 53/192 indicates that we are quoting p. 53 of the German edition of Heidegger's *Humanismusbrief* listed below, a translation of which is found on p. 192 of the English translation listed beneath it. So too Q, 180,5-6/ Bl., 126 means that we are quoting Quint's modernized German version of Eckhart's treatises and sermons, p. 180, lines 5-6, an English translation of which is provided by Blakney, p. 126. By consulting these translations the reader will see for himself where we have adopted the translation entirely, adapted it to our own translation, merely consulted it, or even translated the text quite differently. In the case of Meister Eckhart, we will usually cite Quint's authoritative modernization of the Middle High German text.

I. HEIDEGGER

AED   *Aus der Erfahrung des Denkens*. 2. Auflage. Pfullingen: Verlag Günther Neske, 1965.
         "The Thinker as Poet." In Martin Heidegger, *Poetry, Language and Thought*. Trans. A. Hofstadter. New York: Harper & Row, 1971. Pp. 1-14.

EHD   *Erläuterungen zu Hölderlins Dichtung.* 3. Auflage. Frankfurt am Main: Vittorio Klostermann, 1963.

pp. 7-30   "Remembrance of the Poet." Trans. D. Scott. In *Existence and Being.* Ed. Werner Brock. Chicago: Regnery Co., 1949. Pp. 243-69.

pp. 31-46   "Hölderlin and the Essence of Poetry." Trans. D. Scott. In *Existence and Being.* Pp. 270-91.

EM   *Einführung in die Metaphysik.* 2. Auflage. Tübingen: Max Niemeyer, 1958.

    An Introduction to Metaphysics. Trans. R. Manheim. Garden City, N. Y.: Doubleday Anchor Books, 1961.

FND   *Die Frage nach dem Ding.* Tübingen: Max Niemeyer, 1962.

    What is a Thing? Trans. W. B. Barton, Jr. and V. Deutsch. Chicago: Regnery Co., 1967.

FS   *Frühe Schriften.* Frankfurt: Vittorio Klostermann, 1972.

FW   *Der Feldweg.* 3. Auflage. Frankfurt: Vittorio Klosterman, 1962.

    "The Pathway." Trans. T. F. O'Meara, O.P. and T. Sheehan. *Listening* VIII (1973), pp. 32-9.

G   *Gelassenheit.* 2. Auflage. Pfullingen: Verlag Günther Neske, 1960.

    Discourse on Thinking. Trans. J. M. Anderson and E. H. Freund. New York: Harper & Row, 1966.

HB   *Ein Brief über den "Humanismus" in Platons Lehre von der Wahrheit. Mit einem Brief über den "Humanismus."* 2. Auflage. Bern, Switzerland: A. Francke Verlag, 1954.

    "Letter on Humanism." Trans. E. Lohner. In *Philosophy in the Twentieth Century.* Eds. W. Barrett and H. Aiken. Vol. 3 *Contemporary European Thought.* New York: Harper & Row, 1971. Pp. 192-224.

Hw   *Holzwege.* 4. Auflage. Frankfurt am Main: Vittorio Klostermann, 1963.

pp. 7-68   "The Origin of the Work of Art." In Martin Heidegger, *Poetry Language and Thought.* Trans. A. Hofstadter. New York: Harper & Row, 1971. Pp. 15-87.

pp. 69-104   "The Age of the World View." Trans. M. Grene. *Boundary 2: A Journal of Postmodern Literature,* IV, no. 2 (Winter, 1976), 341-55.

pp. 105-92   *Hegel's Concept of Experience.* New York: Harper & Row, 1970.

pp. 248-95   "What are Poets For?" In *Poetry, Language and Thought.* Trans. A. Hofstadter. Pp. 91-142.

xii

pp. 296-343	"The Anaximander Fragment." In: *Early Greek Thinking*. Trans. D. Krell and F. Capuzzi. New York: Harper & Row, 1975. Pp. 13-58.
ID	*Identity and Difference*. Trans. J. Stambaugh. New York: Harper & Row, 1969. The German text, *Identität und Differenz*, appears in the Appendix.
K	*Die Technik und die Kehre*. Pfullingen: Verlag Günther Neske, 1962.
pp. 37-47	"The Turning." Trans. K. R. Maly. In *Research in Phenomenology*, I (1971), 3-16.
KPM	*Kant und das Problem der Metaphysik*. 3. Auflage. Frankfurt am Main: Vittorio Klostermann, 1965.
	Kant and the Problem of Metaphysics. Trans. J. S. Churchhill. Bloomington, Ind.: Indiana University Press, 1962.
N I, N II	*Nietzsche*. Zwei Bände. 1. Auflage. Pfullingen: Verlag Günther Neske, 1961.
N II, 399-490	*The End of Philosophy*. Trans. J. Stambaugh. New York: Harper & Row, 1973. Pp. 1-83.
PLW	*Platons Lehre von der Wahrheit* in *Platons Lehre von der Wahrheit. Mit einem Brief über den "Humanismus."* 2. Auflage. Bern, Switzerland: A. Francke Verlag, 1954.
	"Plato's Doctrine of Truth." Trans. J. Barlow. In *Philosophy in the Twentieth Century*. Ed. W. Barrett and H. Aiken. Vol. 3. *Contemporary European Thought*. New York: Harper & Row, 1971. Pp. 251-71.
SD	*Zur Sache des Denkens*. Tübingen: Max Niemeyer, 1969.
	On Time and Being. Trans. J. Stambaugh. New York: Harper & Row, 1972.
SF	*The Question of Being*. Trans. W. Kluback and J. T. Wilde. Bilingual Edition containing the text of *Zur Seinsfrage*. London: Vision Press, 1959.
SG	*Der Satz vom Grund*. 3. Auflage. Pfullingen: Verlag Günther Neske, 1965.
pp. 191-211	"The Principle of Ground." Trans. K. Hoeller. *Man and World* VII (1974). Pp. 207-22.
Sp	"Nur noch ein Gott kann uns retten." *Spiegel*-Gespräch mit Martin Heidegger am 23. September 1966. *Der Spiegel* (Hamburg), Nr. 26, May 31, 1976. Pp. 193 ff.
	"Only a God Can Save Us: *Der Spiegel*'s Interview with Martin Heidegger." Trans. M. P. Alter and J. D. Caputo. *Philosophy Today* 20, no. 4 (Winter, 1976). Pp. 267-84.
SZ	*Sein und Zeit*. 10. Auflage. Tübingen: Max Niemeyer, 1963.

Being and Time. Trans. J. Macquarrie and E. Robinson. New York: Harper & Row, 1962.

US   *Unterwegs zur Sprache*. 3. Auflage. Pfullingen: Verlag Günther Neske, 1965.

pp. 9-33   "Language." In *Poetry, Language and Thought*. Trans. A. Hofstadter. Pp. 189-210.

pp. 35 ff.   *On the Way to Language*. Trans. P. D. Hertz. New York: Harper & Row, 1971.

VA   *Vorträge und Aufsätze*. 2. Auflage. Pfullingen: Verlag Günther Neske, 1959.

pp. 71-99   "Overcoming Metaphysics." In *The End of Philosophy*. Trans. J. Stambaugh. Pp. 84-110.

pp. 101-126   "Who is Nietzsche's Zarathustra." Trans. Bernd Magnus. In *Review of Metaphysics*, XX (March, 1967), 411-31.

pp. 145-62   "Building Dwelling Thinking." In *Poetry, Language and Thought*. Trans. A. Hofstadter. Pp. 143-61.

pp. 163-85   "The Thing." In *Poetry, Language and Thought*. Trans. A. Hofstadter. Pp. 163-82.

pp. 187-204   ". . . Poetically Man Dwells . . ." In *Poetry, Language and Thought*. Trans. A. Hofstadter. Pp. 211-29.

pp. 207 ff.   "Logos." "Moira." "Aletheia." In: *Early Greek Thinking*. Pp. 59 ff.

WdP   *What is Philosophy?* Trans. W. Kluback and J. T. Wilde. Bilingual Edition containing the text of *Was ist das—die Philosophie?* London: Vision Press, 1962.

WG   *The Essence of Reasons*. A Bilingual Edition containing the text of *Vom Wesen des Grundes*. Trans. T. Malick. Northwestern University Studies in Phenomenology and Existential Philosophy. Evanston, 1969.

WHD   *Was heisst Denken?* 2. Auflage. Tübingen: Max Niemeyer, 1961.

What is Called Thinking? Trans. J. G. Gray and F. T. Wieck. New York: Harper & Row, 1968.

WM   *Was ist Metaphysik?* 9. Auflage. Frankfurt am Main: Vittorio Klostermann, 1965.

pp. 7-23   "The Way Back into the Ground of Metaphysics" (1949 "Introduction"). Trans. W. Kaufmann. In *Existentialism from Dostoevsky to Sartre*. Ed. W. Kaufmann. Cleveland: Meridian Books, 1956. Pp. 206-21.

pp. 24 ff.   "What is Metaphysics?" (1929 lecture, 1943 "Postscript"). Trans. W. F. C. Hull and A. Crick. In *Existence and Being*. Pp. 325-61.

WW *Vom Wesen der Wahrheit.* 4. Auflage. Frankfurt am Main: Vittorio Klostermann, 1961.

   "On the Essence of Truth." Trans. R. F. C. Hull and A. Crick. In *Existence and Being.* Pp. 292-324.

II. Meister Eckhart

DW, *Die deutsche Werke.* Hrsg. im Auftrage der deutschen For-
I-V schungsgemeinschaft. Hrsg. Josef Quint. 5. Bände. Stuttgart: Kohlhammer, 1936 ff.

LW, *Die Lateinische Werke.* Hrsg. im Auftrage der deutschen
I-V Forschungsgemeinschaft. Hrsg. Ernst Benz, Konrad Weiss, Bernhard Geyer, Josef Koch, Karl Christ, Bruno Decker. 5 Bände. Stuttgart: Kohlhammer, 1936 ff.

   Parisian Questions and Prologues. Trans. A. Maurer. Toronto: Pontifical Institute of Medieval Studies, 1974.

Q *Meister Eckhart: Deutsche Predigten und Traktate.* Hrsg. u. übers. v. Josef Quint. München: Carl Hanser, 1965.

Théry Théry, Gabriel. "Édition critique des pièces relatives au procès d'Eckhart," *Archives d'histoire doctrinale et littéraire du moyen âge,* I (1926), 129-268.

Bl. *Meister Eckhart.* A Modern Translation by Raymond Blakney. New York: Harper & Row, 1941.

Cl. *Meister Eckhart: Selected Treatises and Sermons.* Trans. J. M. Clark and J. V. Skinner. London: Faber & Faber, 1958.

Ev. *Meister Eckhart.* By Franz Pfeiffer (Leipzig, 1857). Trans. with some Omissions and Additions by C. de B. Evans. London: J. M. Watkins, 1956.

Serm. *Meister Eckhart: An Introduction to the Study of his Works with an Anthology of his Sermons.* Selected and trans. James M. Clark. London: Nelson & Sons, 1957.

III. Other Works

CW Angelus Silesius. *Der Cherubinische Wandersmann.* Hrsg. u. eingel. v. C. Waldemar. Goldmanns Gelbe Taschenbücher. München: Goldmann, 1960.

   The Book of Angelus Silesius. With Observations by the Ancient Zen Masters. Trans., Drawn and Handwritten by Frederick Franck (New York: Knopf, 1976). (Contains translations of texts from *Cherubinischer Wandersmann* and related Zen texts.)

Herr.   Herrigel, Eugen. *Zen in the Art of Archery*. Trans. R. F. C.
           Hull. New York: Random House Vintage Books, 1971.

Hühn. Hühnerfeld, Paul. *In Sachen Heidegger: Versuch über ein
           deutsches Genie*. München: Paul List Verlag, 1961.

KRV   Immanuel Kant, *Kritik der reinen Vernunft*.

Löw.   **Löwith, Karl.** *Heidegger: Denker in dürftiger Zeit*. 3. durch-
           gesehene Auflage. Göttingen: Vandenhoeck und Ruprecht,
           1965.

Olt.   Oltmanns, Käte. *Meister Eckhart*. 2. Auflage. Frankfurt:
           Klostermann, 1957.

Schür.   Schürmann, Reiner. *Maître Eckhart ou la joie errante*. Ser-
           mons allemands traduits et commentés. Paris: Editions Pla-
           nète, 1972.

Suz.   *Zen Buddhism: Selected Writings of D. T. Suzuki*. Ed. W.
           Barrett. Garden City, N. Y.: Doubleday Anchor Books, 1956.

Vers.   Versényi, Laszlo. *Heidegger, Being and Truth*. New Haven:
           Yale University Press, 1965.

xvi

IDOLATRY AND METAPHYSICS

INTRODUCTION TO THE REVISED REPRINT

Iₙ *The Mystical Element in Heidegger's Thought* I argued that it is misleading to speak of Heidegger as a mystic. At best, I said, one should take note of a certain mystical "element," a certain "analogy" between Heidegger and mysticism, but in the end Heidegger is separated by an abyss from mysticism. I have the sense that it is the "mystical" in my title which some readers have fastened on, while I meant to stress the "element," that it is "only an analogy." For it is important to keep a sense of the distance between Heidegger and the mystics.

For Heidegger, the matter for thought (the *Sache*) is the history of Being as it unfolds in the West, the language of Being as it addresses us across the epochs, while for Eckhart it is the silent and timeless unity of the soul with God, where my ground and God's ground are one. Heidegger's concern is with the event of manifestness, the historical happening of truth from the early Greeks to the present, a "secular" event which has to do with the movement of the *saecula*, while Eckhart's is with the sacred *unio mystica*. At best, one can see a certain structural analogy between the way in which, in Eckhart, God overtakes the soul which remains open to Him and the openness of thinking to Being in Heidegger.

It is certainly true that Meister Eckhart is one of the masters from whom Heidegger learned something about "thinking." In *Der Satz vom Grund* (1957), Heidegger takes up a couplet from the German mystical poet Angelus Silesius, "The Rose Is Without Why," which sets to verse an expression from Meister Eckhart, which Heidegger uses to delimit Leibniz's metaphysical principle "nothing is without reason." For Heidegger, the poet does not violate metaphysics frontally—by putting forth a capricious and irrational proposition. Instead, he steps beyond the sphere of propositional discourse and brings to words an experience of the rose which lies beyond the sphere of influence of the prestigious principles of metaphysics. In the poet's verse a new region is opened up, on the other side of representational thinking. In the poet's experience of the rose, thinking and Being have undergone a transformation and an emancipation from the constraints of objectifying, metaphysical thinking.

But while it is clear that the mysticism of Silesius, and ultimately of Eckhart, is a "model" for Heideggerian thinking, what is most instructive of all, I think, about this comparison is the way in which Heidegger differs from Eckhart. For there is a certain notion of "danger" in Heidegger's thought which is not to be found in Eckhart's religious mysticism. There is a dark and ominous side to *Ereignis*, which is thought at times by Heidegger as a high and dangerous play (*Spiel*), as a game in which the stakes are high, in which we are ourselves the beings at stake, as a game whose outcome is dark and uncertain. The danger, the *Gefahr*, is that the essence of man and of truth will be perverted once for all, that the grip of the *Gestell* will be unbreakable, that the world-night will grow darker. The movements of the *Ereignis*, the sequence of epochal configurations, the rhythm of the *Geschicke* are all groundless. We remember the Heideggerian formulas of a kind of deep redundancy, or tautologousness (always different yet always the same): *Es ereignet weil es ereignet. Es spielt weil es spielt.* It does what it does, groundlessly. It plays because it plays. I found it strange when I later read Derrida's criticism of Heideggerian "hope," for it seemed to me that there is nothing sanguine about *Seinsdenken*.

Now, if the task of an author writing an introduction to a new printing is, like the God of *Genesis*, to look back upon the work of the six days and to declare it good, then I propose that there are two things about the argument set forth in *The Mystical Element in Heidegger's Thought* which are important. In the first place, it stakes out a uniquely religious and non-Heideggerian way out of onto-theo-logic, a religious overcoming of metaphysics. In the second place, it marks off in a striking way what is characteristic about Heidegger's own project of overcoming metaphysics. I want to take the opportunity afforded me by the revised printing of this work by Fordham University Press to address these two points.

I

In Eckhart, one finds a powerful deconstructive effort aimed at undoing the onto-theo-logical God, an unrelenting drive to free us, to free God, from the constructs and idols of metaphysics. Eckhart is always looking for ways to get beyond "God," that is to say, what men call God, whether on the basis of metaphysical theology or even of revealed faith. That is why he even rejects the adequacy of speaking of God in terms of the Trinity of persons, for whatever one can say of God—even if one says it on the basis of divine revelation—cannot be God, cannot be what God is. Whatever we *know* about God is not God, for that is God *insofar as* he has been brought under the sway of human knowledge. Whatever we *want* of God is not God, for that is God *insofar as* he has been brought under the sway of human willing. The only way to God—that is, to the truly divine God, what Eckhart sometimes called the Godhead beyond all God—is to shut down the whole operation of knowing and willing, that is to say, to suspend the operations of subjectivity, to disconnect the *ego cogito*, and let God *be*, let God be *God*. And it was of course at that point that Eckhart invoked the word *Ge-lassen-heit*, letting-be. The highest rule which holds sway in that realm is Eckhart's prayer, "I pray God to rid me of God."

The "truly divine God" is precisely the God Who *recedes* behind everything which is said about Him. The one thing we can say about God which suits Him is that nothing we say about Him suits Him, that is, that He withdraws behind all names, that He has no master-name, no name which masters Him, no proper name which captures what are *propria* to Him. He is not even "God"—neither the "Father Almighty, Creator of heaven and earth" of the Creed nor the *primum ens* of metaphysics. God "is" (*west*) the self-withdrawing. Or, better, God: the self-withdrawing, that which always already remains behind, in *lethe*, always deferring behind the signifier. And the highest work of the soul is to let Him go, to let Him be, to remain open to the *lethe*, indeed to shelter Him from the fire of metaphysical conceptuality, to preserve Him in His withdrawal.

This argument, in turn, sheds light on the Heidegger and Aquinas issue which I addressed in *Heidegger and Aquinas: An Essay on Overcoming Metaphysics* (which Fordham University Press published in 1982), a study which is best read in conjunction with *The Mystical Element in Heidegger's Thought.* For a long time the students of St. Thomas have been arguing that, by privileging *esse* over *essentia*, Aquinas alone among all the great metaphysicians is pre-eminently alert to the question of Being, pre-eminently free of *Seinsvergessenheit*. That, I argued, is false. For the metaphysics of *esse*, far from constituting an exception to metaphysics, is in many ways paradigmatic of what Heidegger means by metaphysics. While it distinguishes Being (*esse*) from beings (*ens*), the Open (*Lichtung*) in which such a distinction opens up remains withdrawn and out of view. Instead of thinking the groundlessness of this Open, it carries out *within* it a sustained exercise in founding and grounding beings upon Being, organized around the grounding power of *esse* as *actualitas*.

But worse still, this Thomistic rallying around *esse* misses an important opportunity to respond to Heidegger. For it is systematically blind to the resources within Thomas for answering Heidegger in a different and suggestive way. It tries to meet Heidegger's critique of metaphysics frontally, with a restated version of Thomistic metaphysics—and hence plays right into Heidegger's hands—instead of seeing that there is a deep momentum *within* Thomas himself *beyond* metaphysics, a suggestive movement of transgression, excess, delimitation, of overcoming metaphysics. For there is a "mystical element" in Aquinas, too, a deep tendency within his texts in virtue of which metaphysical science gives way to an experience of divine things, a *pati divina*, which exposes the "*debilitas*" of reason and confesses the inexpressibility of *esse*. I argued that the mystical sermons of Meister Eckhart—who held the same Dominican chair of theology at Paris held by "brother Thomas" a quarter of a century earlier—work out a possibility which is latent in Thomas, but with a more critical, more deconstructive vigilance about onto-theo-logical conceptuality, about claims to vision, a more resolute sense of the self-withdrawing, recessive, "lethic" Godhead in

God. Whence the argument of the first book comes home to roost in the second book as well, that there is another, a rival, a religious way out of onto-theo-logic, of the sort found in the religious mysticism of Eckhart, and that insofar as this represents the retrieval of a genuine possibility within Thomas, this is the way to go about responding to Heidegger's critique of St. Thomas.

This entire project about a religious way out of onto-theo-logic has been subjected to a welcome, thoughtful, and incisive line of criticism in reviews of both books by Thomas Sheehan.[1] Even in the most deeply lethic mysticism of Eckhart, even in this Eckhartian Godhead, this abyss of withdrawal, Sheehan argues, there is a residual metaphysics of presence. For God is self-present to Himself, self-coincident, self-identical, stabilized, *noesis noeseos* (what Rahner calls *Bei-sich-sein*, self-presence). To that I make a series of dialectically ascending responses. To begin with, the work of *Gelassenheit* is to let God be God. We cannot prescribe what God is, nor do we have to find some way of breaking the bad news to Him that Heidegger and Derrida have recently delimited Being as presence. That is, God might very well be self-present, if that is what He wants. What is God? Anything He wants to be.

Furthermore, and more soberly, what Nietzsche, Derrida, and Heidegger and the other masters of suspicion in what Derrida calls this era of *différance*[2] have shown us that *we* are not God, that *our* consciousness is wounded, vulnerable, exposed to illusion and self-delusion, to the unconscious. They have shown that our contact with the world is not naked, but mediated by signs; that the world is an interpretation, a rendering. They have forcefully reminded us that we have no way of knowing that faith in God may not spring from guilt, sexual displacement, or hidden economic interests. We have no absolute point of view; we are not gods—all of which seems to me a salutary exercise in the critique of philosophical idolatry. But that is not to say that *God* is not God, that the absolute does not have an absolute point of view. Are we to hold it against God that He is God? Is God refuted, are we to read Him out of existence, because of His perfection? Is that not a new version of the metaphysics of resentment?

Furthermore, and more soberly still, I think the point is to give up the notions of Being and presence in speaking of God, to pray God to rid us of the idolatrous God of presence. Eckhart himself is full of strategic reversals whose point is precisely to achieve that effect: if you call God "Being," he will call Him Nothing (not even a little bit); if you call Him ground, he will call Him abyss. I think we learn from Heidegger, Nietzsche, and Derrida to speak of God in terms of play and e-lusiveness, singing and dancing, the ludic and the choric. We require a God of the dithyrambic, not onto-theo-logic. We learn to think Him in terms of giving and withholding, sending and withdrawing, addressing and keeping silent.

But Sheehan will press on and ask whether the loving trust of the religious mystic does not spring from a hardline metaphysical dogma that God is reliable because He is self-present, and hence whether Eckhart is not a closet metaphysician after all. I would say decidedly not, that he trusts God because God is love and he asks you to leave your metaphysics in the antechamber, if you please. If you insist on calling God presence, he will call Him absence; but if you call God love, he will concede that you are getting warm. But he will insist that "love" is not some onto-theo-logical predicate, but something you "understand" only if you *do* it. Ultimately, the only way you really get warm is to stop calling Him anything and to let Him call you, to stop calling Him anything and start doing something. Eckhart's delimitation of onto-theo-logic lands Him in an abyss, as does every critique of foundations, a point where things are "without why." But the highest case of life without why is love. Love is without why, groundless, without reason. The lack of foundations is the way of love, which does not proceed by a calculus of profits and debits, rules and violations. *Dilige, et fac quod vis.*

II

The other point that emerges clearly from *The Mystical Element in Heidegger's Thought* is how much this religious mysticism differs from Heidegger's own path, how much Heidegger is *not* a mystic. The disconcerting thing about Heidegger, the thing about Heidegger which gives no comfort, is not that he *is* a mystic, as the sneering references to *Seinsmystik* made by his critics imply, but the fact that he is *not*, that the path he stakes out is ominous, uncertain, exposed on all sides to the "danger." And that, I think, is something about Heidegger which we today, in the epoch of *différance*, are likely to miss. For we are accustomed to the French critique of Heidegger which singles out Heidegger's nostalgia for Being, for the master name and unique word of Being, his metaphysics of hope. That critique, I would say, springs from an incomplete rendering of Heidegger, one which cuts short his deconstructive critique of metaphysics. it is a reading whose shortcomings can be readily seen by setting Heidegger's *Denkweg* against Eckhart's mystical and religious way beyond metaphysics. Compared to the way of the religious mystic, Heidegger pursues a darker, riskier, more uncertain path, always exposed to the dark play of the *Ereignis*, a path with markedly Nietzschean tones. Vis-à-vis recent French thought and *"Nietzsche aujourd'hui,"* Heidegger looks more like Eckhart; vis-à-vis Eckhart, Heidegger looks more like Nietzsche.[3]

True, Heidegger has his eschatological moments, and it is the merit of Derrida's critique of Heidegger to have pointed them out and so to have prepared the way for a more chastened, disciplined, suspicious reading of Heidegger. For example, Heidegger writes in 1955:

There was a time when it was not technology alone that bore the name *techne*. Once that revealing that brings forth truth into the splendor of radiant appearing also was called *techne*.

Once there was a time when the bringing-forth of the true into the beautiful was called *techne*. . . .

In Greece, at the outset of the destining of the West, the arts soared to the supreme height of the revealing granted them. It [art] was pious, *promos*, i.e., yielding to the holding-sway and the safe-keeping of truth. . . .

What, then, was art—perhaps only for that brief but magnificent time?[4]

There is a dream-like, indeed I would even say Camelot-like quality—replete with the brief shining moment—to this discourse. It has given way to nostalgia; it portrays a world which, if it existed at all, was available only to Greek, male freemen—whose piety was built upon a system of violent exclusion and *différance*. And when Heidegger writes in "The Saying of Anaximander" that thinking the Being of beings "may well bring about a situation which releases a different destiny of Being" (Hw 309/25), when he talks about the transition from the end of philosophy to the "new beginning," then he gives way to the hope which is the other side of nostalgia. Thinking becomes recollecting and aspiring; time is a circle in which what comes about in the primordial beginning traces out the possibility of what can come again. Such thinking is nostalgic, eschatological, a higher-order, more sublated version of metaphysics.

I would say that this rendering of Heidegger is refuted by Heidegger himself, by a deeper, more suspicious, more critical Heidegger. For it is Heidegger's view that withdrawal, *lethe*, concealment is inscribed in the "essence" (*Wesen* as the process of coming into presence) of Being. And in virtue of that very negativity there can be no privileged, primordial sending of Being—neither in the "first" beginning, nor at the end in the transition to a new beginning; nor indeed can there be a clear demarcation of beginning/end. Every age is equally subject to the law of withdrawal, every epoch is equally "epochal." The very *structure* of the giving of Being implies its self-withholding (*epochein*), so that every epoch is equally subject to *différance*, withdrawal, violence, the fury of the *Unheil*. There can be no privileging or hierarchizing of epochs—which is a fundamental gesture of a metaphysical conception of history. To the extent that Heidegger indulges in this sort of thing his "history of metaphysics" remains under the spell of a "metaphysics of history."

On Heidegger's own terms, oblivion, withdrawal, is ineradicable, and possesses what might be called, in a language we can no longer trust, a structural necessity. If withdrawal is the very condition which grants the possibility *of* history, then there can be no point *in* history where oblivion is overcome. To "awaken" to this oblivion, which is what "overcoming" means, can have no historical correlate, cannot be instantiated somewhere

inside history—whether in a "brief but magnificent time" in the first beginning or in some "new beginning." Wakefulness does not emancipate us
from the oblivion, but *to* it. It does not point back to a primal time nor does
it hail a coming future, but it gives us a certain way of reading that history—as the history which is effected by the withdrawal.

And so I prefer a demythologized Heidegger, divested of heroic stories
(*mythos*) about magnificent times and the days to come, divested of the entire metaphysico-eschatological mode. I prefer a more radical Heidegger
arising from the renunciation of Heideggerian *mythos*, issuing in a more
radical thought of *aletheia*, in which *aletheia* is shining glimmer, ef-
fulgence, and light is delimited in favor of *a-letheia*. By inserting the hyphen
Heidegger disrupts the nominal unity of the word, exposing the a-lethic
play, the play of the epochs as they rise up and pass away. *A-letheia* is not
the shine which things take on in any given epoch, past or coming, but the
very granting of the epochs. It is not the truth of Being, but the very granting of Being and truth, and hence their delimitation. *A-letheia* is not an
historical word, but a word deployed in any natural, historical language,
spoken by any historical people. It points to that process by which historical
worlds and languages spring up, that happening (*Ereignis*) which produces
history, Being, world, and truth *as effects*. Thus understood, the matter to
be thought for Heidegger is the opening in which history and metaphysics,
time and Being, are granted. That is why Heidegger wrote in 1964 that today *Being and Time* would bear the name *Lichtung und Anwesenheit*, that
is, the Opening (*Lichtung*) in which Being as presence (*Anwesenheit*) is
granted.

Accordingly the "overcoming of metaphysics" has nothing to do with
pronouncements about Being's story, about great beginnings, promised
comings, or even ominous and foreboding forecasts. Rather, it consists in
awakening *to* the oblivion, which constitutes metaphysics and makes the
history of metaphysics possible, *as* an oblivion. It consists in raising our
level of vigilance about idolatry, about worshipping idols which are the produced effects, the constituted products of the dif-ference, the *Aus-trag*, the
Ereignis. It prays Being to rid us of Being; it thinks beyond Being to that
which grants Being.

Released from all teleological, eschatological story-telling, the history of
Being is such as it is, an unfolding of dif-ference, the unfolding of the manifold senses of Being. There are many senses of Being, many truths of Being,
playing themselves out, playing because they play, none of which enjoys
special privileges and canonical authority. *A-letheia*: that means, the play
of the epochs, released from all metaphysical rule, springing up from the
withdrawal only to recede again.

Now, it is this groundless play of Being, playing because it plays, to
which, I think, *The Mystical Element in Heidegger's Thought* is singularly

attentive. Without fully setting forth the more radical account of Heidegger's thought which I have sketched here, it makes this eschatological Heidegger questionable. It underlines the "danger" to which thinking and Being are exposed, the uncertainty which inhabits the history of Being. The kingdom is in the hands of a child playing a game of draughts with the epochs. And it is the mystery of that play, of what is withdrawing in that play, that seems to me what is deepest in Heidegger (*infra*, pp. 245–54).

III

I would today speak of a "radical hermeneutics" to describe where Heidegger has led me. By hermeneutics I mean reaching a certain understanding of ourselves and the world; by radical, I mean the delimitation of that understanding, throwing it off balance, robbing it of its security. Because "hermeneutics" has to do with meaning, and "radical" with the loss of meaning, "radical hermeneutics" is concerned with the meaning of that loss. St. Augustine captures both sides of this expression for me when he writes of becoming questionable to himself (*quaestio mihi factus sum*). Radical hermeneutics means a certain confrontation with the cold truth, too much of which, Nietzsche said, might well be too much to bear.

Derrida was quite right, I think, to delimit Heidegger's talk about "authenticity." It is Platonic and politically dangerous to go around dividing people up into the authentic and inauthentic; naïve to think that you can keep these categories from crossing over into each other, that such exclusionary, binary oppositions are water-tight (not to mention their complicity with the discourse of self-presence). But I think that Derrida does no more than "de-limit" the idea. He makes us more cautious, puts us on warning about its trap-doors and pitfalls. For how is one to say what one learns from thinkers such as Nietzsche and Derrida, Heidegger and Meister Eckhart? How are we to describe the effect which they produce? What is it that they succeed in doing, when they put us on guard, raising our level of vigilance and suspicion, our readiness for anxiety? How are we to describe that point at which one no longer seeks to arrest the play, to surround oneself with all the comforts of the metaphysics of presence?

It is a sense of what Heidegger calls the groundless play, of what Derrida calls the *ébranler*, and Eckhart the hidden Godhead that I mean to evoke by "radical hermeneutics." In his later writings, Heidegger speaks, not of authenticity, but of "openness to the mystery," an openness which puts us on the alert about the idols of metaphysics and keeps us open to the mystery which withdraws. We are pointers, he says, drawn in the direction of the winds of withdrawal.

In their profound distrust of the idols of metaphysics and their openness to the mystery which withdraws we find the common teaching of Heidegger and Meister Eckhart. Each seeks his own way of staying open to the self-deferring, of sheltering what withdraws from the harsh lights and grasping hands of metaphysics. It is the sameness and difference of these ways that the following pages try to trace out.

Villanova, Pennsylvania
February 1986

NOTES

1. See Sheehan's review of *The Mystical Element in Heidegger's Thought* in *The Review of Metaphysics* 32 (1979), 537–39; and "A Way Out of Metaphysics: A Review of *Heidegger and Aquinas*," *Research in Phenomenology*, 15 (1985), 227–32.

2. Jacques Derrida, *Margins of Philosophy*, trans. Alan Bass (Chicago: University of Chicago Press, 1982), p. 21. Three of the essays collected in this volume—"Différance," "*Ousia* and *Gramme*: A Note to a Note in *Being and Time*," and "the Ends of Man"—are particularly relevant to Derrida's rereading of Heidegger, and their presence can be felt in the present introduction.

3. Since the appearance of *The Mystical Element in Heidegger's Thought* a number of interesting contributions have been made to the Eckhart literature in English. There are two new translations: *Meister Eckhart: The Essential Sermons, Commentaries, Treatises and Defense*, trans. Edmund Colledge and Bernard McGinn, Classics of Western Spirituality (New York: Paulist Press, 1981); and Matthew Fox, *Breakthrough: Meister Eckhart's Creation Spirituality in New Translation* (Garden City: Doubleday Image Books, 1980).

Reiner Schürmann's book has appeared in translation: *Meister Eckhart: Mystic and Philosopher* (Bloomington: Indiana University Press, 1978); see also C. F. Kelley, *Meister Eckhart on Divine Knowledge* (New Haven: Yale University Press, 1977).

A number of fine articles: Donald Duclow, "Hermeneutics and Meister Eckhart," *Philosophy Today*, 28 (1984), 36–43; "'My Suffering is God': Meister Eckhart's *Book of Divine Consolation*," *Theological Studies* 44 (1983), 570–86: Matthew Fox, "Meister Eckhart and Karl Marx: The Mystic as Political Philosopher," *Listening*, 13 (1978), 233–57; Richard Kieckhefer, "Meister Eckhart's Conception of Union with God," *Harvard Theological Review*, 71 (1978), 203–25; Bernard McGinn, "The God Beyond God," *The Journal of Religion* 61 (1981), 1–19; "Meister Eckhart on God as Absolute Unity," in *Studies in Neoplatonism*, III, *Neoplatonism and Christian Thought*, ed. Dominic O'Meara (Norfolk: International Society for Neoplatonic Studies, 1982), 128–39; "Eckhart's Condemnation Reconsidered," *The Thomist*, 44 (1980), 390–414; A. G. Pleydell-Pearce, "Philosophy, Poetry and Mysticism," *Journal of the British Society for Phenomenology*, 10 (1979), 122–29.

The Thomist devoted an entire issue to Meister Eckhart (Vol. 42, April 1978), which contains a number of excellent studies.

4. Martin Heidegger, *The Question Concerning Technology and Other Essays*, trans. W. Lovitt (New York: Harper & Row, 1977), p. 34.

THE MYSTICAL ELEMENT IN
HEIDEGGER'S THOUGHT

CHAPTER ONE

THE PROBLEM OF THE MYSTICAL ELEMENT
IN HEIDEGGER'S THOUGHT

1. *Mysticism, Philosophy and Thought*

HEIDEGGER is a thinker whose thinking is conducted at the limits
of philosophy. Indeed, he even claims to be no longer doing philosophy
at all. His "thinking" (*Denken*) arises, as he has more and more per-
sistently maintained over the years, out of the "end of philosophy."
An English translation of the concluding essays of the two-volumed
Nietzsche book, e.g., is significantly entitled *The End of Philosophy*.
This title is drawn from an important observation in the essay called
"Overcoming Metaphysics":

> But with the end of philosophy, thinking is not also at
> its end, but in transition to another beginning. (VA, 83/96)

Here "thinking" is differentiated from "philosophy." There is a possibility, Heidegger says, that thought can be restored, now that philosophy is at an end. The restoration of thought is a "retrieve" (*Wiederholung*) of the "first beginning" of Western thinking, which took place
"before philosophy" in the great thinkers who antedate Socrates,
Plato, and Aristotle:

> Heraclitus and Parmenides were not yet "philosophers."
> Why not? Because they were the greater thinkers. (WdP, 52-3)

1

Thought has preceded philosophy and can arise out of its end; but thought is always something essentially *other* than philosophy. Indeed, philosophy is one of the dangers which threatens thought (AED, 15/8).

In "The End of Philosophy and the Task of Thinking" (1964), Heidegger tells us that by "the end of philosophy" he does not mean to say that the history of philosophical speculation is over, or that the present age of philosophers will be the last. The role of the "thinker" is not to predict the future course of history, not even of the history of philosophy (SD, 67/60). Indeed, it might very well be, he adds, that the "end" of philosophy will actually last longer than its development up to the present. The end is no "mere stopping" but the "completion" (*Vollendung*) of philosophy. Philosophy is completed in the sense that it has realized all of the possibilities which inhere in its essence; it has unravelled all of its potentialities. Nietzsche had something similar in mind when, in *Beyond Good and Evil*, he refers to the fact that "the most diverse philosophers unfailingly fill out a certain basic scheme of *possible* philosophies. Under an invisible spell, they always trace once more the identical orbit."[1]

The beginning of philosophy is the beginning of the rule of reason. Today, in the age of the atom and the age of technology, the innermost tendencies of philosophical reason are being worked out (WdP, 32-3). In the twentieth century, philosophy has unfolded into the form of the "particular sciences." The appearance of psychology, sociology, anthropology—of all the "natural" (*Natur-*) and "humanistic" sciences (*Geisteswissenschaften*)—does not represent the dissolution of philosophy but its completion, its final development (SD, 63/57). Philosophy in the form of metaphysics gives birth to philosophy in the form of the particular sciences. The demand of metaphysics to "give reasons" (*rationem reddere*) has as its issue the rational and technical sciences of the modern age.

There is, Heidegger observes, one possibility which belongs to philosophy which has not yet been realized in the present age, but this is a possibility which philosophy can never experience or take up *as philosophy* (SD, 65/59). For this has to do with the possibility to "overcome" philosophy, to accomplish the very task which philosophy sets for itself, but which it is in principle incapable of carrying out, viz., the thought of Being (*Seinsdenken*). It is a possibility *in* philosophy but not *for* philosophy.

By "philosophy" in these essays Heidegger clearly means philosophy as "a matter of reason" (*eine Sache der ratio*: WdP, 22-3). He is referring to the tradition which begins most clearly and unambiguously

2

with Socrates and is passed on to Plato and Aristotle and, from them, to the subsequent Western tradition. Thus the expression "Western European philosophy" is, he says, a tautology (WdP, 30-1). Philosophy here is equivalent to Western "rationality" or what Heidegger calls "metaphysics." It is a matter of supplying reasons and argumentation, of entering the forum of rational debate. The paradigm case of a philosopher in this sense is Socrates. Socrates searched for clear and well-formulated definitions, and for the arguments which sustained them. He wanted to give a "rational account" of the virtues, not one which rested solely on the authority of the poets. But Heidegger has intentionally and consciously abandoned this ideal. "Thinking" has nothing to do with "definitions" and "arguments," and it dwells— contrary to Socrates's warning—in the closest relationship with the poets. Thinking is only possible if one makes the leap beyond the sphere of influence (*Machtbereich*) of the Principle of Sufficient Reason, the sphere, that is, in which it is necessary to provide "reasons" for every "proposition."

And in *What is Philosophy?* Heidegger speaks of "philosophy" in an entirely metaphysical sense. If we really listen to what is spoken in the Greek word *philosophia*, he says, then we must understand that philosophy is a striving (*philia*) towards the *sophon* which is the Being of beings (WdP, 50-1, 54-5). Philosophy in this sense is man's attempt to think beings in their common properties, to isolate the "Beingness" (*Seiendheit*) of beings, their most general features, such as *idea* (Plato) and *energeia* (Aristotle). Now "thought" has become "philosophy."

Does our insistence that for Heidegger "thinking" arises out of "the end of philosophy" amount to a merely verbal dispute? Do we not simply find in Heidegger a thinker who has, as Werner Marx says,[2] a "new conception of philosophy," rather than someone who has left the confines of philosophy altogether? I do not think so. Many major philosophers in the past—Descartes, Kant, Fichte, Husserl, Wittgenstein—have called for a "reform" of philosophy and have laid claim to having finally discovered what philosophy truly is. But none of these thinkers has called for the radical upheaval and transformation of thinking which Heidegger proposes. For the revolutions which these philosophers have effected consisted in overthrowing the previous procedures and methodologies which had been in use up to their time in favor of their own newly discovered philosophical method. Kant and Fichte and the others claimed that they for the first time had finally discovered the proper way to decide philosophical issues, to settle disputes which hitherto seemed interminable. They each proposed the definitive way to give an account (*rationem reddere*) of things in philosophy. But Heidegger's revolution is far more radical than any of these. For Heidegger holds that philosophy must cease to be a matter of "deciding issues" and "settling disputes" at all. Heidegger's call is a call to leave the domain of rational argumentation—the sphere of *ratio*—behind. Revolutions in philosophy in the past have been a matter of finding a new way to give a "rationale" for one's views—whether that rationale be *a priori* or *a posteriori*, pragmatic, linguistic, or phenomenological. But Heidegger calls for a leap beyond the realm of giving reasons in order to take up a non-conceptual, non-discursive, non-representational kind of "thinking" which is profoundly divided from any of the traditional varieties of "philosophy."

That is why Heidegger himself has gradually come over the years to surrender the word "philosophy" to the philosophers—just as he has done with the words "metaphysics" and "Being." His thinking is no longer philosophy but arises out of the end of philosophy, just as it is no longer metaphysics but results from overcoming metaphysics, and as it no longer has to do with what metaphysics calls Being, but with the "It" which "gives" Being, the "Event of Appropriation" (*Ereignis*). We need only to observe what happens to the words "philosophy" and "metaphysics" in the course of Heidegger's writings. In 1927 the project of *Being and Time*, which is to raise anew the question of Being, belongs to the province of philosophy where "philosophy is universal phenomenological ontology" (SZ, §7c, 38/62). But twenty years later, in *A Letter on Humanism*, we are told that we need less philosophy and more thought:

> It is time to wean ourselves of the habit of overestimating philosophy and therefore of demanding too much of it. What is necessary in the present time of world need is less philosophy but more of the attentiveness of thought. ... The thinking of the future is no longer philosophy, because it thinks more originally than metaphysics, which is a name for the same thing. (HB, 119/224)

Then in the works which follow *A Letter on Humanism*, the word philosophy tends to disappear entirely as a name for thought. Thus in 1969 Heidegger said:[3]

> Thus I make a *distinction* between philosophy, i.e., metaphysics and thinking, as I understand it.

4

We also observe a similar evolution in the use of the word "metaphysics." The attempt to penetrate to the ground and source of metaphysics which was undertaken in the early writings was so little opposed to metaphysics that it was described in the Kant-book as a "metaphysics of metaphysics" (KPM, 208/238). It was so little opposed to ontology that it was described as a more radical or "fundamental ontology." In 1929, the question "what is metaphysics?" was asked from a standpoint *within* metaphysics which sought to determine its essence more deeply and genuinely. But by the 1930's and '40's, when Heidegger's thought developed by means of an encounter with Nietzsche, Heidegger speaks of the necessity to "overcome" metaphysics. Metaphysics contains the truth of Being, but it contains it by concealing it. Overcoming metaphysics means delivering it over to its own truth (VA, 79/92). Now the question "what is metaphysics?" is asked from a standpoint *beyond* metaphysics. In its final stage of development Heidegger's break with metaphysics is complete. In his celebrated 1962 lecture, "Time and Being," Heidegger advises us to no longer be concerned even with "overcoming metaphysics" but to leave metaphysics entirely to itself:

> Yet a regard for metaphysics still prevails even in the intention to overcome metaphysics. Therefore, our task is to cease all overcoming and leave metaphysics to itself. (SD, 25/24).

Now the question "what is metaphysics?" is presumably not asked at all, for that is to have a regard for metaphysics.

The question of Heidegger's relationship to philosophy cannot therefore be discounted as a merely verbal or terminological dispute. For what Heidegger rejects in philosophy—that it is an affair of reason—goes to the very heart of philosophy in its most fundamental sense. And Heidegger himself has recognized that his own intentions are best preserved by abandoning such words as "philosophy" and "metaphysics." Now the concern of the present study will be to reflect on the character of that "thinking" whose task is imposed upon it by the end of philosophy. We wish to take up with Heidegger the question which he poses in "The End of Philosophy and the Task of Thinking":

> The mere thought of such a task of thinking must sound strange to us. A thinking which can be neither metaphysics nor science?
>
> A task which has concealed itself from philosophy since its very beginning, even in virtue of that beginning, and thus has withdrawn itself continually and increasingly in the time to come?

A task of thinking which—so it seems—includes the assertion that philosophy has not been up to the matter of thinking and has thus become a history of a mere decline? (SD, 66/59)

If thinking is not philosophy, if it thinks upon that to which philosophy can in principle have no access, what is it? How are we to regard it?

The question of the character of Heidegger's thought acquires a special force when one considers that, having stepped back out of philosophy, thinking takes on a likeness to that which lies beyond philosophy—viz., poetry and mysticism. Heidegger has repeatedly said that thinking and poetry dwell in the closest proximity, and this alliance has often been touched upon in the literature on Heidegger. But Heidegger has also said that "the most extreme sharpness and depth of thought belongs to genuine and great mysticism" (SG, 71). Now the relationship of Heidegger to mysticism is never discussed with any detail in the literature. Of course Heidegger's later writings are frequently characterized, and usually unfavorably, as a "mysticism of Being" (*Seinsmystik*), but never with any serious discussion of what mysticism is. As a matter of fact, when one does examine the relationship of Heidegger to the mystic, it becomes quite clear that a deep and far-reaching affinity exists between thinking and mysticism. Are we to suppose, then, that having left the sphere of philosophy, thinking has become a species of mysticism? Is the path of thought (*Denkweg*) a mystical itinerary (*itinerarium mentis*) not, as with St. Bonaventure, into God (*in deum*) but into Being as Being? It is upon this question in particular that the present study focuses.

Our work has accordingly a "topological" character (AED, 23/12), i.e., it concerns itself with the respective "regions" of thinking, mysticism, and philosophy, with their boundaries and the dialectic among them. It raises this basic question: what is the relationship of thinking to mysticism? are thinking and mysticism the same? The thesis of the book is that there is an important and far-reaching kinship between "thinking" and mysticism, a kinship which illumines Heidegger's thought and highlights certain features in Heidegger's work which might otherwise go unnoticed. This likeness of Heidegger to the mystic, this kinship between overcoming metaphysics and the mystical leap, is what we mean by the mystical element in Heidegger's thought. The concern which we will have throughout this study is to identify this element and then to ask ourselves what significance it has. What does it tell us about Heidegger and what he calls "thought"?

6

The question of the relationship of thinking to mysticism is not arbitrarily imposed upon Heidegger. The fact is that Heidegger has had a life-long interest in Western mysticism, a claim which we will document below. This interest appears as early as 1915, in the "Conclusion" to the *Habilitationsschrift* on Duns Scotus. Speaking of the medieval "world-view," which would in his later work come to be interpreted as the medieval "mission of Being" (*Seinsgeschick*), Heidegger remarks:

> If one reflects on the deeper essence of philosophy in its character as a philosophy of world-views, then the conception of the Christian philosophy of the Middle Ages as a scholasticism which stands in opposition to the contemporaneous mysticism must be exposed as fundamentally wrong. In the medieval world-view, scholasticism and mysticism belong essentially together. The two pairs of "opposites," rationalism–irrationalism and scholasticism–mysticism, do not coincide. And where their equivalence is sought, it rests upon an extreme rationalization of philosophy. Philosophy as a rationalist creation, detached from life, is powerless; mysticism as an irrationalist experience is purposeless. (FS, 352)

A philosophy which is not open-ended and receptive to the vision of the mystic is a sterile rationalism; and a mysticism which resists the clarifying reflection of the philosopher is an irrationalism which serves no purpose and accomplishes nothing. Philosophy and mysticism belong together. One can already see, with the power of hindsight, a new kind of thinking gestating in the youthful Heidegger's mind, one which, dwelling in the proximity of mysticism and poetry, is neither rationalism nor irrationalism.

Heidegger had in those early days a special interest in one particular medieval mystic, viz., Meister Eckhart of Hochheim (1260–1327/9). Heidegger's interest in Meister Eckhart is the key to the strategy of the present work. For it provides us with the opportunity to conduct our inquiry into the "mystical element" in Heidegger's thought "in the concrete." Eckhart is not only a "genuine and great" mystic; he is also an author in whom Heidegger had, and by every indication continued to have, the greatest interest, and by whom he was most assuredly influenced, perhaps even decisively. The link between Eckhart and Heidegger therefore is not only "structural"; it is also historical. The question of "thinking" and "mysticism" can thus be specified as the question of Heidegger and Meister Eckhart. We are accordingly spared the difficulty of proceeding "in the abstract," viz., of having first to define mysticism and then to measure Heidegger's work against this abstractly established criterion. We can instead take Meister Eckhart as a paradigm or model of the mystic, and then proceed to relate Heidegger to Eckhart with the added assurance that we are developing a relationship which in fact possesses an historical foundation.

In Heidegger and Eckhart we will meet the most startling and provocative similarities. We will see how each thinker appeals to man to open himself up to the presence of something which surpasses man, yet from which alone man receives his essence as man. For each thinker, access to this presence is gained not by any human accomplishment, but by "letting" something be accomplished "in" man. They are each spokesmen of "*Gelassenheit*," of letting-be—of letting God be God, of letting Being be in its truth. Each teaches a way to find a new rootedness among things, to let the thing lie forth as the thing which it is, to break the shell of creatures to find God within. For neither thinker is man adequately accounted for as the "rational animal"; both call upon man to lay aside conceptual reasoning and representational thinking in order to enter into either the abyss (*Abgrund*) of the Godhead, or the abyss of Being. In the end, there will be no doubt whatever about the proximity of these two thinkers. The only question which will remain is what import their nearness has for those of us who wish to understand Heidegger.

We will thus by means of this confrontation of Heidegger with Meister Eckhart be in a position to determine the respective regions of mysticism and thought. We will, having set off the borders of each from the other, better understand what each is within its own confines. The topology of Being moves through metaphysics back to thought. But we shall show in these pages that there is a comparable movement, a comparable step back, from metaphysics to mysticism. And we will want to know what kinship there is between these two steps, even as we will want to know how the leap of thought differs from the mystical leap. And in order to carry out this guiding aim, of elaborating the analogy between mysticism and thought, we shall have to ask how each of them takes leave of philosophy itself. For as Eckhart's mysticism effected a breakthrough beyond the scholastic metaphysics of his day and made a penetration to another realm, so also Heidegger's thought moves through the metaphysics of the modern world, the ontology which is expressed in technology, into a simpler and for that reason all the more difficult sphere, into "thought" itself. Our inquiry then is a topology of the regions of philosophy, mysticism and thought.

The plan of this work is, therefore, as follows. We will, in this opening chapter, offer a preliminary sketch of the "mystical element" in Heidegger's thought and of the "problem" which it presents. Here, after presenting the reader with a tentative look into Heidegger's affinity with Meister Eckhart, we will proceed to examine three important critiques of the later Heidegger in which are crystallized the main difficulties confronting Heidegger's later, apparently "mystical," writings. For the kinship of Heidegger and the mystic has provoked not a little criticism of his later works, criticism which must not and should not be disregarded. Then, in the second chapter, we will examine Heidegger's critique of metaphysical reason—of philosophy as a thing of reason—as it is presented in *Der Satz vom Grund* (*The Principle of Ground*), which is an interpretation of Leibniz's principle, "nothing is without reason." In *Der Satz vom Grund*, which serves as the point of departure of our interpretation of Heidegger in this study, Heidegger not only presents a penetrating critique of "metaphysics," but he also, at the same time, bids us heed the mystical poet Angelus Silesius who has said:

The rose is without why; it blooms because it blooms
It cares not for itself; asks not if it's seen.   (CW, I, 289/66)

According to the philosopher "nothing is without reason." But the mystical poet rejoins: something, the rose, is without why. We must learn to make the leap, Heidegger comments, from the first saying to the second.

In the third chapter we will turn to Meister Eckhart himself and attempt to develop as fully as space permits the main lines of his mystical teachings, particularly as they are contained in his German sermons and treatises. Then, in the fourth chapter, we will elaborate the analogy which we believe exists between Heidegger's later writings and Meister Eckhart's mysticism. We will then be in a position, in Chapter Five, to return to the questions which we will formulate in these opening pages. There we will attempt to resolve the problem of the mystical element in Heidegger's thought, and so to sketch the topology of mysticism, philosophy, and thought.

2.   *Meister Eckhart: "On Detachment"*

In *Being and Time*, Heidegger stressed the need for a certain "fore-conception" (*Vorgriff*) of a subject matter which sketches out before-

9

hand the general dimensions of the matter to be understood (SZ, §32, 150/191). This foreconception does not prejudice the results of further investigation but rather establishes the horizon within which the material can be understood. It is precisely with such a foreconception that we wish to supply the reader of the present study. For the relationship of Heidegger to the mystics is not something with which we are all already familiar, and Meister Eckhart himself, while an important figure in the history of Western philosophy, does not enjoy the ready familiarity of an Aristotle or a Descartes. Thus we lack the terms in which to conceptualize this relationship; we lack the "horizon" which allows it to come into view. And so long as that is so, it will be impossible to formulate with any precision the "problem" of the mystical element in Heidegger's thought, i.e., the precise difficulties that are involved in the kinship of thinking, mysticism, and philosophy. Thus our study will rely upon the dynamics of the "hermeneutic circle": we shall first establish in a preliminary way the kinship between Heidegger and Eckhart; then, we will step back from this relationship in order to formulate our question about it. Then in Chapter Four we will return to this relationship in order to study it in detail and so, on that basis, to assess its import.

The most suitable way to introduce the reader to the proximity of thinking and mysticism is to direct our attention to two equally short and penetrating treatises by Eckhart and Heidegger, which have as their common theme the problem of the "nothing" (*das Nichts*). I refer to a treatise by Meister Eckhart entitled *On Detachment* and to Heidegger's *What is Metaphysics?*, including not only the 1929 lecture but also the "Postscript" which he added in 1943. Heidegger delivered his lecture six hundred years after the death of Eckhart, who must have died sometime between 1327 and 1329. It is a matter of no small wonder how very close these two treatises are to one another, separated as they are by six centuries of German thought. It is as though in these two works—as in these two authors as a whole—the beginning and the end of German thought touch one another. In *What is Metaphysics?* Heidegger in fact illustrates for us how his "thinking" goes back to its origin—in this case to the origin of German thought and of the German language itself—to "retrieve" it, to take it over and make it his own. For Eckhart stands at the fountain-head of the development of German thought and of the formation of the German language. Heidegger's famous essay, enigmatic to so many readers, actually belongs to an old tradition in German thought and is familiar to those who know the ways of the "old masters" of German thought, even as it was to its Japanese readers (US, 108-9/19).

10

I shall attempt in the next two sections of this Chapter, first, to sketch the main lines of Eckhart's reflections in *On Detachment*, and then to show how in *What is Metaphysics?* Heidegger, to a great extent, retrieves in his own way and for his own purposes the thoughts of this "old master of thinking" (G, 36/61). By means of this comparative analysis we will be in a position to see some of the main lines of the relationship between these two thinkers. Needless to say, this comparison will have been worked out only imperfectly in the opening Chapter. It will have to be refined and nuanced in a number of ways in order to portray this relationship fairly and accurately, a task which is reserved for Chapter Four. In the final section of this Chapter, I will formulate the "problem" which is presented by the relationship of Heidegger to the mystical tradition.

On Detachment[4] is an attempt by Eckhart to portray "detachment" (*Abgeschiedenheit*) as the highest of all the virtues. Detachment is the pinnacle and crown of the virtues; if the soul possesses detachment it will possess all the lesser virtues as well. "Detachment" is not one of the usual moral virtues that philosophers traditionally speak of in their treatises on ethics. As a matter of fact, to use a Kierkegaardian distinction, detachment is not primarily an "ethical" category but a "religious" one. Hence it is not only the "highest of" all the virtues, it is also in a sense "higher than" any moral or ethical virtue. It is best approached by examining the word "detachment" itself. Literally, it stands for the state of being "cut off" and "away from" something (*ab-scheiden*). In modern German, *Abschied* means "departure" and "*das Abgeschiedene*" means the "departed" in the sense of the dead. Meister Eckhart used the Middle High German word *abegescheidenheit* as a translation of *abstractus*, that which is "drawn away" and "removed from" matter and the conditions of matter (see DW, V, 438-40, n. 1). He also uses it to translate *separatus*; thus "separate substance" (*substantia separata*)—a substance which exists separately from matter—is rendered by Eckhart as *der abgeschiedene Geist*. Meister Eckhart also gives this word a distinctively "mystical" sense as well, which is the meaning it bears in this treatise. Here *Abgeschiedenheit* means the state of having cut off one's affection from everything created and creaturely, from the "world" and the "self." It is a condition of "purity" from created things, from "attachment" to them. It does not refer to a physical or spatial separation but to a detachment of the "heart" from worldly goods.

The key to Meister Eckhart's claim that detachment is higher than all other virtues lies in the fact that God Himself is pure detachment:

> For God is God because of His immovable detachment; and from detachment He has His purity and His simplicity and His unchangeability.
>
> (DW, V, 541-2/Cl., 164)

God is "detached" for Eckhart because He is the highest, most completely "separate" substance possible—the *ens separatissimum*, if you will. He is the most fully removed from matter and particularity. God is neither "this nor that," Meister Eckhart is fond of saying. He is no particular "being" because He is pure "being" itself or rather—and this amounts to the same thing for Meister Eckhart—because He is a pure nothing. God is separate and detached from every being: he is "nothing." Thus detached from creatures, God is also removed from all change and multiplicity. Hence Meister Eckhart refers to God's "immovable" detachment. He illustrates this paradoxically (as is his wont). God is so fully removed from creatures, so detached and untouched by them, that He is completely unaffected by the fact that He even created them—so much so that He would be just the same if He had not created them. Again, He is so fully removed from creatures that His Being is not affected by the prayers we direct to Him and by the good works we do. Now what these seeming paradoxes really amount to, Eckhart explains, is that God's Being is a perfectly immutable simplicity which is totally untouched by all the fortunes of creatures. This is because God has, in one eternal moment, created the world and listened to all the prayers and entreaties of creatures and considered the worth of all their good works:

> And so God has in His first eternal look regarded all things; and God does nothing new, since everything is worked out beforehand (*vorausgewirkt*).
>
> (DW, V, 542/Cl., 165)

While changes occur among creatures, God Himself remains the same, standing in immutable detachment. It was for this reason that God told Moses to tell the Pharaoh that "He who is" had sent him. "This is as much as to say," Eckhart comments, "that He who is there unchangeably [remaining] in Himself has sent me" (DW, V, 543/Cl., 166).

If God Himself is pure detachment, then the way of the soul to God is the way of detachment. This is what we might call the "logic" of the way of the soul to God, or what Heidegger would call "the way one moves along the path" (*die Art der Bewegtheit*: SD, 51/47):

Consequently, should a man wish to become like to God, insofar as a creature can have any likeness with God, then this can only come about through detachment. (DW, V, 542/Cl., 164)

Detachment is the key to the mystical union in Eckhart. That is why it is superior to any moral virtue. For the virtues always have to do in one way or another with creatures, whereas by detachment the soul is related immediately to God Himself. There is a rule of inverse proportions in detachment:

You should know this: to be empty of all creatures is to be full of God; and to be full of creatures is to be empty of God. (DW, V, 542/Cl., 164)

In the manner of a mystic who is also a scholastic *magister*—one is reminded of Heidegger's remark in the *Habilitationsschrift* about the unity of mysticism and scholasticism in the Middle Ages—Eckhart provides us with some proofs of the primacy of detachment. Thus he argues that detachment is higher than love and humility. Love is praised above all the virtues by St. Paul (1 Corinthians 13:1); but for Meister Eckhart detachment is higher still than love. For by love, he says, I am able "to suffer all things for God's sake" (DW, V, 540/Cl., 161). But when a man endures something he still retains a relationship to that created thing from which his suffering comes. Whereas by detachment "I am receptive of nothing other than God" (DW, V, 539/Cl., 161) and "completely free from all creatures" (DW, V, 540/Cl., 161). Detachment makes the soul receptive of nothing other than God because, by detaching itself from everything creaturely, the soul brings itself so near to being "nothing" at all that only the Nothing itself, God, can take up residence there:

But detachment is so near to nothingness, that nothing but God is subtle and rare enough to be contained in detachment [in the detached heart].
(DW, V, 540/Cl., 161)

God lives in immovable detachment from everything created, and the soul assimilates itself to God by detaching its affections—its "heart" —from all creatures, including even itself.

The same kind of argument is made against the primacy of humility. By humility, a man lowers himself before creatures and therefore maintains himself in a relation to creatures. But detachment wishes to

13

be neither above creatures nor below them. It wishes to have no relation at all to them. It does not wish to be "this or that," or to be anything at all:

> ... who wishes to be this or that, wishes to be something. But detachment on the other hand wishes to be nothing.
>
> (DW, V, 540/Cl., 162)

By detachment, the soul lets God be all, and it wishes only to let God's will obtain throughout. It purifies itself of itself in order to let God directly inhabit it. That is why Meister Eckhart quotes St. Paul: "I live now not I but Christ lives in me" (Galatians 2:20).

Eckhart's doctrine of "immovable detachment" leads him to make a most important distinction between the "inner man" and the "outer man." The outer man is a man of "sensation," who expends all the energy of his soul in the employment of his external senses. He is a "busy" man, a man of "activity" (*Betätigung*: DW, V, 544/Cl., 167), who is occupied with many sensible things. If his "surrender" to sensuous objects is complete enough, Eckhart says, such a man will be no better than brute animals, who are led about by the desires of their senses. Having fully expended himself on outer things, this man has no inner reserve, no inner life apart from his outward activity. The inner man, on the other hand, does not expend himself entirely on outer things. He allows the higher faculties of the soul—the intellect and the will—to have commerce with the senses only to the extent that it is necessary, and only to that extent that the higher faculties can retain control over the senses. Thus the inner man has to do with the senses only to the extent that he is their "leader and guide" (DW, V, 543/Cl., 166), and can never himself be led about by them. The man of interiority could therefore lead an active life—Meister Eckhart, himself, in fact, was a man of prodigious activity. What constitutes him as an internal man is that he preserves within his soul an inner sphere in which, insulated from all outer works, he my have an interior life. Such a man, says Eckhart with his usual fondness of metaphor, can be compared to a door on its hinges. The door which moves back and forth is like the outer man, while the hinge, which remains unmoved, is like the inner man.

If the inner man wishes to turn his mind's eye to something "high and noble," then the soul can summon all its powers back from the senses and devote them exclusively to the object of inward contemplation. In such a state, the inner man is literally "out of his senses"

(DW, V, 544/Cl., 166), not in the sense of the one who is deranged, but in the sense of the one who is "rapt" (*verzückt*) in a contemplation of divine things. The object of this inner contemplation is described by Eckhart as "a cognitive representation or a cognition without image."[5] According to Quint, Eckhart is alluding to a text of St. Thomas in which Aquinas distinguishes two different ways in which the soul can be "rapt" (*rapitur*) in intellectual contemplation without the use of either senses or imagination:[6]

> In one way, according as the intellect understands God through certain intelligible forms where are given to it (*per aliquas intelligibiles immissiones*), and this is proper to the angels. . . . In a second way as the intellect sees God in His essence.

In other words, in Eckhart's view, the possibility is open to the interior man to rise to a contemplation of the divine essence either by means of a form or idea which is directly implanted in it by God, or by means of a completely non-representational cognition (*ohne Bilde*). By means of his senses, a man dwells among things and the representation (*Bild, Bildvorstellung*) of things. But the detached man, who is the inner man, removes himself from both things and their representations, in order to achieve a union with God Who is Himself "nothing," and of Whom the detached man does not and cannot form an image.

Eckhart concludes this treatise by asking two questions concerning detachment which are quite helpful in determining its true character. The first question is: what is the object of pure detachment? To this Eckhart answers that ". . . neither this nor that is the object of pure detachment" (DW, V, 544/Cl., 167). The object (*Gegenstand; mhd: gegenwurf*) of detachment is "nothing," the nothing; indeed, he says, "it aims at a pure nothingness." Eckhart explains this as follows:

> God cannot work in *all* hearts with His whole will because, while He is almighty, He can only work insofar as He finds or makes a preparation [for Himself]. (DW, V, 544/Cl., 167)

The union of the soul with God is the activity of God, for ". . . God can join Himself to me more closely and can better unite with me than I can unite myself with God" (DW, V, 539/Cl., 160). But while it is God who acts, it is the soul which must be prepared for such action and made ready for it. Sometimes the soul prepares itself, Eckhart suggests, but sometimes—as in the conversion of St. Paul—God

15

Himself must prepare a readiness in the soul. The readiness makes all the difference. Another simile: the same heat in the same oven will make breads of different textures if the doughs are different; it is not the heat which differs but the materials. In the same way God's action differs according as he finds or does not find readiness and receptivity. But the presence of "this or that," i.e., of attachment to created things, to this being or that, prevents God's action, impairs it, and blocks it out. Hence the detached soul must have nothing in its heart, no "object" at all. In being "nothing" at all, in having "nothing" in view, the soul attains the greatest possible level of receptivity and readiness for God's action.

Meister Eckhart also makes this same point in a different way by attaching a mystical significance to Aristotle's theory of the soul as a *tabula rasa*, which is one of the more interesting illustrations of how this thinker was able to fuse mysticism and scholasticism. If I wished to write upon a tablet, he says, then nothing, no matter how noble the sentiment, can be already written upon it. The presence of anything upon the tablet will prevent my own writing. Thus, if I am to write upon the tablet, I must remove everything that is currently written upon it. In the same way:

> . . . if God would write the highest things in my heart, everything which is called a this or that must come out of the heart; and that is exactly how it stands with the detached heart. (DW, V, 545/Cl., 168)

Thus, if God is to work His divine action upon the soul, the soul must prepare a readiness for Him, a completely clear and open place, in which He can act. But in order that the soul be clear of all things, it must have as an object "nothing" at all.

The second question which Eckhart asks is equally revealing: what is the prayer of the detached heart? He answers:

> The detached and pure heart cannot pray, because he who prays desires of God that something be given to him, or he desires that God take something away from him. (DW, V, 545/Cl., 168)

Meister Eckhart is not suggesting that the detached man give up the life of prayer. He means that the detached soul has ascended to a level of interiority where his prayer is no longer a prayer of "petition," which is a prayer which asks for *things*. His prayer becomes instead like Mary, the Virgin Mother's *fiat*: "let it be done to me according to your will." The only will of the detached man is that God's will be done. He has no will of his own. He prays for and wills nothing. Thus the answer to the second question is the same as the answer to the first question: the prayer (wish) of the detached heart, as also the object of the detached heart, is "nothing" at all, nothing, neither this nor that.

If the detached heart's prayer is no longer one of petition, it becomes one of union. For desiring nothing, it is united with the Nothing itself, that is, with that which surpasses and transcends everything. By its selflessness it comes to be "uniform," i.e., of one form and substance, with God Himself. This is the "mystical union" of the soul with God which forms the center of focus of every mystical teaching and does so no less in Meister Eckhart. The uniformity of the detached soul with God consists in the fact that both God and the soul are equally removed from creatures, equally separated from every mutable this and that. By becoming thus "of one form" with the divine, the soul opens itself up as fully as possible to the divine influence:

No man is able to make himself receptive of the divine influence except through uniformity with God. (DW, V, 546/Cl., 169)

By this uniformity, the soul subjects itself to God alone and not to creatures. Now the pure, detached heart is devoid of all creatures. Therefore the detached heart is the most receptive of God's influence, the most fully taken over by God's life. The detached heart does not pray for things, but gives up its will for things entirely, and in so doing allows room for God, Who is separated from all things, to unite Himself with the soul.

In bringing our discussion of Meister Eckhart's *On Detachment* to a close, I wish to point out that for Meister Eckhart, detachment is to be equated with "true poverty." For according to St. Augustine, the poor in spirit are those who have so "abandoned" (*überlassen*) everything to God that He now has these things back again just as He did before anything existed—viz., as pure ideas in the divine mind. The poor in spirit, therefore, are those who have nothing, because they have given everything back to God, and there can be no greater poverty than that. They have given up all things for the pure Nothing itself.

Eckhart concludes this treatise with a summary of the merits of detachment:

For this reason, detachment is the best of all, for it purifies the soul and cleanses the conscience and enkindles the heart and awakens the spirit and quickens the desires and lets God be known. It cuts off creatures and unites with God (DW, V, 546/Cl., 170).

3. Martin Heidegger: "What Is Metaphysics?"

Reduced to its essentials, Meister Eckhart made two major claims in his mystical treatise: (1) God Himself, as that which is wholly other than everything created, is pure immovable detachment; (2) the way of the soul which would unite with God is the way of detachment. If we turn now to Heidegger's *What is Metaphysics?*, we will find two parallel claims, even though the terms of the discussion are now no longer "God" and the "soul" but "Being" and "Dasein."

(1) The 1929 text of *What is Metaphysics?*, which was Heidegger's inaugural lecture at Freiburg, is an exposition of metaphysics which attempts to think from *within* metaphysics by letting metaphysics speak for itself. This is done by raising, developing, and answering a metaphysical question, viz., "What about the nothing?" (*Wie steht es um das Nichts?*: WM, 33/337). We will also examine the 1943 "Post-script" which defends the lecture against the charge of "nihilism" and "irrationalism" (cf. SF, 94-5 ff.). The 1949 "Foreword," which is a somewhat more independent essay on the question of "overcoming" metaphysics—for this is what the question "what is metaphysics?" had come to signify by then—will not figure in the present analysis.

Heidegger begins the lecture by situating his question. The audience which fills the auditorium to hear the lecture is a "university" audience. A university is a community which pursues the "sciences" (*Wissenschaften*), both physical (*Natur-*) and humanistic (*Geisteswissenschaften*). "In the sciences we are, in accordance with their most proper intention, related to that which is" (*zum Seienden selbst*: WM, 25/326). The sciences wish to know about beings, their relationships, their causes, their effects. "What is to be investigated is the being, and otherwise—nothing; only the being, and beyond that—nothing" (WM, 26/328). Yet what is this "nothing" to which we constantly have recourse in order to characterize the object of science? And how can we speak of it scientifically, for science of itself wishes to hear nothing of the "nothing"? What about this nothing?

We can already see the basis of a comparison with Eckhart taking shape. Both authors are interested in the problem of the "nothing," and both attach an importance to the "nothing" which suggests that it is more than merely the "null and void" (*das Nichtige*: WM, 26/ 328), the "*nihil negativum*" (KRV, A290-2=B347-9). But let us see if there is more to the comparison than just that.

When we ask about the nothing we tend to treat it as if it were a "being" which "is." "Yet from this," Heidegger adds, "it is precisely differentiated" (*unterschieden*) (WM, 27/329). The nothing is what is "cut off" and "separated" from beings. It is no thing, not any *thing* at all. From the point of view of the logician, "nothing" is a truth-functional concept. That is, it arises by taking the totality of what is (p) and then negating it (not-p). "Nothing" is a concept which arises out of the logical function of negation. But for Heidegger the "nothing" is something "experienced," "encountered," something forceful which we "run into." The nothing for Heidegger is reached by a "fundamental experience" (*Grunderfahrung*: WM, 30/333) which shakes us loose from our preoccupation with "what is," which detaches us from the sphere of things. This can be brought about, e.g., by "boredom." In our "daily running about" (*Dahintreiben*), we fix ourselves to this or that being, as if we were lost in this or that area of beings" (WM, 30/333). But in boredom the totality in which we are lost suddenly pales into indifference, loses "all" significance. We are brought before the "all" itself inasmuch as it is a "lack." So, too, with anxiety. Once again the totality is illuminated, this time as "receding" from us into insignificance. In dread we find ourselves *in* a totality—even if we cannot experience the totality as such—and we experience the totality as a lack, a withdrawal of meaning. Anxiety, then, is not the same as "fear," for "we are afraid in the face of this or that determinate being" (WM, 31/335). But anxiety does not have to do with this or that, but with that which is fundamentally differentiated (*unterschieden*) from this or that.

The analogy with Eckhart grows sharper. Just as with Eckhart, Heidegger defines the "nothing" as that which is neither "this nor that" determinate being. As with Eckhart, there is need of a fundamental experience—for Eckhart it was detachment—by which we sever our ties with beings and open ourselves up to the "revelation" of the nothing. Both thinkers make use of a similar expression. For Eckhart, God subsists in pure "*Ab-geschiedenheit*"; for Heidegger, the Nothing is fundamentally "differentiated" (*unter-schieden*) from beings. Of course, we are using no little hindsight here in picking up Heidegger's use of the word "*unterschieden*" in 1929. For every reader of the later Heidegger knows that in *Identity and Difference* (1957), Heidegger makes

19

explicit use of the term *"Unter-Schied"* to signify the cut-off, the differentiation, the rift that arises, between Being and beings (ID, 132/65). It takes the place of the earlier term "ontological difference." To Eckhart's *Abgeschiedenheit*, then, we can relate Heidegger's *Unter-Schied*.

But there is still an important aspect of this first point of comparison which we have not as yet touched upon. In the 1929 lecture, Heidegger goes on to show that the force of the experience of the Nothing is the revelation of the distinctiveness of the being. The nothing is encountered by anxiety. It is not the product of a logical negation; on the contrary it is the basis of all logical negation. The Nothing is a process which comes to pass in and with beings themselves; it is not a being of our judgments (*ens rationis*). It comes about *in* the being in such a way as to let the being emerge into appearance. In and through anxiety we experience "the wonder of all wonders: that the being *is*" (WM, 46-7/355):

> In the clear night of the Nothing of anxiety the original manifestness of the being as such first arises: that it is a being—and not nothing.
>
> (WM, 34/339)

That is why the scientist kept inadvertently resorting to the "nothing" to sharpen his idea of the object of the "particular sciences." The being stands out—like a star on a dark night—against the backdrop of Nothing. In the experience of the nothing, the fact that something *is* there, that there is something *at all*, first arises. Interestingly enough, Ludwig Wittgenstein describes a similar experience:[7]

> . . . when I have it *I wonder at the existence of the world.* And I am then inclined to use such phrases as "How extraordinary that anything should exist!" or "How extraordinary that the world should exist!"

It is clear then that for Heidegger the Nothing is not something apart from beings. It is not the "counter-concept" (WM, 35/340) to the being, but rather belongs to the essence of the being. Indeed, the Nothing is the same as Being itself:

> In the Being of beings, the negating of the Nothing (*das Nichten des Nichts*) comes to pass. (WM, 35/340)

Heidegger then goes on to point out that this is what Hegel had discovered when he said—for the wrong reason—in the *Science of Logic*:

20

"Pure Being and pure Nothing are then the same" (cf. WM, 39/346). We can thus accurately reformulate the old maxim *"ex nihilo nihil fit"* to read: *ex nihilo omne ens qua ens fit* (WM, 40/346). We have thus been dealing with a "metaphysical" question, for in metaphysics we must get out beyond beings to Being itself, to *ens qua ens*. The question about the Nothing is in fact an approach to the question of Being.

Now it is this point which Heideger returns to and lays stress upon in 1943 when in the "Postscript" he sets out to defend *What is Metaphysics?* from its detractors. For one of the criticisms which this essay, and the parent treatise, *Being and Time*, brought down upon Heidegger was the charge of "nihilism." A philosophy which emphasizes a "negative mood" like anxiety, it was said, which defines man (*Dasein*) as a being "stretched out into the Nothing" (WM, 35/339), attempts to reduce man to the point of self-annihilation. It holds out no higher goal to man than the denial of all reality, and it finds no higher experience in man than anxiety at this prospect.

This is of course a simple misunderstanding of *What is Metaphysics?*. For by the Nothing Heidegger does not mean the simple denial of what is, the negation of all beings, but Being itself, taken as what is *other* than any being (*Andere zu allem Seienden*). The negating of the Nothing *is* the Being of beings:

. . . that which never and nowhere is a being reveals itself as that which differentiates itself from all beings (*das von allem Seienden Sichunter-scheidende*), which we call Being. (WM, 45/353)

Without this Nothing, which is Being, every being would fall into beinglessness (*Seinlosigkeit*), for "a being never is without Being" (WM, 46/354). Now that is the sigificance of the mood of anxiety. Anxiety is not classifiable in any of the categories of psychology—as a "negative" or "positive" mood, a higher or lower mood, etc.—for it is not a psychological but an ontological occurrence (SZ, §40, 190/234). The significance of this mood is to be the revelation of Being as that which is other than every being. There is, Heidegger rightly concludes, nothing "nihilistic" in this philosophy of the Nothing.

Now the point of comparison we wish to make with Meister Eckhart is just this. For Eckhart, too, the "nothing" is not to be understood as something merely negative. And for Eckhart, too, there can be no question of nihilism—of a mystical or religious nihilism—in which the self is called to pure self-annihilation. On the contrary, Eckhart's "nothing" refers to God Himself, to "He who *is*." In virtue of His "immov-

21

able detachment" God transcends every being, every this or that, every determinate being. That is why for Eckhart—as for Heidegger—one can refer to this transcendent reality either as "pure nothing" or "pure Being." "Pure Being and pure nothing are one and the same." That sentence from Hegel aptly depicts the nature of God in Eckhart's metaphysics too. What is essential for Eckhart, however, is that God is *pure* Being and *pure* nothing. God's "purity" consists in being pure of or detached from creatures, from beings, from every "this or that."

Thus Eckhart, like Heidegger, focuses upon a transcendent reality which, because it surpasses every being, is referred to as "nothing," the Nothing itself. What is essential about God for Eckhart, and Being for Heidegger, is that each differentiates itself from beings, is *other* than beings. And if man is ever to gain access to such Being, it can only be by way of realizing, and opening himself to this "difference." There is an "Ontological Difference" in Eckhart as well as in Heidegger, and in understanding this Difference lies one key to the unity—or belonging together—of Being and man in both thinkers.[8]

(2) We said above that Meister Eckhart made two essential points in *On Detachment*. The first, as we have just seen, is that God lives in immovable detachment, detached from creatures. To that teaching we find in Heidegger the analogous proposal that Being is what is "simply other" than every being (WM, 45/353), that which is detached from beings. The second claim that Eckhart makes in *On Detachment* is that the way of the soul to God is the way of detachment. There is likewise something analogous to be found in Heidegger, which is Heidegger's proposal that we undertake a "thinking" which is detached from beings in order to think upon Being itself. Let us consider this more closely.

Towards the end of *On Detachment* Eckhart raised the question "what is the object of detachment?," to which he responds: nothing at all, it has *no* object. So too, for Heidegger, anxiety has no object. For anxiety is never anxiety in the face of "this or that":

> The Nothing is revealed in anxiety—but not as a being. It is just as little given as an object. (WM, 33/337)

In anxiety, Dasein effects a break with the busy work and activity of everyday existence in which it is absorbed. In anxiety, Dasein is drawn away (*ab-trahere*) from the world of things to the realm of that which is no thing at all. Instead of running about amidst beings (*Umtreiben an das Seiende*, WM, 36/341), Dasein is brought to a dead halt before that which leaves it speechless (WM, 32/336). An eerie stillness descends upon Dasein. Dasein is not "agitated"—on the contrary, it dwells in a "spellbound rest" (WM, 34/338), removed from the flurry of everyday activity. Indeed Heidegger adds, "It [anxiety] stands . . . in a secret bond with serenity and the gentleness of a creative longing" (WM, 37/343). Such calm is even compatible with the enjoyment of an active life (WM, 37/343).

One can now see taking shape here a very clear parallel to Eckhart's distinction between the outer and the inner man. In Heidegger, the "outer man" is the man of everydayness who is absorbed with the daily "round" (*Umtreiben*) of activities. The powers of his soul, as Eckhart would have put it, are expended on beings. The parallel to the "inner man" in Heidegger is the man who has undergone "the transformation into his Da-sein, which anxiety always brings about in us" (WM, 33/337). Heidegger's inner man has arrested his everyday activities in order to enter into a calm—an eerie calm—in which he experiences that which is not any being at all.

By the time of the 1943 "Postscript" Heidegger has worked out more fully and carefully the "calm" which possesses the soul in "anxiety." Of course, on the surface, calm and anxiety are opposites. That is because we tend to understand "anxiety" pathologically, as a state of mental unrest and agitation, and not ontologically, as a disclosure of that which is wholly other than every being, which actually "suspends" the daily round of activities. By 1943, Heidegger's thought had made the celebrated "turn" (*Kehre*) which had radically changed the significance which he attached to *Being and Time*. For in *Being and Time*, anxiety was a "call" which called silently to Dasein and which was identified as the call of conscience (§57). Of this call Heidegger says in *Being and Time*:

> The call [of conscience] whose mood has been attuned by anxiety is what makes it possible first and foremost for Dasein to project itself upon its ownmost *potentiality-for-Being*. (SZ, §57, 277/322)

If one "hears" the call of conscience, one does so by "following" it, which Dasein does by letting itself be called forth to the unique possibility for Being which is proper to it (SZ, §57, 287/374). In so doing, Dasein chooses (*wählen*) itself. This choosing is a choosing to have a conscience, a willingness to admit one's "guilt," which Heidegger calls "willing to have a conscience" (*Gewissen-haben-wollen*) (SZ, §57, 288/374). In short, the phenomenon of anxiety in *Being and Time* is tied to Dasein's choice of itself.

23

But after the turn, Heidegger has parted company with the philosophy of willing. He has, by 1943, passed through many years of wrestling with the texts of Nietzsche. He would later say of Nietzsche in *What is Called Thinking?* that Nietzsche's thinking must be first found and then lost (WHD, 22-3/52-3), i.e., first encountered then taken up into "*Seinsdenken*" where it will exist on a higher level. Heidegger "lost" Nietzsche by overcoming his metaphysics of will, a metaphysics which still very much influenced the language of "choosing" and "willing" and "resolving" in *Being and Time*. But by the time of the "Postscript," Nietzsche's metaphysics had been overcome.

At the beginning of the "Postscript," Heidegger adverts again to the "situation" of the 1929 lecture, that it was addressed to those who pursue the sciences. The sciences, he says now, have a special mode of "representing" (*Vorstellen*) and "manufacturing" (*Herstellen*) beings which operates within a specific conception of Being according to which "every being is characterized by the will to will" which is the "will to power" (WM, 43/350). The sciences put an interpretation upon things, subject them to a mathematical formulation, manipulate them to produce results. Thus for the sciences, knowledge is, as Nietzsche describes it in the opening aphorism of *Beyond Good and Evil*, the "*will* to truth.*" We are just beginning to realize, Nietzsche says, that physics is only an interpretation, a perspective taken on things (No. 14), a form of the will to power.

Now for Heidegger, Nietzsche's account of truth holds true generally for the entire history of "metaphysics." The term "metaphysics" is now surrendered to the "oblivion of Being," and Heidegger undertakes to penetrate to the *ground* of metaphysics which is hidden to it:

> Metaphysics moves everywhere within the realm of the Truth of Being, which remains to it an unknown and unfounded ground. (WM, 44/351)

The task of thinking will be to get beyond the "will-fulness" of Western metaphysics which is preoccupied with beings and the manipulation of beings. Its task is to meditate upon Being as such, which metaphysics, despite all its talk about Being, is never able to think—except in terms of beings. This new thinking will have nothing to do with willing:

> Reflection (*Nachdenken*) must merely take everything back in the composure (*Gelassenheit*) of patient meditation. (WM, 44/352)

Now the Heideggerian parallel to the distinction between the outer man and the inner man must be recast. Now we must distinguish "representational thinking" (*vorstellendes Denken*), from "essential thinking" (*wesentliches Denken*). Representational thinking is depicted by Heidegger in the "Postscript" as an attempt to calculate and count up beings, to reckon upon the possible uses to which they can be put (WM, 48/356-7). Essential thinking, on the other hand, "spends itself" (*verschwendet*: WM, 49/458) not on beings but on the truth of Being itself. Heidegger and Eckhart even resort to similar metaphors, for while Eckhart says the outer man "spends" all the power of his soul on outer things and keeps nothing in reserve for inner things, Heidegger tells us, on the other hand, that in essential thinking Dasein lavishes and "spends" itself on Being itself. And just as with Eckhart's inner man, who is "rapt" beyond the use of the senses, the essential thinker puts aside all "images" and "representations" to engage in a non-representational thinking on Being which leaves metaphysical reason behind.

It is with this "turn" from choosing and willing-to-have-a-conscience to "composure" (*Gelassenheit*) that Heidegger's thought takes on its affinity to Meister Eckhart.[9] For Heidegger and Eckhart alike realize that the way to deal with the transcendent and "simply other" reality (of God or Being) is not to deal with it at all, but to let it deal with us. What Heidegger realized along his path of thought—and it is this realization that brings him into the proximity of the mystics—is that Being is nothing that answers to human questions, nothing that submits to human interpretation; it is in no way subordinate to human demands. The only way to gain access to Being itself is to let Being be and to let it address man. Now that is something which every mystic knows. The way of the soul to God is to let God take the lead and to let God effect the unity of the soul with God. For it is beyond the powers of the soul to bring about such a unity itself. Hence Meister Eckhart says at the very beginning of *On Detachment*:

. . . God can join Himself to me better and more closely than I can unite myself with God. (DW, V, 539/Cl., 160)

How similar this remark is to Heidegger's observation in the "Post-script":

Being is no product of thinking. On the contrary, indeed, essential thinking is an event (*Ereignis*) of Being. (WM, 47/356)

What Heidegger had to realize—and what he very likely came to realize in his readings of the mystics—is the impotence of Dasein to *wrest* the

25

truth of Being from Being itself. He had to realize that the only "power" of Dasein lay in surrendering its will and letting Being be. And that there is a nobler power in surrender is well known to every mystic and religious man.

This seems to have been one of the essential implications that Heidegger drew from his early analysis of "anxiety" in 1929. Thus we note these very significant observations in the 1929 text:

> . . . anxiety finds itself completely impotent (*Ohnmacht*) in the face of beings as a whole. (WM, 33/338)

> We are so finite that we are not able by our own decision and will to bring ourselves originally face to face with the Nothing. (WM, 38/343-4)

In the experience of the Nothing, Dasein experiences a "withdrawal" (*Ent-gleiten*) of Being which it is both powerless to stop and powerless to effect of itself. In the Nothing, Dasein experiences its own lack and finitude in the face of that which is "simply other" than every being. This is the same realization which affects every religious, and particularly every mystical, consciousness. That is why Heidegger discussed anxiety in the 1929 treatise in terms of calm, serenity, rest, stillness, and silence. There was already contained implicitly in the early experience of anxiety the later notion of the "composure (*Gelassenheit*) of patient meditation." In both anxiety and *Gelassenheit* Dasein is brought to a halt, withdraws from its outer running about with beings (*Umtreiben an das Seiende*), and enters into relation with that which is other than any being. *Gelassenheit* is not the counter-concept to anxiety; it is its further refinement.

Thus it is interesting to observe Heidegger's defence of his conception of anxiety in the "Postscript" against those detractors who considered it testimony to the morbidity of his philosophy. Anxiety, he says, is a "mood" (*Stimmung*) because it responds to the voice (*Stimme*) of Being. The call of Being is the call to experience the wonder of all wonders, that the being is (WM, 46-7/355), that it stands out over against nothingness. Thus anxiety is in fact akin to "wonder" and "awe" (*Scheu*) at the "abyss" (*Abgrund*) of Being.

Our discussion thus far has attempted to show that with the "turn" in his thinking the later Heidegger has moved into an unmistakable proximity with the mystics, and with Meister Eckhart in particular. Not only do both thinkers posit something like an ontological difference, a detachment of Being from beings, but they also see in "detachment" the way of the soul to God, the way of Dasein to the experience of Being. I find the concluding pages of the "Postscript" to be some of the most striking testimony in all of Heidegger's works to just how far-reaching and penetrating this mystical (or even religious) dimension is in his thought. Heidegger's expressions in these texts have so patently a mystical ring that it is quite impossible to avoid the impression that he means to consciously and intentionally allude to the mystics and the language of the mystics. It is as if he wishes to give us a hint that in the mystics—in the old masters of thinking at the beginning of the German tradition—one can find something like "thinking" (*Denken*). If one wants to learn to think, to learn what thinking is, he seems to say, then go to the mystics. And if that is what he seems to hint at in *What is Metaphysics?*, it is what he explicitly declares in SG:

> . . . one might easily come to the idea that the most extreme sharpness and depth of thinking (*Denken*) belongs to the mystic. This is moreover the truth. Meister Eckhart testifies to it. (SG, 71)

Let us conclude this comparative analysis of *On Detachment* and *What is Metaphysics?*, then, with a study of these pages of *What is Metaphysics?* (WM, 49-50/357-61). Heidegger's expressions in these pages signify a state of mind very like Meister Eckhart's detached and humble heart. He is discussing the attitude and posture of "essential thinking" vis-à-vis Being. By means of this thinking, he says, Dasein "surrenders" its being (*Wesen*) to the simple necessity—a necessity without force—which man is under to think the truth of Being. Now this "surrender" is a "sacrifice" (*Opfer*). The sacrifice is the expending of the human essence for the preservation of the truth of Being. Dasein must become less and less so that Being can become more and more. Man must sacrifice and give itself up to the truth of Being. Now this sacrifice is a "thanking" (*Danken,* WM, 49/358) of Being by Dasein for the "grace" (*Gunst,* WM, 49/358) and favor (*Huld,* WM, 49/358) which Being has bestowed upon Dasein by giving itself up to Dasein as a matter for thinking. Since Being does not submit to human control then, if Dasein has succeeded in thinking, it is because Being has "given" itself to Dasein, has bestowed in effect a grace upon it. The appropriate response of Dasein to a grace is thanking, and its thanking consists in not squandering this gift but in actually engaging in "thinking." Now Heidegger asks rhetorically how else "thinking" is possible for Dasein unless

27

> . . . the grace of Being preserves for man, through [man's] open relationship to [Being] itself, the nobility of poverty in which the freedom of the sacrifice conceals the treasure of its essence? (WM, 49/358-9)

In giving thanks one attains to the "nobility of poverty" and "the treasures of the sacrifice." This is the essential paradox known to every religious man and every mystic: that in giving up all one attains all. It was the lesson which Jesus tried to teach the rich young man. Meister Eckhart himself described the detached heart as living a life of perfect poverty:

> The poor of spirit are those who have so given all things over to God, that He possesses them in the same way as when we did not yet exist.
>
> (DW, V, 545/Cl., 169)

Dasein is poor in spirit because by its essential thinking it knows nothing useful or productive; it has acquired no scientific knowledge. Indeed, it knows "nothing" at all, just as Eckhart's detached heart possesses "nothing" at all.

"Surrender," "sacrifice," "grace," "thanking," "poverty"—the motif of this passage is unmistakable. Now I have reserved the most important text in *What is Metaphysics?* for relating Heidegger to Eckhart for last, because I wished to persuade the reader that I am not forcing it, that the context makes it plain, even unavoidable, that Heidegger is referring to Meister Eckhart. In the sentence immediately following his reference to the "nobility of poverty" Heidegger adds:

> The sacrifice is a detaching from beings on the road to the preservation of the favor of Being. (WM, 49/359)

> (*Das Opfer ist der Abschied vom Seienden auf dem Gang zur Wahrung der Gunst des Seins.*)

"*Abschied*" means "taking leave," "departure" in modern German. Hence the English translators, Hull and Crick, render "*Abschied vom Seienden*" as "valediction to everything that 'is'." That is, to be sure, correct. What we are suggesting is that, in view of the patently mystical ring of this entire paragraph, Heidegger has in mind the mystical sense which has been given to the word "*Abschied*" by Meister Eckhart, where "*Ab-schied*" refers to the "detachment" of the soul from worldly things. On this interpretation Heidegger is speaking of "detachment from beings" for the sake of the truth of Being. I should

28

also point out that a few sentences later he refers to the necessity of maintaining an "equanimity" (*Gleichmut*) of mind "which allows nothing to assail the hidden readiness for the essence of all sacrifice, which is a detaching" (*für das abschiedliche Wesen jedes Opfers*) (WM, 50/359).

I am quite convinced that Heidegger is alluding to Meister Eckhart here. And I am not alone in this conviction. Max Müller refers to this same text, and explains that "*Abschied vom Seienden*" is to be equated with "*Abgeschiedenheit*," which is he says "a well-known expression of Meister Eckhart, who is very highly treasured by Heidegger."[10] But even if—as is altogether unlikely—there is no allusion to Meister Eckhart here, what a great inner sympathy there must be between their thought to allow Heidegger to express himself in a manner so close to Eckhart! What a profound analogy must exist between their work!

This preliminary analysis of Heidegger's relationship to Meister Eckhart has made considerably plainer the character of "thinking," and the way in which it has moved out of the neighborhood of philosophy and into the proximity of mysticism. For like the mystic and unlike the philosopher, Heidegger calls for a non-representational experience of Being, and not, as in *Being and Time*, for a new conceptual determination of it (SZ, §2, 6/26). Like the mystic, Heidegger thinks his way through not to a first cause or ground—for Aristotle, philosophy is a search for grounds (*aitiai*) (WdP, 56-7)—but to an "abyss" (*Abgrund*) or "nothingness." Like the mystic Eckhart, Heidegger's "way" to Being is not the way of "discursive" reason, but the way of meditative stillness and total openness to that which is wholly other than beings, to the "simply transcendent." As with Eckhart, there is the same "ascetic" tone of "surrender" which is expressed in terms like "poverty," "sacrifice," "grace," and, most important of all, "detachment" itself. These are not the categories of philosophers—or even of poets—but of the mystic. And even with all of this, we have by no means explored the full dimensions of this comparison. We have only mentioned in passing, for example, something as basic as the fact that the term *Gelassenheit*, which plays a decisive role in the later Heidegger's work, is taken directly from Meister Eckhart, where it is also a fundamental concept. But we have achieved a preliminary survey of the region in which thinking and mysticism dwell, and we are now in a position to formulate the "problem" this presents.

One must not of course embrace this analogy between Heidegger and Eckhart hastily and uncritically. Not only should we overcome our initial prejudice that there can be no relationship at all between a fourteenth-century Dominican mystic and Martin Heidegger, but we must also resist the temptation to identify them, once the analogy between their work is pointed out. We have pointed out that there is a comparable idea of a "difference" in both thinkers. But let us not neglect to consider that in the case of Eckhart we are referring to the difference between the Christian God and the world He has created, while in that of Heidegger we have to do with his unique conception of the relationship between Being and beings. Eckhart's God is transcendent, self-sufficient, timeless. Eckhart's creatures are created images of their eternal exemplars in the mind of God; their "existence" is a weak copy of their original "essence" in God's essential being. Were creatures to cease to be, God's originating being would not be affected, no more than is the sun if its light is prevented from illuminating a certain spot on the earth. But it is perfectly clear that none of these things holds true for the relationship between Being and beings in Martin Heidegger. For Being is essentially an historical, epochal process, a sending in which the various historical epochs are "cleared" in and for Dasein. Being is not the creator of beings; nor could Being "be" (*west*) without beings. And it would make no sense at all to think of beings as "images" of Being in Heidegger's thought.

Moreover, while there is indeed a likeness between the detached heart in Eckhart and the thinking which is detached from beings in Heidegger, there is also a wealth of differences. Eckhart has in mind the man who has become so thoroughly one with God and God's will that he has no will of his own, a man whose love of God is so perfect that he loves not with his own love, but God's own. Now Heidegger clearly has nothing of this sort in mind at all; for Heidegger means to address himself to the technological world and the will to power which pervades it. And he means to say that we must be brought to the realization that there is a deeper power at work in the history of the West than all human willing and human calculating. Thus the likeness between Eckhart and Heidegger which is taking shape for us is a likeness in difference, a similarity of structures and relationships in the midst, however, of very basic differences in content. For the thinker and the mystic whom we have singled out are separated by centuries and so by differing dispensations (*Geschicke*) of Being. And while there is and can be something the same (*das Selbe*) between them, their views are not identical (*gleich*) (ID, 85-6/23-4).

4. *The Problem of the Mystical Element in Heidegger's Thought*

The problem of the mystical element in Heidegger's thought is seen most clearly by a study of certain of Heidegger's critics. Indeed it is frequently the case, in my judgment, that when we examine carefully enough what Heidegger's critics are criticizing, it is precisely the mystical dimension which his works have taken on since the 1930's. There are three critical studies of Heidegger's thought which are especially pertinent to the present work: Paul Hühnerfeld's *The Heidegger Affair: An Essay Upon a German Genius*, Karl Löwith's *Heidegger: Thinker in a Time of Need*, and Laszlo Versényi's *Heidegger, Being and Truth*.[11] These studies are not only important criticisms of Heidegger in their own right, but they also bring out forcefully and clearly exactly what difficulties the kinship of Heidegger and the mystics presents. The followers of Heidegger are frequently enthusiasts who disregard such critiques as we will examine here as "misunderstandings" of Heidegger. But that I think is a serious mistake. For such an attitude can only result in an unquestioning repetition of what Heidegger has said, which is profoundly out of keeping with Heidegger's often expressed intention to set into motion a thinking which deals with the matter of thought, and not, as Husserl said, with "philosophers" and their "philosophies" (cf. SD, 69/62).

In my view the critiques which have been made of Heidegger's thought by Hühnerfeld, Versényi, and Löwith represent a fruitful way for us to approach the singular difficulty of understanding a thinker who appears to have left the ways of philosophers like Leibniz and to have embraced that of the mystics and poets. My task then, in the remainder of this chapter, will be to rehearse for the reader the main lines of these Heidegger-critiques, and then to formulate six questions around which the problem of the mystical element in Heidegger's thought seems to me to turn.

Hühnerfeld's argument with Heidegger is, from the point of view of the present study, provocative. He does not for a moment contest what we have labored to establish in a preliminary way in this first chapter and what we will attempt to work out in detail in Chapter Four, viz., that there is an unmistakably mystical ring to Heidegger's work, that Heidegger's thought has taken on a likeness to the mystics. But it is Hühnerfeld's contention that the ring is false and the likeness is a mas-

31

querade. The later work is a pretentious and arrogant attempt on Heidegger's part to align himself with a profound and great tradition. Thus, for Hühnerfeld, Heidegger is "the false Eckhart." Let us see how Hühnerfeld is led to this conclusion.

Hühnerfeld's book is, according to its author, an attempt to penetrate behind the veil which Heidegger has thrown over his own biography. His intention is to uncover the peculiar "danger" which inheres in a "German genius." Heidegger permits this veil to exist in order to distract attention from his personal life, not because it is the matter of thought (*die Sache*) which is alone of concern to him, but because he realizes that a close scrutiny of his life would reveal the inevitability of his association with the Nazis (Hühn., 9-11; Sp., 3/267). For according to Hühnerfeld:

> The common roots of German fascism and of Heideggerean thought lie clearly for anyone to see. It was the same irrationalism, the same dangerous romanticism, mixed with nationalism and intolerance toward those who think differently. (Hühn., 103; cf. Löw., 49ff.)

Heidegger's relationship with the Nazis was not an isolated "error," as Heidegger's defenders would have it, but a logical and necessary move.

According to Hühnerfeld, Heidegger's biography reveals three characteristically German flaws. He was first of all possessed of the *arrogance* of the genius who knows his own worth. As a young man "he breathed the air of philosophical authority" (Hühn., 48) from Rickert and Husserl; as an independent philosopher, he developed a theory which condemned all criticism beforehand to a "misunderstanding." Indeed, he even takes a perverse delight in insisting that he is misunderstood. Heidegger has moreover maintained that every philosophical thought from Plato to Nietzsche is a falling away from the truth of Being which it is the special advantage of his own thought to restore. Secondly, Heidegger is unmistakably *nationalistic*. This is manifested first of all in his provincialism. Heidegger twice turned down an appointment to the University of Berlin precisely because he did not wish to leave the provinces (the *Schwarzwald*) for a city which was becoming rapidly cosmopolitan (Hühn., 110-4). His love of the simple and the rough, his contempt for the urban and refined, goes hand in hand with an exaggerated love of everything German—e.g., his delight in uncovering the archaic meanings of German words. It is therefore not surprising that Heidegger moved from speaking of the destiny of Dasein in *Being and Time* to the destiny of the German people in his *Rektoratsrede*.

32

Finally, Heidegger is for Hühnerfeld an *irrationalist*. An academic himself, Heidegger early on repudiated academic philosophy, turning away from the Neoscholasticism and NeoKantianism of his youth and turning instead towards Pascal and Dostoievsky, Kierkegaard and Nietzsche (Hühn., 35-6, 54-6). Written in the milieu of Germany in the 1920's, *Being and Time* gave philosophical form to the subterranean themes of anxiety, death, and the nothing, which were the predominant motifs of the Expressionist poets of that same decade, which explains in part the instantly favorable reception which his book enjoyed (Hühn., 73-84). Heidegger's is a philosophy of "melancholy nihilism" (Hühn., 66) which has given up the effort to find a rational meaning in things before it even begins and which has always harbored a resentment against reason (Hühn., 15-6).

It is against this background that Hühnerfeld's assessment of Heidegger's mysticism is made. The missing part of *Being and Time* cannot be written, he says:

> . . . because in order to write it down the quality of a prophet, or at least of a genuine mystic would be necessary. But Heidegger is neither, although many [of his] disciples have for a long time draped him out in a mystical way. Moreover, the philosopher himself is not without guilt in this masquerade. There are places, even in *Being and Time*, but really for the first time in later writings, which in fact sound mystical, without being so.
>
> (Hühn., 121)

Heidegger manages to create the disguise of a mystic by drawing upon two classical sources of Western mysticism, Plotinus and Meister Eckhart. From Plotinus, Hühnerfeld claims, Heidegger takes the distinction between that which is seen in virtue of the illuminating power of the sun (things, beings) and the light of the Sun itself (Being). When we look at things, we forget the power by which they are made visible (ontic truth). Only by turning away from sensible things are we able to behold the sun itself (ontological truth). But the difference between Heidegger and Plotinus, Hühnerfeld says, is that for Plotinus the Sun represents God, and visible things stand for His creatures. Now since the Creator does not wish to degrade His own creation, there is in Plotinus no suggestion that those who concern themselves with "things" are lost in a "they"-world; there is no wish to discredit non-mystics as "fallen." The world and reason are preparatory steps for mysticism, not its opposite (Hühn., 122-4).

From Meister Eckhart, Heidegger takes much of his vocabulary, such as the verb "*west*" (Hühn., 121). But once again there are impor-

33

tant underlying differences between Meister Eckhart himself and the use which Heidegger makes of him. Meister Eckhart tells us we must turn away from the crowd if we would unite with God. But this must not be confused with Heidegger's critique of the "they," Hühnerfeld cautions. For Meister Eckhart does not despise the world nor consider it fallen. Moreover Heidegger, like Meister Eckhart, speaks of the necessity of a "leap" away from the world, but in Meister Eckhart this is a leap into the loving arms of God, whereas in Heidegger it is a leap into Nothingness. Of Heidegger, Hühnerfeld says:

> But about the arms into which man must jump, if he is to free himself from fallenness, the philosopher refuses to speak. It is an heroic leap into the Nothing which is demanded here. . . . (Hühn., 125)

From this comparative study of the relationship of Heidegger to Plotinus and Meister Eckhart, Hühnerfeld concludes that Heidegger's mysticism is a pretense and a sham, and this for two reasons. In the first place, the arms into which Heidegger asks us to make the leap are not trustful but ominous, not a plenum of Being but an "abyss of Nothingness." In the second place, Heidegger has never passed through the trial of "beings" and "reason." He has never tried to think the world through philosophically. He has not given reason a full and fair test. He does not see in "things" what the mystic sees: God's creation, God's reflections. For Hühnerfeld, the one thing that is lacking in Heidegger's mysticism is God Himself, but that is the one thing that the history of mysticism teaches us cannot be lacking. Heidegger's mysticism is therefore a "pure vocabulary without content" (Hühn., 126).

In Heidegger's alleged affectation of a mystical attitude we can see running together all of the themes which Hühnerfeld developed in his account of Heidegger's biography: the hauteur of the authority, of the man who knows, and who separates himself from the crowd; the irrationalism of the man who has left reason behind; the nationalistic love of an old German master, the first German theologian, as Alfred Rosenberg called Meister Eckhart in *The Myth of the 20th Century* (though Hühnerfeld never mentions Rosenberg's book).[12]

Hühnerfeld's study, therefore, poses three questions to the present work, three difficulties concerning the "mystical element in Heidegger's thought": (1) The first and clearest problem is whether Heidegger's "experience" (*Erfahrung*)—of language, of thought, of the matter of thought—is something genuine, or whether it is a pretense and affectation. Can we assume with Heidegger—as we have always assumed with

Meister Eckhart—that we are dealing with a thinker who speaks "first hand"? Or is there good reason to believe with Hühnerfeld that Heidegger's experience is a "mere vocabulary without content"? (2) If we decide against Hühnerfeld that Heidegger's experience of Being is indeed authentic, are we to conclude that Heidegger's experience is mystical? Is Heidegger a mystic? Is thinking a mysticism? Or has Heidegger entered into a "region" which is neither philosophy, mysticism, nor poetry? (3) Hühnerfeld insists that Heidegger's appropriation of the mystical leap results in a leap into an abyss and that Meister Eckhart would not have been willing to make such a leap himself as Heidegger describes. Heidegger himself speaks of the difference between the "danger" and the "saving," the withdrawal and the bestowal. Does Heidegger's leap of thought not expose us to the danger without assuring us of the saving? Among Eckhart's writings there is a *Book of Divine Consolation*. But one can hardly imagine a comparable treatise by Heidegger. Is Heidegger's path of thought fraught with danger and despair and helplessness?

It is of course possible to pursue a completely opposite strategy to that of Hühnerfeld in dealing with the problem of the mystical element in Heidegger's thought. One could assume without further ado that the mystical ring in Heidegger's thought is true and that Heidegger has indeed entered the company of such thinkers as Plotinus and Meister Eckhart. One could then argue that it is precisely because of this genuinely mystical turn that Heidegger's thought has become troublesome. This is precisely the kind of criticism of Heidegger which is undertaken by Laszlo Versényi. The difference between these two lines of criticism is rooted in their differing attitudes toward mysticism. Hühnerfeld is sympathetic to the great Western mystics, and he resents Heidegger's pretension to their ranks. For him Heidegger is a self-styled mystic whose allusion to Meister Eckhart is a sign of his own *hybris*. But Versényi is largely unsympathetic to mysticism. It is to mysticism itself—be it that of Plotinus, Meister Eckhart, or the later Heidegger—that he objects. In assuming the mantle of the mystic, Heidegger has, as far as Versényi is concerned, inherited a whole nest of difficulties.

Before examining Versényi's critique of Heidegger, however, we must first turn to Karl Löwith's *Heidegger: Thinker in a Time of Need*. For Versényi was Löwith's student at Heidelberg, and his critique—like that of Hühnerfeld, I might add—is very much in the debt of Löwith (Vers., 190, n. 6). Löwith's work, first published in 1953, only a few years after the appearance of *A Letter on Humanism*, and then expanded in a second edition in 1960, was the first major and knowledge-able critique of the later Heidegger. It is a classic statement of the diffi-culties with which we are confronted by Heidegger's work, particularly as they are related to the present study. Most subsequent criticisms of Heidegger stand in one way or another in the shadow of Löwith's study.

Up to now, Löwith contends, Heidegger has either been revered by uncritical followers or rejected out of hand as an irrationalist. In con-nection with the latter extreme, Löwith notes those in the scientific community who "react with abhorrence at this new mysticism, which reminds one of Eckhart, to whom—according to Heidegger's own state-ment—the most extreme sharpness and depth of thought belong" (Löw., 8). Hoping to mediate between reverence (*Verehrung*) and revilement (*Verachtung*), with the aim of making a genuine critical encounter with Heidegger, Löwith undertakes an interpretation of the "reversal" which is for him an interpretation of the "foundation" (*Begründung*) of Da-sein: is Dasein to be founded on its own authentic being or on Being itself which appropriates Dasein to itself (Löw., 7)?

After examining the radical reinterpretation which Heidegger has made in *A Letter on Humanism* of such basic concepts in *Being and Time* as thrownness, resoluteness, truth, and the term "Da-sein" itself (Löw., 15ff.), Löwith concludes that Heidegger has subscribed not to one but two grounds in the course of his work. The first is Dasein, on the basis of which "there is" (*es gibt*) Being (*Being and Time*). The second is Being itself, on the basis of which there is (*es gibt*) Dasein (the later writings) (Löw., 38). Löwith objects that Heidegger has attempted to conceal this radical reversal in his thought and to give the impression that the interpretation he later put on *Being and Time* was in fact what he intended to say in 1927. Löwith does not hold that Heidegger has "falsified" *Being and Time*, but rather that he has radically overhauled it without acknowledging that fact (Löw., 17-18, n. 2).

Now Löwith has considerable misgivings about the position which the later Heidegger has adopted, and it is here that his critique becomes especially relevant to the problem of the mystical element in Heideg-ger's thought. He wonders with what right Heidegger can assure us that in the "danger" there also lies something "saving," or that a new "root-edness" (*Bodenständigkeit*) can be found amidst technical objects, provided that we adopt a proper attitude toward them. Is this anything more than wishful thinking, Löwith asks. What assurance do we have that if Being conceals itself—as it has from Plato to Nietzsche—it will also be moved to reveal itself (Löw., 17)? Here Löwith raises the difficulty which, we have seen, was posed also by Hühnerfeld, and which we re-ferred to as the problem of the "danger" of Heidegger's path. It is one thing to entrust ourselves to a loving God and an altogether different thing to be "released" to Heidegger's Being. The mystical attitude adopted by Dasein has been detached from its religious matrix, and that is the source of a major difficulty with it.

Löwith also poses another problem which, we will see below, is expanded upon in Versényi's work. Heidegger has formulated in his later writings a more radical form of the ontological difference whereby Being is no longer treated as the Being of beings—for this is now identified with "beingness" (*Seiendheit*) (Löw., 39 ff.). Rather Being is thought of as if it had dissolved its relation with beings, as if it were literally something "ab-solute" or, to use Meister Eckhart's term, "detached." How then, Löwith asks, can this Being come into relation to man and find in man its "there"? In the Christian tradition, in which Being is God Who incarnated Himself out of love for men, it presents no difficulty that that which is wholly other than beings should find a place among them. But Heidegger's Being is not the Christian God. So, too, Löwith asks, how can man "help" and "preserve" such a "Being" in its "truth"? Is the " 'it' which gives so helpless," Löwith wants to know, "that it needs man as a watchman, shepherd and forest-guide in order not to get lost in its own forest" (Löw., 43)? This is a problem of some importance and we shall be able to formulate it even more exactly after a consideration of Versényi's study.

There is one last point which I wish to bring out in connection with Löwith's treatment of Heidegger by way of a postscript to our discussion of his study, and this concerns his explanation of the tremendous influence of Heidegger. This is to be attributed, he says, to the fact that in Heidegger "the power of his philosophical thought is bound up with a religious motif" (Löw., 72). Heidegger's thought is "religious" but not "Christian" (Löw., 10). Indeed, the very indeterminateness of this religious quality is attractive to many who feel vaguely religious but who are unwilling to commit themselves to the specifically Christian doctrine (Löw., 111). Löwith singles out a sentence from the last page of *The Fieldpath* in which Heidegger, referring to the "address" which the "field path" makes to us, asks: "Does the soul speak? Does the world speak? Does God speak?" (FW, 7/39). A thinker like St. Augustine would have no difficulty deciding this question, comments Löwith; for Augustine was clearly interested not in the world, but in the relation of the soul to God. But of Heidegger Löwith observes:

> The post-Christian thinker Heidegger, on the other hand, determines human Dasein as being-in-the-world. And the question remains undecided and ambiguous whether Being in general speaks above all as the world to the Dasein of man, or as God to the soul. (Löw., 112)

37

There is, according to Löwith, something provocative and suggestive about this indefinite religiosity of Heidegger. It suggests the relation of the soul to God, but it leaves it open as to whether it is really the relation of the "world" to "mortals." In my own judgment, Heidegger's work as a whole clears up this ambiguity very definitively in the direction of the "world" and "mortals." His concern is in the end clearly not with God and the soul but time and history. Rather than an indefinite allusion to God and the soul it seems to me that what Löwith has discovered is that for Heidegger the mystical relationship of God to the soul has become an implicit "model" (SD, 54/50) for the relationship of Being and thought. Thus, what Löwith calls the "religious motif" in Heidegger is in fact founded upon the "mystical element" in his thought, viz., the fact that he has articulated the relationship between Being and Dasein in a way which is strikingly like the relationship between God and the soul in mystical literature. This is not only the explanation of Heidegger's great influence—for mysticism and the mystical have always exerted a great influence on Western thought—but it is also the source of the great difficulty which so many thinkers experience with his work.

Versényi's book carries out and sharpens Löwith's line of criticism. For Versényi, Heidegger's work has developed in three stages, and it is in the third and final period (in *Gelassenheit* and *Der Satz vom Grund*), that Heidegger's thought takes on an openly mystical character. It is at this point, he thinks, that serious difficulties arise with Heidegger's thought. Like Löwith, he sees an abrupt reversal between the standpoint of *Being and Time* and the point of view defended in *A Letter on Humanism*. For Heidegger's position in *Being and Time* "is so Dasein-related, man-bound and relativistic" that it is "surprising" to see Heidegger a decade or so later take "strong exception to what he considers to be humanistic, subjectivistic, and relativistic theories of truth" (Vers., 52-3). Still, on the whole, Versényi does not see the first two stages of Heidegger's thought as contradicting one another. They form instead a "balanced whole" (Vers., 136) in which Heidegger tries to compensate in the later writings for the overly subjectivistic position he adopted in *Being and Time*. Heidegger wanted to develop an idea of Being which is not defined in terms of man (Vers., 83). "*Prima facie*," Versényi says, Heidegger does succeed in overcoming the "humanization of truth" and Being, of which Western metaphysics and *Being and Time* itself are guilty (Vers., 126). It is not man who brings about the truth; on the contrary, thought or truth is an "event" which happens to man, issuing from Being itself. But while it is true that Heidegger has succeeded in "dehumanizing" thought, he has in the process "humanized" Being. For Being still needs man: "the word still needs speakers, truth still needs sayers, the Message still needs messengers" (Vers., 137). Thus although the later writings shift all the emphasis to Being, still there is in both *Being and Time* and the later work a bond between Being and Dasein which is such that "there is" Being only while "there is" man, and there is man only so long as there is Being. Between Being and Dasein there exists a "correspondence"—Being "addresses" man and man "responds"—a living interchange.

But with the publication of *Gelassenheit* (1959) and *Der Satz vom Grund* (1957), in Versényi's view, Heidegger upsets this delicate balance. These works "overcompensate for the shortcomings of *Being and Time*" and "in the end . . . flatly contradict the results of the existentialistic analysis" (Vers., 142). The movement of the "dialectic of correspondence" (cf. Löwith, pp. 37-8) between Being and man is "slowed, its outlines are blurred." With these works Heidegger moves into the proximity of the German mystics:

> In its original use, by the German mystics, *Gelassenheit* denoted the attitude and state of mind of a man who had resigned his own will, taken leave of himself and the world, and, relinquishing all that is earthly, had devoted, entrusted, and abandoned himself totally to God. The word had the connotation of a double movement: away from oneself and the world, and to God. In spite of Heidegger's reluctance to speak of God—"we come too late for the gods and too early for Being" ([A]ED 7)—his use of the word carries the same overtones and refers to a relationship structurally the same as mystic *Gelassenheit*. (Vers., 143)

In *Gelassenheit*, the active life of "responding" to Being which Versényi attributes to the "middle" Heidegger (1930 to the early '50 s) is destroyed. *Gelassenheit*—the very word of course is Meister Eckhart's—refers to a state of total self-denial and self-repression. It is a condition of such passivity that the most noble attitude Dasein can adopt toward the "region"—Heidegger no longer calls it "Being"—is to remain "open" and to "wait" upon it. The promise of a disclosure is a "shadowy hope," Versényi observes, which cannot be clarified.

In *Der Satz vom Grund*, the blurring of the lines which Heidegger had drawn between Being and Dasein is, according to Versényi, carried out even further. Being and man still need one another, as in the earlier works, but it is "difficult to say why"; indeed, in this work Heidegger discourages us from even asking why:

39

. . . the fate of Being and man has become so much of a Mystery that those who want to follow Heidegger on his path can no longer ask questions. They have to abandon philosophy as reflective, self-reflective thought altogether, and find consolation and reassurance in mystical poetry and faith. (Vers., 158)

Versényi singles out for consideration from *Der Satz vom Grund* Heidegger's analysis of the verse from the mystical poet Angelus Silesius:

Without Why

The rose is without why; it blooms because it blooms;
It cares not for itself, asks not if it's seen.

(CW, I, 289/66)

This saying of Silesius is opposed by Heidegger to Leibniz's Principle of Sufficient Reason: nothing is without reason. The philosophical principle is subjectivistic, because it demands that a reason be rendered to the thinking subject, but in the saying of the mystic poet there is a recognition that man most truly is when he is, like the rose, "without why," i.e., when he surrenders all questioning and lets the Ground—Being—be. (Versényi rightly traces the expression "without why" back to Meister Eckhart, who to a great extent is being set to verse by Angelus Silesius.) Versényi points out that according to Heidegger the "ground" revealed to a thinking which is without why is a groundless ground, an abyss (*Ab-grund*). As such it is a mere "play":

It plays because it plays.

The "because" submerges in the game. The game is without "why." It plays while (*dieweil*) it plays. It remains only play, the highest and the deepest. (SG, 188; cf. Vers., 154)

When Heidegger calls for abandonment to a groundless play, he has effectively destroyed the living dialogue between Being and Dasein, according to Versényi. While "Being and Dasein still belong together even in Heidegger's last, most prophetic and mystical writings" (Vers., 155), the dynamic interchange between them is destroyed, and man is reduced to a helpless suppliant "waiting upon" the movements of an enigmatic "mystery." The "impotence" of Dasein which Heidegger discussed in *What is Metaphysics?* (WM, 33/338) now returns in his latest writings to haunt the relationship between Being and man.

From this important—and often ignored—critique of *Gelassenheit* and

Der Satz vom Grund, Versényi draws four conclusions pertinent to the present study. (1) In the first place, he argues that "Heidegger's position as a prophet or mystic" has put him in "an impregnable methodological position," one indeed which is so impregnable that philosophical discussion with him is impossible. If a philosopher wishes to approach Heidegger he can do so only by means of reason, but reason has been ruled out beforehand by Heidegger as "humanistic and therefore invalid" (Vers., 162). Now if one has no mystical vision of one's own with which to challenge Heidegger's view, one cannot raise any question about what Heidegger has said. One should simply accept it, or leave it alone. But if one does claim a "rival inspiration," one has *ipso facto* granted in principle the possible authority of Heidegger's own thought. And one has oneself left philosophy behind. The argument is a "closed circle" which "offers philosophy no point whereby to enter it" (Vers., 163).

This same difficulty can be illustrated further by consulting the exchange that took place between Versényi and Walter Biemel at the Heidegger Colloquium at Pennsylvania State University in 1969. Biemel prefaces a paper on "Poetry and Language in Heidegger" by issuing a warning to his listeners. There are only two possible ways to make an interpretation of Heidegger. The first is to analyze or criticize Heidegger's thought from without. In this case one will inevitably adopt the language of metaphysics and retranslate what Heidegger has said back into the language of metaphysics and, in so doing, distort what is important about it, viz., its very overcoming of metaphysics. The alternative to this, Biemel notes, is "to arrive at Heidegger's position with a leap and then to remain there."[13] But there is a difficulty in doing this, too. For the leap demands a long preparation, and there is a "presumption" involved in this approach in which the "interpreter" of Heidegger "passes himself off as Heidegger," as one who knows what Heidegger knows, while at the same time he spared himself the toil which led up to this leap. Both possible approaches to Heidegger are inadequate, and so we must concede, Biemel concludes, that no interpretation of Heidegger is possible for us:[14]

> To this day a genuine dialogue with Heidegger has never taken place because the partner to such a dialogue is lacking and because, strictly speaking, we remain strange to his thought.

The lecture that follows, Biemel adds, is but a preparation for some future genuine dialogue.

Biemel has been effectively describing the "methodological im-pregnability" which Versényi attributes to Heidegger. Only another "thinker" who is also beyond philosophy can possibly dialogue with Heidegger. Philosophers cannot break into this "closed circle." In his comments on Biemel's pages, Versényi not surprisingly takes up Biemel's "preface." If one examines Versényi's reply to Biemel care-fully, one sees that he does not really disagree with Biemel, at least with regard to Heidegger's "third" stage. For there, Versényi concurs, no interpretation is possible, and philosophy is out of order. Versényi's only real criticism of Biemel's position is that a dialogue and in-terpretation of Heidegger's work before that point is possible and indeed necessary. But once Heidegger's thought takes a mystical turn, his thought becomes a closed circle which forever excludes philosophi-cal interpretation.

Once again we find ourselves brought back to the remark with which we began our study, that Heidegger is a thinker who conducts his thinking at the limits of philosophy. What relation and "dialogue" can there be between thinking, insofar as it has taken on a kinship to the mystic, and philosophy, insofar as it is a matter of reason (*eine Sache der ratio*)? This problem was also broached in a somewhat different way by Hühnerfeld, too, when he agreed that Heidegger has not passed through the trial of reason, that he has not put reason to a "fair test," before he made the leap of thought. What is the relation of thinking and reason?

(2) The second conclusion which Versényi draws which is of interest to us concerns the much debated problem of "humanism" in Heideg-ger's later thought. Heidegger "claims to speak with a more than human—and therefore non-humanistic tongue," Versényi argues (163). Because his thought is "a kind of negative theology and mysticism" (163), his only message is the rejection of all human experience and thought. In leaving humanistic metaphysics behind, Heidegger has sacrificed the human significance of his work. Thinking is opposed to humanism, for Versényi, because thinking is mysticism, and mysticism is the denial of everything human.

Versényi defends this view as follows. Heidegger has rightly pointed out the danger which consists in the forgetfulness of Being and pre-occupation with beings. But he is himself a victim of the opposite danger, which is a forgetfulness of beings which tries to occupy itself with Being "alone." Being and beings form the two poles of the philosophical universe of discourse which "cannot be transcended *within philosophy*" (Vers., 168). The more one is occupied with beings alone, the more one moves outside philosophy to the empirical and

42

technical. But the more one gravitates towards Being alone, the more one moves into a void which is "empty and formal," however "emotionally charged and mysticoreligious" it may be (Vers., 168).

Following up Löwith's suggestion about the radically detached character of Heidegger's "Being" in the later renderings of the ontological difference, Versényi argues that Heidegger searches for something in his later writings which no man can hope to attain, viz., "the Immediate immediately." (EHD, 59), something indeed which, as these words from the Hölderlin book indicate, Heidegger himself once expressly forbade us to seek (Vers., 165). An immediate knowledge of the Absolute is both impossible and undesirable for man. It is a "void which the intellect cannot endure," a "sheer terror to the intellect" (Vers., 169). Being can never be given ab-solutely, as "absolved from all beings" (Vers., 170). Being can only be attained in beings—as the Heidegger of *Being and Time* well realized. "Pure light as such," Versényi comments, "is invisible; light has to be reflected in and by something to be seen" (Vers., 172-3). Indeed, the whole project of trying to think Being "detached" from beings and fully dehumanized is in principle impossible. For any utterance about Being by man would have to be comprehensible to man "and would then have to be given in human rather than non-human terms" (Vers., 190). If Being is "wholly other," then if it speaks to us in a "wholly other tongue," we will understand nothing that it says (Vers., 190). Indeed, to the extent that Heidegger's mystic utterances do have meaning, Versényi comments ironically, it is because of Heidegger's *failure* to detach Being from beings, his failure to expunge the residue of meaning which still clings to his words (Vers., 173). In the end, Heidegger has submitted to a transcendental illusion, having pushed Being beyond its limits in beings (Vers., 176).

(3) Versényi raises a third objection against Heidegger's efforts to assume the position of a "mystic poet," as he puts it (Vers., 164), and this has to do with Heidegger's originality. What Heidegger is doing in his later works is nothing new; indeed, it is even a "commonplace" outside philosophy itself:

Negative theology has done for a long time what Heidegger now attempts to do, and his call out of the world (of everyday existence, of rational questioning "why?") into another realm is a commonplace to all mysticism and religion. (Vers., 164)

If Heidegger has succeeded in getting beyond metaphysics, he has only managed to say what has been said many times before by non-metaphysicians.

In his comments on Biemel's paper, Versényi seems to suggest that even *within* philosophy Heidegger has discovered nothing new. For what Heidegger has accomplished by his sustained attempt to push language to its limits is to discover the very limits of language. But that is a familiar philosophical insight. It is quite similar to Plato's account of the impossibility of adequately saying anything about the Good, to Kant's argument that outside of the conditions of experience the categories of the Understanding are meaningless, to Kierkegaard's contention that philosophy cannot think what Christian faith is, and to Wittgenstein's attempt to critically establish the boundaries of language. Heidegger's critique of Western metaphysics is therefore nothing novel even within philosophy itself. It is a familiar position to be found in any number of major Western philosophers.

(4) The final difficulty which Versényi points out concerning the mystical turn in Heidegger's later thought deals with the problem of ethics. Heidegger has failed to supply us with criteria for determining what is and what is not to be done (Vers., 176 ff.). This is already a problem even in *Being and Time* itself, where Heidegger's thought was in its most man-related and subjectivistic stage. In *Being and Time* we are told to resolve, but we are given no means to decide upon what to resolve. This problem grows worse in the "middle period" when, having turned from man to Being, Heidegger's only advice to us is to listen to the directives which are elicited by Being itself (HB, 114/222). But by the final stage, Versényi holds, Heidegger's concern with ethics has completely deteriorated. For in the latest writings, all human actions—ethical, political, social, or whatever—have been so devalued that the question of ethics cannot even arise (Vers., 186-7). For Versényi, mysticism amounts to passivity, self-diremption, the loss of the self. Thus in taking a "mystical" turn, Heidegger has inevitably abdicated the sphere of activity and the rules that govern activity. Not only is Heidegger's thought "beyond philosophy," according to Versényi, it is also "beyond good and evil."

Versényi's work thus poses four questions to our study of the mystical element in Heidegger's thought: (1) the problem of reason: what is philosophy to make of a methodologically impregnable mysticism? (2) the problem of humanism: in attempting to speak with a more than humanistic tongue, has not Heidegger destroyed the human significance of his work? (3) the problem of originality: what does Heidegger say which has not been said by non-metaphysicians (and even metaphysicians) before him? (4) the problem of ethics: has not all human action and all conduct become a nullity vis-à-vis Being?

When we line up the questions which we have drawn from Versényi's work, along with the difficulties which Hühnerfeld's study has posed to us (remembering the debt of both these authors to Löwith himself), we can see that "the problem of the mystical element in Heidegger's thought" can be broken down into six distinguishable issues:

(1) Is Heidegger's experience of Being genuine, or are we confronted in the thought of Heidegger with a "false Eckhart"?

(2) If Heidegger's experience is genuine, is it a "mystical" experience? Is Heidegger a mystic?

(3) If Heidegger has, in the later work, taken on a likeness to the mystic, what has become of the *homo humanus*, the humanity of man?

(4) Does Heidegger's way of detachment (*Abschied vom Seienden*) and "letting be" (*Gelassenheit*), having removed itself from any specifically Christian or religious context, become a dangerous and ominous path?

(5) What is the relation of thinking to ethics?

(6) What is the relation between thinking, insofar as it has a kinship with mysticism, and philosophy, insofar as it is a matter of reason?

We shall in Chapter Five take up each of these difficulties in turn.

But before we can begin to deal adequately with these important and basic questions about Heidegger, we must make extensive preparations. These questions cannot and must not be answered apart from a careful consideration of Heidegger's critique of metaphysics and of the special kind of relationship which exists between Heidegger and Meister Eckhart. If there is anything to blame in the works of Hühnerfeld, Löwith, and Versényi on Heidegger, it is the somewhat casual and offhand way in which they speak of mysticism in general and of Meister Eckhart in particular. In none of these works does the critique of "Heidegger's mysticism" proceed from a careful analysis of Heidegger's relationship to Meister Eckhart. While Löwith is more than a little familiar with the relationship between philosophy and Christianity, he does not in his book on Heidegger subject the religious-mystical attitude to a close study, although he considers this "motif" to be of the utmost importance for understanding Heidegger. Hühnerfeld relegates Heidegger's affinity to Meister Eckhart to a "masquerade," but his examination of Meister Eckhart himself is literally limited to a few paragraphs. Versényi uses the term "mystical" as a description of, and often as a charge against, the later Heidegger, and gives us the unavoidable impression that, for him, mysticism is to be equated with contempt of the world and of the self. But this equation, which is never questioned, is not supported by a study of mysticism. Neither Hühnerfeld's sympathy, nor Versényi's lack of sympathy, for mysticism is founded upon a close examination of mysticism.

It will be the special strategy of the present study to work out the relationship between "thinking" and "mysticism" in detail and in the concrete. When we turn in Chapter Five to the questions which we have posed here, we will be prepared to answer them, because we will have examined with care Heidegger's critique of metaphysics (Chapter Two), Meister Eckhart's mysticism (Chapter Three) and the subsequent alliance which is formed between the leap of thought and the *unio mystica* (Chapter Four).

CHAPTER TWO

NOTHING IS WITHOUT GROUND: HEIDEGGER'S
CRITIQUE OF METAPHYSICS

THE point of departure for our study of the mystical element in Heidegger's thought is the course of lectures which Heidegger gave at Freiburg in 1955-56 and which he published under the title *The Principle of Ground* (*Der Satz vom Grund*). The text consists of a series of thirteen course lectures and a concluding address on the subject of this famous principle of Leibniz, "nothing is without reason" (*nihil est sine ratione*). These lectures, which are a lucid and penetrating exposition of Heidegger's view of the nature of ground and reason, are not often accorded the attention in the literature on Heidegger that they merit. But as our discussion of Versényi's critique of Heidegger already suggests, SG[1] is a work of special pertinence to the present study, and this for two reasons.

(1) In the first place, Heidegger's critique of the Principle of Ground is for him not merely a critique of Leibniz. Rather, Leibniz's principle is a touchstone of the entire Western metaphysical tradition, i.e., of the history of philosophy and reason in the West. For Leibniz's principle is not *Leibniz's* principle (SG, 47-8), but an expression of the mission or destiny (*Geschick*) of Being in the West. Being speaks in and through Leibniz. What comes to a head in Leibniz's thought has been there from the beginning in Western philosophy and is with us still today, viz., the demand that a rationale or a ground be brought forth for whatever is held to be "true."

The importance of SG is that it contains Heidegger's analysis of this most basic principle of metaphysics. After a close examination of just what this principle meant in Leibniz's own philosophy, Heidegger moves forward, with a great show of virtuosity, to demonstrate how this principle exerts a decisive influence on Kant and, beyond Kant, on the twentieth century, the age of the atom, our own "time of need." As Löwith remarks about SG:

> . . . in the lecture *Der Satz vom Grund*, the discussion of the traditional principle of thought is not broken into by chance and incidentally by a dramatic allusion to the historical situation, but rather it is essentially inspired by this allusion, and indeed in such a way that the reference to the need of the time the established danger of the atom bomb must explain the abyssal (*abgründige*) danger of thinking according to the authority of the Principle of Ground (according to which every being must have a ground in another and ultimately in a highest **being).**
>
> (Löw., 110)

From Leibniz's formulation of the Principle of Ground Heidegger also moves backwards to the Greek *logos*, of which *ratio* and *Grund* are the translations. In the Greek *logos* Heidegger will find a more primal sense of "ground." SG then orchestrates all of the important themes in Heidegger's interpretation of the history of Western thought, and allows him to develop in a penetrating way his critique of philosophical reason.

(2) The second reason we attach such great importance to SG lies in the fact that in no other work does Heidegger so openly make use of the mystical tradition. The pivotal lecture in this book (Lecture V, SG, 63 ff.) is an "elucidation" (*Erläuterung*) not of Hölderlin but of the verse from the mystical poet Angelus Silesius, "The Rose Is Without Why." By means of this verse, Heidegger will show us the necessity of a "leap" (*Satz*) out of the Principle of Ground as it has been understood by metaphysics into a new and deeper understanding of it. This leap is a leap away from the metaphysician's understanding of "why" and "because," represented by Leibniz, towards the mystic's understanding of it, represented by Angelus Silesius. It is in this work—along with *Gelassenheit*—that Versényi claims Heidegger's thought enters into a third and decisive stage which disrupts the balance or "dialectic of correspondence" between Being and Dasein of which he and Löwith speak. In this work, Versényi claims, the capacity of Dasein for a dynamic response to Being is destroyed. Dasein becomes a humble, passive suppliant waiting upon Being's

48

next inscrutable move. Thus a close study of this text is essential if we are to evaluate this critique of Heidegger's later and seemingly mystical writings.

Before we begin this analysis, however, we must pause to consider a certain translation problem which any discussion of SG must face. The principle which Heidegger is here discussing has become familiar to English speakers under the title "the Principle of Sufficient Reason." This of course is a rendering of the Latin, *principium sufficientis rationis*. "The Principle of Ground" has a harsh sound for English ears. So also we are used to hearing the formulation "nothing is without reason," and not "nothing is without ground." We are thus faced with a decision between the more standard English usage and a rendering which though not quite as smooth in English stays somewhat closer to Heidegger's train of thought. After some debate with myself on this point I have decided to take the more literal (and less literary) route of "ground." For one thing, this has the advantage, as Keith Hoeller points out in his translation of the concluding lecture of SG (207, note), of saving the word "reason" for the German *Vernunft*. But more important, the English "ground" will allow us to see somewhat more easily how *Sein* and *Grund* belong together, that is, how the being emerges into presence out of its "own grounds," and does not require that a ground be rendered for it. And establishing that insight is one of the main intentions of SG. The English "reason" will help us to express Leibniz's principle as an assertion of human subjectivity—we are always demanding reasons—but it does not help us get from *Grund* to *Sein*. Thus in the hope of staying closer to the matter to be thought, we must be prepared to sacrifice a certain elegance.

SG is a series of reflections which takes as its text a metaphysical principle. Its aim is to "think" this principle "through," not only in the sense of understanding it "thoroughly," but in the sense of thinking all the way through the metaphysical proposition down into the source from which the metaphysics springs. There is therefore in SG something of the flavor of a medieval "commentary" on the Scriptures in which a text from the sacred writings is savored and lingered upon. In his *Commentary on the Gospel of St. John*, e.g., Meister Eckhart takes the first sentence of St. John's "Prologue" and weaves around it a lengthy and elaborate commentary (cf. LW, III, 3-44/Cl., 231-57). Heidegger chooses his texts not from the Scriptures but from the history of metaphysics; the words he meditates upon are not the words of God but the words of Being. And if the text is basic enough he will find in it an expression of the basic movement of Western history. Leibniz's Principle of Ground is just such a text for Heidegger. And as Meister Eckhart and other medieval commentators could see in the small four words of the opening line of John's "Prologue" —*in principio erat verbum*—the world-historical fusion of Greek wisdom and Christian revelation, so Heidegger sees in Leibniz's four small words—*nihil est sine ratione*—a principle of world-historical importance. Reflecting upon Leibniz's saying with the patience of a medieval commentator, Heidegger, like Meister Eckhart, even employs the device of varying the inflection of the saying in order to bring out its full meaning.

We are not listening to the words of God in Leibniz's principle, but neither are we merely listening to Leibniz (SG, 68). For if we hear Leibniz's saying properly, we will hear not only a familiar metaphysical assertion, but we will also overhear the fundamental movement of Being itself as it speaks to us in the metaphysics of the modern age. Leibniz's principle is therefore the speaking of language itself. The whole meditation of SG takes place in the "region" of "language," in the realm in which language (*die Sprache*) speaks and addresses (*spricht*) itself to us:

> The path of thinking followed in these lectures goes towards the Principle of Ground, towards that which the principle says, about which it speaks and how it says it. (SG, 25)

The Principle of Ground originates in a primordial call (*Ruf*) or saying (*Spruch, Sage*) which "addresses" (*anruft, an-spricht*) modern man and to which the Principle itself is a response. Notice then the questions which Heidegger poses in SG: what does the Principle of Ground say? Where does the call originate? Do we hear everything it has to say? Or do we listen to it only long enough to conclude that what it has to say is simple and self-evident?

Accordingly, Heidegger's program in SG may be articulated as follows: (1) In the first place he listens attentively to the Principle of Ground as it is formulated in Leibniz's philosophy. (2) Then he gives a hearing to Angelus Silesius's saying, which is apparently out of harmony with Leibniz. (3) On the basis of listening to the mystical poet, he proposes a way to hear Leibniz's principle in a "new key." (4) From the listening point established by hearing the Principle in a new key, he tells us how to hear Leibniz's saying as it is reverberated throughout the history of Western metaphysics. (5) Finally, we are told to listen to a "playing" in the Principle (*Satz*) of Ground, a "high" and "danger-ous" playing which is inviting us to play along with it.

1. *The Principle of Ground in the Metaphysics of Leibniz*

Heidegger begins his analysis of the Principle of Ground by listen-ing as closely as possible to the way in which this Principle, after a long period of "incubation" lasting some two thousand years, was finally formulated by Leibniz. What is said by Leibniz is evident to everyone: nothing is without ground. Is it not strange, then, Heideg-ger asks, that it took so long to formulate this principle? The Principle of Ground is so transparent to us that we are already finished with it as soon as we hear it (SG, 16). But this very fact should give us pause. For, as has been Heidegger's constant view from *Being and Time* on, we tend to be thoughtless about that which is most familiar to us. And so it might well be that the Principle of Ground is the most "enigmatic" (*rätselvollste*: SG, 16) of all propositions. Indeed it will be Heidegger's strategy, in these opening lectures of SG, to throw us into confusion about a principle we all take to be self-evident. As with the concept of Being in the opening pages of *Being and Time*, Heideg-ger will show that the Principle of Ground is only superficially simple and devoid of difficulty. When it is understood more deeply, it will turn out to be clouded and confusing.

The difficulties which Heidegger sees in the Principle of Ground have to do with its "formal" character as a "principle" (*Grundsatz*). In the first place, Heidegger holds, this "first principle" throws us into a perplexing circle. Inasmuch as it is a "principle," it is the "foundation" (*Grund*) of other propositions (*Sätze*). The proposition which asserts that everything must have a ground is itself a "funda-mental proposition" (*Der Satz vom Grund ist ein Grundsatz*: SG, 21). Thus in order to clarify the Principle of Ground we need to know what a "principle" is. But in order to know what a "principle" (*Grund-satz*) is, we need to know what "ground" or "fundamental" means (cf. WG, 10-3). Yet where are we to find what "ground" means except in the Principle of Ground (*Satz vom Grund*: SG, 23)? In order to assure the reader that he is not simply exploiting a peculiarity of the German language, Heidegger shows that the same difficulty inheres in Leibniz's Latin expression *principio rationis*, for a "principle" according to Christian Wolff is "that which contains within itself the reason for another." A "principle" thus contains the "reason" for what follows from the principle (SG, 30-1).

In the second place, Heidegger points out, the Principle of Ground is itself "something," viz., a proposition. Are we then to say that as such it falls under its own scope and that it must itself have a ground? But if there is a ground for the Principle of Ground then we may also ask what is the ground for the ground of the Principle of Ground? The result is an infinite regress. But if we deny that the Principle of Ground has itself a ground, then we are left with the disconcerting result that the very assertion which claims that nothing is without reason is itself without reason. On either alternative, we are unable to produce a firm and stable ground, and so we fall into the groundless (SG, 27-8).

While one may quarrel with the way in which Heidegger has formulated the difficulty which first principles present us, his point is clear, and it is a bit like Johannes Climacus's critique of the "system": there is no absolute beginning for speculative philosophy. Every beginning, every first principle, involves some kind of faith or arbitrary decision.[2] We have thus entered into what Heidegger calls a "dangerous region," a "twilight zone." "This region is known to many thinkers although they rightly say very little about it" (SG, 28). The most important observation laid down by one who knows his way around these dangerous waters was made by Aristotle, who observed that if one does not know what needs to be proved and what does not, then one is lacking in *paideia* (*Met*, IV, 1006 a 6 ff.). To have *paideia*, according to Heidegger, is to know what is suitable and what is not. And for Heidegger it is a mark of *paideia* not to be taken in by the apparent self-evidence of the Principle of Ground, which is the evidence only of "average everydayness," but to realize, instead, that a reflection is needed upon what "ground" means, even at the risk of "groundlessness."

Heidegger claims that the obscurity which envelops the Principle of Ground arises from the fact that modern thought has located the essence of ground in a "fundamental principle" (*Grundsatz*) to begin with. As a fundamental principle, the Principle of Ground belongs to the realm of propositions (*der Bezirk von Sätzen*: SG, 40). In the sphere of propositions the *Grundsatz* is first. This is reflected by the fact that "*Grundsatz*" was adopted in the eighteenth century as a translation of the scholastic "*principium*." A principle is what stands first in a series of propositions, the other members of which are derived from the principle. Today we call such a series an "axiomatic system." Like Leibniz himself, who said that "axioms are propositions which are held to be evident by everyone," we all agree today that axioms are propositions. In modern thought it is self-evident and beyond question that principles (*principia*), basic propositions (*Grundsätze*), and axioms (*axiomata*) are interchangeable and equivalent terms.

But in Heidegger's view, while "*principium*" and "*Grundsatz*" are translations of "*axioma*," they contain nothing of the original force of that Greek word. *Axioma* is derived from the Greek *axio*, a verb meaning to value or appreciate something ("axiology" is the science of "values"). Thus an axiom is that which is held in the highest esteem. However, the Greeks had no "theory of values," in which a "value" is something added on to a "fact" by the representational (*vorstellend*) thought of the ego.[3] To value something for the Greeks means, according to Heidegger:

> . . . to bring something into that regard (*Ansehen*) in which it stands, to bring it to appearance, and to preserve it in this. (SG, 34)

"*Ansehen*" in German means the "look" or "appearance" of an object, but it also means the "respect" or "regard" in which it is held. Like the English "regard" it means at once the way in which a thing looks from a certain point of view ("in this regard"), and also the esteem with which it is held ("in high regard"). Now for the Greek a thing stands in the highest regard, not because man has conferred a value upon it, as in modern theory, but rather because it stands forth of itself:

> The thing which stands in the highest regard (*im höchsten Ansehen*) brings this view (*Ansicht*) from out of itself. This look rests on its own visage (*Ansehen*). (SG, 34)

Inasmuch as an axiom is something from which other things are in some way derived, then, in Heidegger's interpretation of the authentic sense of *axiom*, that which stands forth in the highest view, and which is viewed with the highest regard, provides the "prospect" (*Ansicht*) or view from out of which other things receive their look (SG, 34-5).

Hence if Euclid speaks of certain "axioms," like the axiom that two things which are similar to a third are similar to one another, then, according to Heidegger's interpretation, Euclid did not mean to lay down a proposition whose merit consisted in the deductive possibilities which it opened up. Rather the axiom is an "objective meaning" (this is certainly not Heidegger's language) which is so "luminous" (illuminating) that other "geometrical objects" stand in its "light." Human thought is enabled to "see" what these objects mean in the light of the "axiom" and to see what the axiom means in its own light. Heidegger's view is very much like the theory of mathematics and logic which Husserl puts forth in the *Logical Investigations* (a book which Heidegger seems to regard as Husserl's best), and which he himself defended in his 1916 *Habilitationsschrift*. It lays stress upon meanings which stand forth on their own and disclose themselves, rather than upon an inventive human subject which constructs the most deductively supple and fruitful assumptions for his "system" (of propositions).

Thus the riddles to which the Principle of Ground falls prey are only symptomatic of a deeper-lying difficulty, viz., the fact that the essence of ground (*Grund*) has been located in a proposition (*Satz*) to begin with. When Leibniz translated *axioma* by *Grundsatz*, this was, according to Heidegger, no innocent linguistic convention. On the contrary, what lies behind it is the fundamental movement of Western history (SG, 40). *Grundsatz* and *axioma* belong to fundamentally different dispensations of Being (*Seinsgeschick*), fundamentally different ways in which "language" itself speaks to us. In order to locate the essence of ground—it is already apparent—we will need something deeper and more original than a proposition, even a "fundamental proposition." But we are not yet ready to make the "leap" (*Satz*) from this "proposition" (*Satz*) into such seemingly bottomless depths.

In order to hear everything that is being said in Leibniz's principle, Heidegger next turns to Leibniz's characterization of his principle as a *principium grande* i.e., a principle of "great power" (*grossmächtig*: SG, 43). What is the "great power" of this principle, Heidegger asks? And—just as important—do we today still experience it? In answering these questions Heidegger will bring the seemingly abstract problem of the Principle of Ground into relationship with the "pressing needs of the present age" (SG, 42). In following this discussion we will come to understand Löwith's comment, above, upon Heidegger's ability to relate the most abstruse metaphysics to the present time of need (Löw., 110).

In order to comprehend the "great power" of this principle, Heidegger tells us, we must reflect upon another formulation which Leibniz gave to this principle. Up to now we have spoken only of the *principium rationis* (*Satz vom Grund*). But the Principle can also be put into what Heidegger calls its "strict" form: *principium reddendae rationis*, the Principle of "Rendering" a Ground (*Satz vom zuzustellen-den Grund*). In this formulation the principle runs "for every truth, a reason can be given" (SG, 44).

What has been added to Leibniz's principle by the introduction of the *ratio* "*reddenda*"? *Reddere* means literally to "give back." Thus, in keeping with his respect for the elemental meaning of words, Heidegger raises, in the address which he gave in May, 1956, at the end of this lecture course, three basic questions about the *ratio reddenda* (SG, 193-5/209-211; cf. SG, 45-6, 53-4). (1) What does the ground which is to be given back lay the ground for? Of what is it to be the ground? We have seen that the ground is the ground of "every truth." But truth for Leibniz means a true proposition, and a proposition is that in which a subject and a predicate are bound together. The ground supplies the justification for the binding of one predicate rather than another to the subject. Not any combination of subject and predicate is true, but only that for which there is a "reason" (SG, 194/209). (2) The second question asks: why must a ground be "given back" at all? The answer is clear: because without a ground, the proposition is "baseless," "unjustified." Without it, any arbitrary combination of subject and predicate would be true.

(3) The third question is decisive, and provides the clue for understanding the "great power" of this principle: to whom or to what must this ground be given back? Heidegger's all-important answer: to man, to the one who judges and composes propositions, the one who "represents" (*vorstellt*) "objects" (*Gegenstände*). The necessity to give a ground back to man arises from the fact that, ever since the time of Descartes and Leibniz, man has not been understood as being-in-the-world. Rather the "I" (*ego*), which is thought of as something worldless, is brought into relation with the world only inasmuch as the ego "represents" it by its concepts and judgments. The world is given the status of an object (*Gegenstand*), that which "stands forth" as the correlate of a proposition, that which is given standing by the proposition. The world is not given directly to the ego; it is only represented. Hence a sufficient reason must be given to the ego in order to guarantee the ego that its representations are genuinely "representative" of the world, that they genuinely bring the world back "before" (*gegen*) the ego.

The power (*Macht*) of the Principle of Ground lies in the fact, then, that all knowledge (*Erkennen*), all representations, are subject to its demand. No proposition escapes its sphere of influence (*Machtbereich*). But we must not think that the power of this principle is limited to the realm of knowledge alone, as Schopenhauer suggested, for it extends to all that *is*, as well. According to Leibniz and Descartes, and to all modern thinkers, that which "is" is an "object," that which has been given "objective standing" (*stehen*) by the proposition. Leibniz's principle then means that something "is," i.e., is certified as a being, only by being expressed in a proposition which satisfies the Principle of Ground (SG, 47). The great power of Leibniz's principle consists in the fact:

> . . . that the *principium reddendae rationis*—apparently only a principle of knowledge—becomes precisely and simultaneously as a principle of knowledge the principle for everything which *is*. (SG, 47)

One might think that with this conclusion Heidegger has completed his analysis of the great power of Leibniz's principle. But there is still one final—indeed critical—step to be taken. Is it Leibniz himself, Heidegger asks, who has endowed this principle with its power (SG, 47-8)? Is its power a human power? "Or does the ground itself, of itself as a ground, put such a claim upon our thinking" (SG, 74)? Heidegger's answer, to those who are at all familiar with the later writings, is not surprising. "The greatness and the enduring thing in the thought of a thinker," he says, "consists simply in this, that he brings into words that which has all along been sounding (*immer schon anklingt*)" (SG, 48). Thus when Leibniz enunciated this principle, he was expressing something that was already being sounded forth. He "heard" an address which was already there but had never been articulated before. The important thing which Leibniz heard, according to Heidegger, is the "claim" (*Anspruch*) which the Principle of Ground makes upon us, the "demand" it puts upon us. In the saying (*Spruch*) "nothing is without reason," Leibniz heard the demand (*Anspruch*) which it contains. "*Reddenda*" means "that which is to be rendered," "that which must be brought forth." The *reddenda* signifies therefore that a reason must be delivered to the thinking subject. This demand is still being made today, and we are today still in its grip.

Now Heidegger has at last uncovered the great power of Leibniz's Principle. It is the power of an inexorable and unconditional demand under which our thought—even today—still stands. The Principle of Ground is not just a proposition (*Satz*), not even a basic proposition (*Grundsatz*), but a decree (*Spruch*) which lays claim to our thought and makes a demand of us (*in Anspruch nehmen*). The power of this decree is nothing human, but the power of Being itself, for it is clear that for Heidegger Leibniz's principle is the address of Being to man. To the extent that we today are everywhere searching for reasons we live under the influence of Leibniz's principle and hear its calling. Yet we do not really hear what this principle says, because with all the receivers and transmitters which we have invented for listening to the most distant sounds, we do not hear the "claim" it is making upon us, the "decree" it lays upon us. We must all confess to having failed to hear this:

All, I say, even those who have from time to time worried themselves about the "essence of ground." (SG, 48).

Even the author of *The Essence of Ground* (*Vom Wesen des Grundes*), Heidegger admits, did not—in 1929—hear the Principle of Ground as the voice of Being itself.[4]

It is thus no accident for Heidegger that our times are called "the age of the atom" (SG, 57 ff.). We have without blinking an eye designated our historical existence, he says, by our ability to harness the powers of nature. It is as if the distinction between nature (*Natur*) and the human spirit (*Geist*) has been eliminated. The atomic age is founded upon nuclear physics, which is the science of elementary particles. The role of the nuclear physicist, according to Heidegger, is to construct an explanation of the atom which will "sustain" (*tragen*) the diverse properties of the various particles and so allow them to cohere together. The scientist proposes a "rational" or "unitary ground" of the diverse phenomena of sub-atomic physics. Thus, even if the physicists of today no longer invoke Kant's "principles"—of substance, causality, and reciprocity—they have not freed themselves from Leibniz's *principium grande*. For even the post-Newtonian is driven by a desire to explain and rationalize, i.e., to give grounds. The demand which Leibniz's principle puts upon us all is the element in which modern science lives.

In the present age, the great power of Leibniz's principle is not merely "felt"; it has been "unleashed" (*entfesselt*: SG, 60) upon us. Its effect has been so great as to have provoked an enormous upheaval in human existence. The demand we live under today to give grounds has taken away from us the ground and basis of our human dwelling, robbing us of our rootedness (*Bodenständigkeit*) in the ground and soil upon which we have always stood. The more we pursue grounds, the more we lose our footing. The more energy we harness, the less

57

we know how "to build and dwell" (*zu bauen und zu wohnen*: SG, 60). We are thus caught up in a fearful "play" (SG, 60-1). The more we search for grounds, the more groundless our existence becomes. It is as though the history of Being is playing with us, tantalizing us, indeed enticing us on to our own destruction. This is the first reference to the "play" of Being which Heidegger makes in SG, and I take it to be of the greatest significance. For one can see taking shape here the problem of the danger of Heidegger's path, which we discussed in Chapter One. The "Being" to which Heidegger invites us to be "released" appears to be a dangerous and destructive force which plays with the essence of man. We shall, at the end of this chapter, bring together Heidegger's utterances on the "play of Being," for they will prove to be of the utmost importance for understanding the relationship between Heidegger and Meister Eckhart.

The word "rootedness" (*Bodenständigkeit*) in the passage above also calls for some comment. In its ordinary sense, it means indigenous, springing from the native soil, and by extension, that which "has roots" or a firm foundation. In Heidegger's usage, the true "ground" of human existence is Being itself. Thus man is uprooted if he is preoccupied with beings, to the neglect of Being. But by the "leap" (*Satz*) of thought (*Denken*), which we will learn to make by listening to Leibniz's principle more carefully, we will arrive at a new ground, a new rootedness which is Being itself, although to metaphysical reason this ground must needs appear as an "abyss." In so doing we will attain a new way of thinking which is not confined to "giving reasons." And as to the question of whether it is possible to attain a new rootedness in the atomic age, the answer is to be found in Heidegger's address to the people of Messkirch in October, 1955. For there Heidegger describes the possibility of living amidst technical things while using them in a way which does not disrupt our essential nature (G, 26/55). His message is like Meister Eckhart's in *On Detachment*: to live in the world, but not to be "attached" to it in one's heart.

In considering Leibniz's principle first as a "fundamental principle" (*Grundsatz*) and then as a *principium grande*, Heidegger has moved from one consideration to the next without following a clearly laid out plan. He himself characterizes these initial considerations as "detours" (*Umwege*: SG, 75). Instead of making straight for the essence of the principle, he follows first one path then another in the hope of gradually letting everything be heard in this saying. Of course we must not be misled by this method, for Heidegger is following a logic of his own. By the time he is finished, he will have made, in an unimposing way, a penetrating historical and problematic critique of Leibniz's principle.

In keeping with this informal procedure, Heidegger next decides to listen to still another formulation of the principle, this one to be found in Leibniz's "Notes of a Student of Spinoza," written in 1676, six years after composing his first formulation (SG, 64 ff.). Here Leibniz speaks of the principle that "nothing exists unless a sufficient reason for its existence is able to be rendered" (... *nihil existere nisi cujus reddi potest ratio existentiae sufficiens*).

The operative word here is "sufficient." As we mentioned above, this is the form in which the principle has become familiar to English readers, viz., as "the principle of sufficient reason" (*der Satz vom zureichenden Grund*). What then is added by the further specification "sufficient" reason? For Heidegger, "*sufficiens*" must be understood in connection with Leibniz's notion of "*perfectio*." In Leibniz's metaphysics, whatever comes to be must have some measure of perfection. Therefore the ground which serves as its foundation must be a "sufficient" ground. The sufficient reason of any object (*Gegenstand*) is that which brings the object into its completion (*Voll-ständigkeit*) as an object. That which allows an object to stand forth at all (*ratio*) must also allow that object to stand forth fully and wholly (*ratio sufficiens*).

For the perfection (*perficere*) of an object the sufficiency (*sufficere*) of its cause is required. Thus if we "listen" to this latest formulation of the Principle of Ground we discover that it is formulated in the language of "making" (*facere*), and that enables us to understand how Leibniz's principle provides the foundation of modern technology. An object is that which has been "brought forth" or "made" (*ex-facere, factum*), i.e., it is the product of a making. As something made, it must be made fully, "through and through" (*per-facere, per-fectum*). This making itself must be sufficient to bring out this perfection, to steep or "suffuse" the object in its fullness or completion (*sub-facere*). This particular formulation of the Principle of Ground is no linguistic accident; rather it brings out the inner "tendency" of Leibniz's thought.

The author of the Principle of Ground is not just by chance the forerunner of modern logic and one of the first to envisage the possibility of the computer. The logical and historical upshot of Leibniz's work is to have provided the direction and the impulse for the development of what Heidegger calls "calculative thought" (*Rechnung*). Calculative thought is the style of thinking which characterizes the mathematical–technical sciences and modern technical philosophy, the style of thinking which today holds us in its grip. For the present age stands dedicated to a technical understanding of reality and to the control of reality which this makes possible. "Technology" is the "making" (*facere*) which lies within the sphere of influence of Leibniz's demand for sufficiency (*sub-facere*). Leibniz's principle, therefore, is no abstract formula belonging to the historical movement we nowadays call "Rationalism." Nor is it merely one of the principles which belongs to "Leibniz's philosophy." It is on the contrary the power by which the modern age is held:

> The thought of Leibniz sustains and stamps the basic tendency of that which, if it is thought out amply enough, we can call the metaphysics of the modern age. The name of Leibniz, therefore, does not in our considerations stand for a characterization of a past (*vergangen*) system of philosophy. The name is a name for the presence (*Gegenwart*) of a thought whose strength has not yet been endured, a presence which is still making itself really present (*entgegenwartet*) to us. Only by looking back at that which Leibniz has thought out can we characterize the present age, which is called the atomic age, as that which is dominated (*durchmachtet*) by the power (*Macht*) of the *principio reddendae rationis sufficientis*. (SG, 65)

2. *A Verse from Angelus Silesius*

Heidegger's method of following "detours" has allowed him to work out three successively more determinate formulations of the "Principle of Ground." We can summarize these as follows:

	Principle	*Formulation*
(1)	Principle of Ground (*Satz vom Grund*; *principium rationis*)	"Nothing is without ground."
(2)	Principle of Rendering a Ground (*Satz vom zuzustellenden Grund*; *principium reddendae rationis*)	"Nothing is unless a ground can be rendered for it."
(3)	Principle of Rendering a Sufficient Ground (*Satz vom zuzustellenden zureichenden Grund*; *principium reddendae rationis sufficientis*)	"Nothing is unless a sufficient ground can be rendered for it."

The first of these he calls the "common" or "short" form. The second is the "strict" form, because it introduces the "*reddere*," which is the decisive characterization of the principle, revealing to us, as it does, the dispensation of Being (*Seinsgeschick*) in the modern age. The third formulation Heidegger calls the "complete" form, because it further specifies the *ratio reddenda* as a *ratio sufficiens*.

Heidegger now introduces another variant of the principle, not one that Leibniz uses, but one which Heidegger himself has devised. This formulation is derived by developing a shortened version of the strict form. According to the strict form, a reason must be given back to the thinking subject for any proposition which is put forth. Whenever any assertion is put forward, the thinking subject asks "why is this so rather than not?" Nothing can be certified as true unless an answer to the question "why?" is forthcoming. In other words: "nothing is without why." There thus arises a fourth form, which can be called the "short strict" form. All four formulations are logically equivalent variations of the same principle; they all hold true under the same conditions. But, Heidegger suggests, there seems to be a counter-example to the short strict form, whereas we can find no counter-examples to the other three formulations (SG, 67).

It is at this point that Heidegger's discussion takes for Versényi, and indeed for most philosophers, a very disconcerting turn. For the counter-example in question is drawn, as we have seen above, from the mystical poet Angelus Silesius. Though according to Leibniz nothing is without why, Silesius has written:

Without Why

The rose is without why; it blooms because it blooms;
It cares not for itself; asks not if it's seen.

Ohne Warum

Die Ros' ist ohn' warum, sie blühet weil sie blühet,
Sie acht't nicht ihrer selbst, fragt nicht, ob man sie siehet. (CW, I, 289/66)

Those who have been trained in philosophy and logic are inclined to think that Heidegger may well have found a counter-example to the Principle of Ground in Silesius's verse only because mystical poets are "irrationalists" to begin with and rather flagrantly violate the principles of logic at will. That is, we hope to show in this study, a gross misrepresentation of what mysticism is. But even more to the point, that is not what Heidegger himself thinks. On the contrary, he introduces the text of the mystical poet, not because the poet has no regard for the laws of logic, but because one finds in mystical poets thoughts which are "astonishingly clear" and "sharply formulated" (SG, 71). "Angelus Silesius," a pseudonym for Johannes Sheffler (1624–77), is a contemporary of Leibniz. Indeed Heidegger points out a text in Leibniz's letters in which Leibniz refers to Silesius's poetry as "beautiful" but, "extraordinarily daring, full of difficult metaphors and inclined almost to godlessness" (Dutens, VI, 56; SG, 68-9). Scheffler is also mentioned with favor in Hegel's *Lectures on Aesthetics* (*Werke*, Glockner, XII, 493).

We must now "listen" to Angelus Silesius's verse to find out if it is truly out of harmony with Leibniz's Principle. On the face of it, Scheffler has flatly contradicted Leibniz. Leibniz says (in effect): nothing is without why, but Scheffler says: the rose is without why. Now "reason" and "sound common sense" hasten to point out that the poet is wrong about the rose. (Heidegger thinks that reason is "obstinate" [Hw, 247] and that its continual rationalizing blinds it to more subtle points. The present discussion will illustrate this vividly.) The rose, after all, is the flower of a plant and the botanist can surely tell us the conditions and the causes of the growth of plants. But the poet, Heidegger rejoins, did not say that the rose is without a ground or cause (strict form), but that it is without why (short strict form). We must distinguish, he says, between "because" and "why," for each has a different relationship to a "reason" (*Grund*):

> "Why" is the word for the question into the ground. "Because" contains the answer which indicates the ground. The "why" seeks the ground; the "because" brings it forth. (SG, 70)

Thus Angelus Silesius never denies that the rose has a ground. Indeed, the second half of the first line indicates that clearly, for it says that the rose blooms *because* it blooms. The rose is "without why," but it is not "without because." The rose has a ground but it does not consider (*achtet nicht*) it, nor does it question (*fragt nicht*) it.

What the mystical poet means to point out, then, is that the rose is not like men. Men are continually considering reasons and asking questions, deliberating and calculating. But the rose blooms without reflecting upon the grounds of its blooming. Men never act without motives, however ill-conceived they may be. But the rose is not like that; it blossoms without concern. The rose therefore does not obey the Principle of Rendering a Ground; it feels no obligation to respond to the demand or claim which is put upon men, viz., to deliver a sufficient ground for its blooming.

The reader might be inclined to raise the following objection against

Heidegger's interpretation. The Principle of Rendering a Sufficient Ground does not demand that every being render a sufficient reason *for itself*, but only that it be *in principle* possible to render a reason for it. It need not justify itself, so long as it can be justified. Now a sufficient reason can be rendered *for* the rose, but not *by* the rose. Thus it does not, as Heidegger claims, fall outside the range of the Principle of Rendering a Sufficient Ground. But this much Heidegger is prepared to admit. He says:

> The rose, insofar as it is something [i.e., a thing, some particular object] does not fall outside of the sphere of influence of the principle of great power. (SG, 72)

A reason can be rendered for the rose, but the rose cannot render it for itself:

> Nevertheless, the way in which it does belong within this sphere of influence is unique to it, and consequently different from the way in which we men make our residence within the sphere of influence of the Principle of Sufficient Ground. (SG, 72)

The rose belongs within the range of the Principle of Rendering a Sufficient Ground because the principle holds true *of* the rose. But men belong within the sphere of influence of Leibniz's Principle because the Principle holds true *for* them, i.e., they are themselves under the necessity to render a reason for themselves as well as for all other things.

What then have we learned from this distinction between the "why" and the "because"? We have seen that the rose has a ground (short form), has a ground which can be rendered *for* it (strict form), and that it has a sufficient ground (complete form). We have found that the rose does not raise the question of its own grounds. It does not ask "why?" on its own behalf (short strict form), hence the rose differs from men who live under the demand to render reasons. But for Heidegger this is a paradox:

> We see ourselves brought before a remarkable state of affairs: something, the rose, is to be sure not without ground and it is nevertheless without why. Something falls in the range of validity of the commonly conceived Principle of Sufficient Ground. The same something falls out of the range of the strictly conceived Principle of Sufficient Ground.
>
> (SG, 73)

63

Now the man of "obstinate" reason can easily explain Heidegger's feeling of paradox. Heidegger has all along been assuming that the fourth formulation which he proposes is logically equivalent to the first three. In that case it would indeed be "paradoxical" to have found a counter-example to the fourth formulation which is not a counter-example to the others. But Heidegger is wrong to think, our man of "reason" would continue, that the fourth form is equivalent to the other three. What is logically equivalent to the other propositions is this:

> Nothing is unless the question "why" can in principle be raised and answered in its regard.

But Heidegger has been reading the proposition "nothing is without why" to mean "nothing is unless it can raise the question why *on its own behalf.*" And of course the rose does not fall inside the scope of this new, but considerably narrower, principle. All Heidegger has shown, "reason" concludes, is something quite trivial, viz., that men think and roses do not. The paradox is of Heidegger's own devising; he has been trying hard to "mystify" us.

The man of reason would, I think, be acting rashly to judge Heidegger's discussion thus. For what Heidegger means can be learned if we listen more patiently. He says further:

> How does it stand with the *principium reddendae rationis?* It is valid *of* the rose, but not *for* the rose; of the rose insofar as it is an object of our representing; but not for the rose insofar as this stands in itself and is simply a rose. (SG, 73)

What Heidegger is now suggesting is that the Principle of Sufficient Ground does indeed hold absolutely for "representational" thinking —which is of course the sphere of "reason." Every "object" which "stands before" (*gegen-steht*) "consciousness" must have a ground. But the importance of the mystical poet for Heidegger is that he speaks of the rose not as it stands before the representing subject, but as it stands in itself (*in sich selber steht*). The poet lets the rose be the thing which it is (SG, 78), without reducing it to the status of an "object." He detaches the rose from the demands of representational thinking. For the poet, the "rose remains without a relationship to the ground, a relationship which questions and which expressly represents the ground" (SG, 78-9). He lets the ground stand forth of

64

itself: the rose is not an "object" for a "subject" but that which stands on its own grounds. The mystical poet therefore has made a startling discovery of a region *outside* the sphere of influence of the Principle of Rendering a Sufficient Ground, because he has discovered a region altogether outside of "representational" thinking itself. So long as one remains within representational thinking there are no exceptions to the Principle of Sufficient Ground: every *object* must have a sufficient ground or reason delivered up for it. But the mystical poet has opened up access to a region where there are no "objects" but only "things" (*Dinge*) which are left to "stand" (*stehen*), not "before" (*gegen*) a subject, but "in themselves" (*in sich selber*). In this region, grounds are neither sought after nor supplied because "things" rest on their own grounds. In this region, thinking is not under the obligation or "demand" to supply grounds at all.

The man of reason would thus have missed the point quite thoroughly had he concluded that all Heidegger has shown by means of this verse is the difference between men and the rose. Indeed, Heidegger had actually been leading up to exactly the opposite conclusion:

> We would certainly be thinking too summarily if we thought that the meaning of Angelus Silesius's saying is spent in pointing out the distinction between the ways in which men and the rose are what they are. What is unsaid in this saying, and everything depends upon this, is that man, in the most concealed depths of his being, first truly is when he is in his own way like the rose—without why. We are not [however] able to pursue this thought any further here. (SG, 72-3)

The mystical poet is not trying to tell us what is transparent to all to begin with—that men and roses differ because men think and roses do not. On the contrary, Scheffler takes the rose to be a model for the soul (man), and he wants to say that the soul should become like the rose, that man should free himself from the preoccupying search for "grounds" and "reasons." The poet, for Heidegger, is inviting us to enter this other region outside representational thinking where the Principle of Rendering a Sufficient Ground does not hold. This is an invitation which it is hard to accept because man has, from of old, been conceived of as the *animal rationale*, i.e., as the being which gives reasons and engages in representational thinking (SG, 79). The region in which representational thinking is suspended will seem to him a strange and forbidding place. On Versényi's reading this region is an absolutely uninhabitable land in which no one can dwell.

It is important to point out that Heidegger does not construe this verse from Angelus Silesius "irrationalistically." He does not say that the poet is free to *violate* the Principle of Ground. Rather, the effect of the verse is to have shown us the way to a realm which is completely *outside the scope* of Leibniz's principle, where the demand to deliver reasons is neither obeyed nor disobeyed. He does not say that the rose has no ground, but rather that the rose stands forth on its own grounds, and has no need of the representational subject to supply grounds for it. The verse is taken in a "supra-rational" or "non-rational" sense, i.e., as describing a region beyond the sphere of influence (*Machtbereich*) of the principle of "great power" (*grossmächtige*) (SG, 72). As such, this discussion tends to contradict Hühnerfeld's charge of "irrationalism" against Heidegger and to support what Heidegger says in his own defence in *A Letter on Humanism* and in the "Postscript" to *What is Metaphysics?* Still, one cannot fail to be provoked by the introduction of this verse. For one can only wonder what place there is for philosophy in a region where there is no giving or asking for reasons. It is the land of mystics and poets, like Angelus Silesius, not of philosophers like Leibniz, who thought it might even be a "godless" land.

Before leaving Heidegger's discussion of the verse from *The Cherubinic Wanderer*, we must add one last observation. Heidegger said that he would not have the opportunity in this lecture course to pursue further the thought that man must be like the rose, without why. His intention is instead to continue listening to Leibniz's principle until he has heard everything it says to us. We will, however, on Heidegger's behalf, follow up that thought on our own in Chapter Four. There we will work out in some detail just how Dasein, like the soul in *The Cherubinic Wanderer*, must live "without why." Thus we will begin Chapter Three by taking up again this verse from Angelus Silesius and then tracing it back to its origin in Meister Eckhart. We will then (Chapter Four) go on to show the elaborate analogy that exists between the relationship of the soul to God in German mysticism, and the relationship of Dasein to Being in Heidegger's later writings.

3.   *Leibniz's Principle in a New Key*

When reason comes to a "first principle" like the Principle of Ground, it is expected to stop (SG, 83-4). That is what metaphysics has always done. But Heidegger wants to do something simpler and more basic than metaphysical reason. Metaphysics "hears" (*hört*) the Principle of Ground by "obeying" (*gehorchen*) it. But Heidegger wants to "listen" (*erhören*: SG, 86 ff.) to Leibniz's principle so closely and attentively as to hear the very source from which it speaks (SG, 105-6). Heidegger wants to hear what is drowned out for the rest of us —i.e., the philosophers and scientists—by the louder ringing of the Principle of Sufficient Ground as a "first principle," viz., the primal voice which is "speaking" (*sprechen*) in it. We have then, in SG, a paradigm case of Heidegger's critique of philosophy, which consists in "lifting out" and "setting off" the limits (FND, 92-3/119-20) of philosophical reason. Unlike Kant and Wittgenstein, who attempt a similar undertaking, Heidegger does not remain on "this side" of these limits, but rather, by what he variously calls a "leap," a "step back," a "transformation of thinking," he traverses these limits and sets up a position on the "other side" of them. He penetrates to the ground from out of which metaphysics springs, and from that vantage point he looks back upon philosophy and metaphysics. That is the task which Heidegger now sets for himself in SG: to make the leap out of the Principle of Sufficient Ground as a metaphysical first principle into the source from which it springs. The leap has been made possible by listening to Angelus Silesius, who speaks from a region which does not lie within the sphere of influence of the principle of great power. The leap from "metaphysics" to "thought" is opened up by a "mystical poet."

Up to now, Heidegger tells us, we have been listening to Leibniz's principle in its old—or familiar—"key" (*Tonart*: SG, 82):

(1) *Nothing* is *without* ground.

But if we are to hear what that familiar intonation tends to drown out, Heidegger suggests, we must change the key. Now we hear:

(2) Nothing *is* without *ground.*

In the second version, something is sounded which we did not hear before, viz., the ringing together of the "is" and "ground." In the first version, the logico-grammatical subject of the proposition is the "thing," the "being" (*ein Seiendes*). The proposition speaks about the *being*, not about ground. It does not seek to determine what "ground" is, but what the being is, which it determines as something which needs to be "grounded":

> The Principle of Ground, understood in the usual way, is not an assertion about ground, but rather about the being insofar as it is in each case a being. (SG, 82)

In fact, the Principle of Sufficient Ground presupposes what ground means. It takes it as something "self-evident," and then applies this supposedly self-evident predicate to "every being." But the new intonation gives a new stress:

> The stress [now] lets us hear a harmony between the "is" and "ground," *est* and *ratio*. (SG, 86)

In the new key the emphasis is on the "is," not the "being." Of course Heidegger does not mean to say that the logico-grammatical subject has changed, but that our attention is drawn away from the logical subject to the "is." The change of emphasis from "the being" to "is" is also for Heidegger a transition from the being to its Being:

> The "is" names, although completely indeterminately, the Being of that which is ever a being. (SG, 90)

The "is" is no mere copula, but signifies the Being of beings. And in letting us hear a harmony between the "is" and ground, the new intonation is speaking to us of the unity of Being and ground. In its new intonation the Principle says:

> To Being, there belongs something like a ground. Being is ground-like (*grundartig*), ground-related (*grundhaft*). (SG, 90)

Being in some way belongs together with ground in the being.

Now let us pause to compare the two intonations. In its familiar key, the Principle of Ground is a statement about beings. It claims that beings must have a ground, and it simply assumes that the essence of ground is self-evident. In its new key, the Principle of Ground is not a statement about beings but about Being, and it claims that Being and ground belong together. It does not take the essence of ground to be self-evident but tells us that the essence of ground is to be found in its connection with Being (SG, 92-3, 89-90). Heard in this less familiar but, for Heidegger, more penetrating way the Principle of Ground (*Satz vom Grund*) is a principle which speaks about Being (*Satz vom Sein*).

In the new key, the Principle tells us that Being and ground are to be understood in terms of one another:

> Being and ground belong together. Ground receives its essence out of its belonging together with Being as Being. Conversely, Being as Being holds sway out of the essence of ground. (SG, 92)

In saying that Being and ground belong together, Heidegger does not mean to say that Being "has" a ground but that Being "is" ground. Being does not have a ground but itself serves as the ground for every being. Being is itself ground-less (*grund-los*) (SG, 93), i.e., not grounded by anything else. Otherwise we would face an infinite regress, always looking for the ground of the ground of beings, etc. Inasmuch as Being is a ground without ground, Heidegger calls it the "abyss" (*Abgrund*), that which lacks a basis and ground. Being then is both ground and abyss.

We have thus learned two things from the new intonation of the Principle of Ground:

(1) Being and ground are the same.
(2) Being is an abyss.

But our use of language in these two propositions is careless, Heidegger remarks. For we should employ derivative forms of the verb "to be" (*sein*), such as "is" (*ist*) and "are" (*sind*), only with respect to beings. The being is, but Being is that in virtue of which the being is. Thus we must restate what we have learned as follows:

(1) Being and ground: the same.
(2) Being: the abyss.

In other works, Heidegger meets this difficulty by reserving the verb "*west*," which is the third person singular of the archaic verb *wesen*, to refer to Being. Thus he will say "*ein Seiendes ist*," but "*das Sein 'west'*." "*Wesen*" is a Middle High German word and was used by Meister Eckhart, as Hühnerfeld has already pointed out (Hühn., 121), and so contributes to the "mystical tone" of his later writings. It is clear, however, that sentences (1) and (2) above are no longer propositions, for they have no copula. They are "paratactical," not "syntactical" utterances, as Heidegger explains elsewhere of his translations of Parmenides, Fragment 6 (WHD, 111-2/183). But to think a sentence which is no longer a proposition demands a complete "trans-formation of thinking" (*Verwandlung des Denkens*: SG, 94). We have entered thereby into an entirely different region than that wherein propositions are true or false. Thus a new and decisive difference arises between the old and the new intonation of the Principle of Ground. In the traditional key, the Principle of Ground is a proposition; in the new key it is not. In the traditional key, the Principle of Ground belongs to the realm of "representational" thought. But in the new key we have entered into the region which the mystical poet Angelus Silesius discovered. The familiar intonation had to do with the "representation" of "beings," but the new intonation demands a more simple kind of "thinking" of Being itself, of "Being *as* Being, i.e., as ground" (SG, 96).

Now Heidegger raises the important question of how one makes one's way from the old to the new key, how one leaves the meta-physical principle concerning the being for the non-representational thought of Being:

> The change of key is something sudden. Behind the change of key there is concealed a leap of thought. The leap brings thought into another region and into another way of saying, and it does this without a bridge, i.e., without the steadiness of an advance. (SG, 95)

The Principle (*Satz*) of Ground is no longer to be understood as a "proposition" (*Satz*), but as a "leap" (*Satz*). A leap always involves a discontinuity in which one reaches a point where one can only throw oneself over to the other side. But we must not get the idea that the leap can be made easily, or straight off, without preparation. That is the role of the "detours" which Heidegger followed before he changed the intonation of the principle:

> We went around the Principle of Ground with detours, and this was often and intentionally remarked upon. However, these detours have brought us nearer to the leap. Of course, the detours could neither replace the leap nor even carry it out. But in a certain respect they retained its problem, viz., as a preparation for the leap. (SG, 95)

If the "detours" constituted a preparation for the leap, then they were not merely detours but contained, as we remarked above, a "method" of their own. The preparation is difficult and it cannot be dispensed with. This is a point which, we recall from above, Biemel points out in his dialogue with Versényi. Heidegger's leap is not arbitrary because it demands extensive preparation. That is why there is something offensive about the Heidegger commentators who speak like Heidegger speaks, who assume the posture of one who knows what Heidegger knows. They seem to have attained in an instant what Heidegger took a lifetime to make, the "leap of thought." They well illustrate what Hegel calls "that enthusiasm which, as shot from a pistol, begins immediately with absolute knowledge."[5]

Heidegger is now in a position to look back upon the transition from the initial considerations of a "first principle" in "Leibniz's metaphysics" to the "thought" of "Being as Being" which we now hear calling to us in Leibniz's principle. This review, which is only now possible *after* we have taken the leap (SG, 108), sees the transition as taking place in five steps. The steps are not five continuous steps, like the steps of a "logical discourse," because the first four steps have to do with the preparation for the leap, providing the "jumping-off" ground (*Absprungsbereich*) for the leap, while the fifth has to do with the leap itself. There is thus an essential discontinuity between them.

(1) The first step, which Heidegger concedes was touched upon only in passing, concerns the "incubation-period" of the Principle of Ground (SG, 96-8). For twenty-three hundred years, before Leibniz finally enunciated it, this principle "slept." Now since the Principle of Ground is indeed a saying about Being, as we have learned from the leap of thought, it is clear that this period of incubation is also a period in which Being itself, in its "truth," was likewise sleeping. The period of incubation is an epoch of Being, a period in which "Being withdrew itself as Being" (SG, 97). The time of incubation is a "dispensation of Being" (*Seinsgeschick*: SG, 98), a sending which withdraws. (2) The second step is the explicit formulation of the Principle of Ground as a "fundamental principle" (*Grundsatz*). With Leibniz the period of incubation came to an end. The principle is awakened from its slumber and becomes a "first principle." But still, what the Principle of Ground really means is not thereby awakened:

With the end of the period of incubation of the Principle of Sufficient Ground, by means of the thought of Leibniz, the incubation of the principle which will henceforth be well-known ceases, to be sure, but in no way does the period of incubation of the Principle of Ground as a saying about Being (*Satz vom Sein*) come to an end. (SG, 100)

While the dormancy of the "fundamental principle" is broken, the sleep of Being continues. Indeed it is precisely because the Principle of Ground is awakened as a "fundamental principle" that Being falls into "a still deeper sleep and into an even more decisive withdrawal" (SG, 100). Being now hides itself under the guise of the "objectivity of objects" and conceals itself from us in its truth even more radically.

(3) The third step consists in the characterization of the Principle of Ground as a *principium grande*. In this characterization, Heidegger heard the "claim" or "demand" which thinking was under to supply reasons. And so, in this all important step, we were able to detect the "mission-ary" (*geschicklich*) movement of Being itself, and we were also able to understand that the demand to deliver reasons issued from Being itself. The great power of Leibniz's principle is the power of Being itself, of the mission of Being. The voice of Being is the primal voice which is speaking in Leibniz's metaphysical assertion. (4) The fourth step consisted in listening to the verse from Angelus Silesius. This was a critical step in taking the leap and its most immediate preparation. For in listening to Angelus Silesius we heard a thinker who had found a new way of considering things—e.g., a rose—not as an "object" but as "grounded in itself":

> The blossoming of the rose is grounded in itself; it has its ground in and by itself. The blossoming is a pure emerging out of itself, pure shining.
>
> (SG, 101-2)

The mystical poet discovered the region in which the being stands on its own grounds. The mystical poet speaks from the region in which Being and ground belong together, in which things rest in themselves, in their own grounds. (5) The fifth step can now be taken: to hear in Leibniz's own saying what the mystical poet had already discovered, that Being and ground belong together, that beings stand forth in their Being, upon their own grounds. Things do not need to have grounds delivered up for them. They do not have to be "certified" as beings by having grounds "supplied" for them. Rather, insofar as the being *is*, it emerges out of its own grounds, its own Being. It stands forth of itself; it shows itself from itself. This is what the Greeks originally meant by *physis* (EM, 11-2/11-2) and what the author of *Being and Time* meant by a *phainomenon*.

The significant thing for our study is that it is the mystical poet, according to Heidegger, who has opened our eyes—or, better, our ears—to this revelation. The way from metaphysics to thought, from beings to Being, Heidegger seems to be telling us, is to take as our model the example of the mystic. An attentive hearing of the sayings of the mystics is the decisive "preparation" for the leap of thought. Mysticism is not opposed to thinking; on the contrary, ". . . the most extreme sharpness and depth of thought belong to genuine and great mysticism" (SG, 71). Mysticism dwells in the closest proximity to thought, in the region where representational thinking has been left behind and the Principle of Sufficient Ground has no influence. It is the mystic who teaches us to hear what the metaphysician can never detect. The mystic has "thought" the relation of Being and ground more "sharply" and "deeply" than the metaphysician. Thus the questions which concern this study, whether it is possible to make any distinction at all between "mysticism" and "thought," and what either can have to do with philosophy, can be seen even more clearly.

4. The Principle of Ground and the History of Being

By means of the attentive hearing which he has given to Leibniz's Principle, Heidegger has been able to detect the voice of Being itself speaking in it. Heidegger now turns his attention to the way in which Being has addressed itself to Western man both after Leibniz had brought this address to words, in the philosophy of Kant, and before Leibniz, in ancient thought. For the address or language of Being (*die Sprache des Wesens*: US, 200/94) is historical, not merely in the sense of having a history (*Geschichte*), but more fundamentally, in the sense of arising out of the mission of Being (*Seinsgeschick*) itself (SG, 161). The mission of Being is the way in which Being sends itself while at the same time withdrawing over the ages of Western history (SG, 109-10). The clue which Heidegger follows in pursuing the mission-ary (*geschickliche*) movements of Being which come to expression in the Principle of Sufficient Ground is, therefore, a linguistic one, viz., the seemingly innocent translations of *logos* by *ratio*, and of *ratio* by *Vernunft* and *Grund*. These translations (*Übersetzungen*) are not harmless human conventions for Heidegger, but contain within themselves an entire tradition (*Überlieferung*), i.e., a process by which Being itself "hands itself over" from one age to the next (SG, 163-4, 171). These translations are not human decisions at all (SG, 161), but the way in which language itself is speaking to us. Thus each translation bespeaks its own age, its own distinctive epoch of Being. The task which Heidegger sets for himself now is to "hear" (*erhört*) what these words genuinely say, to hear the words *logos* and *ratio* in their Greek and Roman accents, and to listen to *Grund* and *Vernunft* as words which can be spoken only in the modern age.

Only by following these lectures can we understand Heidegger's critique of philosophical reason, for Heidegger's critique is essentially historical. That is, he thinks that what philosophical reason means is what it has come to mean by way of an historical process. The limits of philosophy are limits which it has assumed by its translation into the words *ratio* and "reason." For there was once and there can be again a more original kind of speaking and thinking—before *ratio*, *Grund*, and *Vernunft* were spoken—which, being simpler than philosophy, is more fundamental than it. Thus the thinking which listens to Leibniz's principle which we have so far undertaken must be both a thinking back on (*andenken*: SG, 107) the primal source from which philosophical reason derives, and a thinking forward to (*Vordenken*) a new beginning, at the end of philosophy, in which the ringing together of Being and ground can be heard again.

In the course of these lectures (SG, 143-7) Heidegger raises the important question—which philosophers would call "methodological" —of "how he knows" that it is the voice of Language itself, i.e., Being, which he hears in Leibniz and Kant and the ancient philosophers. This, he says, quite disconcertingly, is something we "accept" (*an-nehmen*). But this does not mean, he hastens to assure us, that it is a mere presupposition (*Annahme*), i.e., something more or less arbitrary which represents his "opinion." Rather it is something we receive from Being itself. For as we saw in discussing the "great power" of Leibniz's principle, we are all "taken in" (*genommen*) by the claim which this principle makes upon us (*uns in Anspruch nehmen*). We receive (*vernehmen*) the mission in which Being sends itself to us; we "accept" what it sends. Thus, Heidegger holds, one does not "prove" that history rests upon the mission of Being. One can only *experience* it. This is something "undergone" or "lived through." In the contemporary age, the testimony to the mission of Being as essentially "technological" (*Technik*) is the "pull" (*Zug*) which we all feel as Being withdraws (*ent-zieht*) itself in its truth and draws us all into the total technologicalization of the earth. Technology is a power which overpowers us, because it is the power of Being itself which is making itself felt in it. In other words, Heidegger says of his "method," i.e., his "way" (*Denk-weg*), what every mystic and religious man must also say; it is a matter of hearing (*er-hören*) for those who have the ears to hear and of seeing (*er-sehen*) for those who have the eyes to see. This is the "methodological impregnability" which has all the earmarks of the "mysticism" of which Versényi complains above.

In sketching the mission of Being which is at play in Leibniz's principle and which can be felt throughout the entire history of the West, Heidegger first moves forward from Leibniz to Kant. In *What is a Thing?* (*Die Frage nach dem Ding*) Heidegger had determined that Kant's thought remained within the Cartesian tradition (FND, 144/184). He remarked also that Leibniz himself "received his decisive inspiration" from "his sojourns in Paris from 1672-76," where the spirit of Descartes held sway and where "the mathematical foundations of modern existence" were established (FND, 76/98). In keeping with this mathematical spirit, Leibniz sought to "axiomatize" philosophy, and he located these axioms in the "subjectivity of the subject." In SG, Heidegger shows how the Cartesian tradition was mediated to Kant through Leibniz's Principle of Sufficient Ground. For if we listen carefully enough to the title of Kant's book—*Critique of Pure Reason*—we shall see that it is only possible on the basis of the Principle of Ground (SG, 125).

"Reason" (*Vernunft*) is the "faculty of principles" (*Prinzipien*), i.e., of "fundamental propositions" (*Grundsätze*). Reason is the faculty which provides the principles or "grounds" for nature (theoretical reason), freedom (practical reason), and judgment. "Critique," from the Greek *krinein*, is not only a negative laying down of limits (*Schränke*) but a positive bringing together (*versammeln*) of a thing into its ideal boundary (*Grenze*) and form. The contours of a Greek statue are not the limits at which the statue is cut off but the form into which the Greek artist was able to bring the marble. A "critique" makes the form of a thing stand out, i.e., it makes it possible (SG, 125; cf. FND, 46-7/61-2). The *Critique* supplies the conditions under which nature and freedom are possible:

> Behind the formula "*a priori* conditions of possibility" is hidden the rendering of the sufficient reason (*Grund*), the *ratio sufficiens* which, as *ratio*, is pure reason (*Vernunft*). (SG, 126)

Kant's *Critique of Pure Reason* stands under the demand which Leibniz's Principle of Ground makes on all thinking: the demand to supply grounds. And if it is objected that Kant almost never refers to this principle, Heidegger's response is that that is because Leibniz's principle stands as the "unspoken" and "unthought" presupposition of Kant's work.

But in Leibniz's principle there is—as we have understood from the leap of thought—a ringing together of ground with Being. What then does ground, understood as "*Vernunft*," have to do with Being? Kant's "reason" (*Vernunft*), like Leibniz's Principle of Ground and like Descartes's *ego cogito*, belongs to the sphere of the "subjectivity of the subject." This means it is a faculty which posits itself as a self-sufficient frame of reference and which defines everything else as that which stands "over and against" (*gegen*) it itself. Thus the ground which reason (the subjectivity of the subject) lays is the ground of "objects":

> Objectivity is the Kantian understanding of the Being of the beings of experience. (SG, 132)

That which makes an object to be an object is that it is brought to stand (*stehen*) under the conditions that reason lays down. Thus the way in which ground and Being belong together in Kant's philosophy is to be found in the belonging together of "reason" and "objects," of the "conditions of possibility" and what they make possible. "Philosophy" from the time of Descartes on is, according to Heidegger, the name for the attempt of human subjectivity to prescribe to things their nature and meaning. "Philosophy" means subject-ism, i.e., the unleashing of the demand of the ego for conformity to its own *a priori* prescriptions.

Heidegger's attention now shifts back from Leibniz and Kant to the epoch before the modern age, his effort now being to hear the voice of Being, which always speaks of the harmony of Being and ground, in the ancient mission of Being. There is a diversity of names for Being (*physis*, *Gegenständlichkeit*) and ground (*ratio*, *Vernunft*, *Grund*), and Heidegger's task is to hear what is the same in them (SG, 153). This multiplicity of words is nothing "bewildering," for behind it lies the "sameness and simplicity of the mission of Being and accordingly a solid constancy of the history of thought and of what is thought by it" (SG, 153). One might think that Heidegger is looking for the "rule" or "logic" in the history of Western thought, that like Hegel he wishes to find the idea which is relentlessly unfolding in history. But Heidegger immediately waylays this suggestion:

> The epochs cannot be derived from one another and reduced to the course of a continuous process. (SG, 154)

While there is a unity to the history of the West, it is not the unity of a continuous development, but the unity of a common source in the mission of Being, a common root, from which the diverse epochs spring up "suddenly" (SG, 154, 160) and unpredictably, like buds on a branch. The epochs arise from the "selfsame," and the selfsame is "concealedly revealed" in them. Heidegger thus is looking for the place of "rest" (SG, 144) behind these epochal fluctuations, for that which is "enduring" (*Währende*: SG, 160) in the missions, the "constant" (*das Stets*: SG, 161) in them, that which has "solid constancy" (*gediegene Stetigkeit*: SG, 153). This enduring constancy is not free from the flux of the missions in the sense of being the end or cessation of them, the final and exhaustive mission, but rather in the sense of being their source. One can see in these expressions very clearly the problem which Löwith underlines, viz., that Heidegger's latest writings have taken a turn away from the historical and towards the atemporal. To the extent that this is so, his writings have surely acquired a more and more "mystical" tone. But we will have more to say of this problem below (Chapter Five).

In Kant, Leibniz's *ratio* received a two-fold translation as *Vernunft* and *Grund*. Now *ratio* is itself a Roman word which received a decisive formulation in Cicero, who writes:

> I call a cause the reason for effecting and the result that which is effected (*causam appello rationem efficiendi, eventum id quod est effectum*).
>
> (SG, 166)

But we must not rashly assume, Heidegger warns, that *causa, ratio*, and *effectus* have here the modern meanings of "cause" (*Ursache*), "reason" (*Grund*), and "effect" (*Erfolg*). Rather we must give these words their own "world-historical bearing" (SG, 167). "*Ratio*," Heidegger observes, comes from the deponent verb *reor, reri, ratus sum*, which means "to reckon, think, or suppose"; hence Heidegger says it means "to hold something for something" (*etwas für etwas supponiert*), to "impute" (*unterstellen*), to suppose (*supponieren*), to "reckon with" or "reckon on" (*mit etwas rechnen, auf etwas rechnen*) (cf. FND, 49-50/64-5). What lies behind all these meanings, according to Heidegger, is "to arrange or order one thing after another." If one "reckons" x to be y, one has ordered x under y so that it is brought forth into public view as y. To calculate with numbers is, therefore, only one restricted sense of "*rechnen*" and "*reor*."

Now to give a "reckoning" or "account" (*Rechenschaft*) of a thing one points out that upon which it depends in order to be manifest. Thus if one speaks in the Roman language of *rationem reddere*, that is a natural, even a redundant expression, for it is of the essence of *ratio* that it bring forth that to which a thing is ordered. In its Roman sense, this expression means to display a thing in terms of that which lets it appear as it is.

This is clearly a long way removed from the meaning this expression has acquired in the philosophy of Leibniz. Leibniz speaks Latin, but not the language of the ancient Romans (SG, 173). The Roman *ratio* was "handed over" to the modern world in a "bifurcated" way, in the form of *Grund* and *Vernunft* (SG, 173-4). It was possible for *ratio* to become *Grund* because, in imputing (*unterstellen*) y of x, one sets (*stellt*) x under (*unter*) y, and x becomes the "basis" or "ground" of the attribute (y). It was possible for *ratio* to become *Vernunft* because *Vernunft* refers to the way in which we receive (*ver-nehmen*) something. *Vernunft* means the acceptance of a thing in the way that it is put forth or "supposed" to be. It was this modern dispensation of the word *ratio* which Leibniz inherited and absorbed into his "subjectistic" metaphysics.

But Heidegger has yet to explain how *ratio* belongs together with Being in the Roman language. "To what extent 'are' Being and *ratio* the same?" he asks (SG, 175). Here we reach an impasse. For there is nothing about the word *ratio* which suggests a connection with Being. But this impasse arises only because we have forgotten that the word *ratio*, like every other fundamental word, "speaks historically" (SG, 176). Thus we must look back further to the Greek *logos*, of which *ratio* is itself the translation. To what extent, then, Heidegger now asks, does *logos*, in its Greek sense, belong together with the Greek conception of Being? *Logos* comes from the verb *legein*, which means, as Heidegger has consistently maintained over the years, "to collect together," "to lay one thing beside another," "to arrange one thing after another" (SG, 178); hence its translation by the verb *reor*.[6] Thus *legein* means to let something lie forth (*vorliegenlassen*) and so come into appearance. In "arranging" a thing one sets it into the proper context within which it can emerge as the thing that it is. Now that which itself lies forth (*das Vorliegende*) is that which comes to presence of itself (*das von-sich-her-Anwesende*):

> *Legein* and *logos* are the letting lie forward of the thing which comes to presence in its presence. (SG, 179)

But that which comes to presence in its presence (*das Anwesende in seinem Anwesen*) is what the Greeks mean by the being in its Being. Thus "*logos* means Being" (SG, 179). Now insofar as that which lies forward (*das Vorliegende*) is that upon which "properties" may be based, and "about which" there can be talk, *logos* also means "ground." Thus in *logos*, both Being and ground are named together.

Thus the ancient Greeks—before Socrates, Plato, and Aristotle— knew what the mystical poet Angelus Silesius also knew—that things lie forth of themselves, that they emerge from out of their own grounds, and that there is no need for the "ego" to "supply" grounds for them. In hearing the ringing together of Being and ground in the new intonation of Leibniz's principle, and in hearing the saying of the mystical poet, we were, it turns out, listening to the resonances of the ancient Greek word *logos* to which Heraclitus beckons us to listen:[7]

> If you have heard not me, but the *logos*, then it is wise to say accordingly: all is one.

But this insight of the early Greek thinkers was soon corrupted:

> The belonging together of Being and ground comes into the word which is called *logos* only for a moment which, in terms of the mission of Being, is uniquely lofty and perhaps the highest of all. (SG, 180)

There was a flash of lightning, a flash of Being itself, which took place in the thinking of Heraclitus (VA, 227), but as is the case with lightning it passed away as soon as it happened. The subsequent history of Being, instead of unfolding what the early Greeks experi- enced (as in Hegel's view), did precisely the opposite, viz., it covered over its beginnings all the more completely (SG, 180; cf. EM, 136-49/ 149-64). The original belonging together of Being and ground was lost and the two were separated. Instead of being thought together with Being, ground becomes a determination of the being, and the search is undertaken to find the ground of one being in another. Thus there is born the whole enterprise of "onto-theo-logic," of "meta- physics," of philosophy itself as a "rational" inquiry into the cause of beings. Things now must be founded upon the solid ground and firm foundation of a causal explanation. The self-evident validity of this rational search for causes rests upon the now no longer heard ringing together of the unity of Being and ground in the Greek word *logos*.

Thus Heidegger's "historical critique" of philosophy is completed. Philosophy "as a thing of reason" (*eine Sache der ratio*: WdP, 22-3) is the result of an oblivion; it is a fall from a primal time in which it was recognized that the thing lies forth of itself, that it rises up and stands before us on its own grounds. Philosophy is an oblivion of the fact that things do not depend on human justification but that they emerge before us on their own. Philosophy is a tyranny over things which insists that nothing is unless human reason has certified its existence. What is needed instead of philosophy is a thinking which learns from the mystical poet to be like the rose, without why, i.e., to let things be. But there is one final difficulty to which we must now turn. The fallenness of philosophy is not a human error, but a withdrawal on the part of Being itself. Man is caught up, Heidegger said above, in a fearful "play" (SG, 60-1) which is not of his own making, the play between the sending and the withdrawal of Being itself. It is, therefore, with a discussion of the play of Being, to which Heidegger devotes the final pages of SG, that we must conclude our analysis of SG, and so of Heidegger's critique of philosophical reason.

5.   *The Play of Being*

By means of the leap of thought we have learned that the search for grounds is appropriate in the sphere of beings—every being has a ground—but that Being itself can in no way be thought of as grounded:

> Insofar as Being is, it itself has no ground. Yet this is not so because it is self-grounded, but rather because every form of grounding (*Begründung*), even and precisely that [which occurs] through itself, remains inappropriate to Being as ground.   (SG, 185)

To think Being we must surrender the search for grounds for which the Principle of Ground calls. We cannot hope to think Being by "explaining" it in terms of something else or even itself. To think Being adequately we must let Being be, let it lie forth (*vorliegenlassen, legein*) and emerge of itself (*physis*). Being *is* ground—i.e., Being and ground: the same—there is no need to supply a ground for it. As that for which every kind of ground and explanation remains inappropriate, Being is thus the "abyss" (*Ab-grund*).

Have we not then, by the leap of thought, fallen into a bottomless pit (*Bodenlose*), Heidegger asks? This is so only for the thinking which cannot understand anything unless it is explained on the ground of another being. In other words, only for metaphysics or philosophical reason is this "abyss" something "baseless." But for those of us who have, after listening to the mystical poet, made the leap into a region where things lie forth of themselves, we have only now for the first time come into correspondence with "Being as Being, i.e., with the truth of Being" (SG, 185). In acknowledging Being as that which lies forth of itself, we have recognized Being as that which cannot be measured by rational standards, as that which to rational thought is "unmeasurable" (*das Unermessliche*) and which itself gives the measure (*das Mass-gebende*) to thought. Heidegger thus has completely reversed the Sophist dictum. It is not man or human reason which is the measure of things, but Being itself which is the measure of thought.

The leap of thought "brings thought into play with that in which Being as Being rests, although not with that on which it rests as on its ground" (SG, 186). Being rests in itself, in its own "play." And not only that: but man too rests, i.e., is "posited" and "staked" (*gesetzt*) upon this play. But what "play" is this of which Heidegger is now speaking? It is not any play with which we are familiar. For Heidegger tells us straight off that up to now Western thought has been quite unable to comprehend the essence of play, because it has always considered play only as a being and, as such, something which is to be explained in terms of "ground, *ratio*, rule," etc. (SG, 186). In metaphysics, to illustrate what Heidegger seems to be saying, play is considered to be a form of "leisure" whose purpose is to allow us to return to "work," a break in the "seriousness" of life, a flirtation with "unreality" which provides an "inter-lude" from the harshness of reality. In every case, play is "founded" upon and justified in terms of work and seriousness as the *telos* which supplies it with its sufficient reason.

But the play which Heidegger has in mind is not the play of a "being," but of Being itself.[8] As such, it rests in itself and it cannot be rationalized or explained in terms of something else. This play is, like the rose, without why:

The play is without "why." It plays for the while that it plays. There remains only play: the highest and the deepest. (SG, 188)

Rather than being accountable for in terms of some cause or purpose, the play is a "mystery" (*Geheimnis*: SG, 186). The play of Being: a "mystery" and an "abyss." The play is a groundless ground; the abyss is a mysterious play. Are we to think the "play" in terms of the "abyss" or the abyss in terms of the essence of play? In the final pages of SG Heidegger adapts the latter alternative: to think the truth of Being, which we have attained by a leap, in terms of play.

He turns then to Heraclitus to defend his injection of the idea of play into his final pages of SG. It is nothing "playful and frivolous" (*spielerisch*) which has led us to speak of the play of Being, he says, but a necessity arising from our attempt to think in terms of the mission of Being. In listening to the Principle of Sufficient Ground, we have ultimately been led to hear the Greek word *logos* ringing through it. But what Heraclitus called *logos* he also called by other names: *physis*, that which emerges from out of itself; *kosmos*, the ordered totality of all things; and finally *aion*, which is usually translated as "world-time." But, for those of us who have taken the leap of thought, *aion* is the name for what we call the mission of Being. Now let us hear what Heraclitus has to say of *aion*:[9]

> Time (*aion*) is a child playing a game of draughts. The kingship is in the hands of a child.

"Time" means the mission of Being; the "kingship" refers to what is first, the *arche*, the *principium* (the "prince"), i.e., the Being of beings. Thus the fragment says the mission of Being is a child who plays. The child-king is the mystery of play upon which Being itself rests and upon which the life of man also rests. The mission of Being sends itself to us in a mysterious, play-like way. The way in which Being speaks to us in the Principle of Ground, and in the history which leads up to and follows upon the formulation of that principle in the philosophy of Leibniz, is itself a play:

> Nothing *is* without *ground*. Being and ground: the same. Being as grounding has no ground, but as the abyss plays that game which, as mission, plays to us Being and ground. (SG, 188)

If one player throws a ball to another, then he "plays" the ball "to" the other. Heidegger says, then, that the mission of Being "plays Being and ground to us" over the history of Western metaphysics. This it does by means of the play which is at work in language in the translation from *logos* to *ratio*, and from *ratio* to *Grund* and *Vernunft*. The history of metaphysics is a vast "language-game" played not by man but by Being, a language-game in which we do not play with words, but words play with us (WHD, 83/118-9). The history of philosophy is the playing of Being with man. Thus we are led back to what Heidegger said above about the sequence of the epochs of Being:

> The epochs cannot be derived from one another and forced into the course of a continuous process. (SG, 154)

The epochs spring up unpredictably; they are a "free play." There is no "why" for the sequence of epochs. Thus in the address given at the end of the lecture course Heidegger cites the following verse from Goethe:

How? When? and Where? The gods remain silent!
You hold yourself to *because* and do not ask *why?*. (SG, 206/219)

One cannot ground the sequence of epochs in a higher explanation. One can only let them be, accept them as they are. Thus in the minutes of the seminar on "Time and Being" it is asked:

How is the sequence of epochs determined? How does this free sequence determine itself? Why is the sequence precisely this sequence? One is tempted to think of Hegel's history of the "idea." For Hegel, there rules in history necessity which is at the same time freedom. For him, both are one in and through the dialectical movement as the essence of the Spirit exists. For Heidegger, on the other hand, one cannot speak of a "why." Only the "that"—that the history of Being is in such a way—can be said.
(SD, 55-6/52)

The play of Being means that we must surrender every "why?" and remain content with "because."

Heidegger's identification of the play of Being as the mission-ary movements of Being confirms what he said above about the play in which modern man is caught up: the more he searches for grounds the more groundless his existence becomes; the more fully he masters the energies of the earth, the less he is able to truly build and dwell upon the earth. The play is thus a counter-play (*Widerspiel*):

There is an enigmatical counter-play between the demand for delivery of a ground and the withdrawal of the basis (*Boden*). (SG, 60)

The "mystery" is the "enigma" of the counter-play. The counter-play is the play between the way Being sends itself (*zuschicken*) and its withdrawal (*entziehen*). The play of Being is the revealing–concealing process within Being. It is a game of "hiding" itself from us in the very act by which it reveals itself. In addressing itself to us as the *ratio sufficiens* it has concealed the original belonging together of Being and ground in the Greek word *logos*. Every self-giving of Being is a disguise behind which Being escapes "in its truth." The mission of Being is an "elusive" (*e-ludens*) game by means of which the truth of Being eludes the grasp of metaphysics.

83

Man is thus in no way a mere "spectator" or onlooker in this "game." On the contrary, he is "drawn" (*gezogen*) into it and his whole essence is "staked" and placed upon it. Thus Heidegger refers to the play:

> . . . in which we mortals are brought, which [mortals] only we are, while we dwell in the nearness of death, which, as the most extreme possibility of Dasein, is capable of the highest illumination of Being and its truth. Death is the still unthought measure of the immeasurable, i.e., of the highest play in which man is brought on earth, upon which he is staked. (SG, 186-7)

Man is caught up in a play which hides the truth of Being from him. But in the above passage Heidegger tells us that the way for man to measure the immeasurable and to uncover the long forgotten truth of Being is to return to his essence as a "mortal." In returning to our mortality a clearing will be made for Being to disclose itself. In returning to our mortality the disguise under which Being has passed itself off—*ratio sufficiens, Grund, reine Vernunft*—will be unmasked and Being will be allowed to lie forth of itself as man's sustaining ground. Thus in the last sentence of this lecture-course Heidegger says of the play of Being:

> The question remains whether and how we, hearing the movements (*Sätze*) of this playing, play along with and join in the playing. (SG, 188)

If Being is a play then the role of Dasein is to play along with it. Dasein cannot, as in Leibniz, lay down first principles which Being must obey, nor, as in Kant, submit Being to reason's own *a priori* synthesis, nor, with Nietzsche, expect Being to submit to its will. Dasein must give up philosophy and metaphysics altogether in order to "play along with" (*mitspielen*) the play of Being. That is the only measure we can take of the immeasurable.

But the way in which Heidegger suggests we play along with Being is to return to our mortality, to dwell in the nearness of death, to become what we alone are, mortals. That is apparently the strangest of advice. It is, however, not so strange to the reader of *Being and Time*, for the only way to resolute, self-possessed existence in that treatise is to open oneself to that ownmost, individualizing possibility which is not to be outstripped (SZ, §50, 250-1/294). Nor is this unfamiliar advice in the religious tradition, in which the contemplation of mortality has always played an indispensable role in reminding the soul of its eternal vocation. But what does this suggestion mean for the later Heidegger? There is no doubt from Heidegger's reference to "mortals," "dwelling" "on earth" (*irdisch*) in the above passage that Heidegger is alluding to the "play" of the world, the mirror-play of the Fourfold. Thus the way to play along with the play of Being is to enter into the ring-dance of the Four together. Let us see what that means.[10]

By entering into his mortality man takes up a genuine dwelling in the "world." Now the world in Heidegger's writings, both early and late, is not any being but the totality, the all. But since the search for grounds is appropriate only in the sphere of beings, the world, like Being, must be thought without why; we must not seek to found it upon some being, to explain it in terms of some cause:

> . . . the world's worlding cannot be explained by anything else nor can it be fathomed through anything else. This impossibility does not lie in the inability of our human thinking to explain and fathom in this way. Rather, the inexplicable and unfathomable character of the world's worlding lies in this, that causes and grounds remain unsuitable for the world's world-ing. As soon as human cognition here calls for an explanation, it fails to transcend the world's nature, and falls short of it. The human will to explain just does not reach to the simpleness of the simple onefold of worlding. (VA, 178-9/179-80)

The "world" too must escape the sphere of influence of the Principle of Ground if it is to be thought properly. The world is freed to be the world, to lie forth as the world, when "things" are free to appear. The "jug" is such a "thing" (cf. VA, 171/172 ff.). Its essence lies in the "giving" which takes place when it pours out its contents and gives us its gifts. The jug's gifts are water and wine, in which Heidegger finds the "marriage of sky and earth." For the rain is received from the sky and stored in the earth, and the wine is brought from the vine which is nourished by the sky. Water and wine are drinks for mortals, providing nourishment and refreshment. Wine is also a consecrated drink which we offer to the gods. Both together—mortals and gods—are found in the drink which the jug gives. Thus all four—earth and sky, mortals and gods—abide together in the jug.

The jug is an exceptionally good example of what Heidegger means by that which lies forth of itself (*das Vorliegende*: SG, 179). The jug is not described in terms of the sturdiness of the materials out of which it is made, the requirements of balance, its weight, resistance to heat, etc. It is instead left to be the thing which it is, to show itself

85

from itself, to rest on its own grounds. As such, it collects "the four" together. Thus it represents the essential features of Heidegger's interpretation of *logos* as that which collects together (*versammeln*) and lies forth of itself (*vorliegen*: SG, 182). The worlding of the world is the revelation of *logos*. In Heraclitus, we recall, *kosmos* and *logos* name the same thing. The "jug" thus is not an "object"; it has not been subjugated to the demands of representational thinking. The jug abides in the region which lies outside the sphere of influence of the Principle of Ground. In the jug, Being and ground belong together, for the jug lies forth on its own. It does not need to have a reason rendered for it.

Now we can understand why Heidegger says that Dasein must enter into its own mortality if it hopes to be brought into relationship with the truth of Being itself. The truth of Being is to be found in Being as the groundless ground. And this recognition is possible only to the thought which has given up the search for grounds and abdicated the demand that a sufficient reason be rendered for every object. It surrenders itself to that for which every kind of ground and cause is inappropriate—the worlding of the world, the play of the Four together. But such a surrender is what characterizes "mortals."

For metaphysics, man is the rational animal, the living being which calculates and reckons and which demands reasons. But in comprehending man as a mortal, Heidegger departs from this metaphysical determination of man and sets up in its place an idea of man as finite and perishable, in tune with the earth and its rhythm. Mortals do not dominate the earth; they "tend" and shelter it. They do not regard the sky as a challenge to aeronautical engineering but as the measure of the day. For mortals, God is one before Whom we can bend our knee, not the *prima causa* (ID, 127/60, 140/72). Mortals let the four come together; they let "things" be; they let the four intersect in the "thing." And in the thing which collects together and lies forth of itself we can hear the *logos* to which Heraclitus bids us listen, and so the belonging together of Being and ground. Mortals, like the mystical poet, know that things are only things when they are without why. For the rose too is a "thing."

Before turning to some concluding reflections on the significance of Heidegger's views on the "play of Being," I should like to introduce a parenthetical but highly relevant observation. We have throughout our reading of SG insisted upon the importance of the motif of "language" and of "listening to language" in this work. Now since Being for Heidegger is a play, and since the essence of language lies in being the language of Being—Being's own language—it follows that the mission of Being is a great, cosmic language game played by Being. Thus in Leibniz's saying *nihil est sine ratione*, language itself conceals what is really being said beneath the demands of representational thinking for a sufficient reason. Now Heidegger tells us that mortals must learn to play along with the play of Being. That means that we must learn to play along with the play of language, to play "back" what Being plays "to" us. Thus if Being "plays to us Being and ground" (SG, 188), we must learn to make a "return play." And there is no better example of such a return play than SG itself. For the central move in SG is a change of key in Leibniz's principle—from "*nothing* is *without* ground" to "nothing *is* without *ground*"—a linguistic, auditory shift of stress which allows us to "hear" something we did not hear before. Heidegger thereby "returns" the play which language itself is playing to us. The "*Satz vom Grund*," in the course of this playing along with Leibniz's principle, has become a "*Satz*" in a fourfold sense: heard in its traditional accents, it is an "assertion" (*Aussage*) concerning beings; inflected in a new way by the playfulness of thinking it becomes a "saying" (*Sage*) about Being, a leap (*Sprung*) from a principle of metaphysics into the primal source from which metaphysics originates, and finally a musical "movement" (*Satz*) of the playing together of Being and ground (see SG, 151). There is a playing on words at work here, but in a higher and deadly serious sense. So too in *Was heisst Denken?*, Heidegger subjects the question which constitutes the title of this volume to a similar change of accent, this time by exploiting the various senses of the verb "*heissen*." In this work Heidegger explicitly comments on the play of language:

> If we may talk here of playing games at all, it is not we who play with words, but the nature of language plays with us, not only in this case, not only now, but long since and always. For language plays with our speech—it likes to let our speech drift away into the more obvious meanings of words. (WHD, 83/118)

But there is nothing amusing about this game:

> This floundering in commonness is part of the higher and dangerous game and gamble in which, by the nature of language, we are the stakes.
> (WHD, 84/119)

Indeed, not only in the expressions "*Satz vom Grund*" and "*Was heisst Denken?*," but in all of his later writings Heidegger is engaged in heeding the game which language plays with us and so in playing with it in return in order to hear what language really says (WHD, 84/119). This is the proper explanation of the extraordinary quality of Heidegger's language, one of which those critics who speak of his constant "play on words" are often unaware.

In the expression "the play of Being" the central motifs in Heidegger's thought come together. Being is no longer conceived according to a "rational model"—such as *eidos, ousia, substantia, res extensa et res cogitans, Vernunft, Begriff*—but according to a model which philosophers have usually avoided—a game, a play, which gives the appearance of something arbitrary and capricious. Philosophers speak instead of the "four causes" and "first principles," not play. But for Heidegger Being is a high and dangerous game. Now if it is shunned by philosophers the model of play is often adopted outside of philosophy. Thus it is no surprise to find it in Angelus Silesius's mystical poem *The Cherubinic Wanderer:*

> God Plays With His Creatures
> It is all a game which God is playing,
> He has devised creatures for His own sake. (CW, II, 198/55)

Creatures originate in God, not as in a first cause, but as in a being who out of His own superabundance and goodness, needing nothing outside of Himself, has freely and spontaneously chosen to communicate Being to them. Creation is a game God plays for His own pleasure. And the creature who would make his way back to God must employ not "words" but "play" (CW, I, 194) and realize that those who are pure and innocent, like the maid and the child, are "God's closest playmates" (CW, I, 296) (cf. also CW, I, 184; III, 216; V, 141; see SG, 118 and CW, V, 366). The relation between God and the soul is a dialectic of playing, a game of love and grace. It is neither a metaphysical-causal nor an ethical-juridical relation.

Now for Heidegger the relationship between Being and Dasein is also depicted as a play. Being is not a cause but a mysterious giving which simultaneously withdraws. Dasein is not an effect but that which must learn how to "hear" the mission-ary "movements" (*Sätze*) of Being and learn how to play along with its playing. There is a dialectic of address and response between Being and Dasein in SG, but the question is whether it is a true and genuine dialectic. For Heidegger writes:

Whatever becomes a thing occurs out of the ringing of the world's mirror-play. Only when—*all of a sudden*, presumably—world worlds as a world, only then does the ring shine forth. . . . (emphasis mine) (VA, 180/182)

The reversal from "technology" to the "world" of the "four" together will occur only "suddenly," like a stroke of lightning (K, 43/11). Pöggeler (*Denkweg*, 36 ff.) tells us that Heidegger was, as a young man, very interested in the following passage from Paul's First Letter to the Thessalonians:[11]

You will not be expecting us to write anything to you, brothers, about "times and seasons," since you know very well that the day of the Lord is going to come like a thief in the night. It is when people are saying, "how quiet and peaceful it is," that the worst suddenly happens.

(1 Thess. 5:1-3)

Pöggeler shows how Heidegger saw in this passage, for the first time, the experience of "facticity." But we can see how it retains a parallel significance for the later Heidegger. For the sequence of epochs is not rule-governed but a play, whose movements come about "suddenly" and unpredictably. The history of Being is not a human doing at all; it is beyond man's control and calculation. Indeed Heidegger even says, as Versényi points out, that in the end we can only wait (G, 37/62) upon this play. The play between Dasein and Being is not the loving play between God and the soul described by Angelus Silesius. It is a "dangerous game" in which we are the stakes.

In moving beyond the categories of both reason and religion, Heidegger's play has become enigmatic and troubling, leading his critics to claim that he counsels self-surrender to a blind and purposeless power. And the work which Heidegger dedicates to a critique of the Principle of Ground, to which all philosophy must subscribe in one way or another, concludes by hearing in it the playing of a groundless play. Nothing could sound stranger to the philosopher's ear.

Appendix: Heidegger's Critique of "The Essence of Ground"

No discussion of SG would be complete without a reference to the self-criticism which Heidegger makes of his own earlier attempt to think through the nature of ground in 1929 in the essay entitled *On the Essence of Ground (Vom Wesen des Grundes,* hereafter WG). For SG contains a penetrating critique of the earlier treatise. Heidegger writes:

> Have we, we who are here now, felt that which displays its force (*dieses Machtende*) in this high and mighty Principle of Ground, have we experienced it properly and considered it in a completely sufficient way? If we do not throw dust in our eyes, we must all confess: no. All I say, even those who have from time to time troubled themselves about the "essence of ground" (*das "Wesen des Grundes"*). (SG, 48)

While the Principle of Ground was discussed in WG, it was not "experienced," for the power which pervades it was not "felt." Two lectures later in the same work, WG is again criticized for having taken the Principle of Ground too lightly, for having failed to hear what is genuinely being said in Leibniz's saying:

> It lies clearly before the eyes of this treatise (WG) that the principle "nothing is without ground" asserts something about the being (*das Seiende*) and gives no clarification as to what a "ground" is. But this insight into the content of the principle did not succeed in becoming an insight into what lies nearest. Instead of this, it (WG) took a step which is almost unavoidable. (SG, 85)

This step Heidegger represents as follows:

> The Principle of Ground is an assertion about the being. Accordingly it gives no information about the essence of ground. Thus the Principle of Ground, particularly in its traditional form, is not suited as a guide for a discussion of that towards which we aspire when we consider the essence of ground. (SG, 85)

The expression "nothing is without a ground" is an assertion about the being: no *thing*, no *being*, is without a ground. In the affirmative mode: every*thing*, every *being*, has a ground. The sentence presupposes that what a "ground" or "reason" is, is self-evident. It tells us nothing about the essence of ground, but asserts instead that this supposedly obvious predicate applies to everything. Thus we are inclined to drop the principle from any further consideration if our aim is to discover the essence of ground—which was the "almost unavoidable" step taken in WG. The author of WG did not appreciate the full implications of the Principle of Ground; he did not experience the "power" contained in the principle nor did he suspect that there was something "unsaid" trying to make itself heard in the principle. I should like to analyze what this criticism of WG by the later Heidegger amounts to, in order to throw light not only on Heidegger's own "path of thought" but also upon our understanding of the Principle of Ground.

In WG, the Principle of Ground serves as a "point of departure" (WG, 12/13), an "occasion" (WG, 8/9) for raising the larger problem of the essence of ground. There is, however, Heidegger observes, a kind of suffocating self-evidence about this principle which tends to extinguish every trace of a "problem." "Nothing is without ground"— what could be more obvious? What puzzle does this present? In terms of its content, of what it has to say, the Principle of Ground simply assumes from the start that what a ground is is familiar to everyone. In terms of its form as a "principle"—as a "Grund-satz"—it again presupposes that we know what something "ground"-like or "fundamental" is.

Still, Leibniz's principle does make a limited contribution to the discussion by giving us a clue as to what direction we should take in search of the essence of ground. Heidegger cites an opusculum of Leibniz in which Leibniz claims that the Principle of Ground originates in the nature of truth. For Leibniz "truth" is the truth of propositions. A proposition is a relationship of subject and predicate whose nexus is an identity-function (*inesse, idem esse*). Thus to say that 'S is P' is true is to say that P is discoverable by analysis in S. That is the "ground" or "foundation" of truth. The "sufficient reason" for the truth of a proposition is the discoverability of P in S. If the Principle of Ground did not hold, any predicate could be asserted of any subject, and there would thus be no truth at all. Hence the idea of "ground" is inseparable from the idea of "truth."

Heidegger then goes on to show that while Leibniz had made an important discovery—of the connection between truth and ground—his idea of truth was defective. For the truth of propositions depends upon the "pre-predicative" manifestness of the being about which propositions are made ("ontical" truth), which itself depends upon Dasein's understanding of Being ("ontological" truth). But Dasein's understanding of Being is its capacity to "transcend" (*über-steigen, transcendere*) beings to their Being, to transcend innerwordly entities to the horizon of the World itself. Thus the proper framework for discussing the essence of ground is "transcendence" ("transcendental" truth).

91

In the end, the essence of ground as transcendence is identified in WG as a threefold process called "grounding" (*Gründen*) (WG, 104/ 105ff.). Grounding is the process by which Dasein "grounds" or "founds" its world, the process by which it creates for itself a living space in which it can work out the task of becoming a "self." As such this discussion of grounding parallels very closely *Being and Time*, §§ 28-34, in which Heidegger discusses the way in which Dasein constitutes its own "there," the "there" of its world. The first moment of "grounding" Heidegger calls "establishing" (*Stiften*), which is Dasein's projection (*Entwurf*) of the "for the sake of" (*Umwillen*). "Establishing" is the act by which Dasein, which exists for the sake of itself, projects the "World" as the horizon within which its projects and possibilities as a self can be realized (WG, 84/85 ff.; 106/107 ff.). The second moment of grounding is identified as "gaining a footing" (*Bodennehmen*). The world would not be manifest to Dasein if, in projecting the world-horizon, Dasein were not already situated in the midst of (*sich befinden inmitten*) worldly things. Thus while Dasein projects the world, it is simultaneously "taken in" (*eingenommen*) by innerworldly entities and so is "tuned" and "disposed" (*durchstimmt*) by them (WG, 106-8/107-9). These first phases of grounding are clearly identical with "understanding" (*Verstehen*) and "disposition" (*Befindlichkeit*), projection and thrownness, in *Being and Time*. And as in *Being and Time*, the two belong together; the being which "establishes" the world is at the same time grounded amidst inner worldly beings.

Indeed it is this very unity of the first two moments which gives rise to the third moment. Heidegger explains this as follows. By the "project of the world" Dasein has no relation to any particular *entity*. By "gaining a footing" it has no *relation* to entities, because the horizon which allows entities to appear is lacking. In order to have a full and definite relationship with inner worldly entities—which is in fact what is meant by "intentionality" (WG is a contribution to a Husserl *Festschrift*)—the unity of the first two moments is required. This unity constitutes the third moment called "founding" (*Begründen*). "Founding" is not a theoretical attitude of the mind, by which it lays a "theoretical foundation" for entities. Rather founding concerns Dasein's very "existing," which is the way it conducts itself (*sich verhalten*) towards inner-worldly entities, towards other Dasein, and towards itself (WG, 112-4/113-5). Founding is what is called "care" in *Being and Time* (WG, 122/121). And, just as in *Being and Time*, Heidegger asserts that every theoretical question and proof arises from this more primordial (existential) founding. Every question "why" arises from the understanding of Being and of world—which is the inner core of "founding"—which lets things be manifest to begin with.

Only at the end of the treatise does Heidegger return again to his original point of departure, the Principle of Ground. Now we know, he claims, "why" the Principle of Ground holds. We know the "ground" or "reason," in the sense of the condition of possibility, for the Principle of Ground. By its transcendence to the world (its understanding of Being), Dasein lays the foundation for the appearance of every being. The being is manifest only on the ground of Dasein's understanding of Being. Apart from Dasein's transcendence, nothing is manifest; nothing is without its ground in transcendence—which is Leibniz's principle:

> Thus we see that the "birthplace" of the Principle of Sufficient Ground lies neither in the essence of the assertion nor in its truth, but rather in ontological truth, i.e., in transcendence itself. (WG, 122/123)

The essence of ground lies in Dasein's transcendence; the Principle of Ground has been given a transcendental explanation.

With the main line of argument in WG now in mind, we may return to Heidegger's self-criticism of this early text. No one, he said, not even those who have meditated on "the essence of ground," may assume that he has sufficiently experienced the "great power" of Leibniz's *principium grande*. For the principle is no mere proposition (*Satz*) but a decree (*Spruch*) which puts a claim (*Anspruch*) upon us all to deliver "grounds" and "reasons" and "causes":

> The *reddendum*, the demand for the delivery of grounds, is that which displays its might (*machtet*) in the Principle of Ground as the principle of great might. The *reddendum*, the demand for the delivery of grounds, now speaks unconditionally and incessantly throughout modernity and sweeps over us contemporaries. The *reddendum*, the demand for the delivery of grounds, has slipped in between thinking man and his world in order to take possession of human representing in a new way.
>
> (SG, 48)

The Principle of Ground is thus a power which permeates the modern world, a power which, holding us all in its grip, forces "thinking" to take the form of "demanding reason." The power which inheres in Leibniz's principle is the will-to-power itself of modern technology which represents an unprecedented assault upon man and nature.

Science is "reason," the demand for a "rationale," and its aim is the rational control of entities. Science dwells within the Principle of Sufficient Ground as within its own natural element (SG, 58-61).

In WG, the Principle of Ground was given short shrift. It served only as a point of departure which directed the inquiry into the realm of "truth" and "transcendence" as the sphere within which the essence of ground could be found. Having offered this clue, however, the principle itself dropped out of sight until the end of the treatise when Heidegger returned to it again in order to supply an explanation of how the principle arises in the first place. But in SG, Heidegger stays with the Principle of Ground more persistently, searching throughout the lectures for its more hidden depths. Hence we are told to "listen" more carefully to what it has to say.

By this more attentive hearing of the Principle of Ground in SG we hear in it not merely the voice of Leibniz, but that on behalf of which Leibniz speaks:

> The name Leibniz does not in our considerations stand as a characterization of a past system of philosophy. The name names the presence of a thought whose strength has not yet been endured, a presence which is still making itself present to us. (SG, 65)

Leibniz sounds the leit-motif of the metaphysics of the modern world. Leibniz is not an isolated speaker but a spokesman of the history of Being itself. In Leibniz's principle Being itself is speaking. In Leibniz's metaphysics, we come in contact with that sending (*schicken*) and withdrawing (*entziehen*) which Heidegger calls the "mission of Being" (*Seinsgeschick*) (SG, 108). It is Being itself which sends itself to us in Leibniz's metaphysics under the form of the "objectivity of objects"; it is Being itself which announces itself in the form of a "first principle" which lays claim over every "representation" and object. But in sending itself thus to us, Being simultaneously withdraws in its truth, i.e., in its belonging together with ground. The silent peal of the ringing together of Being and ground in the Principle of Ground can be heard only by those who have the ears to hear. It can be heard only by those who are willing to make the leap from the first to the second intonation of this familiar principle, a leap which, consisting in a simple shift of emphasis, is all the more difficult to make.

More than anything else, in our estimation, Heidegger's critique of WG in SG amounts to a criticism of the failure of the former treatise to think through Leibniz's principle in terms of the history and mission of Being. The idea which animates SG, and sets it off decisively from WG, is that of the mission of Being. For in SG Heidegger shows that, beginning with the Greek *logos*, and passing through the Latin *ratio*, which is used to translate *logos* by the Romans, the medievals, and by Leibniz himself, up to the German *Grund* and *Vernunft*, the "self-same" thing has been speaking. In each of these words belonging to the Western metaphysical tradition the belonging together of Being and ground has been concealedly addressing itself to us. In these translations (*Übersetzungen*) the Western tradition (*Überlieferung*), which stems from the history of Being itself, hands itself over to us (SG, 163-4). These translations are not innocent human conventions; they are nothing human at all. They are the speaking of language itself (SG, 164), the address of Being to man who, in giving utterance to these words, is responding to the primal word of Being. In WG, Heidegger remained in a sense in the "natural attitude" about Leibniz's principle. He took it to be the expression of an historical individual. But in SG the natural-historical (*historisch*) attitude is broken and it is replaced by the critical-historical (*seinsgeschichtlich*) thinking which thinks this principle in terms of the history of Being itself.

It is this failure to attain the perspective of the history of Being which lies at the basis of Heidegger's two criticisms of WG. In WG, the Principle of Ground is not understood as the first principle of the metaphysics of modernity; the straight line which leads from Leibniz's interest in the "calculus" of thought to modern logistics and technical-calculative thought is not perceived. Hence the great power which this principle harbors is not grasped. Secondly, because the Principle of Ground is not understood to issue from the mission of Being in WG, there is no suspicion that it contains within it a more primordial depth, that it is in a concealed way a saying about Being itself. In WG, there is no attempt to think what is left unthought in the Principle of Ground, to hear what it leaves unsaid.

Lacking the perspective of the mission of Being, the essence of ground is determined in WG as a "condition of possibility," an idea which for the later Heidegger belongs to the metaphysics of subjectivity. The essence of ground is the "condition of possibility" of the manifestness of the being, of all "intentional" behavior, and of every question "why?". But this is, as Heidegger argues in SG, the Kantian understanding of "ground" (SG, 126) which, instead of letting the being emerge on its own grounds, instead of living without why, makes it dependent on human thought. In WG, founding is the process by which Dasein supplies the horizon within which the being is allowed to appear. Founding in WG is still confined within the limits of what is criticized in the *Discourse on Thinking* (*Gelassenheit*) as "transcendental-horizonal" thinking. In WG, grounding is a transcendental *a priori* which renders beings possible and which, even if it is more fundamental than "representational" thought, still does not attain to the pristine simplicity of letting-be. As a contribution to a Husserl *Festschrift*, WG is still affected by Husserl's own transcendental phenomenology.

Heidegger's self-criticism of WG in SG provides thus an instructive insight into the relationship between the early and later works, revealing in a forthright way the path Heidegger's thought had followed in the intervening three decades.

96

CHAPTER THREE

THE ROSE IS WITHOUT WHY: MEISTER ECKHART'S MYSTICISM

IN listening to Angelus Silesius's saying "The Rose is Without Why," Heidegger claims that Silesius is really telling us that man must learn to be like the mystical rose. Man first enters into his essential nature (*Wesen*), Heidegger says, when he too is "without why." The present study has undertaken to meditate upon the kinship which Heidegger is thereby suggesting between what he has called "thought" (*Denken*) and the mystical life of the soul. But before that kinship can be discussed, we must form for ourselves as clear an idea as possible of Meister Eckhart's own doctrine. The task of the present chapter, then, will be to discuss Eckhart's teachings, to develop them on their own and largely without reference to Heidegger. We shall try to examine Eckhart in his own terms, to capture not only the meaning of his ideas but the spirit and flavor of his unique and original spirituality. Then in Chapter Four we will raise the question of Eckhart *and* Heidegger; we will confront these two masters of the German tradition in order to see whether and how these opposite ends of the history of German thought touch one another. But first we must let Meister Eckhart speak.

1. *Meister Eckhart and Angelus Silesius*

In SG, Heidegger mentions Meister Eckhart only once (SG, 71), for his attention is directed towards *The Cherubinic Wanderer*. How-

97

ever, as we mentioned briefly above, the writings of Angelus Silesius, in particular *The Cherubinic Wanderer,* are very much rooted in Meister Eckhart's thought. While the mystical rose of Angelus Silesius is the literary creation of Silesius, the thought which lies behind it derives from Meister Eckhart, as Heidegger himself is certainly aware. Let us begin our effort to understand the significance of Heidegger's reference to the kinship of Dasein with the mystical rose by turning first to Angelus Silesius and to the way in which he leads us back to Meister Eckhart himself.

Born and raised a Lutheran, Johannes Scheffler (1624–77), who held a medical degree from the University of Padua, was one of the leading religious figures in seventeenth-century Germany.[1] He spent an important period in Holland, where numerous religious and mystical groups had taken refuge from persecution elsewhere. Spinoza, e.g., went to Holland as a result of his difficulties with Jewish religious authorities, and he came into contact there with the pantheistic Jewish caballa. In Holland, Scheffler almost certainly was exposed to the works of Jacob Boehme (1575–1624), who is also a fertile source of German mysticism and a figure one sees occasionally linked with Heidegger.[2] It is well known that Schelling had taken up Böhme's notion of *Ungrund* in his *Philosophical Investigations on the Nature of Human Freedom,* and that Heidegger taught a lecture course on that important work of Schelling which was published in 1971. A connection may well exist between Böhme's *Ungrund* and Heidegger's *Abgrund.*

By means of Scheffler's friendship with Abraham of Franckenburg, by whom he was personally influenced, Scheffler became familiarized with the German mystical tradition from late medieval German mysticism up to the numerous mystical writings of his own day. In 1653, Scheffler converted to Roman Catholicism, an event which did not follow by long a bitter dispute between Scheffler and the Lutheran Church over the censorship of a book in which he had expressed himself in openly mystical language. Thereafter he became one of the leading Catholic spokesmen for the Counter-Reformation. It was by means of some Jesuit friends that he was able to secure an *imprimatur* for *The Cherubinic Wanderer,* which was published in 1657. In 1661, he was ordained a priest.

The importance of *The Cherubinic Wanderer* lies in the unexcelled poetic expression which Scheffler gave to the common stock of mystical ideas that had been accumulating since the late Middle Ages in Germany. He had made a careful study of a work by a Jesuit writer named Maximillian Sandaeus, which was an anthology of the major ideas in the German mystical tradition. *The Cherubinic Wanderer* seems then to have been the product not of a personal mystical experience but of a poetic inspiration which articulated an already established mystical tradition.

The rose in *The Cherubinic Wanderer* serves as the model of the soul. As the rose is sustained by the sunlight and mild temperatures of the Spring, so the soul is counseled to rely solely upon God's grace and favor:

The Mysterious Rose

The rose is my soul; the thorn the pleasures of the flesh;
The Spring is God's favor; His scorn the cold and frost;
Its blossoming is doing good without paying mind to its
thorn, the flesh. (CW, III, 91)

Accordingly, the deepest obligation and highest life of the soul—as of the rose—is to open itself up (*sich auftun*) to its gracious benefactor:

Open Up Like a Rose

My heart could receive God if only it chose,
To open itself to Him as does the rose. (CW, III, 87/119)

This is the pivotal metaphor: God rushes in upon the soul like the sunlight upon a rose provided only that the soul "open" itself up to God's gift. The soul is "closed" by self-love; it contracts upon itself in the narrowness of self-will (*Eigenwille*) and attachment to its own desires (CW, V, 186). The "openness" of the soul, on the other hand, consists in what Scheffler, following a long tradition in German mystical literature, calls "releasement" (*Gelassenheit*), i.e., an unselfish surrender to God's will. As the rose opens itself to nature and lets the powers of Spring work in it, so the soul must abandon its own will to God's and let Him work His ways in it. In such consummate resignation the soul, like the opened rose, attains its greatest beauty. Thus in the couplet preceding the one that Heidegger cites in SG, Scheffler says:

Released Beauty

You, O man, learn from the little meadow flowers
How you could please God and be beautiful all the same. (CW, I, 288)

One can see how openly Scheffler borrows from Meister Eckhart. Not only is the term "*Gelassenheit*" originally Meister Eckhart's, so too is the phrase "without why," which is the center of our interest in Scheffler. In his vernacular sermons, Meister Eckhart writes:[3]

> . . . God's ground is my ground and my ground is God's ground. Here I live on my own as God lives on His own. . . . You should work all your works out of this innermost ground without why. Indeed I say, so long as you work for the kingdom of heaven, or for God, or for your internal happiness and thus for something outward, all is not well with you.
>
> (Q, 180,5-13/Bl., 126-7)

The life of the soul which is "released" and so "without why" is a life which does not act for the sake of any external purpose—not even the kingdom of heaven itself. Rather, it acts out of God's own indwelling presence within the soul. Its life is an overflow of the divine life within it. It does not act for any rewards, temporal or eternal. It is "disinterested" in and "detached" (*abgeschieden*) from every external purpose, every *telos*, however exalted it may be. For every act which has a "why" is moved by a "material principle," as Kant would say, and so is rooted in self-love.

Thus the ultimate source of the mystical tradition to which Scheffler falls heir is Meister Eckhart, the greatest of the "Rhineland Mystics." Scheffler himself did not acknowledge Eckhart (in the "Preface" to *The Cherubinic Wanderer*) because the Church had condemned the great medieval mystic in 1329. It is clear, however, that if we wish to fully understand the kinship between Dasein and the mystical rose, and so to see how "thought" and "mysticism" dwell in the same neighborhood, we must go back to Meister Eckhart himself, in whom the whole notion of living "without why" first originates. That Heidegger himself realized the source of Angelus Silesius's sayings in the work of Meister Eckhart is beyond question, as we shall see below.

Eckhart, whose surname is "von Hochheim" and who is sometimes wrongly referred to as "Johannes" Eckhardus, was born in 1260 in the former state of Thuringia in Central Germany.[4] He entered the Dominican Order, the "Order of Preachers," and became himself the most celebrated preacher of his day. He also held for most of his mature life responsible administrative positions in the Dominican order. He was, for example, the first "Provincial" of the Saxon province. He was also chosen to represent the order as a "master" (*magister*) at the University of Paris, whence the name by which he is known to us today, because of his singular abilities as a scholastic theologian and philosopher. Thus he was to be one of the successors, by a little over a quarter-century, of another, somewhat better known Dominican master at Paris, Thomas Aquinas—"brother Thomas," as Eckhart calls him.

Eckhart's writings fall into two groups. In the first place, there are the Latin works: commentaries on the Scriptures, Latin sermons, disputed questions, etc.—the standard fare of a medieval theologian. These works are enormously original, however, and they reflect a distinctive blend of Plotinus and Augustine with the more recent Dominican tradition, above all, Albertus Magnus and Thomas Aquinas. Eckhart's ability to take familiar medieval notions and give them a distinctive reinterpretation in accord with his own "speculative mysticism" is extraordinary. It was not, however, by these Latin works that Meister Eckhart would achieve a lasting place in the history of Western thought, but rather by his "vernacular" works. Like Heidegger himself, Eckhart was an innovator in his use of the German language and is numbered among the creators of the German language. There have been numerous studies of Eckhart by Germanists who are primarily interested in the history and formation of the German language. These vernacular works consist primarily of sermons which Eckhart delivered. The Dominicans were charged by the Pope with the task of preaching to the religious orders of women in the thirteenth century. Since these women did not receive the formal theological training accorded to the men and could not read Latin, the sermons of the preachers were one of the few sources of instruction they would receive. Accordingly, Eckhart does not express himself abstractly in these sermons. His intent is to put his ideas vividly, resorting to numerous analogies and comparisons, always choosing the best German word to translate the Latin terminology of the schools. His intention was primarily to inspire these women in the practice of Christian piety and the virtues of the convent, and it is often necessary to recall this when interpreting his sermons.

Eckhart was a masterful writer with a great affection for paradoxes. He was also an extremely daring writer who frequently couched his mystical ideas in a language which, if taken literally, was certainly heretical. It is hardly a surprise that he ran afoul of the ecclesiastical establishment. His orthodoxy was challenged by the Archbishop of Cologne in 1325, and the final upshot of this challenge was a Bull issued by Pope John XXII, on March 27, 1329, sometime shortly after Eckhart's death, condemning some twenty-eight propositions extracted from his works. Eckhart's defence against these charges in his last days contains important refinements of his meaning, and is also quite useful in separating authentic from spurious writings.

As a result of the condemnation, Eckhart's Latin writings fell into almost total neglect, except for an edition of them by Nicholas of Cusa (1401-64), who was deeply influenced by Eckhart. It was not until 1885, when the German Dominican scholar H. S. Denifle published lengthy portions of the Latin writings,[5] that interest in them would be revived. The vernacular writings on the other hand went underground. They were incorporated, in part, into the works of two of Eckhart's foremost disciples, who had not been condemned—Henry Suso (1295-1366) and John Tauler (ca. 1300-1361). Suso and Tauler were fellow Dominicans and Germans who, with Eckhart, constitute the main figures in "Rhineland Mysticism." They perpetuated Eckhart's teachings in their own writings; indeed, Eckhart's own sermons are often confused with those of Tauler.

By means of Tauler and Suso, Eckhart would exert a decisive influence on the development of German mysticism, religion, and philosophy. His influence reaches to Jan Ruysbroeck (1293-1381), to the author of the *Imitatio Christi* (ca 1441), to the author of *Eyn Theologie Deutsch* (ca. 1350), and, by means of the latter work, to Luther himself and to the entire Protestant tradition, including Jacob Böhme. It was this tradition, at the head of which stood Eckhart, that Angelus Silesius was to inherit. Franz von Baader (1765-1841) introduced Eckhart's works to Hegel; and we know that Schopenhauer praised the appearance, in 1857, of the once standard edition of Eckhart's sermons and treatises by Franz Pfeiffer. A remark by Hegel in his *Lectures on the Philosophy of Religion*, in which Hegel compared nineteenth-century theologians unfavorably with Meister Eckhart, occasioned a response by Carl Schmidt, which took the form of a monograph on Eckhart in 1839. Schmidt's study lent impetus to a modern revival of interest in Eckhart which has lasted to the present day.[6] In 1936, a massive critical edition of Eckhart's Latin and German works was begun, and its work continues even today.

Nietzsche said in *The Antichrist* that "the grandfather of German philosophy is the Protestant minister" (*Antichrist*, No. 10). He might have added that the German mystic is its great-grandfather. For there are the most interesting, even startling, likenesses between Eckhart and the subsequent German tradition. Thus the comparison which we will work out in the following pages between Heidegger and Meister Eckhart is a very suggestive one for the historian of German thought. It brings together the "ends"—the *terminus a quo* and the *terminus ad quem*—of the German tradition. It suggests a fundamental continuity in the German tradition whose "middle term" is the great idealist systems of the nineteenth century. In Eckhart, Hegel, and Heidegger one finds a fundamental "concern" (*Sache*) for thought: God, the Absolute, Being. In all of them, "man" is conceived of not "anthropologically" (as a higher species of animal), but "ontologically," viz., as a pure relationship to the matter to be thought: as what Eckhart calls the "ground of the soul," as Hegel's "*Geist*," as Dasein. For each thinker man is the place where something essential comes to pass and is realized, a place which this essential event "needs and uses." This is a compellingly interesting theme, but, we should add, one of such proportions that it cannot be developed in these pages.[7] Like the question of Heidegger and Eastern mysticism, it deserves a separate, full-length treatment. We shall be content in this work to offer suggestions here and there, where space permits, concerning this larger continuity from Eckhart through the Idealists to Heidegger. For the task of the present work has already been set: to go back to the hidden origin of the German tradition in Meister Eckhart, and to bring out into the open the way in which Heidegger is repeating and retrieving this beginning.

Let us now turn to the main task of the present chapter, which is to set forth the main lines of Meister Eckhart's mysticism. We shall begin with an exposition of his teachings on the nature of God, leaning for this rather heavily on his Latin writings. From there we will turn to the German sermons and treatises in order to discuss his teachings on the soul, the birth of the Son, and the other elements of what has been called his "speculative mysticism."

2. "*Being is God*"

In the "Prologue" to the *Opus Tripartitum* Eckhart sets out the "first proposition" from which, if one is careful, nearly all that can be known of God can be deduced (LW, I, 168/85). The proposition is: being is God (*esse est deus*). He does not say, as did Aquinas, that God is being (*deus est suum esse*), but he adopts instead the more extreme expression that being is God. Aquinas, realist and Aristotelian, emphasized that creatures possessed their own proper and proportionate share in being, while God possessed the unlimited fullness of being itself. But the mystic Eckhart stresses instead the radical dependency of creatures upon God. Of itself, he says, the creature is "absolutely nothing" (*nihil penitus*), a "pure nothing" (*ein reines Nichts*: Q, 171, 9/Serm., 173) not even a modicum. The creature does not have being "in itself" at all, but only "in God." Created things have being, Eckhart holds, the way air has light (LW, II, 274-5). The air does not "possess" the light; it simply receives it for as long as the sun illuminates it. The light is not "rooted" in the air, but in its source, the sun. In the same way, the creature does not "possess" being, has no "hold" on it, but instead continuously receives being from its source, being itself. Being is God, that is to say, being belongs properly only to God, in Whom alone it is originally "rooted" (LW, II, 282).

The proof which Eckhart gives for the proposition that being is God is as follows. The relationship between being itself (*ipsum esse*) and a particular being (*ens hoc aut hoc*) is like the relationship between whiteness itself and any white thing. As white things are white by sharing in whiteness itself, so individual beings exist in virtue of being itself. But if being were not God, but something other than God, then God Himself would exist in virtue of something other than Himself, and other beings would exist in virtue of something other than God. But if this is so, God would not be (what we mean by) God. It also follows from this that God exists. This can be shown by Eckhart's own version of the ontological argument. Nothing is more evident than an identical proposition. But if it is true that "being is God," then it is true that God is. For the two terms, being and God, are identical.

Furthermore, if being is God, then nothing of the perfection of being is lacking to Him. God is the purity and plenitude of being (*plenitudo esse*, *purum esse*: LW, III, 77). He precontains and includes (*praehabeat et includat*: LW, I, 169) in a preeminent way the limited and multiple perfections which have been "lent" (Q, 119, 20-20, 6/Cl. 128) to creatures. Finally, if being is God, then God is "one." He possesses His being in a timeless simplicity which entirely excludes the successiveness and multiplicity, i.e., the "negativity" of creatures:

> Everything which falls short of God, inasmuch as it falls short of being, is both being and non-being, and something of being is denied of it. For it is beneath being and falls short of it. Therefore negation befits it.
>
> (LW, II, 77)

But one must deny every negation in God Himself. God is the "negation of negation":

> Therefore no negation, nothing negative, befits God except the negation of negation, which is what the one, taken negatively, signifies: God is one. But a negation of a negation is the most pure and full affirmation.
>
> (LW, II, 77)

The phrase "negation of negation" is, linguistically at least, a remarkable anticipation of the later Idealists' formulation. However, Eckhart does not intend to use this expression "dialectically," i.e., he does not mean to say that God has overcome otherness and returned to Himself. He is referring to the pristine simplicity and undividedness of the divine nature. If there is anything in the later Idealist movement to which it bears a resemblance, it is the self-identical One in Schelling's "*Identitätsphilosophie*." But it must be insisted that Eckhart's "One" stands in no *need* of diversification and enrichment, because it is already the fullness of Being (*plenitudo esse*). It is important to keep this point in mind in discussing below the disanalogy between Eckhart and Heidegger. For Eckhart's God is the fullness of Being, the lack of every negation, and therefore in no sense in "need" of man. Man is not needed in order to bring God into His "own" as in Heidegger's view of the relation of Being and man. It is true, as we shall see below, that Eckhart's German sermons sometimes suggest something different. But that is why we must read the Latin writings, for these always provide a corrective which prevents a misinterpretation of Eckhart's daring language in the vernacular writings. It must never be forgotten that Eckhart conceived himself to be a faithful son of the Church and of St. Dominic, and that he had not the slightest intention of teaching a heretical metaphysics which denied the orthodox doctrines concerning God, creatures, and the human soul.

The neoplatonic emphasis which Eckhart places on the "unity" of the divine being reappears in the German works in terms of the distinction between the "Godhead" (*Gottheit, divinitas*) and "God" (*Gott, deus*). "God" refers to the divine being insofar as it is related to creatures and so insofar as it is named on the basis of these relationships. Hence "God" is called good as the cause of the goodness of creatures, wise because of the order He has established in the universe, etc. But the "Godhead" is the divine being insofar as it remains concealed behind all the names which are attributed to Him. The Godhead is the "one" which is purer than goodness and truth, which is even prior to the Son and the Holy Spirit. The "one" refers to God:

> . . . there where He is in Himself, before He flows out into the Son and the Holy Spirit. . . . A Master has said: the one is a negation of negation. (Q, 252, 32-5/Serm., 230)

105

The Godhead is the absolute unity of the divine being, the negation of all multiplicity, not only of the multiplicity of creatures but even of the multiplicity of Persons in the divine Trinity. The Godhead is the deeper "ground" (*Grund*: Q, 264,7/Ev., 258) from out of which even the Persons of the Trinity flow. But because this ground is "hidden," it is just as much an "abyss" (*Abgrund*: Q, 213,34/Serm., 224). Eckhart also speaks of the hidden Godhead as a divine "wasteland" (*Wüste*: Q, 213,18/Serm., 223) and as the "naked being" of God (Q, 210,13/Serm., 220). The Godhead totally transcends the power of thought to represent it. Eckhart says this is not the God of thought but God Himself as He is in Himself, "the divine God" (*der göttliche Gott*: Q, 60,26/Cl., 70), who cannot be reduced to the dimensions of human intelligence.

The doctrine of the divine Godhead is one of the most characteristic and original of Meister Eckhart's teachings, and one which deserves a fuller development than we have accorded it here. Our intention, however, is to return to it a bit later in this exposition of Eckhart in order to examine the special problem it presents in the interpretation of his thought. For we shall see in the pages that follow a certain tension developing in Eckhart between the more recognizably Christian themes in his writings and the Neoplatonic ones. Indeed it will turn out that there are two different ways of formulating the mystical union in Eckhart's sermons, one Christian and the other Neoplatonic, each of which seems to exclude the other. We shall in the pages that follow develop Eckhart's thought in terms of its Christian and indeed Johannine motifs, and then towards the end of this chapter raise the question of the place of the neoplatonically inspired doctrine of the divine Godhead in his mystical teachings.

Eckhart's statement that being is God may appear to be borrowed from Thomas Aquinas's teaching that God is his own act of being. But while Eckhart will often vest his thought in the language of Aquinas, the basic tendency of his thought is quite different. For Eckhart denies the central tenet of Thomistic metaphysics, the primacy of *esse*. Thus in an astonishing set of disputed questions held at Paris, Eckhart appears to flatly contradict himself and to deny being of God. After accepting Aquinas's arguments for the identity of being (*esse*) and understanding (*intelligere*) in God, he states in his *Parisian Questions* that he has reached a very unthomistic conclusion:

> . . . I am no longer of the opinion that He understands because He is, but that He is because He understands, so that God is intellect and the act

of understanding, and the act of understanding is the ground of being itself. (LW, V, 40/45)

There is something higher—or deeper—in God than "being," and that is "understanding." God is *not* being, formally speaking:

> . . . in God there is neither being (*ens*) nor the act-of-being (*esse*), because nothing is formally present in both the cause and that of which it is the cause, if the cause is a true cause. But God is the cause of all being. Therefore being is not formally present in God. (LW, V, 45/48)

Eckhart attempts to reconcile this position with the one he adopted in the *Prologues*—that *esse est deus*—by arguing that being does not belong to God "formally" but rather in a "higher" sense. This is because God is "a true cause," i.e., one which is of an essentially higher kind than its effect, in this case creatures. Now creatures have "being" properly speaking, for to be "created" is to receive being. But God is the cause of the being of creatures. And since He is a "true" or transcendent cause, He does not share "being" with creatures in an "univocal" sense (LW, V, 45/48). Thus God does not have being, properly speaking, but the "purity of being" (*puritas essendi*: LW, V, 45/48).

But the purity of being is identified by Eckhart as understanding. The understanding is *not* being, but that by which being is known. Ideas are not things but the means by which things are known. For we have seen above that Eckhart follows Aristotle's teaching that in order to know the soul must be "pure" of or "unmixed" with that which it knows. If the eye were colored it would see all things under that color. The understanding must, if it would know all things, be separate from all beings. But God is what we have called the *ens separatissimum*, the most removed of all from every "this or that." Hence God knows all beings but is not Himself a being. He is the "purity" of being, viz., understanding.

The notion that the understanding is in some way "non-being" while its object is "being" is another suggestive theme for the historian of modern philosophy. One finds a similar idea in Fichte's "First Introduction to the *Wissenschaftslehre*," and it is also this same duality which is behind Hegel's famous observation in the "Preface" to the *Phenomenology* that the true is both substance (being) and subject (*negativity*). The subject for Hegel is "pure simple negativity," the "tremendous power of the negative." A similar idea is even to be found in Jean-Paul Sartre, for whom to know is to negate.

107

The "naked essence" of God, the pure, simple, inner life of God, is the life of understanding, or, as Eckhart translates *intellectus* in his vernacular sermons, the life of "Reason" (*Vernunft*):

> If we take God in His being, then we take Him in His vestibule, for being is the vestibule in which He dwells. But where is He then in His temple, in which He shines forth as holy? *Reason* is the temple of God. God dwells nowhere more authentically than in His temple, in Reason. As that other master said, God is His Reason, which there lives in knowledge of Himself alone, abiding there only in Himself, where nothing ever troubles Him. For He is there alone in His stillness. In His knowledge of Himself, God knows Himself in Himself.
>
> (Q, 197,25-33/Serm., 207-8; cf. Q, "*Einleitung*," 23).

By assigning such primacy to the understanding, Eckhart is defending the traditions of his order against the Franciscans who emphasized the divine will.[8] Eckhart takes over the "self-thinking thought" of Aristotle and contours it to the needs of his Christian metaphysics. As such, Eckhart's *Vernunft*, the life of God knowing Himself, provides a neglected link in the familiar connection between Aristotle and Hegel. When Hegel identifies the Absolute as the absolute "Idea," he agrees with the Dominican–Aristotelian intellectualism of the Middle Ages, and with the German Eckhart in particular.

The activity of thought thinking itself is entirely self-contained, beginning and ending in the divine mind itself. Hence it is for Eckhart the supreme form of "life." With Aristotle, Eckhart held that a living thing is

> . . . that which is moved from itself as from an inner principle and in itself. But that which is not moved except by some external thing neither is nor is said to be living. From this it is evident that everything which has an efficient cause prior to and above itself, or a final cause outside of or other than itself, does not live in the proper sense. But such is the case with every creature. Only God as the ultimate end and first mover lives and is life. (LW, III, 51)

God requires no efficient cause to set Him into activity, nor does He act for the sake of any end outside of Himself. He is the cause and principle of all things, but He requires no cause or principle for Himself. Hence Eckhart cites with approval Proposition VII of the *Liber XXIV Philosophorum*:

108

God is the principle without principle, the process without variation, the end without end. (LW, III, 16, n. 1/Cl. 239)

The life of the self-thinking thought is self-sufficient, self-complete. It is in this context that Eckhart says that the life of God is "without why." While it is the explanation (or "why") of all other things, it itself stands in need of no explanation of its own being (LW, III, 41/Cl. 255). Thus God created the world, not out of any lack in Himself which He hoped to fill up (a "why"), but out of the welling up within Himself (*ebullitio*) of His own life which spills over into creatures. In an unusually rhapsodic passage for the Latin writings Eckhart says:

Life means a certain overflow by which a thing, welling up within itself, first completely floods itself, each part of itself interpenetrating every other, before it pours itself out and wells over into something external. (LW, II, 22/Cl., 226)

While it would be an exaggeration to see in Eckhart the first process theory of God, it is true that he emphasized the living and active quality of the divine nature.[9] He was at home with the Christian doctrine of the Trinity, for he saw there a process of life giving birth to life. And he regarded the act of creation as a further extension of the inner life of the Trinity (LW, II, 22/Cl. 226). The Father is the one, the beginning (*principium*) of life; the Son is the begotten; the Spirit is their mutual love and ardor for one another. Creation is the overflow, the spilling over of this inner life-process into time and number and multiplicity.

Thus—to recapitulate Eckhart's doctrine of God—God is *esse*, *unum*, *vivere*, and *intelligere*. But only the last name penetrates beyond the vestibule into the naked essence of God, and provides the foundation of the other names.

3. *The Ground of the Soul*

The transition from Eckhart's interpretation of the nature of God in his Latin writings to his mystical doctrine may be made by returning to the pivotal text from the German sermons which we cited above, in which Eckhart spoke of the divine Reason. It continues:

Now let us take it (=knowledge) as it is in the soul, which possesses a trickle of Reason, a little spark, a twig. (Q, 197,34-5/Serm., 208)

109

Eckhart sets up a correlation between God and the soul. As God in His hidden ground is Reason itself, so the soul in its own hidden ground possesses a "little spark" (*Fünklein*), a drop, a small share, in the divine Reason. In virtue of this divine spark, the soul alone among all creatures is able to penetrate to the hidden center of the divine being. Because it shares in the divine intellectuality, the soul is akin to God and is able to unite with God:

> . . . intellect properly speaking belongs to God and 'God is one'. To the extent, therefore, that each thing possesses intellect or intellectual powers, to that extent it is one with God. . . . To ascend to the intellect, therefore, and to be subjugated to it, is to be united to God. . . . All being apart from the intellect, outside the intellect, is creature and creatable, is other than God, is not God. (LW, IV, 269-70/Cl., 212)

Because the soul possesses an intellectual nature, there is an intimate and profound correspondence between it and God. As God's Reason is the hidden sanctuary of His Being, so the soul's spark of Reason is its inner temple (Q, 153,11-3/Serm., 127). Here God and the soul unite:

> Here God's ground is my ground, and my ground is God's ground.
>
> Q, 180,5-6/Bl., 126)

When Eckhart speaks of the "little spark" of Reason, he does not refer to the faculty of discursive reasoning, the power that moves from premises to conclusions and which uses concepts and representations. In the vernacular sermon "*Impletum est*" he distinguishes three kinds of knowledge:

> The one is sensible: the eye sees things, even at a distance, which are outside of itself. The second is rational and much higher. But with the third is meant a noble power of the soul, which is so high and noble that it grasps God in His own naked being. This power has nothing at all in common with anything else. (Q, 210,9-14/Serm., 220)

The first two powers are directed outward to creatures, the first in terms of their sensible properties, the second in terms of their essential or intelligible properties. The second power, which Eckhart calls "rational," proceeds by means of representations and concepts (*Vorstellungen*: Q, 138, 30/Cl. 147; *Begriffe*: Q, 318,10/Ev., 32; in Latin *species*), which in the classical Aristotelian theory are signs of external things and are themselves symbolized by words. But of the third power, which is "the ground of the soul," he says that it "has nothing in common with anything." It is not concerned with creatures, nor is it in any way like creatures; it is related solely to God, and to His "naked Being" (the Godhead).

By means of its "faculties"—sensation, will, and (discursive) reason —the soul is related outwards to creatures. By the use of these faculties it performs "outer works," not only of laboring and eating, say, but also of praying and fasting (Q, 76,32-3/Cl. 85). The ground of the soul, the very "being" (*Wesen*) of the soul, on the other hand, is prior to the emergence of the faculties and is the "root" (*Wurzel*: Q, 318,17/Ev.32) of all outer works. Hence Eckhart says that one should be holy in one's being, not merely in one's works; if a man "is" holy, his "works" will be holy. We are not sanctified by our works, our works are sanctified by us.[10] There is no "activity," no commerce with creatures, in the ground of the soul, because the ground of the soul is prior to the faculties by which one "acts." Aquinas had taught that the faculties of the soul "flow from the essence of the soul as from a principle,"[11] but for Thomas the essence of the soul apart from its faculties is a truncated and immobilized substance which stands in need of the further actualization of its faculties. It is in the German Dominican tradition—in Albert the Great (d. 1280) and Dietrich of Vrieberg (d. 1310)—that Eckhart found the idea that the essence of the soul was a "hidden recess of the mind" (*abditum mentis*).[12] In this innermost ground, the soul is still and silent (Q, 238,26-35/Serm., 164). and ready for a union with God which is denied to the "faculties," inasmuch as they are immersed in "outer works" and the daily business of life.

In a sermon entitled "*Intravit Jesus in quoddam castellum*" ("Jesus entered a little town," Luke 10:38) (Q, 159 ff./Serm., 133 ff.), Eckhart gives a series of characterizations of what this innermost ground of the soul, which has stripped itself of all relationships with creatures, is like:

> I have also said already that there is a power of the soul which touches neither time nor flesh. (Q, 161,19-20/Serm., 135)

Because the ground of the soul is removed from all contact with creatures, it is withdrawn from the realm of space and time. In the hidden "ground" of the soul, therefore, there is an eternal now in which the soul is removed from the sequence of "now's" which constitute its conscious or "outer" life. But God Himself dwells in eternity. Thus this eternal now is a meeting place in which God and the soul dwell together in a single timeless "moment":

> . . . God is in this power as in the eternal now. Were the spirit at every moment united with God in this power, man could never grow old. . . . Now, look, man dwells in the light with God; consequently there is in him neither suffering nor the sequence of time but an eternity which remains the same. (Q, 162,2-9/Serm., 136)

Nothing "new" can happen to such a soul, for it has risen above the fluctuations of time. Eckhart continues:

> I have said on occasion that there is a power in the spirit which is alone free. (Q, 163,13-4/Serm., 137)

But in what does its "freedom" consist?

> It is free of all names and bare of all forms, wholly untrammelled and free, as God is untrammelled and free. (Q, 163,21-2/Serm., 137)

Having detached itself from all outer commerce with creatures, the soul is "free" and "unfettered" by creatures. Its freedom is its "purity" from everything created. The soul is at once free from attachment to created things and free for union with God. In the ground of the soul, the soul is like God Himself: absolutely simple and detached. Like God, the ground of the soul is neither "this nor that":

> Up to now I have said that it [the ground of the soul] is a shelter (*Hut*) of the spirit; up to now I have said it is a light of the spirit; up to now I have said it is a little spark. But now I say: it is neither this nor that; despite that, it is something which is raised above this and that as heaven is above the earth. Consequently, I have named it in a more noble way than I have ever named it. . . . (Q, 163,14-9/Serm., 137)

The ground of the soul is no determinate thing, no particular being. It has nothing in common with anything. It is a silent, still, inner reserve, a "shelter" of the spirit which allows the spirit to detach itself from everything outward. The soul becomes like God in the treatise *On Detachment*: so detached from every "thing," that it is itself "nothing"—yet in such a way as to be raised above every "thing." It cannot be identified by any "property." Like the Godhead itself, the ground of the soul is entirely nameless.

Eckhart goes so far in assimilating the ground of the soul to the Godhead that he even says the ground of the soul is uncreated:

> . . . as I have often said, there is something in the soul which is so akin to God that it is one [with God] and not [merely] united with Him. It is one; it has nothing in common with anything; nor does anything which is created have something in common with it. Everything which is created is nothing. But this ground of the soul is distant and alien from all created things. Were a man wholly like this, he would be completely uncreated and uncreatable. (Q, 215,9-15/Serm., 225)

If the soul were wholly what it is in its ground, it would be uncreated. Of course, the ground of the soul is not the totality of the soul, for there is also the outer life of the soul in and through its faculties (cf. Théry, p. 214/Bl., 285). But the ground itself, in and of itself, is like the uncreated: timeless, eternal, pure, detached. Eckhart is not saying the soul is composed of two parts, one created and one uncreated. His view is that in the innermost ground of this creature, the soul, there is a purity and detachment from creatures which is exactly like the uncreated Being of God Himself.

There is thus a special correspondence, an exclusive reciprocity, between God and the soul. Only the ground of the soul is pure enough and simple enough to receive God; and only God is pure and simple enough to enter the ground of the soul (Q, 164, 18-21/Serm., 138; 252, 23-8/Serm., 229). "God is nearer to the soul," he says with St. Augustine, "than it is to itself" (Q, 201, 15-6/Serm., 198). And again:

> Where God is, there is the soul; where the soul is, there is God.
>
> (Q, 207,2/Serm., 2-3)

The soul is the place of God, as God is the place of the soul. The ground of the soul is a "place" among creatures into which God may come, a "clearing" for God's advent into the world. An "event"— God's coming—can happen in the soul because the soul has "cleared" a place in which it may take place.

4. *The Birth of the Son*

The advent of God into the soul, the event that takes place in the soul, is described by Eckhart as the "birth of the Son."[13] The place that the soul makes for God, he says, is God's "birthplace" (Q, 415, 22/Bl., 95). The point of departure for this central doctrine in Eckhart's writings is St. John. St. John's gospel of love and divine sonship, of the love of the Father for his children, animates Eckhart's work and moves him to some of his most enthusiastic and extreme formulations. There can be no doubt about the Christian and Johannine inspiration of these passages. The celebrated "Prologue" of St. John's Gospel begins: "In the beginning was the Word" (*In principio erat verbum*). For Eckhart, the being of God is the process of life giving birth to life. The First Person of the Trinity is the "*principium*," the first principle and beginning of the life-process; hence He is called the "Father." The essence of the Father is to give birth. "The Father works only one work" (Q, 185,32/Serm., 189), he says, and that is to bear His Son "incessantly" (Q, 185,20/Serm., 188). The essence of the Son, correspondingly, is to be born, to be the offspring and image of the Father, to receive life "incessantly." Hence the first sentence of the "Prologue" refers to the process by which the Eternal Father conceives the co-eternal Word (*logos, verbum, Wort*) in which He knows Himself. The sentence means: in the Father, the Son is born. The "Prologue" continues:[14]

> But to all who did accept Him [the Son] He gave the power to become the children of God, to all who believe in the name of Him Who was born . . . of God Himself. (John 1: 12)

It is upon this text and similar ones—such as the following from John's First Letter—that Eckhart bases his teaching about the mystical birth of the Son:

> Think of the love that the Father has lavished on us, by letting us be called God's children; and that is what we are. (1 John 3:1)

For Eckhart, John is to be taken at his word, and John says that we are not only "called" God's children, but "that is what we are." This can mean only one thing: "As little as a man can be wise without wisdom," he says, "so little can he be a son without the filial being of the Son of God . . ." (Q, 317,19-21/Ev., 32). And even more strongly:

> The Father bears His Son in eternity like to Himself. 'The Word was with God and the Word was God'. He was the same as God and of the same nature. Yet beyond this I say: He has begotten Him in my soul. . . . The Father bears His Son in the soul in the same way that He bears Him in eternity, not in any other way. He must do it, whether He wishes to or not. The Father bears His Son incessantly, and I say still more: He bears me as His Son, and as the same Son. (Q, 185,13-21/Serm., 188)

Eckhart means to say that the process by which the Father bears His Son in eternity is extended to the ground of the soul so that the Father bears His Son in the soul. Moreover, He bears the soul itself as that very Son. The Son is born in the place that the soul makes for Him and the soul is assimilated to that Son. The generation of the Son in eternity and the Incarnation of that Son as man is a universal event for Eckhart which is extended to the soul itself:[15]

> It would mean little to me that the 'Word was made flesh' for man in Christ, granting that the latter is distinct from me, unless He also was made flesh in me personally, so that I too would become the Son of God.
>
> (LW, III, 101-2; cf. Q, 415,6-8/Bl., 95)

Although Eckhart's formulations are in the strongest possible language, his position is essentially orthodox. For not only is there a doctrine of mystical union expressed in terms of the divine sonship in the Johannine Gospel, but the notion that the Son is born in the soul has a long history in orthodox Christian theology before Eckhart. Hugo Rahner has shown in a lengthy study that the sources of this idea go all the way back to the early patristic theology of grace. It was, for example, Origen who in his *Homilies on the Gospel of St. Luke* first asked:[16]

> What does it profit you if Christ comes in the flesh unless He would also come to your soul?

For Origen, as for the early Fathers in general, this birth is accomplished in the soul by grace, in Baptism. The same doctrine is found later in Cyril of Alexandria and Gregory of Nyssa among the Greek fathers. In the Latin tradition, Rahner points to its role in Ambrose and in the Augustinian doctrine of the "Body of Christ." In medieval theology, it reappears in Richard of St. Victor, with whom Eckhart was quite familiar. As Rahner concludes:[17]

> The idea flowed to him from a thousand sources; it is age-old; it is one of the essential pieces of Christian mysticism of all centuries.

In keeping with this tradition, Eckhart distinguishes between the Son by nature and the Son "by grace" (Q, 120,22-9/Cl., 128; 208,11-5/ Serm., 218). The Son by nature is the Eternal Word Himself; the Son by grace is the soul itself which has been "formed over" (*überbildet*: Q, 103,31/Cl., 111) into the Son in its very ground by reason of the residence which the Son takes up in the soul. By grace, the Son "dwells"

115

in the ground of the soul, "unites" with it: "Grace is rather an indwelling and co-dwelling of the soul in God" (Q, 398,26-7/Ev., 200). By grace, the Son resides in the soul, not as a cause is present to its effect, but personally, as the beloved is present to the lover.

Eckhart elaborates the doctrine of the birth of the Son in two important ways: first, in terms of an "image," and secondly, in terms of a "word."

A father is one who generates his "image" (*Bild*) or likeness. For an image, there are two requisites (Q, 224,33 ff./Serm., 145 ff.). First, there must be a likeness between the original model and the image. But while this is a necessary condition, it is not a sufficient one:

> There can be no image without likeness, but there can indeed be a likeness without an image. Two eggs are equally white, yet one is not the image of the other. (Q, 224,28-30/Serm., 144-5)

The second requirement is stronger, viz., that the image be sustained in its very being as an image by the model:

> An image takes its being immediately and solely from that of which it is an image. (Q, 226,21-3/Serm., 146)

The image of a face in the mirror, e.g., is not only like the face of which it is the image, but it also derives its being from the face, in the sense that the image persists only so long as the face is present; if the face were removed, the image would vanish. Now the relation of a son to his father fulfills both these requirements. Yet even here a distinction is to be made. A human father brings about the being of his likeness, his son, but because of the disunity between a human father and son—they are distinct and separate substances—the human son may continue to live after the father has died, thus impairing the perfection of the second requirement. The divine Father on the other hand is essentially a process of giving birth, the divine Son essentially a process of being born. The being of each is their relationship to one another. (The medieval theologians held that the divine Persons or "hypostases" constituted a set of "subsistent relations.") And since it is the same eternal birth process which is extended to the ground of the soul, the soul too is an authentic and true image of the Father. The soul is formed and made in the image of the Father (*überbildet*) by the Father Himself.

For the Father to bear His Son is also, according to Eckhart, for Him to speak the eternal Word. According to medieval theology, the essence of the Second Person is to be the "thought" in which the Father knows Himself. The "Son" is the "concept" or that which is "conceived" by the Father. The Second Person is thus the "Word" in the sense of a *"verbum cordis,"* a silent inner word (or "concept") of which the vocal word (*verbum vocis*) is the outer sign. If the Father bears His Son in the soul precisely as He does in eternity, then He also "speaks" His Word in the soul just as in eternity (Q, 238,17-35/ Serm., 164; 287,5-10). What good would it be, Eckhart might have asked in this context, too, if God would speak His Word only in eternity and not speak it to the soul?

One should stress that the Word (*verbum cordis*) has nothing to do with a spoken sound (*verbum vocis*). Indeed, it is even opposed to such. The Word which God speaks in the soul is "hidden" and easily overlooked. To hear what is spoken in silence, one must be silent oneself:

> . . . all voices and sounds must be put away and a pure stillness must be there, a still silence. (Q, 237,9-10/Serm., 162)

> In stillness and peace . . . there God speaks in the soul and expresses Himself fully in the soul. (Q, 238,28-30/Serm., 164)

The truest word, the most perfect language, is silent. In the best tradition of negative theology, Eckhart denies the ability of human language to express the divine nature; he quotes St. Augustine:

> What one says about God is not true; but what one does *not* express is true. (Q, 242,36-243,1/Serm., 159)

But not only "voices and sounds" disrupt the silence that Eckhart has in mind, but all concepts, images, and representations:

> . . . the best and most noble thing of all which one can attain in this life is to remain silent and let God work and speak. Where all the powers have removed all their works and images, there is this Word spoken.
> (Q, 419,34-420,1/Bl., 99)

Nothing created is able to express the divine being. Not only spoken or written words, but even inner concepts, are incapable of comprehending the simplicity and plentitude of God (Q, 242, 15-7/Serm., 158). The only "concept" which adequately expresses the likeness of the Father is the uncreated "Word" itself, which the Father speaks.

117

All human language, interior and exterior, must be silenced in order to let the Father speak.

If the soul attains perfect silence, emptied of all words and deeds, sounds and concepts, then God will work and speak in it. And since this word is spoken "in" the soul itself, there is some sense in which this Word is the soul's own. When the Father speaks, Eckhart says, the soul is thus able to "answer" with the living Word itself—by letting it be spoken. In the same Word, the Father "speaks" to the soul, i.e., bears His Son in the soul, and the soul "responds," i.e., allows the Word to be spoken. The soul's language is the language of response.

5. Letting-be (Gelassenheit)

While the birth of the Son in the soul is the work of God, it cannot be accomplished without the soul's cooperation. The soul must prepare itself for God's action; it must make ready a "place" in which the birth can occur. The role which the soul plays in this process, then, is not passive. Indeed, Eckhart says that the soul "co-bears" (mitgebiert: Q, 161,28/Serm., 135) the Son, that it "co-works" (mitwirkt: Q, 94,27/ Cl.,102; 176,10/Serm., 235) with God. There is only one work—which the Father works in the soul and with which the soul cooperates.

To understand Eckhart's position in this matter, one must, as Alois Dempf points out,[18] place him in the historical tradition of Bernard of Clairvaux, by whom Eckhart seems to have been influenced. Both Eckhart and Bernard compare the soul to Mary, the "virgin" ("pure" of affection for creatures) and "mother" (who bore the Son in the flesh). In a sermon entitled "Super missum est," Bernard teaches that it was not enough for God simply to announce the Incarnation to Mary, but it was also necessary for Mary to consent to the action of the Holy Spirit, which she does in the famous words: "Let it be done unto me according to your word" (Fiat mihi secundum verbum tuum). Bernard contends that Mary's "fiat" is the expression of Christian freedom—Bernard was also the author of a treatise on free will—the freedom not to bear the Son "at will," but to let the Son be born. Bernard and Eckhart agree that the soul must actively "ready" itself for God's coming. The soul is not to be compared to wax upon which a stamp is impressed (which is suggested by the model of the "tabula rasa"), but to one who, like Martha, busily prepares a house for the coming of the Lord. The perfection of the wax is passivity to the stamp; the perfection of Martha is the diligence with which she prepares a clean and pure dwelling for the divine guest.

118

The soul readies itself for God's coming by the practice of "detachment" (*Abgeschiedenheit*) and "letting-be" (*Gelassenheit*). We have already examined Eckhart's treatise *On Detachment* in detail in the first chapter. Here it is appropriate to add only that in this introductory discussion of the treatise we entirely omitted any reference to the birth of the Son in the detached heart, without which we cannot fully understand what "detachment" means for Meister Eckhart, as should be obvious by now. For what the detached heart accomplishes is to "clear" itself of all affection for creatures ("to be empty of creatures") precisely in order to prepare a place for the birth of the Son ("to be full of God").

We may give our undivided attention in this chapter, then, to the idea of "letting-be" (*Gelassenheit*), which is the best-known word in Eckhart's vocabulary to the readers of the later Heidegger. The root of this word, *lassen*, means to let go, to relinquish, to abandon. The soul in *Gelassenheit* must relinquish everything which would impede God's advent into the soul. But "*lassen*" also means to "let" or "permit," and so it suggests openness and receptivity. Thus the soul which has left behind all the obstacles to the birth of God can at the same time permit or let the Father bear His Son there. The first moment is negative—to relinquish creatures—and the second is positive—to permit the Son's birth. Thus *Gelassenheit* and *Abgeschiedenheit* seem to be identical ideas in Eckhart's mystical theology. For "detachment" too has this same two-fold structure: negatively, it means to be empty of creatures, and positively, to be full of God.

Unlike Heidegger, Eckhart maintains that if the birth of the Son fails to take place in the soul, it is entirely man's own fault. God is a God of love and St. John tells us that, in Christ, the love of God is revealed to us. Upon this Eckhart comments:

> Nothing other than we ourselves bear the responsibility for the fact that [the love of God] is concealed from us. *We* are the cause of all our obstacles. (Q, 177,17-9/Serm., 236)

Now the obstacle which prevents God from revealing His love to us —by bearing His Son in us—is "self-love" (*Eigenliebe*) or "self-will" (*Eigenwille*):

> People say: Ah, Lord, I would very much prefer that I stood as well with God and that I had as much devotion and peace in God as other people have. And I would also prefer that things would go along for me in the same way as with others or that I too might be as poor.
>
> (Q, 55, 14-7/Cl., 65)

119

Eckhart's diagnosis of such complaints is this:

> In truth, it is your "I" which is protruding. It is self-will and nothing else.
> (Q, 55,21-2/Cl., 65)

and his remedy:

> Consequently, begin first with yourself and abandon yourself (*lass dich*).
> (Q, 55,31/Cl., 65)

The "self" is the principle of evil in the soul, and the way to union with God is to suppress the desires of the self. Eckhart is both philosophically and mystically *pre*-Cartesian. He wants to surrender the self to God in his mystical theory just as he wants to subordinate consciousness to reality in his metaphysics. In either case it is the presence of the *ego cogito* which conceals true being.

The self is "surrendered" by overcoming self-will. This does not mean that the soul "does" nothing, for Eckhart is not referring to the soul's "outer works" but to the "ground" from which they issue. He means that the ground upon which we act cannot be our *own* will, but God's. Thus the sphere of outer works is not affected by "letting-be" (*Gelassenheit*). Like Kierkegaard's knight of faith who looks and lives outwardly like a tax collector,[19] Eckhart's just man may lead a life which is outwardly industrious. For it is not what a man *does* which matters, but what he *is* in his essential being (*Wesen*). Again: it is not *what* he does which matters, but the grounds *upon which* he does it. A man should do nothing because it is his own will, but only because it is God's will. Thus it is better for a man to earn money, if it is God's will, than to give alms if it is his own will. It is better for a man to marry if it is God's will, than to enter a monastery if it is his own will. If a man abandons (*lässt*) all his possessions but not his own self-will, then he has given up nothing. But if he gives up self-will, then he has relinquished everything, even if he retains his possessions outwardly (Q, 185,10-2/Serm., 188).

The "released" (*gelassen*) soul gives up its own will entirely. Eckhart goes to great lengths to emphasize the "will-lessness" of such a soul. He wants the soul to have radically purged itself of every vestige of "willing," which is one reason why he is such an attractive thinker to Heidegger. It would be a superficial misunderstanding of Eckhart to think that he means by this only that the soul should will eternal goods (heaven) rather than earthly ones. For clearly such a soul still has a *will* of his own. Nor does Eckhart mean that we should will not our *own* but God's will:

> . . . so long as a man has it in himself that it is his *will* to fulfill the most beloved will of God, then such a man does not have the poverty of which I speak; for this man still has a will, with which he wishes to satisfy God's will. . . .   (Q, 304,22-7/Bl., 208)

What Eckhart demands is perfect "will-lessness," the complete emptying of willing so that God's will simply steps in and takes over for our will. Thus in the sermon on the "just man," he says that the worst are those who have ill-will, i.e., who disobeyed God's will. They are better who will what God wills and do not disobey His law. Still, if the latter were sick, they would want it to be God's will that they get better, and so they have much "self-will." The best of all, therefore, are the "just":

> The just have no will at all; it is all the same to them what God wills, however great a hardship it be.   (Q, 183,18-20/Serm., 186)

When the soul has "left" (*gelassen*) all willing behind, it thereby opens itself to God's influence. Having relinquished creatures, it lets God be God:

> Where the creature ends, there God begins to be. Now God desires nothing more of you than that you go out of yourself according to your creaturely mode of being and let God be God in you.   (Q, 180,32-4/Bl., 127)

The soul with *Gelassenheit* has become, to use one of Eckhart's simple but illustrative comparisons, like a good vessel; it is closed on the bottom—to creatures—and open on the top—to God (Q, 227,35-228,1/Serm., 148). It has become an empty receptacle (Q, 114,24-7/Cl., 122), i.e., a receiving place, for the birth of the Son.

Now since the soul is completely emptied of creatures and of all affection for creatures, and since it lets God be God, it is clear that for Eckhart the "released" (*gelassen*) heart receives God just as He is, free of any distortion. The soul in *Gelassenheit* is "nothing"; it has completely emptied itself of its "creaturely mode of being." Thus it is a pure medium in which God can be as He is, in His "unconcealed" (*unverhüllt*: Q, 147,4/Cl. 156) being. The soul which has achieved the heights of *Gelassenheit* receives God

> . . . in such a manner as God is existent in Himself, not in the manner of something received or won, but rather in the very Being (*Seinsheit*) which God is in Himself. (Q, 215,3-5/Serm., 225)

It is with the unconcealed God Himself, not the God of our images and representations, that the soul is united in *Gelassenheit*.

It is in connection with "letting God be" that Eckhart speaks of the necessity for the soul to live "without why," the phrase which is of course picked up first by Angelus Silesius and then by Martin Heidegger. We have seen Eckhart use this expression in connection with the being of God. A living thing is that which moves from within, of itself. But that is preeminently the case with God, Who is life itself (*ipsum vivere*). God is the beginning of all things, without Himself having a beginning (*principium sine principio*). Thus God has no "why," no external cause or aim for His being. He lives "for His own sake," His own honor and glory. Now Eckhart wants the soul to take on this same divine fullness and superabundance.

Eckhart tells us that every work which is performed for the sake of something outside of oneself has a "why." If I take nourishment this has a "why"—my sustenance. If I keep the civil law, this has a why, to be regarded as a good citizen. If I perform good works to please God, this has a why: to earn eternal salvation. But Eckhart wants the soul to be entirely without why:

> . . . one should not serve or work for the sake of some "why," neither for the sake of God, nor of honor, nor for anything which is outside of oneself, but only for the sake of that which is one's own being and one's own life in oneself. (Q, 186,26-9/Serm., 189)

Thus the soul cannot so much as "seek God" in its actions—i.e., by doing good works hope to someday be united with God. For this is to *will*, and it is to will something *external* to the self. The soul must become like God Himself who lives out of the plentitude of His own Being, needing nothing, lacking nothing, and acting "for the sake of" nothing. Yet how is this possible for a creature which is finite and limited, with "ends" and "needs" and which is so bound to act for a "why"? This question makes the mistake of assuming that God and the soul are two different things, each external to the other:

> One should not look upon God and comprehend God as outside of oneself, but rather as that which is my own and that which is *in* oneself.
>
> (Q, 186,24-6/Serm., 189)

122

Thus God *is* our own life and our own being. We live through Him:

> What is my life? That which is moved from within out of itself. That does
> not live which is moved from without. If we live with Him [God], then
> we must also co-work with Him from within, so that we do not work from
> without. Rather, we should be moved by that out of which we live, that
> means, through Him. Now we must and we can work from within out of
> our own. If we then live in Him or through Him, then He must be our own
> and we must work out of our own. Thus as God works all things through
> Himself and on His own, so must we work on our own, which He is in
> us. (Q, 176,7-17/Serm., 235)

Thus the soul is able to attain the plentitude and sufficiency of God's
life because it becomes one with the divine life. The soul has become so dispossessed of its own will that God takes up residence in
the soul and becomes the source of its life. "I live now not I," said
St. Paul, "but Christ lives in me." This has become quite literally true
for Eckhart. God and the soul are one life welling up from one
"ground" (Q, 180,5-10/Bl., 126).

Thus the soul no longer acts "for the sake of" God, as if it would, by
such and such an action, take a step towards attaining union with
God. Rather it acts out of God's indwelling presence. It does not act
for God, but from *out of* the God within it. Its life becomes free and
unfettered; it is "released"—to use a term from the Heidegger translators—from the "calculating" mentality which weighs up whether a
certain course of action will produce eternal rewards. It acts for the
sake of the action itself, for the sake of itself. Hence Angelus Silesius
had captured something essential when he said of the rose that "it
blossoms because it blossoms." We find in Eckhart a comparable expression:

> If someone asked life for a thousand years, "why do you live?" then if
> it could answer, it would say nothing other than "I live because I live"
> (*Ich lebe darum, dass ich lebe*). This is so because life lives out of its own
> grounds and wells up of itself. Consequently it lives without why by the
> fact that it lives for itself. If someone asked a truthful man who works
> out of his own ground, "why do you work?" then if he answers rightly,
> he would say nothing other than, "I work because I work" (*Ich wirke
> darum, dass ich wirke*). (Q, 180,23-31/Bl., 127; cf. Q, 384,6-19)

The just man, the detached man, acts because he acts, like Silesius's
rose. He can savor an action for itself, and he need not subordinate
it to an external purpose. I can love my friend because of what loving a

friend is, not because it produces eternal rewards (Q, 299,19-26/Bl., 188). This is so because the act of loving my friend is an act that wells up (*quillt*: Q, 180,27/Bl., 127) from the life of God within me. It needs no further "rationale" (no "why") than that. The act is "justified" of itself. It does not need to be given a teleological explanation.

Thus Eckhart had already—before Silesius—discovered the realm outside the sphere of influence of the Principle of Ground. He discovered the realm in which the soul may act without giving an account of itself. These acts are not "without ground" (*ohne Grund*), because they spring up out of their own grounds, which is the innermost ground of the soul, where the ground of the soul and the ground of God are one. But they are "without why"—i.e., they do not need to be explained and justified in terms of some external purpose—or ground. A ground need not be rendered for these acts (e.g., such acts lead to God), because they already rest in their own ground (the God with which the soul is already united).

There is one last point which must be discussed in connection with Eckhart's conception of "*Gelassenheit*." Eckhart seems to say at times that God is under some "necessity" to bear His Son in the soul which is truly released, that God "needs" the truly detached heart:

> It is God's nature that He give, and His being depends on the fact that He give to us, if we are submissive to Him. If we are not and we receive nothing, then we do Him violence and kill Him. (Q, 172,27-32/Serm., 174)

God appears to be under the same necessity of nature to bear His Son in the soul as He is in eternity:

> The Father bears His Son in the eternal knowledge, and He bears Him as fully in the soul as He does in His own nature. And He bears Him in the soul as His own, and His being depends on the fact that He bear His Son in the soul, whether He wishes to or not. (Q, 172,4-8/Serm., 174)

The soul apparently provides a necessary complement, an indispensable medium, in which the divine life is completed and fulfilled.

But this is not exactly Eckhart's view. It is quite clear that the divine life is a self-contained and self-sufficient process. Even the process by which God creates is a "welling over" and an overflow (*antequam effundat et ebulliat extra*: LW, II, 22/Cl., 226), not an attempt to fill up a lack. Moreover the birth of God is the result of grace (*gratia*), which is a free giving, and not of the necessity of nature.

Finally, even in the vernacular sermons, where Eckhart states his position in the most extreme manner, he eventually qualifies his assertions. Hence the passage in which he spoke of "killing God" continues:

If we are not able to do this in Him Himself, still we may do it in ourselves and as far as it concerns us. (Q, 172,30-1/Serm., 174)

The death of God in question turns out to be a death in and for the soul, not in God's own being. We are able to stop the flow of God's life into our souls. No Dominican master at Paris, and certainly not the author of the "Prologues," would hold that anything of the perfection of *esse* could ever be lacking to God.

But what the German preacher—*Equardus praedicator*—did mean by this bold language is to be found in his defence (Théry, 241-2/Bl., 296) of such texts as we have cited (Q, 172,4-8,27-32/Serm., 174; Q, 185, 13-34/Serm., 188-9). In the first place, he says, this is an "emphatic expression, commending God's goodness and love." This is the assertion of a preacher who means to inspire the soul to the "highest virtue" of detachment. Because Eckhart demanded a perfect abandonment—without why—to God, he found it necessary to assure his listeners of the goodness of God and of the fact that it belongs to the necessity of the divine nature to return love with love. Thus Eckhart's sermons do not belong to the realm of "objectivistic" theology, theology as a *scientia*—or what Heidegger calls "onto-theo-logic." They belong instead to the existential order, the order of what Heidegger called in the *Habilitationsschrift* the "living spirit." If Eckhart's formulations in the sermons are taken as formulations of the doctrine of a scholastic "onto-theo-logic," then they will certainly appear—as they did to the medieval churchmen—as unorthodox. They can only be seen in a true light if they are recognized to belong outside the "sphere of influence" of metaphysical theology. The second explanation Eckhart advances in defence of his expression about God's need of the soul has to do with the identity between the ground of the soul and God. He wants to say that it is the same divine life of the Trinity which has been extended—by grace—to the soul. Thus the same Son Whom the Father bears in eternity is received by the released soul through grace. It is the same necessary process of divine filiation which takes place in eternity and in the soul which has prepared itself for it. The soul comes to be by grace the self-same thing which the Son is by the necessity of his divine nature.

125

Whatever Eckhart's own intentions may have been, his expressions have fathered a long tradition of the divine "need" of man in the German tradition. Among the mystics, God's need of man is found in Jacob Boehme and in Angelus Silesius in *The Cherubinic Wanderer*, where it receives its classic expression:

God Does Not Live Without Me

I know that God cannot live an instant without me;
Were I to become nothing, He must give up the ghost. (CW, I, 8)

In the philosophical tradition, God's need of man certainly recalls the nineteenth-century idealists. Where Eckhart says that the "highest striving of God" (*Gottes höchstes Streben*: Q, 208, 9/Serm., 218) is to bear the Son in the soul, for Fichte the Absolute Ego will also be a process of striving (*Streben*), not for the birth of the Son in man, but for the achievement of moral order in and through him. And perhaps the most important representative of this tradition of all is Hegel himself, for whom the Absolute is estranged from itself until it attains self-knowledge in and through speculative thought.

Thus Hegel, in his *Lectures on the Philosophy of Religion* (*Sämtliche Werke*, Bd. XV, p. 228), cites the following text of Eckhart:

The eye with which God sees me is the eye with which I see Him; my eye and His eye are one. In justice, I am weighed in God and He in me. If God were not, I would not be. If I were not, then He would not be. But it is not necessary to know this, since there are things which are easily misunderstood and which could be grasped only in a concept.

For Hegel, Eckhart seems to say that the Absolute comes to know itself in the same act in which man rises to a knowledge of the Absolute. In fact, Eckhart is alluding to the Aristotelian doctrine that the knower-in-act and the knowable-in-act are one, and to *De trinitate*, Bk. IX, c. 12, in which Augustine says that the knower and the known, when thus united, conceive a common offspring—for Eckhart, the Word which is born in the soul (Théry, 224-5, 238). Moreover, Hegel's text appears to be corrupt. I find in Quint this version of the first sentence:

The eye in which I see God is the same eye in which God sees me. My eye and God's eye are *one* eye and *one* seeing and *one* knowing and *one* loving. (Q, 216,24-7/Serm., 226-7)

I do not find the second sentence in Quint at all, although the same sentiment is there (Q, 267-9). The third and fourth sentences, which would be easily misunderstood if one were unfamiliar with the distinction between "*Gott*" and "*Gottheit*," can be found as follows in an altogether different sermon:

> . . . but if I were not, so also would "God" not be. I am the reason that God is "God." If I were not, God would not be "God." It is not necessary to know this. (Q, 308,21-4/Bl., 231)

"*Gott*" is a name assigned to the divine being in virtue of its relationship to creatures. Hence if I were not—i.e., if I were not created— God would not be called "God," i.e., the cause of being. Eckhart also refers to the ideal pre-existence of the self as an Idea in the Divine Mind. The last half of the fourth sentence, which represents Hegel's but not Eckhart's views, I find nowhere in Quint.

Thus Eckhart is not a German idealist who maintains that God needs the human "spirit" in order to be actualized as God. He means to say only that God extends to the soul—by grace—the opportunity to attain a knowledge of Himself in precisely the same medium in which He already knows Himself in Eternity: the divine Word. But Eckhart's bold language, coupled with our metaphysical predisposition to take his sermons as essays in "onto-theo-logic," produced a serious, even if historically fruitful, misunderstanding of his own intentions.

6.   *The Breakthrough to the Godhead*

The reader who has followed this exposition of Eckhart's thought closely may have detected in Eckhart what appears to be an inconsistency. On the one hand, we have said that for Eckhart the deepest ground and essence of the soul, as of God Himself, lies in a nameless region from which all properties and attributes (*Eigenschaften*) are excluded. Thus the ground of the soul is the hidden recess of the soul about which we can say nothing except negative things: it is timeless, simple, motionless, divested of faculties, without relation to creatures, etc. The highest thing we can say of this "ground of the soul" is to say that it is nameless. By the same token, there is a comparable namelessness in God. There is an inner recess of the being of God which also eludes any properties or attributes we can affirm of Him.

127

This we have seen Eckhart calls the divine Godhead (*Gottheit*). We cannot say of the Godhead that it is either good or wise; we cannot call it creator or even Father, Son and Holy Spirit. The Godhead is the nameless One which eludes all names. Even the names of the Holy Trinity refer to properties of God—power (Father), wisdom (Son), and love (Holy Spirit)—and therefore do not name the Godhead itself. The ground of God and the ground of the soul: both are alike a nameless unity prior to any attribute or faculty. Indeed both are one: "Here God's ground is my ground, and my ground is God's ground" (Q, 180,5-6/ Bl., 126).

Yet we have seen that for Eckhart the *unio mystica* is identified as the Birth of the Son in the soul. But how is that possible? How can the union of the soul with God be a union with the Son? Is not union with the Son something less than the union of the ground of the soul and the ground of God? In other words, when the soul unites with the Godhead, has it not as it were surpassed the Son? Does not the Son belong to the "attributes" of God, and does not union with the Son fall short of union with the Godhead? Does not such union fail to penetrate to the ultimate, innermost wasteland of the Godhead?

The fact of the matter is that there is another formulation of the mystical union of the soul with God in Meister Eckhart which does indeed appear to be more radical than that expressed by the birth of the Son. This formulation is found in those sermons of Eckhart which discuss the "breakthrough to the Godhead" (*der Durchbruch zur Gottheit*). In these passages we come face to face with another dimension of Eckhart's thought, another "motif." This can be explained as follows. Up to now we have been discussing the more characteristically Christian side of Meister Eckhart. We have emphasized the scriptural foundations of his thought in the teachings of St. John, according to whom God lovingly engenders His only begotten Son in our hearts, and indeed engenders us as that same Son. Eckhart's conceptual framework, his "understanding of Being" as Heidegger would say, has in the writings we have examined up to now been Christian, personal, vitalistic. Thus Being has been conceived as a process of emergence, of life welling up into life and flowing over into more life. Moreover this life is personal; indeed it is the life of love itself, the life which a father engenders in his son.

But there is another side to Eckhart, and if the first side is typically Christian, the second is predominantly Neoplatonic. For the focus of this second motif is the idea of unity, of absolute simplicity, nakedness. The reader may already have noticed the contrast between the two basic metaphors that Eckhart uses in articulating these two motifs. The "Godhead" is a divine wasteland, a barrenness, a naked unity. How different this is from the "birth" of the Son, the process by which the life of the Father wells up and spills over into the Son and then over into creation and then into the heart of the detached soul. The Godhead is the divine "substance," in contrast to the Trinitarian and extra-Trinitarian "relations." The Godhead is stillness and unity; the Trinity and birth of the Son is a process. The Godhead is silence; but in the birth of the Son the Father "speaks" His Word.

I should like in this section then to do two things. First, to examine in some detail the idea of the breakthrough to the Godhead; and then secondly to discuss how the two themes of breakthrough and birth, the one Neoplatonic and the other Christian, relate to one another.

The most forceful exposition of the breakthrough to the Godhead is to be found in Sermon 32, "Blessed are the Poor in Spirit." In this sermon Eckhart teaches that he alone is poor in spirit who "*wills* nothing, *knows* nothing, and *has* nothing" (Q, 303,26-7/Bl., 227). The first two notions are already familiar to us. To will nothing refers to the will-lessness which lets God be God in us; to know nothing means to have surrendered all human concepts and representations in order to let God's own knowledge fill the mind. In other words, the poor in spirit are those who practice detachment and letting be. But what is this third thing, having nothing? Eckhart gives us a hint of it early on in the sermon:

> For if a man should truly have poverty, then he must be so devoid of his created will as if he did not yet exist. (Q, 304,7-9/Bl., 228)

Eckhart here refers not to Christian immortality, to life *after* death, but to a Neoplatonic *pre*-existence. A few lines later he adds:

> When I still stood in my first cause, then I had no God, and there I was the cause of myself. I willed nothing; I desired nothing, for I was a pure being and a knower of myself in enjoyment of the truth.
> (Q, 304,34-305,1/Bl., 228)

The soul antedates its own earthly existence (*esse secundum*) insofar as it is contained as an idea (*esse primum*) in the mind of God. There, in that existence before this one, the soul was "pure" of all earthly stains, free from all contact with creatures, completely "detached." The soul's own preexistence in the mind of God is a kind of purity which it should strive to regain, an original condition that it should try to reconstitute. Thus we begin to see what having nothing means, viz., to return to the state when the soul *was* nothing, to return to the primordial and first (*ur*) thing from which it drew its substance (*Sache*), to its primordial source (*Ursache*): to stand in one's first cause.

But God insofar as He is "God" is not the primordial being (*Ursache*), for God is the "creator," the "first cause" (*prima causa*). Now we have already seen that to penetrate to the hiddenmost recess of God we must get beyond God to the divine Godhead. That is why Eckhart says:

> Consequently I ask God that he may rid me of God. For my essential being is beyond God insofar as we grasp God as the beginning of creatures.
> (Q, 308,4-8/Bl., 231)

We see in this text something of what might be called Eckhart's mystical "a-theism." Of course we do not mean by this that he no longer believes in a divine being, but that, in a deeper and more significant sense, "God" is not enough, that everything which we call "God" in philosophy and theology does not suffice. For a man whose heart has been touched by the mystical grace, who has entered into the depth of that depth-experience of the "Godhead," the whole structure of "first cause" and "highest being" must be laid aside in order to unite with the truly divine God (*der göttliche Gott*: Q, 60,22,26/Cl., 69-70). It is difficult to conceive a more complete freedom from what Heidegger calls the "onto-theo-logical" conception of God (ID, 60/127).

To get back to God in His innermost Godhead then means two things: it means that God ceases to be God, that is, the creator; but it also means that the soul ceases to be a creature, for it makes a regress back into its primal origin. In other words, the mystical union consists in the *undoing* of the whole creation process, in reversing its direction, in overcoming creation on both ends, so that there is neither creature nor creator.

We thus can see that at the basis of Eckhart's mystical teaching there is a fundamental movement, an original motion "out," by which the Trinity and the whole created world first come to be. Then there is a subsequent movement "back," a movement of regress, by which the soul traces its way back into its primal source. These two movements are called by Eckhart "flowing out" (*Ausfliessen*) and the "breaking through" (*Durchbrechen*) or in Latin *exitus* and *reditus*:

A great master says that his breaking through is more noble than his flowing out, and that is true.   (Q, 308,25-6/Bl., 231)

The two movements are not equal. The first is less noble than the second. But why?

> When I flowed out all things spoke out: God is. But this cannot make me blessed, for I know myself in this way as a creature.
>
> (Q, 308,26-7/Bl., 231)

The first movement terminates in creation, in creatures, and so in a division or distinction. In the first movement a distinction is set up between the creature and "God." In bringing forth creation, God becomes "God."

> But in the breakthrough, where I stand divested of my own will and of the will of God and of all His works and of God Himself, there I am beyond all creatures and I am neither "God" nor creature, but rather what I was and what I will remain now and ever more.
>
> (Q, 308,28-32-/Bl., 231)

But in the breakthrough the distinction between "God" and "creatures" is overcome; the division is healed. The creature divests itself of its creatureliness and makes its way back into its primal ground in the Godhead where there is neither God nor creature, but only the abyss of the nameless One.

But where does this regress into the Godhead and unity with the Godhead take place? In that nameless ground where God and the soul are one, where God's ground is my ground and my ground is God's ground. A simple diagram can help to make Eckhart's teaching more plain:

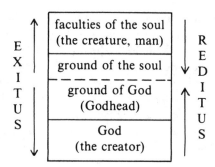

There is a movement "out" from the innermost ground which terminates in division and separation, which posits the difference between God and creatures. But then there is the movement "back" towards the innermost ground in which the division is overcome in a nameless unity. The dotted line signifies the unity of the two grounds and illustrates what Eckhart sometimes says of the ground of the soul, viz., that the ground of the soul is more united with God's ground than it is to its own faculties (Q, 315,25-7/Ev., 153).

What then, to return to the original point of this sermon, is true poverty of spirit? It is to "have nothing" in the very primordial sense that the creature has completely divested itself of its very created being. The creature in its *esse secundum,* in its being outside God as something created, is an "actuality" (*Wirklichkeit*); God on the other hand is the creator, the creative activity (*Wirken*). But in the breakthrough the whole conceptual framework of act and actuality, cause and effect, is overcome. The creature divests itself of its very being as creature. There can be no greater unity than this, Meister Eckhart says, that a man attain to that which he was before he existed (Q, 309,4-7/Bl., 232). And the remarkable thing about this mystical poverty which Eckhart speaks of in this sermon is that not only must the soul become poor, and divest itself of its will and its knowledge and of its very being, but so too must God become poor. For in a passage which in another author might surprise us, Eckhart writes:

> In all truth and as truly as God lives: God Himself will never look into it [= unite with the ground of the soul] and never has looked into it, insofar as He exists in the mode and "property" of His Persons. . . . If God should ever look into it, it would cost Him all His divine names and His personal property. He must leave these out altogether if He wishes to look in. (Q, 164,8-15/Cl., 138)

Let us now return to the problem which we originally posed in this section. How are we to understand the relationship between the birth of the Son in the soul and the breakthrough to the Godhead? Are these not two different accounts of the mystical union? For the birth of the Son is discussed in personalistic language and speaks of the soul's being born again as the Son. This account is Christian, Trinitarian, personalistic. But the breakthrough takes place in the region prior to the emergence of the Persons, and it does not speak of a process of birth but of entering into a deathly stillness, an abyss, a wasteland where nothing stirs. It is Neoplatonic, Unitarian, pre-personalistic.

132

Shizutera Ueda, in his remarkable book on this problem, suggests the following resolution.[20] The Christian element in Eckhart is a product of his personal, historical circumstances. He was a medieval Dominican monk who never wished to be anything else. He was loyal to the Church and protested vigorously against those who thought otherwise. He dispensed the sacraments, partook of the Eucharist and, in a word, belonged fully to what Heidegger might call the medieval-Christian "*Geschick.*" The birth of the Son in the soul is an idea which moves within this Christian framework. But this idea is incapable of expressing everything that Eckhart means to say. And so the doctrine of the birth of the Son must be completed and radicalized by the doctrine of the breakthrough, which surpasses the conceptual framework of Christianity, and specifically the Christian teaching of the Trinity. Only when Eckhart speaks of the breakthrough does he move in his own element. Untrammeled by the conceptual heritage of Christianity, he is able to formulate a more radical understanding of the unity of the soul with God.

For my own part I am disinclined to separate Eckhart's Christianity from his understanding of the breakthrough. For Eckhart himself the breakthrough and the birth of the Son were not exclusive of one another. He did not see one as more important than the other, nor did it ever occur to him to separate or distinguish one from the other. Indeed, as Ueda points out, sometimes his expressions blended the two ideas in one, as when he tells us that the Son is born in the ground of the soul. I think he saw the two ideas as forming a living unity, united, that is, as the root is to the flower. I believe that Eckhart was as deeply touched by the love which the Father has shown for us by making us his children, as he was inspired by the Neoplatonic doctrine of being one with the One. And what he attempted to do was to synthesize these ideas into a single doctrine. The synthesis consisted in seeing the breakthrough to the Godhead as the base or ground upon which the birth of the Son takes place, from which the latter originates. In Eckhart's view unity is the ground from out of which the trinity of persons flows. Thus in uniting with the ground of God, the Godhead, the soul catches the life of the Trinity at its source and so can fully enter into it. Thus for the soul to enter into the inner life of the Trinity, for it to be born as that same Son, it must unite with the ground of the Trinity, the Godhead, and then it too will give birth to the Son. Indeed in uniting with the Godhead and so with the ground of the Trinity, the soul also unites with the Father and so can itself give birth to the Son. Thus the breakthrough also explains the "active" birth of the Son. For not only is the soul born as that same Son; it also gives birth to Him (Q, 258,19-31/Cl., 214).

In other words, if there is, as Ueda says, something incomplete about the birth of the Son, if it does not give expression to a radical enough unity of the soul with God, there is also something incomplete about the breakthrough, viz., it does not give birth; it does not tell of the love the Father has for us. The incompleteness of the breakthrough is expressed vividly in the image of the "virgin," the barren one who does not give birth. In the "wasteland" there is desert solitude; but the wasteland is barren. That is why Eckhart writes:

> If a person were always a virgin, then no fruit would ever come from him. If he is to become fruitful, it is necessary that he be a *wife*. "Wife" is the noblest name which one can apply to the soul, and it is much nobler than "virgin." That man should *receive* God in Himself is good; in this receptivity he is a virgin. But that God should become fruitful in Him is better. For becoming fruitful by a gift is alone thankfulness for the gift. And the spirit is a wife in the thankfulness of rebirth when it bears Jesus back again in God's fatherly heart.   (Q, 159,33-160,8/Cl., 134).

I believe that Eckhart understood the breakthrough and the birth of the Son to form a living complementarity. If the breakthrough is more basic and more radical than the birth of the Son, it is also incomplete. For it must be crowned with the "living" unity of the soul with God in the birth of the Son. The birth of the Son is the "focal" point of Eckhart's sermons; it animates them, inspires them. But the breakthrough to the Godhead is the "depth" point of his spiritual teaching. It grounds and founds the birth of the Son. To use the image of the root and the flower: the root is more basic, but the flower is the fulfillment. But there is no choosing between them; each is needed for the other.

7.   *"All Creatures Are a Pure Nothing"*

No treatment of Eckhart's mystical teachings can be considered complete without a discussion of the relationship between God and creatures as Eckhart sees it. Eckhart has long been considered a "pantheist" who ascribes no being at all to creatures other than the being of God:

> You find *nothingness* only because of the fact that you seek *nothingness*. All creatures are a pure nothing. I do not say that they are of scant worth but rather that they are not anything at all. That which has no being is nothing. But all creatures have no being since their being depends on the presence of God. If God were for only a moment to turn away from creatures, they would all become nothing.   (Q, 171,8-14/Serm., 173)

This statement was included in the list of twenty-eight propositions taught by Eckhart condemned by Pope John XXII in his Bull "*In Agro Dominico*" of March 27, 1329. Such metaphysical pantheism would seem to go hand in hand with a mystical theology of "detachment," of severing oneself from creatures:

> That is pure which is separated and detached from all creatures, for all creatures contaminate because they are a nothing.
>
> (Q, 175,32-4/Serm., 235)

Eckhart has frequently been cast as a pantheist, but a careful study of the Latin writings and of the critical edition of the vernacular works dispels any such interpretation. It is true that Eckhart says that *esse* is God, and that things exist by having the being of God. But one must be careful to give these words their genuine Eckhartian sense. If they are given a Thomistic reading, they are surely pantheistic. But Eckhart does not have the same notion of being, or of the analogy of being, that Aquinas did. Eckhart wanted to say that since God is being, anything other than God is absolutely nothing, and that if anything other than God came to be, it could only do so by coming to be "in God," i.e., "in being":

> . . . God created all things, not that they might stand outside of Himself or alongside of Himself or beyond Himself, the way other artifacts [stand outside of their human makers], but He calls them from nothing, i.e., non-being, so that they may come into and receive and dwell in Himself. For He is being. (LW, I, 161-2)

Eckhart is emphasizing that a creature "of itself" is nothing and that when it comes to be, it exists in and through God. A creature does not "have" being; it does not have being "of itself." Rather its being is "lent" to it, the way the sun lends light to the air. The air has light only so long as the sun shines and interpenetrates it. It does not have light absolutely and of itself. So too the creature exists only so long as it receives the divine influx and is sustained by and in God. Unlike Aquinas, who attributes to created things their own proper and proportionate share of being, Eckhart, in keeping both with his mystical tendency and his "Christian Neo-Platonism," holds that creatures are only by the being of God, as white things are white only by whiteness itself. He does not mean to say that creatures are God, but that they are *in virtue of* God and that they are absolutely dependent *upon* God. For if the creature were anything—even a modicum—of itself, then it would not be created at all. "Of itself" the creature is nothing at all. It is whatsoever it is, totally and absolutely by the power of God (Q, 171,12/Serm., 173).

Eckhart's mystical teaching therefore goes hand in hand with this Christian Neo-Platonic metaphysics:

> In God's will all things *are* and are *something* and are pleasing to God and perfect; *outside* of God's will, on the other hand, all things are *nothing* and *not* pleasing to God and *im*perfect. (Q, 379,30-3/Ev., 140)

To pursue the creature for its own sake is to pursue it outside of God's will, and because it pleases our self-will. But outside of God's will things are nothing, i.e., of no worth in attaining unity with God, just as for the metaphysician creatures considered "in themselves," apart from God's creative power, do not exist. However, one does not find in Eckhart anything of the "flight from the world" which is often associated with mysticism. It is worse to go to a monastery out of self-will than to remain in society because it is God's will:

> When we think that a man should flee from this and seek that—these places and these people and these ways of life or this crowd or this activity—it is not really the fault of the ways or the things if you are hindered. Rather you are yourself the very thing by which you are hindered, for you are related to things in an inverted way. (Q, 55,25-30/Cl., 65)

The soul has an "inverted" (*verkehrt*) relationship to things because it views them as things in themselves, independent of God, whereas they are nothing at all, not even something small, outside of God.

God is concealed by things only if one is related to them in the wrong way. Hence Eckhart does not advise leaving the world but learning how to find God in things, so that someday one may find things in God (in Heaven):

> A man does not learn this [finding God] through flight by running from things and turning to a solitude of an outward kind. He must rather learn an inner solitude wherever and with whomever he may be. He must learn to break through things and to seize God in them and to hold His image steadfastly in himself in an essential way. (Q, 61,16-21/Cl., 70)

The perfectly detached heart is able to "break through" to God in all things. This is a difficult art, one acquired after a long struggle. That is why there is nothing "quietistic" about Eckhart's account of detachment. "One should not begin in peace," he says, "one must run forwards to it" (Q, 188,10-1/Serm., 191). The wood does not surrender to the fire without a struggle (Q, 117,28-118,4/Cl., 126). The soul must be in *labor* to give birth to the Son (Q, 118,24-6/Cl., 126). God is "*in*" things, and the soul's labor must be to "find" Him there, to "break through" to His presence.

8. *Mary and Martha*

I should like to conclude this survey of Meister Eckhart's mysticism with a short account of one of his most startling and inventive sermons, which lays to rest once and for all the charges of quietism which, while they may sometimes apply to other mystics, have nothing whatever to do with Eckhart's genuine teaching. I am referring to Eckhart's interpretation of the story of Mary and Martha ("Intravit Jesus in quoddam castellum," Q, 280 ff.). This story served as the point of departure in the Middle Ages for the scholastic theory of the relationship of contemplation to action (cf. VA, 54-5). The Dominicans were students of Greek metaphysics on this point, and they ranked *theoria* before *praxis*. Thus Thomas Aquinas, following Aristotle, identified contemplation as the highest end of man. And Thomas, like the other scholastics of the same mind, pointed to the story of Mary and Martha to support his position.[21] The story, we recall, goes as follows. Jesus entered a small village and there visited two sisters, Mary and Martha. The one sister, Martha, kept herself busy serving Jesus, while the other sat at Jesus's feet and listened to his every word. When Martha asked Jesus to chide Mary for letting all the work fall on her, Jesus responded by saying, "Martha, Martha, you worry and fret about so many things, and yet few are needed, indeed only one. It is Mary who has chosen the better part; it is not to be taken from her" (Luke 10:41-2).

However, Aquinas's position on this point was actually somewhat more complicated than we have so far said. For while St. Thomas thought that the contemplative life is higher than the active life considered "in themselves," he nonetheless thought that in *this* life, on earth, where the contemplative does not have an immediate vision of the very being of God (as do the blessed in heaven), the "mixed" life is better. The mixed life refers to a life which combines action and contemplation. The practitioner of the mixed life does not merely contemplate but he also engages in good works. Now this position of "brother Thomas" led Eckhart to a most unorthodox interpretation of the Mary and Martha story. For if on earth the mixed life is better, then in some

137

sense Martha, who symbolized the active life, was superior to Mary, the symbol of contemplation. In other words, contrary to Jesus's literal words, Martha had chosen the better part.

Eckhart expounds this as follows. When Jesus addressed Martha he spoke her name twice. This signified, according to Eckhart, that Martha possesses two gifts (Q, 282,30 ff.). The first gift is a temporal perfection, viz., that Martha is well exercised in virtue and good works. But the second gift is an eternal gift, according to which Martha is united with God in the ground of her soul. Hence when Jesus said that Martha was concerned with many things, he meant that she kept herself busily occupied with her duties, but that none of these duties were obstacles for her. "You stand *amidst* things," Eckhart paraphrases Jesus, "but things do not stand *in you*" (Q, 283,1-2). The created things with which Martha occupies herself do not enter the ground of her soul; they do not disrupt her unity with God. Martha therefore is seasoned and exercised in "life." She has learned that which only a long life of virtue can teach, viz., to dwell in the world and to concern oneself outwardly with created things, all the while retaining an inner calm.

Mary on the other hand does not represent for Eckhart pure contemplative unity with Christ. Rather Mary is related to Martha as potency is to act, or as the imperfect is to the perfect. Mary sits at the feet of Jesus because she does not have the strength of Martha to deal with things. Mary would be hindered by creatures; Martha is not. Moreover, Mary listens to Jesus's words; she wants to learn about union with God. But Martha already knows what such unity is, because she has been taught in the school of life, the only school indeed in which this can be learned. Thus when Martha asks Jesus to have Mary "stand up" and help with the work, she does so out of love for Mary and out of a desire to see her achieve a higher state of perfection. She is asking Jesus to dispel Mary's illusion that perfection can be achieved by wishing for it and by basking in religious feelings. She is asking Jesus to show Mary that true perfection in this life is not withdrawn from activity but that it nourishes itself in the midst of activity.

Thus Eckhart proposes to us in this startling reinterpretation of the Gospel story the paradigm of a religious inwardness which is completely at home with the world. The paradigm in fact anticipates the Reformation critique of monastic Christianity, that is, the conception that God could be found only by withdrawing from the world. It also reminds one strongly of the problem which torments Joannes Climacus in the *Concluding Unscientific Postscript*: if without God a man can do nothing, how am I to take a walk in the Deer Park? Eckhart's reading of the story of Mary and Martha shatters once and for all the complaint that mysticism—at least Eckhart's mysticism—is quietism and *contemptus mundi*. For Eckhart vividly shows that it is quite possible, indeed it is to be expected, that a man may be concerned with many things while still preserving the one thing necessary. The ground of the soul is the source from which the faculties flow. Thus the man whose soul is united in its ground with the Godhead takes creatures "in God," not in themselves. He sees the creature not with secular eyes, not as a distraction and an obstacle, but with the eyes of eternity. Angelus Silesius aptly expressed this theme in Meister Eckhart when he wrote some four centuries later:

The Rose

The rose that with mortal eye I see,
Flowers in God through all eternity.

(CW, I, 108/42)

Martha sees things in God, and sees God in them. She is at home with the world and with created things; she has learned to understand them in their essential being. She leads a life not of passivity and withdrawal but of active and robust commerce with things. For Eckhart the depth of mystical union is completely compatible with the bustle of virtue and good works. That is why the author of this austere doctrine of will-lessness and mystical poverty can at the same time enjoin a life of moral activity. Hence the concluding line of this sermon reads, "May God help us to follow Him [=Christ] in the exercise of true virtue" (Q, 289, 17-8).

139

CHAPTER FOUR

HEIDEGGER AND MEISTER ECKHART

1. *Preliminary Considerations*

HAVING carried out our survey of the main lines of Meister Eckhart's spirituality, we are now in a position to turn to the central focus of this work, that is, to the kinship between thinking and mysticism, between Heidegger and Eckhart. For we must not forget the provocative statement which Heidegger made in SG and which gives impetus to this study. Speaking of Angelus Silesius's verse "The Rose Is Without Why," Heidegger writes:

> What is unsaid in the saying—and everything depends on this—is rather that man, in the most hidden ground of his essence, truly is for the first time, when he is in his own way like the rose—without why. (SG, 72-3)

Here Heidegger himself tells us that the mystical rose in Silesius's poem, which is as we have seen a poetic expression of Eckhart's teaching on the soul, is also a model in terms of which we can understand man and thinking. Thinking can be understood by meditating upon the model of the mystical rose. Then, after making such a provocative suggestion, Heidegger adds:

> We cannot pursue this thought any further here. (SG, 73)

140

It is in a sense the whole aim of this study, and particularly of this chapter, precisely to pursue this thought further. We have a much fuller sense of what Silesius's verse means because we have gone back to its origins in Meister Eckhart's mysticism. Now our task is to relate what we have learned by listening to Meister Eckhart's sermons to Heidegger's later writings. Now we must undertake an explication of the analogy between Heidegger and Meister Eckhart. But before we plunge into that task I would like to address myself to two preliminary considerations.

The first of these consists in taking into account Heidegger's occasional disclaimers that his thought is some form of mysticism (cf. SD, 57/53; 79/71). Even in SG itself he says that his talk of the withdrawal of Being is not to be construed as a dark, "mystical" utterance (SG, 183). Heidegger's strongest statement in this regard, and the one that appears to be the most damaging for the present study, is to be found in the *Nietzsche* lectures, where he criticizes mysticism as "the mere antitype (*Gegenbild*) to metaphysics" (N II, 28). This appears to be an especially serious remark for the thesis of this book. For if mysticism is the mere antitype to metaphysics, then it does not represent a model for the overcoming of metaphysics. Rather mysticism is itself caught up within metaphysics and represents the mere inverse of metaphysical coin. Heidegger appears then to be taking two different positions. On the one hand he criticizes mysticism as a form of irrationalism and obscurantism and as a flight from the sensible world. But on the other hand, in SG, he suggests a positive parallel between the thinker and the mystic and lets a mystical poet be guide of the leap beyond Leibniz's metaphysical principle. The solution to this dilemma is not hard to find. Heidegger writes of Silesius's saying about the rose:

> The whole saying is so astonishingly clearly and tightly constructed that one might come to the idea that the most extreme sharpness and depth of thought belong to genuine and great mysticism. For that is also the truth. Meister Eckhart proves it. (SG, 71)

In other words Heidegger is making a distinction between genuine, great mysticism (*echte und grosse Mystik*) and mysticism of the other sort. If mysticism means a flight from reality and the sensible world, if mysticism means irrationalism and an obscurantism which throws everything into confusion, then mysticism is devoutly to be avoided. Such mysticism clearly has nothing to do with thought. Like all irrationalism, it remains within the sphere of influence of the Principle of Ground. It

141

continues to use propositions but it uses propositions arbitrarily and capriciously. In genuine mysticism, on the other hand, sentences are formulated "sharply" and they are "tightly constructed." False mysticism does not give up "representations" but it prefers confusing and contradictory representations. Genuine and great mysticism does not make use of "representations" at all, but rather it lets the rose rise up in its simple presence, the way the rose "is," prior to the categories of representational thought.

Genuine and great mysticism participates in the sharpness and depth of thought itself. It is not irrationalistic (cf. FS, 352), but neither is it a matter of reason. Like thought itself, it is able to effect the step back out of reason and representations into a sphere which is simpler than that, which is prior to the distinction between reason and unreason. Great and genuine mysticism is neither metaphysics nor the mere antitype of metaphysics. And we have it on Heidegger's own assurance that Meister Eckhart is to be numbered among the great mystics, and therefore, we take it, that Meister Eckhart's mystical thought is, in Heidegger's view, akin to thought itself. Our task in this chapter will be to show how this is so.

We might add one further point in this connection. Heidegger's assurance that Eckhart's mysticism shares in the sharpness and closeknittedness of thought itself appears to betoken a growing appreciation on his part of the significance of Meister Eckhart's mysticism. For in his most well known reference to Eckhart—in the *Discourse on Thinking* (G, 35-6/61-2)—Heidegger's allusion to *"Gelassenheit"* in Eckhart is tempered by the criticism that for Eckhart *"Gelassenheit"* still belongs to the realm of willing, and so to metaphysics. Now I will show below that this criticism of Eckhart is unfounded. One can hardly say that the naked unity of the ground of the soul with the ground of God, a union which represents the utter dissolution of the relationship between "God" and "creature," cause and effect, above and below, yonder and hither, belongs to the realm of metaphysics. But be that as it may, what is more important is that there is no hint of criticism in Heidegger's treatment of the mystical poet Angelus Silesius or in the reference he makes to Meister Eckhart in SG. In fact the whole tone of the work exhibits a certain reverence towards the mystic and mystic poet. Now one must recall that the discourse on *"Gelassenheit"* was composed in 1944-45, some twelve years before SG. And it seems to me that in SG Heidegger's attitude towards Eckhart had become somewhat more appreciative, that he had come to realize more keenly the inner likeness of his thought to Meister Eckhart. We should remember too that in 1944

Heidegger had only recently completed the critique of Nietzsche and of the metaphysics of the will, and that he might therefore have been inclined to find the spectre of willing everywhere in the Western tradition, even where willing had been overcome, as I believe is the case with Meister Eckhart.

The second preliminary consideration that I wish to discuss before taking up the analogy between Heidegger and Eckhart has to do with the very idea of such an "analogy." For we must clarify exactly what the term "analogy" means as it applies to the relationship between Heidegger and Eckhart. Heidegger himself provides the best clue to the nature of this analogy. In 1960, in one of his meetings with the "old Marburgians," Heidegger recommended the following "analogy" to those theologians who wished to make use of his thought in their theological work—Being : thinking :: God : the thinking conducted within faith.[1] Heidegger is borrowing this analogy from the medieval tradition which he knows so well. We have already seen, above, his interest in the medieval doctrine of analogy (cf. FS, 197 ff.). Cardinal Cajetan, who codified the Thomistic theory of analogy, refers to this analogy as the "analogy of proportionality" (*analogia proportionalitatis*), which he distinguished from the analogy of proportion (*analogia proportionis*).[2] The analogy of proportion, which Aristotle called a *pros hen* analogy, signifies a direct relation or proportion between the two terms. Milk, e.g., because it contains calcium, is a cause of good bone development, and so bears a direct, because directly causal, relation to bone development. One could, thus, by the analogy of proportion, call milk "bone food," not because it is or is composed of a boney substance, but because it is the cause of good bones. The analogy of proportionality, on the other hand, is employed to relate things which are not immediately or directly related to one another but share only a certain similarity of proportions. This analogy is at work, e.g., in metaphors. If the poet calls the moon the "candle of the eve" he does not mean that the moon is composed of wax, wick, and flame, or that it either is caused by or is the cause of such. Candles have no direct relation at all to planetary satellites. What he means is that the moon "is to" the dark night the way a candle "is to" a dark room. Even the most disparate entities—half a dollar and half a century—can be related by this analogy, for they need have nothing to do with one another intrinsically, so long as they have a similarity of relationships (a proportion of proportions, a relation of relations).

Now Heidegger is suggesting to the theologian that the relationships between Being and thought and between God and the thought

143

conducted within faith are comparable. By only a slight modification, we can adapt this suggestion to our own needs: Being : thought (Dasein) :: God : the soul. This suggests that the relationship, the dialectic, the interchange, between God and the soul in Meister Eckhart is similar to the relationship between Being and Dasein in Heidegger. As God takes the initiative in Meister Eckhart, so Being takes the initiative in Heidegger. As the soul must stay open and receptive to God, so Dasein must stay open to Being. This in no way suggests that the terms of the relation—Being and God, Dasein and the soul—are directly related to one another, no more so than are the candle and the moon. It suggests a similarity of structures, not of content. It is not *what* is related but the *how* which is comparable. In each relation, one term "addresses" and the other "cor-responds"; one sends itself, and the other stays open for its coming. But *what* is related in each case is quite different: for in one case we have to do with the *unio mystica*, the purification and divinization of the soul; in the other with the epochal event of truth. Thus we are in no way committed by our study of this analogy to saying that for Heidegger Being is "really" God, a disguised form of the divinity, and Dasein is "really" the soul. We simply claim that the *relationships* into which Being and God enter in Heidegger and Meister Eckhart are similar; each plays a similar role within a similar structure.

It will be important to the reader to bear this element of disanalogy in mind as we pursue this study. For the proportionality in question is compatible with profoundly different "*contents.*" That is to say, it must all along be borne in mind that the *Sache* in Heidegger and in Eckhart differ greatly. When we say that this or that is the "same" in Heidegger and Eckhart, we mean to say only that the *structure* is the same. Let us give an example of this. We have seen in the first chapter that in both Eckhart and Heidegger we find a comparable structure of detachment (*Abgeschiedenheit*), of cutting off from beings (*Abschied vom Seienden*). But in Eckhart this means that the soul withdraws its affection from creatures in favor of the love of God. It means that the soul no longer takes creatures as if they are something of themselves but only in reference to their primal being as ideas in the mind of God. But in Heidegger the cutting off (*abscheiden*) is the *differentiating* (*unter-scheiden*) between beings and Being. It is the thought of Being qua Being, without constricting it to any of its modes, to anything entitative (*seiend*). It is a matter of rising to an understanding of Being in all its purity from beings. Clearly we have to do here with two different things, with differing concerns (*Sachen*), but the relationships that each thinker sees within his own concern are interestingly akin. That is the advantage of "proportionality" over "proportion"; the former kind of analogy articulates a likeness which is compatible with the most basic kind of unlikeness.

2. *Heidegger and Medieval Mysticism*

The first step in elaborating the relationship between Heidegger and Meister Eckhart must consist in documenting the great interest which Heidegger has shown in Meister Eckhart from his earliest days as a student in Freiburg through his "later" writings in the 1950's and '60's. For one of the legs upon which this study stands is that the relationship of Heidegger to Eckhart is not only "structural," like the relation of Heidegger to Eastern thinkers, but also "historical," i.e., rooted in the direct acquaintance of Heidegger with the work of Meister Eckhart. In explaining the extent of Heidegger's interest in Eckhart we will also acquire a better idea of the nature of this relationship, and so of the significance that the mystic of Hochheim holds for understanding Heidegger.

The first indication of Heidegger's interest in Meister Eckhart is to be found in his 1915 *Habilitationsschrift* at Freiburg, *The Doctrine of Meaning and Categories in Duns Scotus.*[3] Here Heidegger expresses great concern with medieval mysticism in general and with Meister Eckhart in particular. In a note in the closing pages of this work Heidegger promises us a future study of the problem of truth in Meister Eckhart. It will be worth our while to investigate this remark in some detail, for in it lies a clue to the importance which Heidegger attached to Meister Eckhart.

Heidegger's *Habilitationsschrift* is a study of a medieval treatise entitled *De modis significandi*, composed by a fourteenth-century Scotist (Thomas of Erfurt), though wrongly attributed by Heidegger to Scotus himself.[4] An essay in "speculative grammar," this treatise held to the theory that every empirical language obeyed universal, *a priori* rules. As a Catholic and short-lived aspirant to the priesthood, Heidegger was interested in the medieval tradition; his interest in medieval logic in particular was stimulated by Husserl's *Logical Investigations*, in which Husserl had himself defended a similar idea of a pure, *a priori* grammar.[5] Before undertaking an analysis of the theory of pure grammar (called by Husserl the "doctrine of meaning") contained in *De modis significandi*, Heidegger first attempts to locate the "sphere" of "meaning." This he does by determining that "meaning" (*Sinn, Bedeutung*) belongs to the irreducible realm of the "logical," of "logical being" (*ens verum, ens logicum*). The "is" in a proposition has nothing to do with real existence (*Wirklichkeit*), but with "being valid of," "holding good for" (*Geltensein*). Such considerations, in which one determines the logical "place" (*Ort*) or "sphere of Being" (*Seinsbereich*) of meaning, are called the "theory of categories."

In the light of Heidegger's mature interests, both in *Being and Time* and in the "later" period, it is surprising to see how technical in nature the *Habilitationsschrift* is.[6] The youthful Heidegger himself, conscious of the abstract nature of his study, remarks upon the need to show:

> . . . that in a field of investigation so seemingly poor in ideas of great value and of the fullness of life, deep and ultimate problems have their ground and basis. (FS, 238)

However technical the problems of philosophy, he says, they cannot be divorced from the living personality from which all philosophical questions ultimately arise:

> The value of philosophical thought is more than that of a scientific matter with which one occupies oneself out of merely personal preference and for the purpose of furthering and sharing in the formation of culture. Philosophy lives at the same time in a tension with the living personality and draws its content and claim to value out of its depths and fullness of life. A personal stand on the part of the philosopher concerned is for the most part the basis of every philosophical conception. Nietzsche, in his pitilessly sharp method of thinking and plastic capacity of presentation, has put the fact that philosophy is determined by the subject in the well-known formula, "the impulse which philosophizes."
>
> (FS, 137-8)

The "living personality" of whom Heidegger speaks in the *Habilitationsschrift* is further identified in the "Conclusion" as the "living spirit," i.e., concrete, historical man, with all of the needs, both theoretical and practical, of his time. Heidegger is raising a protest here against the predominantly Neo-Kantian epistemology of his day, which reduces man to the epistemological subject:

> The epistemological subject does not represent the most metaphysically significant meaning of the spirit, let alone its entire content. (FS, 349)

146

Heidegger must now show the "living" or—to use a later term—"existential" basis of the *grammatica speculativa.* This he does in the "Introduction" to the *Habilitationsschrift* where he says that, while medieval man lacks the modern capacity for self-reflection and introspection, still he possesses a talent of his own. For the scholastic thinker is oriented towards the world, the object, reality itself; hence he achieves an insight into "intentionality":

> ... scholastic psychology, precisely inasmuch as it is not focused upon the dynamic and flowing reality of the psychical, remains in its fundamental problems oriented towards the objective and noematic, a circumstance which greatly favors setting one's sight on the phenomenon of intentionality. (FS, 147)

While he lacks a sense of "subjective experience" the medieval thinker possesses a strong sense of "being." The scholastic, in Heidegger's interpretation, makes an "absolute surrender" to the "content of knowledge." For him, "the value of the subject matter (*Sache*) (object) dominates over the value of the self (subject)" (FS, 140). "Intentionality" in the Middle Ages refers to the "tendency" (*tendere*) of consciousness "into" (*in*) being, the act by which consciousness subordinates itself to the demand of the subject matter, to its unchanging structures and objective meanings. That explains why one rarely catches a glimpse of the personalities of the authors of the great medieval *Summae.*

Accordingly, scholastic thought is uncontaminated by the "unphilosophy of psychologism" (FS, 147). "Scholastic psychology" has nothing to do with "subjective introspection" in the manner of English Empiricism. It is instead an ontological theory of man which subordinates knowledge to being. The living basis of this psychology is medieval man's experience of belonging to an unchanging order which has been established independently of him. Hence Heidegger says:

> In order to reach a decisive insight into this fundamental character of scholastic psychology, I consider a philosophical, or more exactly, a phenomenological examination of the mystical, moral theological, and ascetical literature of medieval scholasticism to be especially urgent. In such a way will one really push forward to what is living in the life of medieval scholasticism. (FS, 147-8)

147

The surrender of thinking to the object, the subordination of knowledge to being, both spring from a frame of mind which is best understood in terms of the spiritual attitude of the mystic and the ascetic. Heidegger is not suggesting that the mystic is a typical medieval man. He is in any age an extraordinary occurrence. But for the Middle Ages, as Heidegger understands it, the mystic represents the life of medieval man intensified and "writ large." The mystic is the complete flowering and highest expression of medieval values. The mystic is the man in whom the virtue of the "absolute surrender" of the "individuality of the individual" is practiced to an heroic degree. Thus the cognitive, or epistemological theory of intentionality, which is described in terms such as "surrender," represents on the speculative-philosophical level the way the living, historical man in the Middle Ages experiences life. The highest virtue in the Middle Ages was reverence or piety—both in epistemology and in life. Thus in Meister Eckhart's *On Detachment*, Eckhart associates the mystical-ascetical notion of purifying oneself of all affection for creatures (detachment) with Aristotle's *tabula rasa*, which is the "emptiness" or receptivity necessary for cognition. In both the "detached heart" and the "passive reason" there is the same necessity of the subject to purify itself of its subjectivity.

The existence of a medieval theory of pure, *a priori* grammar is now easily explained. In the Middle Ages, language and grammar were thought to be subject to a timeless and universal set of rules and to give expression to unchanging meanings, precisely because reality itself was thought to constitute an eternal order. Language, in its essentials at least, could be no more a matter of a man-made convention than nature itself. Language is instead stamped throughout with unchanging structures to which every empirical language must subordinate itself.

The reference to Meister Eckhart in particular occurs in the "Conclusion" of the *Habilitationsschrift* where Heidegger once again takes up the question of the relationship of abstract logical problems to the concrete experience of medieval man. Here Heidegger tells us that the problem of "categories" must be further situated. In the first place, it must be given a fully "metaphysical setting." No logical problem can be successfully dealt with unless it is set within a perspective which is "translogical" and metaphysical:

Philosophy cannot for long dispense with its true optics, metaphysics.

(FS, 348)

148

The realm of logical meaning must be given "ontical significance" (*ontische Bedeutung*: FS, 348). Philosophy must effect a "breakthrough"—a favorite word of Eckhart's, as we have seen—into "real truth and true reality" (FS, 348). The categories must therefore be grasped as determinations of objects, modes of being. For in the Middle Ages truth means the "*verum*," the knowability of being, being in its relationship to intellect. The categories are not merely epistemological but ontological structures.

In the second place, the problem of categories must be rooted in the historical life of the Middle Ages (FS, 351-2). This is accomplished by showing the connection between the problem of categories and the principle of "analogy" in medieval thought. The doctrine of categories in Duns Scotus expresses the medieval experience of the "manifold sense of Being." Being is said in many ways (*ens dicitur multipliciter*), according to the scholastics. In *Being and Time* itself, Heidegger singles out the doctrine of analogy, which originates in Aristotle and is developed by the schoolmen, as putting the problem of Being on a "new basis" (SZ, § 1, 3/22; cf. § 20, 93/126), even though the scholastics failed, in Heidegger's view, to show the unity of the diverse modes of being (or categories).

The principle of analogy, according to Heidegger, is no mere "schoolroom" concept; rather it is

> . . . the conceptual expression of the world of experience of medieval man, [a world which is] qualitatively fulfilled, charged with values and drawn into relationship with the transcendent; it [analogy] is the conceptual expression of the determinate form of inner existence anchored in the primordial and transcendent relationship of the soul to God. . . .
>
> (FS, 350-1)

According to scholastic philosophy, the analogicity of being means that being is differentiated into various levels which are, as the scholastic put it, "somewhat the same and somewhat different." "Being" is thereby amplified so as to include not only sensible but also supersensible reality: the soul, angels, and God. The medieval theory of analogy, in Heidegger's interpretation, conceptualizes what the medieval man "lives through" (*er-lebt*).

The life of medieval man, Heidegger says, is "anchored" in a "transcendent and primordial relationship of the soul to God" (FS, 351). Medieval man is not lost in the flowing world of sensible experience, for this world is but one kind of reality for him, and not even the

149

highest, inasmuch as it is itself dependent upon "uncreated" being. "Stretched out into the transcendent," he seeks a goal which transcends everything earthly, and this transcendent aspiration unifies his earthly existence. Modern man, on the other hand, suffers from the "insecurity and disorientation" of a life which is caught up in the flowing, sensible world.

The "transcendental and primordial relationship of the soul to God," we should add, is a relationship between two spiritual individuals and hence it is not achieved at the expense of, nor by the destruction of, the individuality of the soul. For while, on the one hand, the absolute value of the transcendent is affirmed, the value of the soul is, on the other hand, enhanced by its participation in the life of God (FS, 351).

The transcendent relationship of the soul to God is achieved in a perfected form in the mystic. Hence the more closely we study medieval mysticism the more perfectly we will understand the living basis from which the speculative problems of scholastic philosophy issue:

> In the medieval world-view, scholasticism and mysticism belong essentially together. The two pairs of "opposites" rationalism–irrationalism and scholasticism–mysticism do not coincide. And where their equivalence is sought, it rests on an extreme rationalization of philosophy. Philosophy as a rationalist creation, detached from life, is powerless; mysticism as an irrationalist experience is purposeless. (FS, 352)

The speculative thought of the Middle Ages is not to be opposed to the mystical tradition but, on the contrary, is to be seen as its conceptual articulation.

It is in this context that we must understand Heidegger's reference to Meister Eckhart. In a footnote in the "Conclusion" of the *Habilitationsschrift*, Heidegger promises us a study of the problem of truth in Meister Eckhart:

> I hope to show on another occasion how, in terms of this [the correlativity of subject and object], and in connection with the metaphysics of the problem of truth, which we will discuss below, Eckhartian mysticism first receives its philosophical interpretation and evaluation.
>
> (FS, 344, n. 2)

The investigation of Eckhart's thought will be philosophical. Thus it will not concern Eckhartian mysticism as mysticism. Rather, it will

150

examine the significance which Eckhart's mysticism holds for the study of philosophical problems, viz., the problem of the "metaphysics of truth." A metaphysics of truth, as we have seen above, adopts a translogical perspective. It considers consciousness as a faculty of being, a faculty which seizes true reality and real truth. Heidegger also characterizes this metaphysical interpretation of consciousness as "metaphysical-teleological." By calling it teleological, he means that it will investigate the living subject with its concrete historical goals and aspirations, and not merely the abstract, lifeless subject. Heidegger's reference to Eckhart, moreover, speaks of Eckhart's work in connection with the correlativity of subject and object. He is referring to the medieval conception of the *verum*, according to which every being is or can be related to intellect, and, conversely, the intellect is or can be related to every being ("the soul is in a way all things"). We have also seen above that, in the medieval mystic, we find in an intensified way the primordial and transcendent relationship of the soul with God which constitutes the highest ideal of medieval life.

If we put all these considerations together, then we can interpret Heidegger's reference to a projected work on Meister Eckhart as follows. The personal relationship between the soul and God in Eckhart's mysticism contains a clue to the solution of the problem of truth, where truth is taken to be the correlativity or belonging together of thought and being. The way the soul makes its way to God in Eckhart's mystical doctrine tells us something about how thought makes its breakthrough into true reality and real truth. Now exactly what Heidegger meant by this in 1915 we cannot know, but we might hazard the following guess. Heidegger might still at this time have been under the residual influence of scholastic realism. We know that the work which has always seemed to him to have been Husserl's best was the *Logical Investigations*, in which Husserl said he was unable to find an "*ego cogito*." With the appearance of *Ideas I*, however, Husserl's thought took a turn towards "transcendental subjectivity," which Heidegger would always disavow. Thus Heidegger hoped in the *Habilitationsschrift* to bring the *De modis significandi* into line with the Husserl of the *Logical Investigations*, who spoke of "objective meanings," independent of the "psychological" state of the subject. Now Heidegger might be referring to the connection, which we discussed above, between Eckhart's demand to be "detached" from the desires of the "self" in his mystical works and his acceptance of the *tabula rasa* of Aristotle as the model for consciousness in his the-

151

ory of knowledge. Heidegger might have wanted at that time to develop a theory of knowledge which would have clear traces of his early training in scholastic realism while casting it more in the form of the "objective" realism and theory of "intentionality" of Husserl's *Logical Investigations.*

By the appearance of *Being and Time* in 1927, this "realism" had been both abandoned and retained. It was assuredly abandoned inasmuch as Heidegger's theory of truth in *Being and Time* was patently "Dasein-related" (*Daseinsmässig*): only as long as Dasein is, is there truth (SZ, § 44c, 230/272). But it had been retained inasmuch as *Being and Time* is a profoundly un-Cartesian work which has no theory of the "*ego cogito.*" Instead it takes a view of man as immersed in the world from the start, and it adopts as its task the description of what shows itself "as it shows itself from itself."

But it is only in his later works that Heidegger's reference to Meister Eckhart would acquire its full force. For in these writings, where the primacy of Dasein in *Being and Time* is replaced by the primacy of Being itself, Heidegger returns to a position which, in a strange way, resembles the realism of the *Habilitationsschrift.* Thus how appropriately the following remark from the Scotus book characterizes the "later" writings:

> The value of the subject matter (*Sache*) (object) dominates over the value of the self (subject). (FS, 140)

In the writings which appear after 1930 Heidegger develops a theory of truth as *aletheia* to which the mystical relationship of the soul to the "unconcealed" God (Q, 147,4/Cl., 122) bears the most striking resemblance. For Dasein, like the soul, must make a clearing in itself by detaching itself from beings (*Abschied vom Seienden*: WM, 49/359), in order to "let" Being itself come to pass "unrefracted" and undistorted by human subjectivity. Dasein must prepare an open "place," not for God, but for Being. "Being" "needs" the "clearing" Dasein provides, even as Meister Eckhart will say that God needs the detached heart. The most extensive and even startling analogy can thus be built up between the "birth of God" in the "ground of the soul" in Meister Eckhart and the primal event (*Ereignis*) of Truth in Heidegger's later thought.

Now it may seem to the reader that we are attaching an undue significance to a footnote which makes a promise that is not kept in a work which seems to bear little resemblance to Heidegger's mature views. In order to dispel that impression let us document further Heidegger's great interest in Meister Eckhart at this time. To begin with, the 1915 inaugural lecture, "The Concept of Time in the Science of History," in which Heidegger differentiates the "time" of the historian from the "time" of the physicist in a way which strongly anticipates the notion of authentic temporality in *Being and Time*, begins with a motto taken from Meister Eckhart on the distinction between time and eternity:

> Time is that which transforms and multiplies itself; eternity keeps itself simple. (FS, 358)

Now in citing Meister Eckhart at the beginning of his lecture, Heidegger is following the example of his mentor at Freiburg, Heinrich Rickert. Rickert prefaced his article "*Das Eine, die Einheit, und die Eins*" [*Logos II* (1911-12), 26 ff.], with a quotation from Meister Eckhart (FS, 160). This article, incidentally, was of much importance for Heidegger in his interpretation of the *unum* in the *Habilitationsschrift*. Perhaps Rickert was instrumental in introducing the young Heidegger to the works of Eckhart; perhaps he encouraged an already present interest.

Moreover, while Heidegger never produced the promised work on Meister Eckhart, he did give a lecture-course in 1919 entitled "The Philosophical Foundations of Medieval Mysticism."[7] It is regrettable that none of the manuscripts of this course, if any are still extant, have ever been published, and that they are not planned for appearance in the *Gesamtausgabe*. Still we can be certain that Meister Eckhart was given a prominent place in these lectures from the fact that a student in this course, Käte Oltmanns, would in 1935 publish a study entitled simply *Meister Eckhart*. The point of view of this book is thoroughly Heideggerian, as Oltmanns readily admits (Olt., 10). This book met with something of a cool reception by Eckhartian scholars, and the reason for this is of interest to this study. Hence, after our own comparison of Meister Eckhart and Heidegger, we will take up Oltmanns's work, along with another, more recent study of Eckhart from a Heideggerian standpoint, in order to throw some further light on our subject.

Nor is Heidegger's interest in Meister Eckhart confined to these early years. For while he never refers to Meister Eckhart in *Being and Time*, he does cite Meister Eckhart seven times, to my knowledge, in the works that are written after 1930. Compared to the number of references to Parmenides, Heraclitus, Aristotle, or Kant, this seems like a negligible number. But these references are warm and admiring (even if sometimes critical), and they often are made in connection with the most basic elements in Heidegger's thought. The best-known reference to Meister Eckhart occurs in the book whose title, *Gelassenheit*, is a basic term in Eckhart's vernacular writings (G, 35-6/61-2). We shall have occasion below to undertake a comparative analysis of "*Gelassenheit*" in these two authors. On two occasions (K, 39/7; VA, 175/176) Heidegger displays a familiarity with the Middle High German text of Eckhart's writings. In *What is Called Thinking?*, he refers to one of the most famous teachings in Eckhart's mystical writings, the notion of the *Fünklein* or "little spark" in the soul (WHD, 95-6/149). Twice he points to Eckhart, whom he called a "master of thinking" (VA, 175/176), as a deep thinker from whom technological reason has much to learn (SG, 71; FW, 4/35).[8] Finally (FND, 76/98), Heidegger objects to the tendency sometimes found in histories of modern philosophy, particularly by German historians, to mark off the beginning of "modern" philosophy with Eckhart. In Heidegger's terms, this would classify Eckhart as a "subjectivistic" thinker, a position impossible before Descartes.

There can thus be no question about Heidegger's acquaintance with Meister Eckhart. Eckhart's works are known to Heidegger, apparently quite well. Hence the relationship we are developing in these pages is not arbitrary. It must be taken into account by the historian of German philosophy and by those who are interested in probing into Heidegger's historical "sources." We have established beyond doubt that Heidegger retained a life-long interest in Meister Eckhart which began in his early days as a student of the Catholic medieval tradition. These days, we hold, are essential to his "origin" (US, 96/10).

3. *Dasein and the Ground of the Soul*

In order to articulate the relationship between Heidegger and Eckhart I have singled out four themes in Heidegger's thought, for which, I hope to show, one finds significant analogues in Meister Eckhart. First of all I wish to discuss in this section Heidegger's conception of "Dasein," to which, I believe, there are important and interesting similarities in Eckhart's notion of the "ground of the soul." Then I will take up the question of how the "event" (*Ereignis*) of truth in Heidegger bears an important relationship to the "birth of the Son" in

Meister Eckhart. Next we will turn to the best-known and most frequently commented upon parallel of Heidegger to Eckhart, the one betokened by their common use of the word "*Gelassenheit*," a term which seems to me equally basic to the vocabulary of both thinkers. Finally, I wish to show how the relationship of Being to beings in Heidegger is partly illuminated by a comparable relationship in Meister Eckhart of God to creatures.

Of course, I must hasten to add, these similarities manage to subsist along with the most radical dissimilarities. For these two thinkers are separated by centuries, and so by different dispensations of Being (*Seinsgeschick*). In a sense the differences between them are plainly seen. Heidegger is not interested (focally) in God, but rather in the history of Being. Heidegger is not seeking "holiness," or unity with God. Rather he seeks to prepare the clearing which must be made in human history for the event of Being. Heidegger expresses no interest whatsoever in the Blessed Trinity, the immortality and spirituality of the soul, or the Christian-neoplatonic doctrine of the preexistence of things in the mind of God, all of which ideas are of central importance to Meister Eckhart. Heidegger's Being is not the "creator" or first cause of beings. Heidegger does not take the life of Jesus as a model for man's relationship to Being. He does not invoke the scriptures. And so on. The differences between Heidegger and Eckhart are so clear and so numerous that they threaten to inundate us before we even begin.

Indeed it is because Professor Martin Heidegger is so patently different a figure and thinker from "frater Equardus, ordo praedicatorum" that we will devote most of our labors in this section to finding their similarities. While we will point out the differences, we will not dwell on or thematize them in this chapter. Important as these differences are, we must first learn what sort of kinship exists between these two German masters. We will leave it primarily to the next chapter to draw out the disanalogy between Eckhart and Heidegger. Because it is there that we will assess the significance of this whole analogy for understanding Heidegger's thought. There we will undertake to determine whether thinking is a kind of mysticism, and if it is not, how we are to understand it. In the end the difference between Heidegger and Eckhart will be decisive; but in the beginning we must first establish the likeness. And of course it is the very nature of "analogy," particularly of the "analogy of proportionality," to articulate sameness in difference. It is analogy which allows us to say, Eckhart and Heidegger: the same but different.

155

Neither Eckhart nor Heidegger speaks of "man." For both thinkers, there is something deeper within man, something which is not merely human, which constitutes man's true dignity and worth. For both, there is a hidden ground in which man's truest being and essential nature (*Wesen*) lies. "Here is man a true man," writes Eckhart (Q, 215,7/Serm., 225). In his *Talks of Instruction*, Eckhart says:

> Do not think to base holiness on doing; one should rather base holiness on being. For works do not make us holy, but we must make works holy.
> (Q, 57,15-8/Cl., 67)

Holiness has to do not with our action, but the ground of our action, our being. The truly great are great in their being:

> Nothing will come of whatever works they work who are not great in being. (Q, 57,22-3/Cl., 67)

It is in the inner ground of the soul, the very being (*Wesen*) of the soul, that genuine greatness is to be found. Heidegger singles out this text of Meister Eckhart in "The Reversal," citing it in the Middle High German. He then adds this commentary:

> We consider that the great being (*Wesen*) of man consists in the fact that it belongs to the essence (*Wesen*) of Being, that it is needed and used by the latter to preserve (*wahren*) the essence of Being in its truth (*Wahrheit*). (K, 39/7)

Heidegger himself thus draws the first point of comparison for us. He, like Meister Eckhart, finds in man something deeper than his everyday commerce with the things around him. This primal being of man is called by both Heidegger and Eckhart man's "*Wesen*." As for Eckhart, so for Heidegger, *Wesen* has a verbal sense. Eckhart usually translated the Latin *esse* by the Middle High German *wesen* (he often employed *wesenheit* and *wesunge* as translations of *essentia*) (cf. Q, "*Anmerkungen*," 538). This term means for him the "essential being," the "primal being" of a thing, that by which a thing *is* what it *is*. Heidegger picks up this original sense of the word and uses it to refer to the very Being of a being.

Now in both cases the very being of man, which is nothing anthropomorphic, lies in its relationship to something which, for lack of a better word, we say "transcends" man. The essential being of man is

156

not to be found in his relationship to beings but in his relationship to that which transcends beings, viz., to Being. Thus for Eckhart, the essence of the soul is the ground of the soul, which is timeless, nameless, and uncreated. This ground is a "place" in which God and the soul unite, in which the transcendent being of God comes to pass in man. The "true man" is the man who "lets God be God," who provides a dwelling place which can shelter and preserve the birth of the Son. So too in Heidegger, the essential being of man rests in something more radical than man—"the question into the essential being (*Wesen*) of man is not a question about man" (G, 31/58). For the great being of man is to be a relationship to Being itself—to provide a "place" (*Ortschaft*, HB, 77/204; *Stelle*, WM, 13/213) in which Being itself can come to pass. The great being of man is to provide a shelter and a preserve for the being of truth.

Eckhart and Heidegger do not often use the word "man"—they speak instead of "Dasein," the "little spark," the "little castle," the "ground of the soul." This arises not out of a desire for terminological inventiveness but out of what Heidegger would call the attempt to play along with the play of language. For this more radical dimension of man's being is something which continually tends to slip out of sight and be forgotten. When we speak of "man," language is imperceptibly accustoming us to think that all there "is" to man is something human, something "anthropological." Heidegger and Eckhart subvert this drift towards the easiest and most superficial meaning of the word "man" by avoiding the word and using in its place a language which will not conceal but reveal what there "is" (*west*) in man.

In both cases, then, the anthropological interpretation of man is "overcome." Man is not understood "zoologically"—as an animal with the specific difference of rationality. Nor is he given any of the other, equally anthropological, specifications of man in Western philosophy —such as "spirit" or "person" (HB, 66/199; SZ, § 10). All of these determinations of man are "metaphysical," i.e., they take man as a species of beings which must be differentiated from other species. They are "ontic" determinations of man. Eckhart, indeed, is quite insistent about the fact that the ground of the soul belongs in no classifiable category, that it is no determinate mode of being. "This power has nothing in common with anything else," he says (Q, 210,13-4/Serm., 220). It is neither "this nor that." It cannot so much as be named:

Consequently, I name it now in a more noble way (*edlere Weise*) than I have ever named it, and yet it rejects such a nobility (*Edelheit*) as well as any way (*Weise*) and is raised above both. (Q, 163,18-21/Serm., 137)

157

The ground of the soul is not a being, or a kind of being, but a place within which God reveals Himself as He is in His truest being.

So too "Dasein" is not merely a being, or a species of beings, which can be differentiated off from other beings (HB, 66/199). Rather Dasein is primarily a "relation" (*Ver-hältnis*) to Being as such. Dasein is not so much a being but a relationship to Being. Dasein is not something which man "has," a property or characteristic of man, but something which possesses man and makes man and his relationship with other beings possible (WM, 16/308-9). "Dasein" is not consciousness, whether empirical or transcendental; it is not the *ego cogito*, the *res cogitans*, the *animal rationale*. Dasein is something more basic and simple than all of these, making all of these possible.

In *What Is Called Thinking?* Heidegger seems to indicate that he is not prepared to admit that Eckhart's conception of the "little spark of the soul" (*Seelenfünklein*) does indeed fully transcend the notion of man as a "living being" endowed with a "specific difference" of "reason" or "thought":

> However, it still makes a decisive difference whether this trait of the living being "man" is merely included in our considerations as a distinguishing mark superadded to the living being—or whether this relatedness to what is, *because* it is the basic characteristic of man's human nature, is given its decisive role as the *standard*. (WHD, 96/149)

It is not enough to speak of man as *anima*—a being possessed of a principle of life, for every living thing ("animal") has *anima*. But neither is it enough, Heidegger says, to speak of man as *animus*. Now *animus* means, according to Heidegger,

> . . . that inner striving of human nature which always is determined by, attuned to, what is. The Latin word *animus* can also be translated with the word "soul." "Soul" in this case means not the principle of life, but that in which the spirit has its being, the spirit of spirit [cf. Q, 319,10/Ev., 33], Meister Eckhart's "spark" of the soul. (WHD, 96/149)

Even Meister Eckhart, in Heidegger's view, fails to understand that man is *basically* and *fundamentally* a relatedness to what is and that this is not simply something "added on" to man.

Heidegger is, I believe, mistaken about this. For Eckhart, the "little spark" or "ground" of the soul refers to the innermost "source" and "root" (*Wurzel*: Q, 318,17/Ev., 32) of the soul's being. It is not something added on to the soul, but that from which the soul draws its

158

life. This is the force of the very word "*Grund*." Moreover, the little spark of the soul is in no way a "distinguishing mark" of the soul because it signifies that realm of the soul where there are no "distinguishing marks" or "names" at all. The ground of the soul is no "thing"; it belongs to no "class" of things, and has nothing to do with any kind of "specific difference." Indeed, "it has nothing to do with anything"—genus, species, or difference. The simple truth is that with his notion of the "little spark of the soul," Eckhart has conceived of man not as man but as a pure relationship to Being, which is—for Eckhart—God.

Indeed, it is because Heidegger and Eckhart have such similar conceptions of man's true being that they can each speak of the need for man to "return" to his innermost essence. Thus, for Heidegger, Dasein is the very being of man by which he is always and from the start related to Being. Dasein is not something which is to be attained but something in which man already stands. Man already *is* Dasein, and his task is to become what he is, i.e., to take it up again and make it truly his own. In the same way, Meister Eckhart tells the soul to stay at home—i.e., to take up residence in its own inner chamber, which is the ground of the soul (Q, 170,10-1/Serm., 172; 393,32-5/Ev., 85). I could not leave home, Eckhart says, if I did not already dwell there. So too man's fallenness out of his ownmost being, his Da-sein, is itself testimony to that from which he has fallen—his inner belonging to Being.

Thus there is in Eckhart and Heidegger a comparable distinction between the being which has truly entered into its ownmost essential nature and the being which allows itself to be occupied with one thing or another. What Eckhart calls the "outer man" is the man who spends all of his energies on external things. He is a "busy" man, occupied with created things—collecting taxes, negotiating in the market place, or even "busily" fasting, giving alms, and visiting churches. Such a man is not "at home"—but outside among things. And the busier he becomes the more likely he is to "forget" the hidden, silent ground of the soul, where "nothing" is happening. For the outer man lives a life of action (*Tun*), constantly employing his "faculties" (intellect, will, sense). But the inner man stays at home in the ground of the soul, which is deeper than and prior to the faculties. Here, then, is no action (*Tun*), but only being (*Wesen*), which to the man of action looks like nothing at all. Such a ground is easily forgotten and covered over.

Heidegger too warns of the danger of becoming so preoccupied with

159

the business of everyday existence as to forget the question of Being. Indeed, the first time Heidegger made such a distinction—in *Being and Time*—he used a religious expression to describe it: fallenness. Dasein is "fallen," not from a state of integrity into a state of sin, but out of its ownmost way of being into a public mode of existence. In the later works, this distinction is given a different shape. He speaks there of those who are concerned with beings, with the rules which govern beings (the sciences) and with the way to control and manipulate beings (technology). He distinguishes this attitude from "thought," a quiet, all but silent meditativeness. Thought is humble and produces no effects (SD, 66/60), hence it is easily drowned out by the noisy success of the sciences. To the sciences, thought appears to be idleness, mythology or romanticism—yet the sciences themselves do not "think" in the special Heideggerian sense of that word.

Thus both Heidegger and Eckhart describe a comparable "fallenness" into everyday existence. For both, man is exposed to the danger of being lost in beings, of getting swept up by a concern with "this and that." Both call for a return to a forgotten ground within man which is deeper than anything human, in which man is opened up to the presence of something which transcends beings altogether.

It is also important to realize, however, that neither Eckhart nor Heidegger looks upon everyday existence with contempt. For both, everydayness is not contemptible but only "derivative," resting in deeper grounds. For Eckhart, the ground of the soul is not the opposite or contradiction of its faculties but the root from out of which they flow. What better testimony can there be to Eckhart's belief in the unity and harmony which ought to exist between outer activity and inner stillness than his unforgettable interpretation of the story of Mary and Martha? Eckhart does not reject the Aristotelian definition of man as the rational animal. He simply denies that this circumscribes the entire being of man. The man who lives an outwardly holy life, and who conforms his will to God's, is good—he is simply not the best of all. By the same token, Heidegger, like Eckhart, is prepared to admit that the definition of man as the rational animal is not "false" (HB, 74-5/203). He contends that while it is a "correct" determination of man from the point of view of "representational" thought, there is a realm beyond representational thinking of which philosophical reason knows nothing. In this realm, man is comprehended as an open relationship to Being itself, and it is on the ground of this relationship that man's relations with beings are made possible (WG, 22-3; WW, 20/314-5). Thus neither Heidegger nor Eckhart wants to rid himself of everydayness, but only to see that it is not made into an absolute and allowed to cover over the deeper ground of man's being.

Let us conclude this section with the necessary admonition not to exaggerate the analogy we have drawn, for we are not suggesting that the ground of the soul is to be equated with Dasein. The ground of the soul is a relationship to God, and if Being is God for Eckhart, this Being is not exactly what Heidegger means by Being as Being, Being in its difference from beings. While we shall discuss this more fully below we should at once point out that for Heidegger Being refers to the epochal coming to pass of the event of truth, the successive clearings opened in the various historical ages. And obviously Eckhart's "ground of the soul" has nothing to do with this. Indeed Eckhart's ground is absolutely timeless and eternal. It does not provide a clearing in which history comes to pass, but one in which the ahistorical root of man's life is recovered. To return to Eckhart's hidden ground is to return to the eternal now, whereas to truly experience the Dasein in man, that is, man's relationship to Being, is to enter into the very rhythm of the historical movements of the "event" (*Ereignis*). It is to feel the movements of and hear the music which Being plays to us (SG, 188).

And one final note. It is quite clear that Eckhart conceptualizes the distinction between the "outer faculties of the soul" and its "inner ground" in the language of scholastic metaphysics, and therefore in a way which appears to leave him caught up within the metaphysical tradition. Thus the distinction is drawn in terms of the outer and inner, the temporal and the eternal, faculties and their substance. In other words, Eckhart's formulations remain captive to the metaphysics of Christian Neoplatonism. Now I have not the slightest desire to argue that Eckhart does not belong to the Christian Neoplatonic tradition, or that one cannot find such a metaphysic formulated in the language of that tradition in his Latin writings. But I do want to argue, however, that in his German sermons and treatises Eckhart achieves a "breakthrough" beyond metaphysics to another realm. I want to maintain that his idea of the ground of the soul gives expression to an experience of a still and quiet sphere which lies deeper than and prior to the hustle and bustle of everydayness and of rational discourse and of all our incessant desires. Thus I want to distinguish what these ideas mean in Meister Eckhart from the unavoidable tendency he had to formulate them in terms of the metaphysics of his day. When we

161

do that, I maintain, we will find that the still realm of which Eckhart speaks is not unlike that outside the cabin when "one morning the landscape is hushed in its blanket of snow . . ." (AED, 20/11).

4. *The Event of Truth and the Birth of the Son*

The great being of the soul is to be the "birth place" of the Son, the "clearing" in which the Father engenders His Son. The great being of Dasein is to be the place of truth, the clearing in which the "event of appropriation" (*Ereignis*), the event of truth, comes to pass. In both cases, the true dignity of man lies in his poverty, i.e., in the humble way in which he provides a shelter and a preserve for a transcendent event. Man can in no way effect this event of himself; he can only make a "clearing" in which it might take place. There is a convincing parallel between the way in which Heidegger articulates the event of truth and the way that Eckhart describes the birth of the Son, a parallel which brings out in a striking way the affinity between the thinker and the mystic.

For Meister Eckhart, the Father and the Son exist in a "subsistent relation" to one another, i.e., their relationship to one another is not something added on to either. Rather, the very being of the Father is to give birth, and the very being of the Son is to be born. Neither Father nor Son subsists apart from their relation to one another. They subsist *in* this relation; they *are* this relation. Now since, in Eckhart's mystical theology, the inner life of the Trinity is extended to the soul, Eckhart is able to speak in the same terms of the relationship between the Father and the soul:

> What is our name and what is our father's name? Our name is that we must be born and our father's name is to bear. . . .
>
> (Q, 220,6-8/Serm., 238)

The essential being of the Father is to give birth; the essential being of the soul is to have the Son born in it. Now it is very revealing to see how closely Heidegger's expression of the relationship between Being and Dasein approximate Eckhart's views. For Heidegger, Being "is" (*west*) the very process of coming to pass in Dasein, and Dasein "is" the very process of letting Being reveal itself. The "relationship" between Being and Dasein is not something added on to either.

162

Rather, the essential being (*Wesen*) of each is to be related to the other. Thus, in a text which from this point of view is most interesting, Heidegger speaks of "mortals" (Dasein) as *"das wesende Verhältnis zum Sein als Sein"* (VA, 177/179). Of course, *"Wesen"* is to be understood verbally, and so this phrase means: the relationship to Being (*Sein*) whose being (*Wesen*) is to be ("*wesen*" taken as an infinitive) a relation. Using Adamczewski's suggestion that *"Wesen"* be translated as "way to be,"[9] the phrase means: the relationship to Being whose way to be is to be related. The Being of Dasein is to be related to Being; for Dasein, to be is to be related (*esse est referri*). Thus Heidegger too proposes something of a "subsistent relationship" (*ein wesendes Verhältnis*) between Being and Dasein.

We have seen, moreover, that the process by which the Father generates the Son in the soul is the process of producing His own "image": "The heavenly Father bears in me His very image" (Q, 220,16-7/ Serm., 239). We recall that it was not sufficient for the Son to be merely like the Father in order to be His Image; it was also required that He be sustained in His being as an image by the Father. Now Heidegger's account of the relationship between Being and Dasein conforms remarkably to what Eckhart demands of a "true image" and relation:

> But how is Being related to ek-sistence, provided that we may so rashly ask this question at all? Being itself is the relationship (*Verhältnis*) insofar as it [=Being] holds (*hält*) ek-sistence (*Ek-sistenz*) in its existential, i.e., ex-static essence (*Wesen*) in itself and gathers it [=*Eksistenz*] to itself as the dwelling place of the truth of Being in the midst of beings.
>
> (HB, 77/204)

Heidegger here and elsewhere (WHD, 1/3-4) exploits the root "*halten*" in the word *Verhältnis*: Dasein is "held" in its relationship to Being by Being itself. In the "Introduction" to *What Is Metaphysics?*, Heidegger refers to "a thinking which has come to pass by Being itself" (WM, 13/213), i.e., which is held up as thought by Being itself. And in the "Epilogue" to the same works he says:

> Being is no product of thought. On the contrary, indeed, essential thinking is an event of Being (*Ereignis des Seins*). (WM, 47/356)

The relation of Dasein to Being is not the work of Dasein, but of Being. The *thought* of Being (where the "of" is an objective genitive) is the

163

thought of *Being* (where the "of" is a subjective genitive). Thinking is not something that man is capable of on his own. Thought comes to pass *in* man, but not *by* man.

Thus in a sentence which could very well have been written by Meister Eckhart himself, Heidegger says:

> A relationship to something would be a true relationship if it [=x] is held in its [x's] own essence by that [=y] to which it is related.   (G, 50/72)

This meets Eckhart's requirement for a "true image" exactly. The relationship of Dasein to Being is not the "doing" of Dasein but of Being. Being itself brings Dasein into relationship with itself, and sustains that relation. For the early Heidegger, Dasein's relationship to Being seems to have originated in Dasein itself and to have depended upon Dasein's ability to sustain that relation. Thus the question of Being depends upon man's ability to raise and answer it, man's ability to break through the accumulation of prejudices and presumptions about Being in order to truly *ask* the question of Being anew. The ability to question is itself a measure of Dasein's capacity to resolve, its *will* to know (EM, 16/17). But it seems to have been one of the decisive realizations of the later Heidegger, and so of the Heidegger who began more and more to take on a likeness to the mystics, that Being does not come as the "answer" to a "question" (SD, 20-1/20; US, 175/71-2). It is the very attempt to interrogate Being, to make it give an account of itself to man, that must be surrendered. "Questioning" submits to the demand in Leibniz's principle to render a sufficient reason. But Being, as we have seen, is without why; we must let Being lie forth of itself. Even the "why" of the question of Being—why is there something rather than nothing?—must be given up. The "why" must give way to "because" (SG, 188). Being comes not as the answer to a question but as a "gift," a "favor" (*Gunst*: WM, 49/358), which is bestowed upon man. Being is thought because Being "gives itself to be thought" (WHD, 1-2/34). We are endowed (*begabt*) with the gift (*Gabe*) of thought by Being itself (WHD, 86/126)

This conforms closely to what Eckhart says of the birth of the Son. The birth of the Son is the work of God, not of the soul, although the soul's co-working and cooperation is required (Q, 94,27/Cl., 102). The image of the Father which is generated in the soul is engendered by the Father:

164

The work is so proper to Him [the Father] that no one other than the Father is able to effect it. In this work, God effects all His works; the Holy Ghost depends on it and [so do] all creatures. If God effects this work—which is His birth—in the soul, then this birth is His work, and the birth is the Son. God effects this work in the innermost part of the soul, and in such a hidden manner that neither an angel nor a saint knows why, and even the soul itself can do nothing other than endure it. It belongs uniquely to God. (Q, 376,32-377,6/Ev., 125)

However, Eckhart does say that the soul itself bears the Son:

In the same stroke, when He bears His only begotten Son in me, I bear Him back in the Father. (Q, 258,30-1/Serm., 214)

But Eckhart means to say that the soul "co-bears" (*mit-gebiert*: Q, 161,28/Serm., 135) and co-works (*mitwirkt*: Q, 94,10-27/Cl., 102) with the Father in giving birth to the Son. The soul has become so totally unified with God that the work of the Father has become the work of the soul as well. God's own work and my own are the same (Q, 176,16-7/Serm., 235). His work is my work, and my work is His. Eckhart does not mean to suggest that the soul *apart from the Father* could bear the Son—no more than Heidegger would suggest that Dasein is in a position to summon up or command Being into unconcealment (G, 65-6/84). Dasein and the soul are humble and poor: they prepare a place of shelter for a guest over whom they have no authority.

Eckhart also formulated the doctrine of the divine birth in terms of the "Eternal Word." For the Father to bear His Son in the soul is to speak His Word (*conceptum, verbum, Wort*) in the soul. When the soul is silent, he says, Jesus comes to it and speaks:

What does the Lord Jesus speak? He speaks that which He is. What then is He? He is the Word of the Father. (Q, 157,8-10/Serm., 131)

The heavenly Father speaks His eternal Word in the soul of the detached man; the Word that he speaks then is the divine Word itself. The soul in which the Father speaks becomes an "ad-verb" (*Beiwort*: Q, 200,25/Serm., 211) of the Word itself. Now since the work of the Father and of the soul is *one* work, the soul can "respond" (*entspricht*) to God by speaking back the Eternal Word to the Father. We thus have a "dialogue" between the Father and the soul, like the

165

co-bearing of the Son by the Father in the soul, and of the Son by the soul in the Father (Q, 258,13-32/Serm., 214). If the Father speaks in the soul, the soul can answer with the living Word itself (Q, 235,18-20/Serm., 168).

Now one finds a remarkably similar structure in Heidegger. For Heidegger, too, the transcendent event—of truth—comes to pass as a primordial language. And as with Eckhart, this language is nothing human. For Eckhart this language is the language of God; for Heidegger it is the language of Being. It is not man who speaks, he says, but "Language"—i.e., Being—itself (*die Sprache spricht*: US, 12/190). The speaking of language, Heidegger says,

> . . . is not anything human. But on the contrary, the human is indeed in its essence linguistic. The word "linguistic" as it is here used means: having taken place (*ereignet*) out of the speaking of language. What has thus taken place (*das so Ereignete*), the essential being of man, has been brought into its own (*Eigenes*) by language so that it remains given over or appropriated (*übereignet*) to the essential nature of language.
>
> (US, 30/207-8)

Language is nothing human; instead, man is something linguistic. Man is the modifier and adjective of language. Man is, to use Eckhart's expression, the "by-word" and adjective of language itself.

And as with Eckhart, Heidegger too characterizes man as the "respondent" or "correspondent" of the language of Being. "Originative thinking," Heidegger says, arises as "echo" of Being's address to us:

> This echo is the human answer (*Ant-wort*) to the word (*Wort*) of the soundless voice of Being. (WM, 49/358)

Meister Eckhart uses exactly the same metaphor of the "echo" to describe the dialectic and reciprocity between the Father bearing and speaking His word in the soul, and the soul responding to Him by speaking and bearing the Word, His Son:

> Out of this purity [of the eternal Godhead], He [God] has given birth to me as His only begotten Son in the likeness of His eternal Fatherhood, in order that I may be a Father and bear Him of Whom I am born. In the same way, if one stood before a high mountain and called out, "are you there?" the echo would answer "are you there?" If you said "come out," the echo would also say "come out." (Q, 258,19-25/Serm., 214)

Man comes to be man by responding to the address which Being makes to Him. Man is a response to the address of Being, an echo of its primal voice, even as the Word spoken in the soul is the echo of the Father's voice.

Like Eckhart, Heidegger too insists that the primal language can only be heard in silence. Too many words drown out what is being said. Thus Heidegger says that the speaking of language is "the peal of stillness" (*das Geläut der Stille*: US, 30/207). The voice of Being is quiet, and so it can only be heard in quiet. The more words, the less likely it is we shall hear Being's address. The only possibility of a "response" (*Entsprechen*) to the silent peal of Being lies in keeping silent (US, 262/131). Thus speaking, having something "to say" (*sagen*), depends upon our ability to listen and hear:

> We do not only speak *the* language, we speak *out of* it. But we are able to do this solely because we have already always heard language. What do we hear there? We hear the speaking of language. (US, 254/124)

And we listen to the speaking of language, Heidegger adds, by "letting something be said to us" (US, 255/124). We thus come back to the same point which Eckhart makes: true language consists in a response to the Word which the Father addresses to us, and this response consists in letting the Father speak His Word *in* us. And in both cases, letting something be said in us is possible only on the ground of silence. The silence, we should add, of which Eckhart and Heidegger speak, is not merely the cessation of spoken words, but also the cutting off of all images, concepts, and representations.

Heidegger and Eckhart are deeply conscious of the language they speak as they speak it. Both are, e.g., great innovators in the use of the German language. Eckhart is a "preacher" of the "word." He is also a commentator on and expositor of the Sacred Scriptures, which are for him the words of God. Now we have seen above, in our introductory remarks on SG, that there is an analogue to the Scriptures for Heidegger in the great writings in the history of metaphysics. Both Eckhart and Heidegger have their "texts"—texts which for one express the words of God, and for the other, the words of Being. It is therefore fitting and important to compare the "hermeneutics" which each employs. "Hermeneutics" means here the method by which one is to read the "message" (*Hermes*) of God—or Being—which is contained in the text. Eckhart writes:

167

Words have great power (*grosse Kraft*); one can work wonders with words. All words have power from the first Word.

(Q, 235, 29-31/Serm., 169)

For Heidegger, too, the words of metaphysicians have "great power" (*grosse Macht*)—the words of Leibniz, e.g., that nothing is without reason. And like Eckhart, Heidegger attributes the great power of words to the "first Word," to Being itself. For the great power of Leibniz's saying (*Spruch*) is the decree (*Spruch*) under which we today all exist to obey the demand (*Anspruch*) to render a sufficient reason. In the *ratio reddenda* the power of Being itself lays claim to us. Both Heidegger and Eckhart, then, have developed a way to "listen" to what is really being said in a text. Let us compare their methods of "interpretation."

The Holy Scripture, Eckhart says, is like the sea; it has various depths. He cites a saying of St. Gregory in this regard: where the lamb sinks, the cow swims; where the cow swims, the elephant runs, for the water is only up to his neck. To this Eckhart adds an analogy of his own: one man goes in to his ankles, a second to his knees, a third to his waist, and a fourth goes in over his head and sinks (Q, 262, 31-3/Ev., 257). Eckhart means to say that in the Scriptures as in the sea there is a proper depth for every man. A child can learn from the Scriptures and be captivated by its stories. A simple man can learn the basic principles of morality that shape his life. But for the learned man, the Scripture is so full of meaning, so rich and complex, that he can never touch bottom, although he studies it for a lifetime. There is always a meaning to the Scripture which is concealed from him; there is always a further sense beyond the one he has discovered:

. . . no one is so wise that if he wished to probe it, he does not find something more and deeper in it. Everything which we are able to hear on earth and everything which can be said to us has within it a further, concealed sense. (Q, 263,4-8/Ev., 257)

This is true not only of the Scriptures, Eckhart adds, but of everything created. Thus Eckhart can say of the Scriptures what he says of all creation:

The shell must be broken and what is contained in it must come out; for if you want the kernel, you must break the shell.

(Q, 265,3-5/Ev., 259; cf. Q, 218,17-20/Serm., 237)

168

All created things, and all the Scriptures, are for Eckhart, a vast "book" which has been authored by God. They are all the offspring of the Father, His Image, His Son, His Word. Thus the task of the one who reads the Scriptures is to break through the shell of the words to the meaning which they conceal, and so to find the Father "in the kernel of His Fatherhood" (Q, 264,7-8/Ev., 258).

Eckhart's "hermeneutics" then consists in breaking up outer and superficial meanings in order to let the concealed, hidden meanings come forth. When we have discovered the hidden meaning we will have found the way to the Father, Who is expressing Himself in all things. This is what is at the basis of the "mystical" interpretation—the "mystical hermeneutics," if you will—which Eckhart employs on the sacred texts. Let us briefly illustrate this. In the sermon based upon Matthew 21:12, "Jesus entered into the temple and began to cast out those who bought and sold" (Q, 153 ff.), Eckhart makes the following interpretation. The "temple" is the soul. Jesus casts out the money-changers because he wants the soul to be empty so that He Himself may dwell there. The money-changers are those who do good deeds, but for the sake of a reward, the Kingdom of God; they are those who live with a "why." The temple cleared of money-changers refers to the soul which lives freely, without why. In the cleared, empty temple, Jesus can enter, that means, the Father can bear His Son in the detached heart.

This interpretation clearly has nothing to do with biblical scholarship —nor is it merely "symbolical." For the Scripture has many meanings of which only one is the "literal" meaning. What Eckhart "hears" in the Scripture is there for those who have the ears to hear. Eckhart reads the Scriptures "out of an experience" (*aus der Erfahrung*) of the divine birth. The Scripture must be read, Eckhart says, in the spirit in which it is written, i.e., the Holy Spirit:

> Consequently, one work—a gloss—very rightly says that no one can teach
> or understand St. Paul's writings, unless he has the spirit in which St. Paul
> spoke and wrote. (Q, 124,28-31/Cl., 133)

Those who read the Scriptures in the Spirit "hear" in them the address of the Father, inviting the soul to be divested of self in order to make ready a place for the birth of the Son. That is what is always and everywhere being said, in one way or another, in the Scriptures. If a man comes to the Scriptures without the Spirit, that is, without the experience of the birth of the Son, then he will understand them

169

only in the most superficial way, and their deepest meaning will remain "hidden" and "concealed" from him.

All of this bears an interesting analogy to Heidegger's method of reading the writings of the great thinkers in the Western tradition. For Heidegger, too, wants to break up the shell to get to the kernel, i.e., to effect a "destruction," a shaking loose, of Western philosophy in order to gain an access to what is really being said in and by it. For Heidegger, too, the deepest meaning of a text is "concealed" within it, for what a text really has to say is "unspoken" in it (US, 253/122). The task of thought is to bring what is unspoken into words, to let it be spoken out. Moreover, with Heidegger, one can approach the history of metaphysics only "out of an experience" of Being. There is always and only one thing being said throughout the history of metaphysics, and that is the address of Being to thought, the call (*Heissen*) of Being to man to take up thought. And as with Eckhart, this address makes itself heard only to those who have the "spirit," i.e., the experience of Being. Thus as Eckhart's reading of the Scriptures has little to do with biblical scholarship, so Heidegger's reading of the history of philosophy is out of accord with the results of traditional philosophical scholarship. There is all the difference, Heidegger says, between the matter of thought and an object of scholarship (AED, 9/5). That is why Eckhart's and Heidegger's interpretations of their texts appear so outrageous to the rest of us. Eckhart's reading of Matthew is as scandalous as Heidegger's reading of Leibniz. This is because Eckhart and Heidegger are listening to another voice in these words; they hear a primal address which can be heard only in silence and detachment. All words for them speak with the power of the first word (*Wort*).

We cannot, however, leave the question of the kinship between Heidegger and Eckhart on the essence of language without mentioning the criticism which Heidegger makes of the "theological" interpretation of language:

> As against the identification of speech as a merely human performance, others stress that the word of language is of divine origin. According to the opening of the Prologue of the Gospel of St. John, in the beginning the Word was with God. (US, 14-5/192-3)

Heidegger may or may not have had Eckhart in mind when he wrote these words, but he certainly has described Eckhart's interpretation of language. It is precisely this text from St. John which Eckhart invokes to support his view of language—indeed his *Commentary on the Gospel of St. John* begins with a lengthy exegesis of just these words (LW, III, 3-44/Cl., 231-57). But what does Heidegger find to criticize in a theory which apparently resembles his own? For Heidegger, the theological interpretation of language is inherently metaphysical and so remains within the traditional conception of language, despite the fact that it attributes a transcendent origin to language. For theology understands language as "expression" (*Ausdruck*). Theology makes the distinction between the inner (conceptual) meaning and the outer (verbal) expression of the meaning. The word is the way the "ideal" meaning enters the "real" world (FS, 232). The main difference between the theological and the traditional metaphysical interpretation of language is that theology refers every "concept" to the "first concept," the One Who is "conceived" of the Father, the "Word" of the Father. Like the tradition, theology maintains that the truest word is the *verbum mentis*, the mental word (the meaning); but unlike the tradition, it holds that every inner word is but an imperfect expression of the Uncreated Word itself, in which all things are understood with simplicity and perfection. Theology thus subscribes to the "meta-physical" distinction between the inner and the outer, the ideal and the real, the supersensible and the sensible. That is why, Heidegger says (US, 15/193), theology stresses the "symbolic" character of language. For theology, language speaks of sensible things which are taken to be symbolic of the super-sensible.

Heidegger on the other hand has rejected this entire metaphysical framework within which language is usually understood. For him, words are not signs of things, nor concepts signs of words (US, 143 ff./45 ff.). On the contrary, the thing first comes to "be," i.e., to "appear," only through language (US, 193-4/87-8) and when there is no word, there is no thing. Language lets things be; it is the "condition" (*Be-ding-ung*) of the "thing" (*Ding*) (US, 232-3/151). As Stefan George writes:

So I renounced and sadly see:
Where word breaks off no thing may be. (US, 220/140)

Now what is important for Heidegger in George's poem is that the poet, having experienced this limitation of language, does not lapse into silence. He writes a poem instead:

171

> . . . this renunciation is a genuine renunciation, not just a rejection of saying, not a mere lapse into silence. As self-denial, renunciation remains saying. It thus preserves the relation to the word. (US, 228/147)

For Heidegger, language is the house—the boundary—of Being. Only within language can Being dwell. As for Wittgenstein, language is the limit of the world. Heidegger does not call for utter silence, but for a *new* language—one tempered by silence and originating from silence. While Eckhart praises a genuinely mystical silence, Heidegger praises the singing of the poet who has, in his view, overcome the extreme rationalism of technological language, on the one hand, and the superficiality of ordinary language on the other. While Eckhart is a classic representative of the *theologia negativa*, Heidegger is a thinker who thinks in the neighborhood of the poets.[10]

To the extent that Eckhart does subscribe to the metaphysical distinction between inner meaning and outer concept and advocates an absolute mystical silence, Heidegger's critique of Eckhart is on target and, indeed, is of the utmost importance for our interpretation of the relationship between "thought" and "mysticism." Hence we will have occasion to return to it in Chapter Five. Still, we must not overlook or underestimate the profound and striking analogy between their respective views of language and between the "hermeneutics" which they each employ.

I wish to conclude this discussion of the analogy between the event of truth in Heidegger and the birth of the Son in Eckhart with the following qualification. While we have been able to construct an analogy of Heidegger to Eckhart's teaching on the birth of the Son, we must not forget that the birth of the Son was not the only formulation which Eckhart gave to the mystical union. We have also seen that Eckhart expresses the unity of the soul with God in terms of the naked unity of the ground of the soul with the ground of God. Here there is no giving birth, no making of an "image," no speaking of the Father's original word, in short, none of those very elements in Eckhart's teachings with which we have been able to compare the relationship of Being and man in Heidegger. The fact is that there is nothing in Heidegger to compare to that dark mystical night in which the ground of the soul and the ground of God merge, no "identity" so naked and undifferentiated.

Heidegger discusses the question of the "identity" of Being with thought in his interpretation of the metaphysical "Principle of Identity" (ID, 85 ff./23 ff.). We recall that at the very beginning of this lecture he rejects the notion that identity means the empty unity of a thing with itself, the logician's A=A. Yet that formula is not nearly so inappropriate to Meister Eckhart who wished to stress the complete union which exists between the ground of the soul and the ground of God. Indeed Meister Eckhart argued that the soul is "one [with God] and not united" (*unum et non unitam*: Théry, 223/Bl., 288). He stressed an identity not unlike the logical unity expressed by the formula A=A. Heidegger on the other hand reinterprets identity to mean "belonging together" and he understands this belonging together to be a process by which man assists Being into its own and Being brings man into his own. "Being and man are appropriated (*übereignet*) to each other" (ID, 95/31). They do not sink into a motionless unity but each brings the other into its own. This unity of Being and thought is not "still" but rather vibrates with the movements of the mission of Being (*Seinsgeschick*). It is not absolutely silent, but rather brings language itself into words. It is not a union which takes place in an eternal now; rather it is an historical coming to pass. Eckhart's expressions concerning the unity of God and the soul are more uncompromising. They point to a different kind of unity than do Heidegger's formulations, more to an identity than a belonging together. And that is only as it should be, for the *Sache* in Heidegger and in Eckhart differ even as they are akin.

5. *Letting-be (Gelassenheit)*

We have discussed above the sense in which the birth of the Son is in some way the work, or better the "co-work," of the soul itself. For this birth cannot take place without the soul's "*fiat.*" By means of this *fiat* the soul becomes so thoroughly "one" with God that its work and God's work are one work; what God does the soul does. Now the *fiat* of the soul consists in the detachment (*Abgeschiedenheit*) and letting-be (*Gelassenheit*) by which it "lets" God come into the soul and become the source of its life. All of this has its parallel in Heidegger's later writings. For in Heidegger too the self-disclosure of Being is the "work" of Being. Thus in "The Reversal," Heidegger says that the essence of "technology" (*Technik*), because it is Being itself, is beyond the control of human action:

If the essential being of technology—the *Gestell* as the danger within Being—is Being itself, then technology can never be mastered, neither

173

positively nor negatively, through a merely self-dependent human action. Technology, whose essential being is Being itself, can never be overcome by man. This would mean that man would be the lord of Being.

(K, 38/5-6)

Still, the "work" of Being cannot be accomplished without the "co-operation" (*Mithilfe*) of man:

> But because Being has sent itself into *Gestell* as the essential being of technology, because the essential being of man belongs to the essence of Being, insofar as the essence of Being needs and uses the essential being of man in order to remain *preserved* as Being according to its own essence in the midst of beings and so to be as Being, because of all of this, the essential being of technology cannot be led into a transformation of its mission without the cooperation of man. (K, 38/6)

The "great being" of man lies in his cooperation with Being in bringing Being into its truth. Dasein cooperates with Being by "letting Being be." This is Dasein's *fiat*. The proximity of Heidegger to Eckhart and the mystical tradition is so great at this point that Heidegger can find no better word to express the relation of Dasein to Being than Meister Eckhart's own term: *Gelassenheit*.[11]

"If only I possessed already the right releasement (*Gelassenheit*)," says the "Teacher" in the *Discourse on Thinking* (*Gelassenheit*), then I would be free of the will (G, 34/60). But we must not set ourselves the "work" of "awakening" releasement. We can only "stay awake for" *Gelassenheit* and "let" it come to us. For every vestige of "willing" must be removed from releasement:

> *Scholar*: Especially so because even releasement can still be thought of as within the domain of will, as is the case with old masters of thought such as Meister Eckhart.
> *Teacher*: From whom, all the same, much can be learned.
> *Scholar*: Certainly; but what we have called releasement evidently does not mean casting off sinful self-seeking and getting rid of self-will in favor of the divine will. (G, 35-7/61-2)

Thus Heidegger's acknowledgment of the source of this idea in Meister Eckhart is couched in the form of a criticism of Eckhart. Eckhart thought of releasement in terms of the will, according to Heidegger. This is so because Eckhart was concerned with uprooting

174

"self-love" (*Eigenliebe*) and "self-will" (*Eigenwille*: Q, 55,22), which are primarily moral or ethical defects. Thus Heidegger does not want to think of *Gelassenheit* within the realm of "morality"—but in the realm of "thought":

> *Scholar*: So now, if I understand correctly, we are to view what we call releasement in connection with the nature of thought. . . .
>
> (G, 38/63)

Heidegger is not interested in overcoming self-love, but what he calls "subject-ism" (*Subjectität*: Hw, 236). The perversion is not "sinful self-seeking" but setting up the thinking "subject" as the highest principle of Being, and subordinating everything to the dictates and demands of the subject. This inversion of the truth, as we have seen from our analysis of SG, is the essential mission of Being in the modern age. It begins with the "discovery" of the *ego cogito* by Descartes and is consummated by the absolutizing of the ego in Hegel. That is why Heidegger refuses to consent to the practice, found principally in some German historians of philosophy, to begin the history of modern philosophy with Eckhart instead of Descartes (FND, 76/98). For Eckhart's position is not subjectivistic; he subordinates the self to God, both in his epistemology and in his sermons. Subjectivism inverts the essence of man (N II, 366), for it refuses to acknowledge the priority of Being and sets up in its place the priority of man. This whole phenomenon of "subject-ism" bears a striking analogy to the religious phenomenon of "pride," in which the creature (the self) sets itself before the Creator (God).

For Heidegger, *Gelassenheit* is not merely a matter of overcoming "self-will," but "willing" in the broadest sense, where willing includes "representational" thinking:

> But thinking, understood in the traditional way, as re-presenting is a kind of willing; Kant, too, understands thinking this way when he characterizes it as spontaneity. To think is to will, and to will is to think. (G, 31-2/58-9)

Heidegger is obviously not talking about the self-will of a "sinful" man, but what he describes does have the same ring of a perverted self-importance. Descartes, Leibniz, and Kant belong within the tradition of subjectivism, in which Being is made an "object" for the thinking subject. Being is expected to conform to the principles (*Grundsätze, Prinzipien, principia*) which are laid down as "self-evident" rules by the *ego cogito*, or as necessary forms of synthesis by transcendental consciousness. The history of metaphysics is a history of rational prescriptions about what Being must be—*eidos*, *ousia*, *Gegenstand*, *Geist*, etc. (ID, 64/66). But for Heidegger, Being is the overpowering (*das Überwaltigende*: EM, 115/126), and it does not obey Leibniz's demand for the *ratio reddenda*. For Heidegger, Being lies forth on its own grounds, outside the "sphere of influence" of metaphysical reason. Man is not the lord of Being (K, 38/6) but a "mortal," cast forth by the "throw" of Being (HB, 84/207; 90/210).

The religious man has always warned of the dangers of unbridled rationalism and regarded the absolutization of reason as the death of faith. Heidegger too shares in this attitude, in his own way and for different reasons. He too advises us that man's true "worth" (*Würde*: HB, 90/210) lies in poverty and humility. He sees in reason something analogous to pride, an obstinate self-sufficiency, a willfulness, a desire to impose its own categories on things. Like the religious man who warns against undue intellectualization, and who praises simple and unlearned men who are pure of heart, Heidegger too praises the simple and the rural. He would make of man the "shepherd of Being" (*der Hirt des Seins*: HB, 75/203) and in no sense a lord, neither of beings (HB, 90/210) nor of Being (K, 38/6). The poverty of Dasein is that it has no power of disposal over Being, that it depends upon the gifts and favor of being. Its true worth lies in guarding and watching over Being, like the shepherd of the night. The fault of the metaphysician is like "false pride." In false pride, a man pretends to be what he is not and so overlooks what he is. In metaphysics, man is exalted as the master of the earth while his true dignity in the service of Being is ignored (HB, 66/199).

Let us now examine the comparative structure of "*Gelassenheit*" in Meister Eckhart and Heidegger. Like Eckhart, Heidegger says that "letting be" is a non-willing, and just like Eckhart he grapples with the ambiguity of this expression. Eckhart writes:

> . . . so long as a man has it in himself that it is his *will* to fulfill the most beloved will of God, then such a man does not have the poverty of which I speak; for this man still has a will, with which he wishes to satisfy God's will. . . . (Q, 304,22-7/Bl., 208)

The man who has reached the highest stage of *Gelassenheit*, for Eckhart, does not *will* God's will, or *will* to have no will. He is simply will-less; he lives outside the sphere of willing altogether. Heidegger too is aware of the ambiguity of "not-willing":

> *Scholar:* Non-willing, for one thing, means a willing in such a way as to involve a negation, be it even in the sense of a negation which is directed at willing and renounces it. Non-willing means, therefore: willingly to renounce willing. And the term non-willing means, further, what remains absolutely outside any kind of will. (G, 32/59)

In the beginning of the conversation Heidegger seems to favor the first sense of non-willing—willing to not will (*willentlich dem Wollen absagen*). But then he adds that it is "by means of" this first sense (*durch dieses*) that we will attain to the "thinking which is not a willing" (G, 33/59-60). Still later in the conversation he says, speaking of "relinquishing" transcendental-representational thought:

> Such relinquishing no longer stems from a willing, except that the occasion for releasing oneself to belonging to that which regions requires a trace of willing. This trace, however, vanishes while releasing oneself and is completely extinguished in releasement. (G, 59/79-80)

Thus it turns out that Heidegger's view is structurally very like Eckhart's: in true *Gelassenheit* every trace of willing has been extinguished; it is not even a will to not-will. In Heidegger, willing to not will is a preparation for the final stage of releasement where we have left the sphere of willing behind altogether, where man, as with Eckhart, has no will at all.[12]

Moreover, Heidegger, like Eckhart, distinguishes a negative and a positive mode of releasement. The negative moment in Eckhart consists in being detached from creatures; the soul abandons or relinquishes its own will and desires. So too Heidegger speaks of the necessity of "being loosened" (*Losgelassensein*: G, 51/73) from beings and the thinking which "represents" beings within the horizon projected by transcendental subjectivity. Thus, as Eckhart said in *On Detachment* that the soul must be "empty of creatures" (DW, V, 542/Cl., 164), Heidegger says we must be "loosened" from transcendental-horizonal thinking. We should of course also recall Heidegger's own talk about "detachment from beings" (*Abschied vom Seienden*: WM, 49/359) which we discussed in the first chapter. We might add here that in German "*die Abgeschiedenen*" refers to those who

177

have "departed" this world (the dead). Thus there is an overtone in this phrase of a mystical death by which Dasein dies to beings and the thinking which is concerned with beings. This first moment of *Gelassenheit* is a negative, "ascetic" one. The asceticism consists in the discipline by which Dasein seeks to free itself from concern with beings.

It is in connection with the "ascetic" overtones of *Gelassenheit* that we may understand Heidegger's frequent insistence that thinking is not arbitrary but, in keeping with Husserl's determination of the nature of phenomenology, something "strict." It does not have the "exactness" of mathematics, nor is it, as Husserl himself demanded, a strict "science." But it does adhere to a rigorous "discipline," for it must resist the temptation to explain Being in terms of "reasons," to produce a "highest being" and a "first cause." The strictness of thought is its ability to let Being be, the great restraint by which it is able to remain "without why." Strict thinking stays within the element of Being itself (HB, 56/194). That is why Heidegger so frequently describes thinking in ascetic terms. He refers to it as "persevering meditation" (*ausdauernde Besinnung*: G, 15/49; cf. ID, 47/51). The thinker must have perseverance, the ability to stay with Being as Being, however much he may be tempted to give it a metaphysical explanation. He must also have a "readiness for anxiety," comparable to the mystic's readiness to endure disconsolation and the "dark night of the soul." This readiness for anxiety Heidegger calls "insistence" or "persistence" (*Inständigkeit*: G, 62/81-2; WM, 15/214; WM, 46/355), the "virtue" which is required of Dasein by the fact that Being is dark and eludes the familiar categories of rational thought. And towards the beginning of the "Memorial Address" Heidegger tells us that thought demands "higher effort" (*höhere Anstrengung*), "more practice" (*längere Einübung*) and "more delicate care" (*noch feinere Sorgfalt*) than calculative reason (G, 15/47), which is very much like what a spiritual director would tell the initiates in a Christian—or Buddhist—monastery about the nature of "meditation."

The first moment of *Gelassenheit* faces beings, cutting itself off from them. It is a negative "being loosened from" which is described in active, ascetic tones. Thus it corresponds with the will to not will. The second moment of *Gelassenheit* is turned towards Being itself. It is a positive being free for, being open to, Being (G, 25-6/54-5). This second moment attains the perfection of *Gelassenheit*, for it is entirely outside the sphere of willing, where every "trace" of willing has been eliminated in favor of a simple openness which "lets Being be" (HB, 111/220). This moment corresponds to the affirmative moment of *Gelassenheit* in Meister Eckhart, in which Eckhart spoke not of being "empty of creatures" but "full of God," not of being detached from self-will but of "letting God be God" (Q, 180,34). Heidegger writes:

> This being released from is the first part of releasement; yet that does not hit its nature exactly, let alone exhaust it. (G, 51/73)

Releasement should not be defined only negatively in terms of what it is released from, but "affirmatively" in terms of that to which it is released and by which it is held in the relation of releasement:

> If genuine releasement is to be the proper relation to that-which-regions (*Gegnet*), and if this relation is determined solely by what it is related to, then genuine releasement must be based upon that-which-regions, and must have received from it movement toward it. (G, 51/73)

Dasein is held in releasement to Being by Being itself. This affirmative mode of pure openness to Being is also described by Heidegger with another term which he borrows from the religious-mystical tradition, "ectasy," understood by him in its fundamental root meaning: *ek-stasis*. Dasein's existence, he says, is ek-static, i.e., it is a standing out in (*aus-stehen*) the truth of Being, a standing open to the Open itself (WM, 15/214). Dasein's relation to Being is ecstatic, even as the soul in *On Detachment* is rapt in ecstasy before God.

We are now in a position to reflect further on Heidegger's observation that Eckhart's idea of releasement remains within the sphere of willing. It is perfectly obvious that if Heidegger means that Eckhart regarded *Gelassenheit* as a *will* to not will, then Heidegger is quite mistaken. For the radical will-lessness of the "released" man is a point upon which they both insist. What Heidegger appears to mean is that for Eckhart *Gelassenheit* is an ethico-religious term, whereas Heidegger uses it to refer to the realm of "thought." But Heidegger is mistaken about this. For Eckhart demanded of the detached soul not only the suspension of its "will" (desires) in the restricted sense, but also the suspension of all "willing" in the broad sense in which Heidegger uses it. For Eckhart demanded that the soul cast off all talk, both inner and outer, all concepts, all images, and all representations, in order to have an "empty temple" into which God could come.

179

When this is achieved, then the soul is privy to an insight into the "unconcealed" (Q, 166,18/Serm., 154) Godhead itself: it attains not the God of thought and representations but the "divine" God, God in His true Being (Q, 60,20-6/Cl., 69-70):

> This power [the ground of the soul] receives God wholly denuded in His essential Being. (Q, 221,14-5/Serm., 240)

Thus Meister Eckhart's *Gelassenheit* has to do not only with eradicating moral defects, but with emptying out all "representations" in order to experience God in his naked Being.

Eckhart thinks of *"Gelassenheit"* as a way to enter into the unconcealed abyss of the Godhead, as a way to be admitted into the being of things prior to their being created. In releasement we see the rose as it has been from all eternity and before it was created; we see the rose in its true being. The detached man in Meister Eckhart is not simply to be understood as one who has divested himself of all self-love, but also as one who, like Martha, is at home in the world of things, who has a new relationship to creatures, who understands them for what they are, who lets them be. "Gelassenheit" in Meister Eckhart is not to be confined within the sphere of morality. It does, to be sure, presuppose moral self-purification. That is obvious from our reading of the treatise *On Detachment* in the first chapter, where Eckhart argued that detachment is the perfection and flowering of all the virtues. It includes all the virtues as a base but it itself is a blossoming into something richer and deeper than moral purity.

Heidegger's critique of Meister Eckhart, I believe, is based on a misunderstanding of Eckhart's views. It suggests that for Eckhart *Gelassenheit* means only willing to not will, that it means passivity, that it is an ethical and moral category. Yet in the sermon on poverty which we discussed above Eckhart does not contrast the detached and poor in spirit with those who are "sinful and self-seeking," but rather with **"good people"** who keep God's commandments. Eckhart wants to go beyond both good and evil, that is, both good wills and bad wills, in order to enter the realm of will-less unknowing in which God's ground and my ground are the same.

However, in his critique of Meister Eckhart in the *Discourse on Thinking*, Heidegger suggests that there are two reasons for thinking that *"Gelassenheit"* in Meister Eckhart remains confined within the sphere of willing. The first, which we have already examined, is that for Eckhart *"Gelassenheit"* is wholly concerned with getting rid of self-

180

seeking. But the second is that, having overcome self-will, "*Gelassenheit*" means giving oneself over to the "divine will." Once again what Heidegger says is not exactly so.

If we understand the distinction between God and Godhead, then the completely detached soul does not reach God as possessed of a will. That belongs to "God," to the creator, to the first cause of metaphysics. The detached soul unites with the ground of God, with a nameless and will-less divine abyss, even as the soul in its ground is nameless and will-less. The faculty of the soul called the will is directed to the will of God. But the soul in its ground unites with God in His ground, that is, prior to any dimension of God's being which can be named "divine will." But Heidegger's remark does bring out the fact that in Eckhart the soul is released to a being of infinite goodness, of perfect love and of boundless care for His creation. Whether one calls this "God" or "Godhead," the "divine will" or the divine "abyss," still as Meister Eckhart says, there is nothing to fear in God; God is only to be loved (Q, 100, 21-3/Cl., 108). For Eckhart, God is a loving Father who engenders His only begotten Son in our hearts. On this issue the work of Eckhart and Heidegger reach an extreme point of divergence. This is a matter of great importance for the present study, and one which we shall develop at length in the next chapter. For we shall see that there is all the difference in the world between being released to the event of Being and being released to Eckhart's God.

There is one last point to be made in connection with the notion of *Gelassenheit* in Heidegger and Eckhart. Eckhart, we noted above, unwittingly fathered a long tradition of God's "need" of man in German thought. Now the relation of Dasein to Being which Heidegger expresses in the word "*brauchen*" seems to stand in the shadows of that tradition. Ordinarily, "*brauchen*" means "to need" or "to use." But for Heidegger it does not precisely signify either of these. Being does not "use" Dasein insofar as this implies "utilizing" (*Benützen*: WHD, 114/187). To "utilize" something is to subordinate it to the user, to make of it a mere instrument, like the hammer. Dasein is no "tool" for the "cunning" of Being. Nor should we think "*brauchen*" in terms of "needing." For it is not appropriate to imagine that Being—Truth itself—is dependent upon man (G, 65-6/84). This is to fall back into the error of Cartesian subjectivism. Nor is Being's relationship to Dasein one of "necessitating" (*Benötigen*: WHD, 115) it, for the "sacrifice" of Dasein to Being must be free (WM, 49/358), just as Mary's "*fiat*" was free.

181

If Being does not utilize or need or necessitate Dasein just what does "*brauchen*" mean? Heidegger answers:

> . . . only proper use (*Brauchen*) brings what is used into its essence (*Wesen*) and holds it there. . . . To use something is to let it enter into its essence, to preserve it in its essence.   (WHD, 114/187)

"*Brauchen*" must be understood in the light of the fact that Being and Dasein belong together, that each complements and provides the proper element for the other. Each "helps" (*hilft*: WM, 50/359) the other into the fullness of its being (*Wesen*). Without Dasein there is no clearing in which the Event of Truth may occur. Yet Dasein does not determine how the Event will come out, which is the sense in which Truth is not dependent upon Dasein. "*Brauchen*" means something like "assisting" or "helping," rather the way God and the soul "help" and preserve one another in *The Cherubinic Wanderer*. Scheffler writes:

One Sustains the Other

> God is as important to me as I am to Him;
> I help (*helf*) Him in His Being, as He protects (*hegen*) mine.   (CW, I, 100)

Heidegger writes:

> Thought is attentive to the truth of Being and so helps (*hilft*) the Being of truth make a place for itself in man's history.   (WM, 50/359)

> Thinking is the genuine doing (*Handeln*), if doing means: to be of assistance to the essential nature of Being (*dem Wesen des Seins an die Hand gehen*).

There is between Being and Dasein, as between God and the soul in *The Cherubinic Wanderer*, the same reciprocity, the same mutual "appropriating" (*ver-eignen*) by which each is assisted into its own essential being. That is why Heidegger says that "*Es brauchet*" is to be thought in conjunction with "*Es gibt*." The "It" which "gives" is the same as the "It" which "uses," and the It which gives is the Event itself. But the Event comes to pass as an appropriation process: it "bestows" upon Dasein its proper essence and, in so doing, the Event too comes about in a manner which is "appropriate" to itself. This mutual self-appropriating is the giving of the "It gives" and the

182

using of "It uses." And while this position is not Eckhart's, it belongs to a philosophical and mystical tradition of which Eckhart is, willingly or not, the forefather.

We say that this position is not Eckhart's for the reasons which we gave above, in the previous chapter, when we discussed those formulations in Eckhart's sermons which do mention a kind of necessity that God is under to bear His Son in the soul. There we saw that Eckhart had in mind only the necessity of love, the necessity that God will rejoin love with love, for God Himself is love. The difference between Heidegger and Eckhart on this point is interesting. Eckhart's conception of God is ultimately orthodox, and he has not the slightest notion that there is an insufficiency and incompleteness about God which needs to be filled up by His extending His divine life to creatures. But in Heidegger, Being as the process of presencing (*An-wesen*), as the process of "emergence" into presence (*physis*), does require a place in which and for which this process can emerge. Being as emergence into presence requires a correlative letting-be on the part of Dasein. Presencing (*An-wesen*) requires letting-be-present (*An-wesen-lassen*); presencing needs the openness of a clearing in which it may be what it is (ID, 95/31). Being and man in Heidegger belong together in a different way than do God and the soul for Eckhart, for Eckhart's God does not ultimately depend upon man for His self-revelation. It is true that Eckhart tends to portray God as needing man to disclose himself to, that he tends to say that the soul is a necessary complement of the Trinitarian life. But when the Inquisition pressed him on this point he allowed that these were "emphatic" expressions which did not imply a dependency of being in God. For Heidegger, on the other hand, Being's need of a clearing is more radical than that.

6. *Being and beings*

The last theme which we have singled out for comparison is the relationship between Being and beings in Heidegger and between God and creatures in Meister Eckhart. Thus alongside the central analogy of proportionality—God : soul :: Being : Dasein—there exists another analogy which is nearly as important—God : creatures :: Being : beings.

It is important to state immediately the sense in which this analogy does *not* hold, in order to prevent misunderstanding the sense in which it does. For Heidegger, Being is always the Being *of* beings, and beings must always be taken *in* their Being (WG, 26-7). Being does not have an independent, separate reality. If it did, it would become "a being," the most real of all (*ens realissimum*) perhaps, the highest being, but a being nonetheless. The most interesting testimony to this is the famous alteration that Heidegger made in the text of *What Is Metaphysics?*, first pointed out by Max Mueller.[13] In the 1943 edition of *What Is Metaphysics?*, an "Epilogue" is added which contains the remark:

> . . . it belongs to the truth of Being that Being may *indeed* (*wohl*) "be" (*west*) without beings, (but) that a being never is without Being. (Emphasis ours)

But in the Fifth Edition, in which Heidegger adds an important "Prologue," the same sentence is modified as follows—without an acknowledgement of the change by the author:

> . . . it belongs to the truth of Being that Being may *never* (*nie*) "be" (*west*) with beings, that a being never is without Being. (Emphasis ours)
>
> (WM, 46)

The emendation, even if unacknowledged, is welcome and in accord with everything that Heidegger had previously said about the relationship between Being and beings. The original text, a very misleading statement which it is not surprising to see Heidegger correct, seems to have meant that the "initiative," as it were, belongs to Being in the process by which Being comes to pass in beings. Being comes to pass in beings, but how this takes place is entirely dependent upon the "advance" or "withdrawal" of Being itself. The corrected version makes it plain that it would be a mistake to "hypostatize" Being on that account, to allow it to subsist apart from beings.

But it is precisely such self-subsistence, on the other hand, which Eckhart attributes to God, Whom we have said can be considered a kind of an *ens separatissimum*. For Eckhart, God is a transcendent creator and first cause Who is above being, i.e., creation, and Who could well subsist without the creature from which He is absolutely distinct. Were the relationship of God to creatures in Eckhart assimilated to the relation of Being to beings in Heidegger, then the absolute transcendence of God would be destroyed and the Inquisition would have rightly charged Eckhart with heresy. Eckhart would see no need at all to emend the first version of Heidegger's "Epilogue"; for God can "indeed subsist" (*wohl west*) without creatures, though creatures cannot be without God.

However, Eckhart did lay the greatest emphasis upon the immanence of God within creatures, or better, of creatures within God. For God creates all things, not in order to have them "stand outside of Himself or alongside Himself or beyond Himself," but in order to have them "dwell in Himself" (LW, II, 161-2). In bringing a creature into being, he brings it into Himself, for "Being is God." What this amounts to, as we have seen, is not pantheism, but a doctrine of the radical dependency of all things upon God, which emphasizes that a creature "of itself" is nothing. Now this metaphysics has a most important bearing on Eckhart's mystical teachings. He stresses to the listeners of his sermons the necessity we are under to "find God in all things." He says that to the detached heart all creatures taste of God, while the worldly man savors nothing in creatures save something created (Q, 230,17-9/Serm.,150; 272,4-9/Serm., 183). This, we will show, is profoundly like Heidegger's own insistence that we find Being itself in beings and his critique of the thinking which understands beings—and nothing else.

Eckhart and Heidegger point to similar dangers. Eckhart warns us against the worldly spirit which takes creatures "in themselves," apart from God. Heidegger warns us not against worldiness, but against metaphysics:

> Insofar as it always represents beings as beings (*das Seiende als das Seiende*), metaphysics never thinks upon Being itself.   (WM, 8/207)

Metaphysical reason is concerned with "this or that," with beings and their causes. Instead of thinking Being as such, it is content to explain beings in terms of the highest being, or in terms of some common property of beings—substance, say, or will. Metaphysics is content with beings, the way the worldly heart is content with creatures. And as Eckhart warned that the desire for creatures was a desire for nothing (Q, 171,8-9), so Heidegger regards the present age, in which metaphysics has run its course to completion (SD, 61 ff./55 ff.), the age of technology (*Technik*), as a time of "nihilism." Nihilism, according to Heidegger, is the age in which Being has become a vapor, a vacuous abstraction (EM, 27-9/29-31), "nothing at all" (N I, 338). The phenomenon of "fallenness" described by the author of *Being and Time* has become in the later writings a matter of thinking what is given

185

while forgetting the "it" which "gives" (SD, 8/8), even as for Eckhart the worldly heart is "fallen," because it considers creatures to the neglect of their Creator.

But just as Eckhart does not recommend that the soul leave the world to find God, so Heidegger thinks it only "foolishness" to suggest that we do away with technology. We are not interested in "some kind of renaissance of presocratic philosophy," he says. This would be "idle and foolish" (WM, 11/210). Nor does he wish to relinquish the use of techological tools:

> The equipment, apparatus, and machines of the technological world are for all of us today indispensable, for some to a greater extent, for others to a lesser extent. It would be foolish to blindly assail the technological world. It would be shortsighted to wish to condemn the technological world as the work of the devil. (G, 24/53; cf. ID, 33/40; K, 24-5)

But neither does Heidegger make the by now familiar suggestion that it is not technology which is evil but the use to which it is put, that technology is "neutral" and that we must learn to master it, instead of letting it master us (K, 5). The essence of technology, which Heidegger calls the "frame" (*Ge-stell*), is not neutral because it is a "mission of Being" (*Seinsgeschick*) in which Being remains concealed. The "frame" is a name for the epoch of Being in which the illusion is perpetrated that Being is nothing more than a "store of energy" which awaits man's use (K, 26), and that logico-mathematical thinking is the uniquely valid kind of thought. This is nothing neutral but a concealment of Being. The real problem that technology presents, according to Heidegger, is the distortion it makes in the essence of truth and therefore in the essence of man (VA, 164/166); the problem is not with "machines and equipment." Now that is a point which parallels Meister Eckhart's observation on the soul which complains of all the obstacles which are being put in its way, all the people and places which are preventing its union with God:

> . . . you yourself are the very thing which hinders you. For you are related to things in a perverted way. (Q, 55,28-30/Cl., 65)

> With those with whom it goes well, in truth, it goes well with them in all places, and among all people. . . . But if someone does well, he has God in truth within him. But whoever has God in truth, has Him in all places, on the street and among people, as well as in church, or in a desert retreat or in his cell. (Q, 58,25-59,3/Cl., 68)

186

Eckhart's advice to the soul is not to leave the world but to change its attitude toward it. The soul should make a change in its "mind" (*Gemüt*) and "disposition" (*Gestimmtheit*) towards the world:

Man should seize God in *all* things and should accustom his mind to have God present at all times—in his mind, in his strivings, and in his loves. Attend to how you are turned towards your God, if you are in church or in the cell; hold this same disposition and sustain it among crowds and in unrest. . . . (Q, 59,21-6/Cl., 68-9)

We find analogous advice from Heidegger with respect to technology. There is no hope or value in trying to rid ourselves of technological equipment. The important thing is to adopt a new attitude towards it:

We are able to use technological objects and yet with suitable use keep ourselves so free of them that we are able to let go of them at any time. We are able to make use of technological objects as they ought to be used. But we are also able simultaneously to let them alone as something which does not concern what is innermost in us and proper to us. (G, 24/54)

The new attitude—which of course is "releasement"—says "yes" to the utilization of technological equipment, but "no" to the distortion it makes of the essence of truth. Because it views technology as a mission of Being, this attitude is alert to a truth which technology conceals: "The meaning of the technological world is concealed" (G, 26/55). But releasement stays open to this hidden meaning:

I call the posture in virtue of which we hold ourselves open for the concealed meaning of the technological world: openness towards the Mystery. (G, 26/55)

As the soul finds God in all peoples and places, so meditative thinking can find even in modern technology the traces of a pristine disclosure of the event of Truth. In Leibniz's principle of sufficient ground, thinking can find the ringing together of Being and ground. In the modern mission of Being as the *Gestell*, thought finds the possibility of another beginning, a new "world" (K, 42/10). In contemporary technology it can find the hint of a pristine *techne* (K, 34). This primal *techne* consists in a making which does not exploit nature but which brings it into its truth. Thus a Greek temple is nothing "technological" but a work in which "truth is set to work" (Hw, 30 ff./41 ff.). So too a painting by Van Gogh, or the "jug" described in "The Thing" are

187

products, but not technological products. They are the issue of a making which belongs together with true dwelling. They belong to a genuine "world" in which man is born, matures, and dies, in which he works and rests and prays, and in which he thereby discovers the sense of being human.

Hence, as the soul for Eckhart is at peace with the world and no longer disturbed by its dangers, so Dasein is reconciled with technology (G, 25/54), while it nourishes the hope of another day (K, 31) in which technology is assigned its proper place and is no longer taken to be "something absolute" (G, 25/54). Both Dasein and the soul will then have acquired the art of "breaking through" (Q, 61,19/Cl., 70; cf. FS, 348) beings in order to discover Being. For both Dasein and the soul, "things" take on a new luminosity which is concealed from those who are not "released." In *The Cherubinic Wanderer* Angelus Silesius writes:

The Rose

The rose that with mortal eye I see,
Flowers in God through all eternity.

(CW, I, 108/42)

Those who have an inner eye as well as outer eye can see eternity in the rose, i.e, they can see the divine beauty itself in the beauty of the created rose. For them, the rose is a "thing" which concealedly reveals the Being of God. So too in Heidegger, a painting by Van Gogh, the bridge at Heidelberg, a Greek temple, a jug, each is a "thing" which concealedly reveals the event of Truth, the playing together of the "four" which is, for Heidegger, the Truth of Being (K, 42 ff./10 ff.)

But once again even here we must introduce a qualification into the analogy which we have drawn. In Eckhart's teaching, all the fault is to be laid at the feet of man himself, of the "ego." It is wholly and solely because man looks upon things in the wrong way that things present an obstacle to him. There is nothing wrong with things or people or places; it is the way we look upon them which is at fault. The world which God "gives" us is resplendent with divine being and beauty. Every creature can, like the rose, be taken in its eternal being in the mind of God. It is man and man alone who is responsible for the God-lessness of the world. But in Heidegger matters stand differently. The technologization of the earth, the darkening in the essence of truth, the mistake about the nature of thought, all of these are errors which we did not commit, for which no man is to be held responsible. The ultimate technologization of man and earth is the "doing" of Being as the *Ge-stell*. The world is posited and framed (*gestellt*) for us as the realm of the manipulable, and we are ourselves posited as the masters of the earth, those who manipulate, calculate and accumulate (1D, 98-9/34-5). Who today has not felt the pull (*Zug*) of Being's withdrawal (*Entzug*) (SG, 143-7)? Accordingly, it will not be by man's efforts that this withdrawal will be reversed. The world of technical things will always present an obstacle to thought so long as Being continues to withdraw. And even if the thinker does learn to say yes and no to the technical world, still the world-night of the *Ge-stell* may persist indefinitely.

7.   *Heidegger, Eckhart, and the Rose*

Our essay on the relationship of Heidegger and Eckhart has thus brought us back to the point from which we embarked: Silesius's rose. And our charge now is to state as clearly as possible what Heidegger had in mind when he wrote in SG:

> What is unsaid in the saying, and everything depends on this, is rather that man, in the most hidden ground of his essence, first truly is, when he is in his own way like the rose, without why.   (SG, 72-3)

The rose of which Silesius writes is simultaneously the model for both God and the soul as these are portrayed by Meister Eckhart. In blossoming without why, the rose exemplifies the fullness and plentitude of the divine being (*plenitudo esse*), which stands in need of nothing outside itself. The rose also portrays the soul which "lets God be God," which lets God enter and become the internal source of its life. The soul acts out of the spontaneity of the God within it. And so, like God, the soul lives a "free and untrammelled" life—without why:

> God does not seek His own. He is free and untrammelled in all His works, and He works them out of genuine love. *That* man who is united with God does exactly the same thing. He also is free and untrammelled in all his works and works them solely for God's honor and does not seek his own; and God acts in him.   (Q, 154,27-32/Serm., 128)

Now Heidegger also sees a two-fold model in the rose. For the rose is the model both of Being and Dasein. The rose is, in the first place, the model for Being. Silesius says the rose blossoms "because" it blossoms. Upon this Heidegger comments:

> The "because" does not here, as it usually does, refer us on to something else which is not a blossoming and which should found the blossoming elsewhere. The "because" in the saying simply refers the blossoming back to itself. The blossoming is founded in itself, has its ground in and of itself. The blossoming is a pure emerging from out of itself (*Aufgehen aus ihm selbst*), pure shining. (SG, 101-2; cf. SG, 73)

But that which emerges from out of itself is what Heidegger means by Being. Being is *physis*, which means the power which emerges and endures (*aufgehend-verweilend-Walten*: EM, 23/24). The shining (*Scheinen*) of the rose is its beauty (*Schönheit*):

> Beauty is a highest way of Being, which means: pure emerging out of itself and shining. The oldest of the Greek thinkers said *physis*. . . .
>
> (SG, 102)

The rose lies forth of itself, resting on its own grounds, emerging of itself into unconcealment. It is in no way an object which has been shaped by the thinking subject.

Heidegger's language at this point reminds one of Eckhart's own talk of God's life in the text from the Latin writings which we cited above:

> Life means a certain overflow by which a thing, welling up within itself, first completely floods itself, each part of itself interpenetrating every other, before it pours itself out and spills over into something external.
>
> (LW, II, 22/Cl., 226)

God is a process of welling up from concealment into self-revelation —first into the Son and the Holy Ghost, then into creation itself. God emerges from the darkness of the "Godhead," the divine "desert," the "abyss" (*Abgrund*)—another word which is important for both thinkers—into the light of day, into "God" and creatures. God is an *arche* for the medieval mystic, not because He is a first cause of beings—although He is also that for the scholastic metaphysician—but because He is the ground upon which beings stand, the source from which they well up. Eckhart says that "*in principio*" means standing on the divine ground from which one emerges, rising up from one's origin (LW, II, 160-2; III, 63; Q, 348,4-9/Serm., 181). Heidegger's

190

physis and Eckhart's "life" (*vita, Leben*) thus are profoundly akin. Each is a process of rising up into presence, of emergence into unconcealment. Moreover, each is a "self-sufficient" process in the sense that each rises up *because* it rises up, needing no external justification. The rose is because it is; it needs no "rationale."

But the rose is also a model for Dasein itself, as it was also a model for the soul in Silesius's poem. Dasein must be without why, not in the sense of that which lies forth of itself (*das Vorliegende*), but in the sense of *letting* the being lie forth (*Vorliegen-lassen*). Dasein must suspend representational thinking in order to let Being arise, emerge, and stand forth. Otherwise Being becomes an object measured by the dimensions of the human subject. Why is there something rather than nothing? Because there "is," because the being emerges and stands forth on its own ground. It simply rises up into unconcealment without having to appear within a horizon which has first been established for it by "reason." The "why?" in the question of Being is submerged in "because."

Eckhart's life without why is a life of perfect love and perfect unity with God, which allows God to enter the soul and become its principle of life. Heidegger's life without why is the renunciation of concepts and representations, of propositions and ratiocinations about Being; it lets Being be Being. Both the soul and Dasein are "admitted" (*einlassen*) into a realm which lies outside the sphere of influence of Leibniz's principle, where rationales and justifications have no place. In this realm things are because they are. They are resplendent—self-resplendent—with their own grounds. Here no questions are asked because things rise up from out of themselves; they are their own "because." Here there is no giving or demanding of reasons. For reasons belong to the realm of the "why?"—the realm of "time" for Eckhart, and of beings and the sciences for Heidegger.

Living without why, Dasein is appropriated by Being as Being's own; it is claimed by Being as the place of the preservation of its truth; it is claimed by the "Region" (*Ver-gegnis*: G, 52/74). Living without why, Dasein admits Being into the "thing," allows Being to "condition" (*be-dingen*) the thing, so that the thing becomes transparent in its Being and the playing together of the four can be seen within it. Thus when Dasein is, like the rose, without why, Dasein is appropriated by the region (*Ver-gegnis*) and the thing is "conditioned" as a thing (*Be-Dingnis*: G, 55-6/76-7). Being, thing, and Dasein are all released into their "own" (*eigen*); all three attain their ownmost essential being (*Wesen*). All three—Being, thing, and Dasein—are, to use

191

Meister Eckhart's expression, *"ver-wesentlicht"* (Q, 62,2; Mhd. *gewesent*: DW, V, 208,12), which means "radicalized in their essence," "brought into their essential being." And Silesius's rose is the model of this three-fold process. "The rose is without why"—this means, all in one: Being emerges of itself and appropriates man and thing; a "thing"—this rose—becomes resplendent in its Being and rests on its own ground, allowing the "four" to "intersect" within it; and finally Dasein, dwelling among things, in the openness of Being, "first truly is, in the most hidden ground of its essence" (SG, 73).

It is of no small importance that the life "without why" plays an exactly analogous role in Meister Eckhart and Angelus Silesius. For in living without why, God, the created thing, and the soul—all three —enter likewise into their ownmost essential being (*Wesen*). "The rose is without why"—this means, all in one: God's Being is without why; it is a welling up and overflowing, a self-diffusion which pours itself out for the sheer sake of communicating itself to others. It means, too, that the created thing—this rose which we see with our outer eye—has become luminous and transparent with the divine being. And it means, finally, that the soul lives with the life of God, with His free and untrammelled Being, which is now the soul's "own," and it finds God in all things.

The poet's words are incomprehensibly rich and mean the deepest things for both thinker and mystic. No wonder Heidegger says of it:

> The whole saying is so astonishingly clearly and tightly constructed that one might come to the idea that the most extreme sharpness and depth of thought belong to genuine and great mysticism. That is moreover the truth. Meister Eckhart testifies to it. (SG, 71)

8. *Two Studies of Eckhart from Heidegger's Standpoint*

Having developed our own analysis of the relationship between Heidegger and Meister Eckhart, we can shed further light on the subject by examining two books on Eckhart which are of unique interest to the present study. The first, which we mentioned briefly above, is Käte Oltmanns's *Meister Eckhart* (1935); the second is Reiner Schürmann's *Maître Eckhart ou la joie errante* (1972). Each of these works is a study of Eckhart which explicitly invokes the language and the thought of Heidegger as a framework for interpreting Eckhart.

Oltmanns, in fact, was a student in Heidegger's 1919 lecture course on the philosophical foundations of medieval mysticism. We shall examine each work in turn, offering some critical remarks of our own on each. In this way, we will be able to define more sharply the relationship between Eckhart and Heidegger which we have developed above. For while Oltmanns and Schürmann are not explicitly concerned with comparing Heidegger and Eckhart, their work does in fact constitute an implicit confrontation of these two German "masters."

In the Foreward to her *Meister Eckhart* Oltmanns states:[14]

> This work owes its origin to the stimulus provided by Professor Heidegger. Just how much on the whole it owes to the philosophy of Heidegger can be judged by each one who is concerned with such a thing. It [Heidegger's philosophy] so much forms the presupposition of this work that it was not possible to refer in particular cases to [such] relationships.
>
> (Olt., 10)

True to her word, no further mention is made of Heidegger, but the stamp of Heidegger's work is plain to see—for those of us who are concerned with looking for it.

Oltmanns announces at the beinning of her study that she intends to consider Eckhart's doctrine of the soul's relation to God as pure philosophy, not as mysticism or theology. As philosophy, it has to do with the being of man, with "ontology." There is nothing specifically Christian about Eckhart, she says, no reliance on the person of Christ, or the specific contents of Christian revelation. The relationship of the soul to God belongs "to the essence of natural man." Oltmanns even intends to prescind from Eckhart's historical context in the Christian Middle Ages. The Eckhart of these pages is neither scholastic, mystic, nor neo-Platonist (Olt., 59-60). Oltmanns's attitude towards Eckhart is inspired by Heidegger's notion of "fundamental ontology" as something more basic than and prior to the "regional" ontology of a particular science, like theology. *Being and Time* is not opposed to theology, but presupposed by it. Thus Oltmanns sees in Eckhart's doctrine of the ground of the soul an ontology which is more fundamental and essential than the contents of Christian revelation. Her attitude towards Eckhart is very clearly a reflection of Heidegger's delineation of the relationship between philosophy and theology in his 1927 lecture *"Phänomenologie und Theologie."*[15]

Eckhart's fundamental idea, according to Oltmanns, is the "dialec-

193

tical relationship" of the soul to God. Her interpretation of this dialectic is made in three steps. (1) In the first place she argues that the
birth of the Son is "the authentic being of man" (*eigentliches Sein
des Menschen*: Olt., 61). Being-one's-self (*Selbstsein*: SZ, § 27) means
being-God's-Son (*Gottessohnsein*). For Oltmanns, the ground of the
soul quite literally *is* God. God "is in the birth of God one with the
soul, that is, He is the soul and the soul is God" (Olt., 66). The soul
is God's Son, *is* the Father's Image (His Son); it is not merely "like"
God. But what of the man who is not just, who has turned away
from God? Such a man, Oltmanns says, has turned away from his
"ownmost" essential Being. He is one with God in the mode of turning away from God. Thus the ground of the soul, as man's authentic
being, is both that which man is and that which he should be. "Man
is that which he should be and should be that which he is" (Olt., 85).
This is the true dialectic in Eckhart's philosophy: "Eckhart says on
the one hand that man is divine and on the other hand that man as
man is not divine, but rather must first come into unity with God"
(Olt., 86). Thus God's being in the soul—the soul's essential being—is
not a "rest," an established "fact" (Olt., 78,82), but a process (*Gesche-
hen*) which the soul must carry out. Like Dasein which has its Being
to be, the soul has its being one with God (which is its Being) to be.

The process by which the Son is born in the soul, by which the soul
attains its true self, is called "detachment." Detachment for Oltmanns,
which she identifies with the birth of the Son, is depicted quite
negatively. It is the process of dying to oneself, of becoming nothing,
of eradicating the self. "God . . . is death for everything which comes
near to Him. Who sees God must die" (Olt., 93). The dialectical life
of the soul can now be defined more sharply. The soul has the choice
either to live its own life, follow its own will—and thus die, for it
thereby turns away from God. Or else it may embrace death and, by
dying to its self, become one with God. The death of man is inescapable (Olt., 98-9). Now these two "ways of existing" (*Existenzweisen*)
(Olt., 98) belong together in a dialectical unity and tension. This tension is freedom, for freedom is essentially dialectical: whoever wishes
freely to manage his own affairs and to make "something" of himself
is unfree; but whoever gives up his freedom and wishes to be "nothing"
is truly free. Freedom is dying (Olt., 101-2).

(2) Oltmanns acknowledges that Eckhart says very little about freedom. She claims that her assertion that the very being of the soul
consists in freedom cannot be textually justified. It is introduced, she
says, with the aim of providing a light with which to illumine Eck-

hart's work (Olt., 104-6). Thus the second stage of her argument consists in substantiating this thesis. Basing her position on Eckhart's *Parisian Questions*, she argues that God is freedom itself. In this work Eckhart claims, as we saw above, that God is pure intellect (*intelligere*) and as such "pure" of being. God is raised up above all being and this purity of being (*puritas essendi*) is His freedom. Now the soul has a "little spark" of God's intellectuality, and so of His freedom. Thus the soul's freedom is not a "pure" freedom, for the soul is situated in the world amidst beings (Olt., 101) and so it is simultaneously unfree. The soul's freedom is a tendency, a drive towards freedom (Olt., 120). Thus when Eckhart says that the soul is the "image" of the Father, that it is the Son "by grace," that it is the Son by "analogy" (Olt., §§ 19-21), he is, according to Oltmanns, stressing the radical nothingness of the creature, that its Being is only "lent" to it. The freedom of the soul, therefore, is sustained by and tends towards pure freedom, which is God. But we must not think, she insists, that "God" is something outside the soul, something external. For we have seen above that God is the innermost essence of the soul. Hence the soul's tendency into pure freedom is its tendency towards its own authentic Being. God is freedom, but God is the innermost essence of the soul. Hence the essence of the soul is freedom (Olt., 134-6). But man never fully attains this inner ground. He remains always in strife towards it. It is never an accomplished "fact" (*Tatsache*: Olt., 137). The soul is no merely factual being, no merely "present at hand" entity (= something "created"). Rather it is characterized by "*Existenz*" (= something "uncreated"), which is its possibility to choose to become itself, to actualize its innermost potentiality for Being (cf. Olt., § 22). The essence of the soul, she says, "is determined out of its *Existenz*" (Olt., 137).

(3) The final stage of Oltmanns's argument consists in showing what idea of "reality" or of the "world" is demanded by the "dialectic of freedom." In brief (Olt., 168-70), she holds that since the essential nature of the soul lies in the choice between "life"—unity with God—and death—asserting one's own autonomy and turning away from God—there must be a comparably exclusive and inverse relationship between God and the world. If God has Being, then the world does not; if the world has Being, then God does not. Each is the "death" of the other. What Eckhart is ruling out, she maintains, is the possibility that there are *two* worlds, two "Beings." If that were so, there would be no need for the soul to turn away from the world (*Abgeschiedenheit*), for it would then be turning away from Being. Thus Oltmanns

reads Eckhart's statement that Being is God (*esse est deus*) to mean that God is the Being and reality of the world. There is no "other" world for Eckhart according to Oltmanns. When Eckhart speaks of "eternity" he means only the ecstatic unity of temporality (Olt., 153-4). The theory of exemplary causality, of the Divine Ideas, which Eckhart held, is for Oltmanns a "foreign body" in which he is not interested, a residue of the tradition (Olt., 172-7). Eckhart had no theory of an afterlife, she says, of another, higher, ideal world. Still, Oltmanns does not regard Eckhart as a pantheist, because Eckhart insisted that God is free of creatures, that Being is no being. Oltmanns has assimilated the relation of God to creatures in Eckhart to the relationship between Being and beings in Heidegger—God is the Being of beings—and she now claims that his position is not pantheism because of the "ontological difference" between Being and beings. Creatures are a continual striving for, and hungering after, Being which they cannot satisfy, for Being is God (Olt., 209-10). The Being of nature, like the Being of man, is "unrest, transiency, dying" (Olt., 211). Both the just man and the unjust, she concludes, live in the same world and must, like the things of nature, perish. The sole difference between them is that the unjust man seeks Being in illusion (the world) and has a false freedom. Why has God destined man to be denied Being and rest? This is our inescapable facticity. There can be no justification for it; Eckhart "wishes only to show us that we have to love Being as it is" (Olt., 213). The end of Oltmanns's book sounds rather like the end of *Being and Nothingness*; the soul, she seems to say, is a useless passion.

Oltmanns's book reads considerably more like a Heideggerian "retrieval" (*Wiederholung*) of Meister Eckhart than an exposition of the Meister himself. Thus, in a review of *Meister Eckhart*, Otto Karrer says, "To be sure, this is no Eckhart-book, as the title lets us believe, but a Heidegger-book."[16] "I recollect," he adds, "having read all of this not in Eckhart, but indeed in Heidegger." Karrer is of course quite right, and the best that can be said for Oltmanns is that she has very skillfully managed to assimilate this medieval mystic to the author of *Being and Time*. But one must agree with Karrer: the apparently innocuous title of her book is very misleading.

Still, our interest is not in judging Oltmanns's book by the canons of Eckhartian scholarship, but in the light which it sheds on Heidegger's relationship to Eckhart. And the first point to be made in this connection is that the later Heidegger himself would certainly disavow

196

any attempt to treat Meister Eckhart's writings as "pure philosophy." Oltmanns approach is inspired by the early Heidegger who, under the influence of Husserl, stressed the radical autonomy of the phenomenological method and so of philosophy itself. But in his later works, the autonomy of philosophy, i.e., the conception of "philosophy" as "strict science," has come under attack. He speaks of the "strictness" of "thinking," to be sure, by which he means that thought must stay strictly within its element, which is Being, but such thinking is no longer philosophy. The autonomy of philosophy is the heritage of Western rationalism, and of modern philosophy in particular, and has led to the age of the atom. Thus the later Heidegger—quite the contrary of what Oltmanns suggests—looks to poets and mystics such as Angelus Silesius and Meister Eckhart, and away from philosophers such as Leibniz, precisely to find a thinking which escapes the sphere of influence of philosophical principles, like the Principle of Rendering a Sufficient Ground. A reading of Eckhart in keeping with Heidegger's later writings would consider Eckhart's vernacular works not as philosophy but as something which has overcome philosophy and metaphysics. Such a reading would have the added advantage of being in keeping, not only with the later Heidegger, but also with Meister Eckhart as well.

In the second place, in centering her study around the motif of "freedom," Oltmanns has cast Eckhart's thought in the language of willing, which is once again precisely what the later Heidegger—not to mention Eckhart himself—wishes to renounce. Thus she says that the freedom of the soul is the freedom to choose itself:

> Man can only be free while he wills to be free, and while he wills to be free he is already free. (Olt., 137)

The detached soul for Oltmanns is a will which wills itself (Olt., 152), a "resolute" will which exists "for the sake of itself" (*um willen seiner selbst*: Olt., 153). Now not only is this a misleading way to present Eckhart, who said that the detached man has no will at all (Q, 183,18-9), it is also profoundly out of keeping with the later Heidegger's interest in Meister Eckhart. Of course, Oltmanns does concede that true freedom for Eckhart is not sheer self-determination but choosing to give up self-will, "willingly to renounce willing," as Heidegger puts it (G, 32/59). Thus there is something prophetic about Oltmanns's "Eckhart-book," for when she does analyze freedom as letting-be, as willing to let God's will be all, she prefigures the very

197

move that Heidegger himself makes in the 1943 publication *On the Essence of Truth* (which is, in all likelihood, a thoroughly revised version of the 1930 lecture of the same name.)[17] While truth is freedom, for the author of *Being and Time*, because Dasein actively discloses the being in its Being (WG, 100-1, ff.), truth is freedom in this later treatise because Dasein frees itself for the openness of what is manifest of itself. Freedom thus becomes *Gelassenheit*, which is the renunciation of willing. Once again Oltmanns would have followed Eckhart more closely had she followed the later Heidegger more closely—a Heidegger who of course in 1935 was only beginning to emerge.

The last difficulty I see with Oltmanns's work is perhaps the most serious of all. In assimilating Eckhart to the language of *Being and Time*, she entirely destroys one of the most essential and fundamental themes in this Christian mystic who was so deeply inspired by St. John. Her "existentialist" reading of Eckhart seems to prefigure the Sartrean–Heideggerian synthesis which would be published eight years later in 1943, under the equally "dialectical" title of *Being and Nothingness*. For she adopts two of the central theses of this point of view: (1) the soul must become what it is (Olt., 85); (2) the soul cannot become what it is (Olt., 209-13). The contradiction between these theses is what Oltmanns means by the dialectic of freedom. The result of her reading of Eckhart is to leave the soul in a singularly disheartening and "disconsolate" position. The distinguished Eckhartian scholar Ernst Benz has written the most eloquent refutation of this distortion of Meister Eckhart. Protesting "against the way in which his [Eckhart's] philosophical concepts are abstracted from the religious power with which they are laden," Benz writes:[18]

> In order to save the Meister Eckhart described by Oltmanns from the self-mortifying consequences of his disconsolate (*trostlosen*) reflection on Being, there would be only one means: reading the *Consolation-book* (the *Book of Divine Consolation*) by Meister Eckhart, who believed in God and in the exaltation of men and in rest and bliss; who lived in the consciousness of having grasped both [rest and bliss] and having possessed both inseparably in union with God, and who on this basis found the courage not to accept the world as it is but rather to transform it in God's image.

Eckhart wrote the *Book of Divine Consolation* precisely in order to show the limitation of every *consolatio philosophiae*, which is ultimately secular and non-religious. What Oltmanns has done to Eckhart therefore is precisely to have turned him into something worldly and God-less. And in so doing she has destroyed one of the most essential differences between Eckhart and Heidegger: that in Eckhart *Gelassenheit* is a surrender to a loving Father, and in Heidegger it is a release into the "play of Being." It is precisely the fact that Eckhart's work is essentially religious which makes what he says so important to the present confrontation of Heidegger and Eckhart. This is a difficulty which was raised in the first chapter of this study and to which we will have to return in Chapter Five.

If the weakness of Oltmanns's book is that it based itself on *Being and Time*, it is the merit of Reiner Schürmann's *Maître Eckhart ou la joie errante*[19] to have undertaken a study of Eckhart from the point of view afforded by the later Heidegger. The premise of Schürmann's book is that Eckhart's work is to be understood as a "peregrinal" rather than an "entitative" ontology. By peregrinal he means a thinking which is ever "underway" (*unterwegs*), i.e., which describes the soul in a state of being underway towards God and which means to show this way to others. Eckhart does not engage in an ontology of "substances," a "natural ontology," as Yves Congar calls it, but an ontology of personal spiritual relationships, which Rombach calls a "functional ontology" (Schür., 170-1). This distinction between an entitative and a peregrinal ontology parallels Heidegger's distinction between metaphysics, as the ontology of the static present-at-hand (*Vorhandensein*), and thought, which is concerned with Being as Event. In dealing with the living relationship between the soul and God, Eckhart is treating not of two "things" but of the "activity" in which God and the soul embrace. Although he is a scholastic, Schürmann holds, Eckhart has taken the step back out of metaphysics.

The "way" of the soul to God according to Schürmann is the way of "detachment," along which path Schürmann marks off four stages (Schür., 159 ff.): (a) dissimilarity: the creature is "unlike" God because, of itself, it is a pure nothing. Like the coal which before it glows with heat must first lack heat, the soul begins by being unlike God. (b) Similarity: after a while the fire makes the coal glow, i.e., like to itself. So the soul becomes by detachment like God. (c) Identity: mere likeness must be overcome in favor of identity with God. But if this identity is taken entitatively, Eckhart's work is confused with pantheism. However, Eckhart does not speak the language of substances but of Event; he speaks of the functional unity, the unity of a single act, in which God and the soul work together. This co-working is a "playing together" of the "three," God, soul, and world. (d) Outpouring: an "overflow" arises from the fact that the soul has made its way back beyond God into the naked Godhead. Here every "reason" and "first cause" is laid aside and the soul lives without why, acting spontaneously and from the overflow of its unity with God.

Schürmann's thesis about a "peregrinal ontology" also has implications for Eckhart's theory of "analogy." It is usually said that Eckhart holds to an analogy of "attribution" which, as we recall from above, is based on Aristotle's *pros hen* analogy. "Fresh air" is "healthy" by this analogy because it has a direct causal relationship to health, not because the molecules of air are "healthy" themselves. So too Eckhart clearly says that creatures are nothing in themselves and have being only in "reference" to God, whereas Aquinas held that creatures have being properly, if imperfectly, in themselves. But Schürmann argues that this interpretation does not get to the heart of Eckhart's teachings (Schür., 340). For the language of "analogy" belongs to the language of scientific explanation (Schür., 338), whereas Eckhart has left entitative ontology behind. What the problem of analogy in Eckhart teaches us is the inadequacy of metaphysical language to interpret his work. We need to discover a language which is suited to understand Eckhart, and this Schürmann claims we find in Heidegger.

The concluding pages (Schür., 340 ff.) of *La joie errante* are given over to a study of the relationship of Eckhart and Heidegger on *Gelassenheit*. For Schürmann, Eckhart and Heidegger speak of the same thing (*das Selbe*), although what they say is not identical (*gleich*). He is not interested in drawing lines of comparison between Eckhart and Heidegger (Schür., 348), or in showing the influence of Eckhart on Heidegger (Schür., 340-2), but in uncovering the "selfsame" to which both Meister Eckhart and Heidegger are "responding" (Schür., 347-8). *Gelassenheit*, in Heidegger, Schürmann says, is to be translated as "letting-be." Letting-be is a transitive movement towards things, a being "destined" to things. But that to which thought is destined simultaneously reveals and conceals itself. Thus Heidegger says "letting ourselves be destined towards things (*Gelassenheit zu den Dingen*) and openness for the mystery (*Offenheit für das Geheimnis*) belong together" (G, 26-8/55-7; Schür., 335). Being is revealed not by grasping but by letting-be. Letting-be is not a human activity but arises from Being itself. Like Eckhart, Heidegger speaks of letting-be, not willing. Like Eckhart, Heidegger speaks of the "identity" of Being and man, not the static identity of two things but the "peregrinal" identity of man and Being as they make their way

200

towards one another. Heidegger even uses central words from Eckhart's vocabulary in the way that Eckhart himself uses them, most notably *Wesen*, which means for both authors the way things come into presence and dwell there. Finally, Being for Heidegger, as for Meister Eckhart, is *ohne Warum*, without reason or explanation, a simple upsurge into presence (*physis*) (Schür., 343-58).

Still, if Heidegger and Meister Eckhart speak of the selfsame, they do not do so in the same way. Underlying all of the differences between these two thinkers is the simple difference that Heidegger is concerned with the nearness of Being to thought, whereas Eckhart is concerned with the nearness of God to the soul. Heidegger's *Gelassenheit* has a "profane" sense which is compatible with abject political causes, whereas Meister Eckhart's "*gelâzenheit*" is identified with morality itself. Heidegger's way is a way which follows the path of Western history whereas history itself—the medieval world-view—held Eckhart back from historical consciousness. Still, Eckhart and Heidegger are kindred minds who seek a deeper understanding of man and his relationship to the "ultimate" than is afforded by their contemporaries—scholasticism on the one hand and modern metaphysics on the other (Schür., 358-67).

We can see at once that Schürmann's approach to Eckhart is eminently more successful than Oltmanns's and that this is made possible because he approaches Eckhart from the standpoint of the later Heidegger. Thus, while Schürmann's study is quite different from our own, while it is a book about Meister Eckhart, not about Heidegger, it indirectly confirms the argument that we have been making in this chapter. In showing how wonderfully adaptable the language and the framework of the later Heidegger is in the interpretation of Meister Eckhart, Schürmann indirectly testifies to the inner relationship of Meister Eckhart and Heidegger. For Heidegger's relationship to Eckhart is not merely heuristic. Heidegger provides us with the language to understand Eckhart because he has himself taken over for his own purposes, viz., the explication of the relationship of Dasein to Being, the very relationship of the soul to God which we find in Meister Eckhart. He provides a language and a framework for understanding Eckhart because this language and framework derives to an important extent from Meister Eckhart to begin with.

Oltmanns on the other hand testifies vividly to the incompatibility of *Being and Time* with the point of view of Meister Eckhart. Thus, what is at work in the difference between these two very different interpretations of Meister Eckhart from Heidegger's standpoint is the "reversal" itself. For there is no celebration of the power of the will or of the autonomy of philosophy, no subterranean reflections on the ineradicable finitude of the self in Schürmann's *Meister Eckhart*. That is because Heidegger himself no longer celebrates the autonomy of philosophy or the power of the will; Heidegger himself has moved into a real and genuine kinship with Meister Eckhart, and not merely an "acoustical" one, as Ernst Benz says in his review of Oltmanns's *Meister Eckhart*.[20] Schürmann's interpretation is able to succeed precisely because there has been a reversal which consists in a movement away from the existential-phenomenological ontology of Dasein in *Being and Time* and a movement into a nearness with the mystic and the mystic-poet.

I have but one main reservation to express about Schürmann's *Maître Eckhart*, and this has to do with the two "ways" of Heidegger and Meister Eckhart. Schürmann holds, and rightly so, that Eckhart's way is one of joy. This does not mean that Eckhart's path of detachment insulates the soul from suffering, for as Schürmann points out the way of detachment is the way of the Cross. It means rather, and this is precisely what Oltmanns ignores, that Eckhart's way is one of "divine consolation," in which the detached soul gives itself over to the loving and absolutely trustworthy power of the Father Himself. But there is plainly nothing comparable to this in Heidegger; indeed Schürmann points out that the "way" of Heidegger is a "travel" (*Fahren*) which is fraught with danger (*Gefahr*: Schür., 362-3). But Schürmann does not pursue this difference; he does not raise the question of how seriously this affects the whole problematic of *Gelassenheit* in Heidegger. For once *Gelassenheit* has been removed from its religious context, the question arises as to whether the way of detachment remains something *viable* at all. It is true, as Schürmann contends, that Heidegger speaks the language of Event and not of substances, but the language of Event is not—for Heidegger at least—the language of "persons" and "intersubjectivity." Indeed, Heidegger's Event is an ominous "It." It is not easy, in the light of this consideration, to assume that Heidegger and Eckhart are speaking of *das Selbe* at all. Oltmanns assimilated Meister Eckhart into the secular categories of *Being and Time*, and so prevents this problem from being seen. Schürmann keeps religion and the "profane" (Schur., 360) apart, but he does not pursue the immense difficulty this presents concerning the danger of Heidegger's "peregrinal" way of Being. This will be, however, a major concern of ours in the next chapter of this study.

9. *Heidegger, Eckhart, and Zen Buddhism*

The question of Heidegger's mysticism cannot be explored solely in terms of his relationship to Meister Eckhart but must also include the intriguing question of Heidegger's relationship to the East. For it may well be that the "step back" out of "Western philosophy"— the very expression is redundant (WdP, 30/31)—results in adopting the spiritual attitude of the East. I have in these pages restricted my analysis to Heidegger and Meister Eckhart, partly in order to keep this study manageable, partly too because Eckhart is something of a "paradigm" case of the mystic, generally considered to be one of the greatest of Western mystics, and finally because of Heidegger's historically certifiable interest in Meister Eckhart. Heidegger and Eckhart share the same tradition—the "Western European"—and even the same language. What has been "handed over" to Heidegger has in part been handed over to him by Eckhart himself. Thus the present work stands on solid grounds; but it needs to be complemented by still another and more difficult study of Heidegger's relationship to those who do not share the tradition which he hopes to "retrieve" (*wiederholen*), and who speak neither Greek nor Latin nor any language which stands under their influence. What is needed for this task is an "experience with" the essence of Eastern languages (US, 113 ff./23 ff.). As Heidegger said in his letter to those who gathered in Honolulu in 1969 to discuss the topic of "Heidegger and Eastern Thought":[21]

> The greatest difficulty in this enterprise always lies, as far as I can see, in the fact that with few exceptions there is no command of the Eastern languages either in Europe or in the United States. A translation of Eastern thought into English, on the other hand, remains—as does every translation—an expedient.

I do not myself profess to have the expertise—let alone the space—to discuss the question of Heidegger and the East with the care I have given to Heidegger and Eckhart. Still, I believe that our study of the mystical element in Heidegger's thought, and of Heidegger's relationship to Meister Eckhart, stands to profit by even a tentative treatment of this issue.

There are some hints that it is to Zen Buddhism that we should look to find an analogue to "thinking" in the East. The broadest hint in that direction is Heidegger's lengthy conversation with the Japanese in *Unterwegs zur Sprache*, for it is in Japan that Zen Buddhism today finds its home. Heidegger has had Japanese students since the

203

1920s, and the Japanese have shown the greatest interest in his work since the first appearance of *Being and Time* (which they have translated five times) and *What Is Metaphysics?* (which they have translated twice).[22] Moreover, Heidegger has also drawn attention to a possible connection between his "way" (*Weg*) and the *Tao*:

> The word "way" probably is an ancient primary word that speaks to the reflective mind of man. The key word in Laotse's poetic thinking is *Tao*, which "properly speaking" means way. (US, 198/92)

Now Taoism, which is indigenous to China, became an essential ingredient in the Buddhism which Bodhidharma brought to China in A.D. 520 and which came to be called "Zen" Buddhism. Again, in "Who Is Nietzsche's Zarathustra?," Heidegger mentions both Schopenhauer and Buddhism in connection with the question of overcoming the will (VA, 117/424).

There is also the much quoted remark of William Barrett in the preface to his anthology of the works of Suzuki, the leading exponent of Zen Buddhism in the Western world:[23]

> A German friend of Heidegger told me that one day when he visited Heidegger he found him reading one of Suzuki's books: "If I understand this man correctly," Heidegger remarked, "this is what I have been trying to say in all my writings." (Suz., xi)

One does not know how much stock to put in this kind of hearsay, but the remark is tantalizing, for once one turns to Zen, one does indeed find striking and revealing similarities to Heidegger.

There is one last bit of evidence which suggests a link between Heidegger and Zen, and this is the fact that Meister Eckhart is frequently pointed to as a Christian mystic whose experience seems to be remarkably like Zen. I am thinking not only of Suzuki's *Mysticism: Buddhist and Christian*, which is a comparative study of Eckhart and Zen, but also of the work of Shizuteru Ueda, to whom we referred in the previous chapter. Ueda is a Japanese who wrote a book in German on Eckhart and Zen, under the direction of Ernst Benz, and who reads both Scholastic Latin and Middle High German.[24] Eckhart then provides something of a "middle term" in our attempt to see the affinity between Heidegger and Zen.

Huston Smith has well described one's initial reaction to Zen Buddhism:[25]

Entering the Zen outlook is like stepping through Alice's looking glass. One finds oneself in a topsy-turvy wonderland in which everything seems quite mad—charmingly mad for the most part, but mad all the same. It is a world of bewildering dialogues, obscure conundrums, stunning para-doxes, flagrant contradictions, and abrupt non-sequiturs, all carried off in the most urbane, cheerful, and innocent style. Here are some examples:

An ancient master when he was asked the meaning of Zen lifted one of his fingers. That was his entire answer. Another kicked a ball. Still an-other slapped the inquirer in the face.

Bearing this in mind, the reader will perhaps be less shocked when I say that I wish to introduce the main ideas of Zen which are relevant to this study by turning to a work entitled *Zen in the Art of Archery*.[26] I readily admit that, on the face of it, our lofty deliberations on the Birth of the Son in Meister Eckhart and the "*Ereignis*" in Heidegger seem to have little to do with archery. I might only add, for whatever help it is at this point, that the Zen masters tell us that "The *Tao* is your everyday mind." This means that the essential experience of Zen takes place in and through the objects and activities of everyday exist-ence—very much in the way that Eckhart tells us there is no need to take flight from the world into the monastery to find God. "Zen" is a branch of "Mahayana" ("the great raft") Buddhism which, like Protestant Christianity, stresses the accessibility of the divine to the layman, despite all of his worldly preoccupations. "Hinayana" ("the small raft") or Theravada Buddhism, on the other hand, holds that Buddhism can be practiced to perfection only in the monastery.

Zen in the Art of Archery is written by Eugen Herrigel, a German professor who was invited to teach philosophy at the University of Tokyo and who used this time in Japan to study Zen. His work is the best introduction to Zen that I have found because it provides a "prac-tical" exposition of a spiritual movement which is profoundly "experi-ential" and which steadfastly eschews metaphysical speculation. Para-doxical as it seems to us, initiates have been introduced to Zen for centuries by studying, under the direction of a Zen master, such prac-tical arts as ink-painting, flower arrangement, swordsmanship, archery, and even ceremonial tea drinking. I wish to briefly chart Herrigel's training in Zen archery, which, I hope to show, is of the greatest interest to Heidegger readers, and then to formulate some general observations about the relationship of Heidegger, Eckhart, and Zen which will serve to further define the mystical element in Heideg-ger's thought.

Archery is not a gymnastic art for Zen, but a spiritual and religious

205

exercise. It is not acquired by toning the muscles and learning certain techniques. The "art" must instead be "artless"; shooting must be "not shooting" (Herr., 20). By means of this artless art we become "aware, in the deepest ground of the soul, of the unnameable Groundlessness"—indeed, Herrigel adds, we become "one with it" (Herr., 22). This "Groundlessness," we will see below, is called by the Zen masters "*sunyata*," the Void, Emptiness. With this essentially spiritual goal in mind, Herrigel took up the six-year course of instruction under a Zen master.

He describes the great difficulty he experienced acquiring the first step, viz., learning how to draw the bow, letting the hands do all the work while the rest of the body is relaxed (Herr., 34 ff.). This puts an enormous strain upon the hands causing them to tremble. Herrigel worked for weeks, unable to draw the bow rightly, while the master's only advice was to "relax." At long last, and only after the master explained to him that he was not breathing correctly, he learned to draw even the heavy bow of the master. His motion was "effortless"; all his bodily muscles were relaxed. Why did the master not teach him to breathe correctly to begin with, he asked a friend:

You had to suffer shipwreck through your own efforts before you were ready to seize the lifebelt he threw you. (Herr., 42)

Herrigel's own "will" and "cleverness" had to be humbled before he could receive instruction. In a similar way, Eckhart says that the soul must be pure of all images and all self-will if it would receive God.

After devoting a full year to mastering the first step, Herrigel advanced to the next stage, viz., learning how to release the bowstring. Strange as it may seem, this "letting go" of the bowstring has everything to do with what Eckhart and Heidegger call "letting-be." The difficulty is to release the string in such a way that the arrow is not jerked and caused to wobble, and so that the body of the archer is not shaken. Learning this would take Herrigel over three years. The master himself discharged the arrow "effortlessly," cushioning the sudden release of the tension (Herr., 46-7). The master had achieved the "effortless effort" (*wu wei*) which is spoken of in Taoism. Hence he admonished Herrigel about exerting too much self-conscious effort:

You must hold the drawn bowstring like a little child holding the proffered finger. It grasps it so firmly that one marvels at the strength of the tiny fist. And when it lets the finger go, there is not a slightest jerk. Do you know why? Because a child doesn't think: I will let go of the finger in order to grasp this other thing. Completely unself-consciously, without purpose, it turns from one to the other. (Herr., 49)

The Zen master is instructing Herrigel in what the ancient Chinese Zen masters called "no mind" (*wu-nien*), the purging of the mind of conscious thoughts, wishes, and intentions. The self must become "empty" of its own goals ("without why"). As Huston Smith puts it, speaking of Taoism:[27]

> One way to create is through following the calculated directives of the conscious mind. The results of this mode of action, however, are seldom impressive; they tend to smack more of sorting and arranging than of genuine creation. Genuine creation, as every artist has discovered, comes when the more abundant resources of the subliminal self are somehow released. But for this to happen a certain dissociation from the surface self is needed. The conscious mind must relax, stop standing in its own light, let go. Only so is it possible to break through the law of reversed effort in which the more we try the more our efforts boomerang.

The master tells Herrigel he must learn to "wait" (Herr., 51) for the moment when the arrow should be released, even as Heidegger tells us in *Gelassenheit* to wait on the regioning of the region (G, 43-4/67-8). But how can he "wait"?

> By letting go of yourself, leaving yourself and everything yours behind so decisively that nothing more is left of you but a purposeless tension.
>
> (Herr., 52)

The master's instructions are to "let" the tension build up, to "wait" until the tension has fulfilled itself "like a ripened fruit," so that the arrow will almost release itself in an "actionless activity" (Herr., 56). For this is required "right presence of mind," a recollected, meditative tanquillity in which the archer becomes "self-less" and "egoless." But frustrated by continual failure, Herrigel commits the cardinal sin: he resorts to a technical trick to loose the arrow smoothly. Instead of leaving the task to the Unconscious, the Groundless, the Void, to carry out through him, he turns it over to his conscious, calculative reason. He decides to ease his grip on the string so that the string will tear the finger loose at a certain point and the arrow will be released smoothly. The result was predictable. The master detected the ruse at once and dismissed him from his instruction. It was only through the intercession of a friend that the master agreed to resume the lessons.

Herrigel continued to practice under the master's eye and still without success, although he was by now in his fourth year of instruction. He became despondent at his repeated failure, and at one point was convinced that he no longer cared whether he learned to release the bowstring correctly or not (Herr., 75-6). The ego was brought to shipwreck once again. Then one day, in the midst of his endless practicing, the master said to him: "Just then 'It' shot." Herrigel had acquired the method! But then again it was not "Herrigel," for his "self" had been purged. "It" shot the arrow, not Herrigel, i.e., the Unconscious, the Void had taken over for his conscious life and acted through him. Thus the master said to him:

> . . . you are entirely innocent of this shot. You remained this time absolutely self-oblivious and without purpose as the highest tension, so that the shot fell from you like a ripe fruit.   (Herr, 77)

In the final stage of his instruction Herrigel was taught to shoot at a target. Once again he had to learn an "aimless aim," to shoot without conscious teleological control—Eckhart would have said "without why." Hence the master taught him no method of "sighting" the target, for "sighting" is another ruse of the calculative mind. After all, what value is it in itself to be able to hit a paper target with an arrow? Zen has no interest in a technically controlled achievement (Herr., 81). So finally, as before, after long practice, "It" began to hit first the edge of the target and then the center. When the master asked Herrigel if he now understood what "it shoots" rather than "I shoot" means, Herrigel said he thought he no longer understood anything. And in this response the master took great satisfaction (Herr., 88).

Herrigel tells us that throughout his lessons everything depended on the presence of the master. He mentions that his own performance would be improved simply by letting the master take a few shots with the bow he had been using. The master had a spiritual power over Herrigel which he seemed to be able to impress directly upon him. This illustrates what Zen means when it says that Zen is passed "from mind to mind," directly, and not by means of Scriptures or an ecclesiastical establishment. Its "apostolic succession" is "mind to mind."

Herrigel's training in Zen archery, I contend, takes place in the sphere of "releasement" (Gelassenheit) and so dwells in proximity to Eckhart and Heidegger. The Zen master says in effect: let go of the

208

ego cogito, with all its willing and desiring and calculating, so that "It" may appropriate you in your essential being, in your innermost ground. The "It" which shoots in *Zen in the Art of Archery* is like the "It" (*das "Es"*) which "gives" in Heidegger's "*Ereignis*" (SD, 19/18) and the Father which bears His Son in Meister Eckhart. Let us examine this more closely.

When Buddha left the court of his father at the age of twenty-nine, it was because he thought there was no solution in the opulent life of the court to the problem of "suffering" (*dukkha*), i.e., of death, illness, and pain. After he emerged from his meditation of forty-nine days under the Bodhi tree, he proclaimed that he had found the root of suffering, and this he called "*tanha*"—desire, craving, self-love. Because he had diagnosed the source of suffering, he could also prescribe for its cure: "release" from self-will and craving, and taking up what is called the "eight-fold path." Now when one turns to Eckhart, one finds a comparable "structure" although the "concern" (*Sache*) of this thought is different. For it is not "suffering" (primarily) which concerns Eckhart but "sin," turning away from God, alienation from the Father and Creator. And by the same token Eckhart too has diagnosed the root of sin: "self-love" (*Eigenliebe*), "self-will" (*Eigenwille*), which is comparable to what Buddha means by *tanha*. Like Buddha, Eckhart prescribes a comparable remedy: abandon yourself, let go of yourself (*lass dich!*: Q, 55,31/Cl., 65). Finally, when we turn to Heidegger, once again the same "structure" is revealed. What concerns Heidegger is neither suffering nor sin (alienation from God), but the forgottenness of Being, alienation from Being in its "truth," or what he calls "metaphysics." Like Buddha and Eckhart, Heidegger knows the root of metaphysics, which he locates not in desire or self-will but in something analogous: "subjectism," the attachment of the *ego cogito* to its own "representations" and "principles." Like Buddha and Eckhart, Heidegger sees in "releasement"—overcoming subjectism—a way out of this time of need. But once again, as we have already mentioned in treating of a similar theme in Heidegger and Eckhart, the neediness of the times in Heidegger, the turn towards subjectivity, does not originate in man himself, but rather in the historical movements of Being's own withdrawal. In Eckhart and Zen, however, the ego is the origin of its own problems. I should now like to spell this structural likeness out in greater detail by first sketching the teachings which the Zen masters have handed down to us, which are so excellently illustrated in Herrigel's book, and then by expounding first the "Eckhartian" character of these ideas, and finally their "Heideggerian" character.

The patriarch who gave definitive shape to the formation of "Zen" was Hui-neng (638-713). The key to Hui-neng's teaching lies in his statement that "from the first nothing is" (Suz., 68, 157). By this he meant to say that no "particular" thing is real; no individual entity has true being; everything particular is epiphenomenal. What is real is the underlying ground and basis of all particularities, that from which they emerge and to which they return. This ground or absolute is completely "unconditioned." It is itself nothing particular, determinate, definite, determinable, or formed. All of these ideas imply a limitation and circumscription of its nature. Hence the Zen masters called it "*sunyata*," the Void, Emptiness. Suzuki writes:

> This unconditioned, formless, and consequently unattainable is Emptiness (*sunyata*). Emptiness is not a negative idea, nor does it mean a mere privation, but as it is not in the realm of names and forms, it is called emptiness, or nothingness, or the Void. (Suz., 190)

As the unconditioned, it is that which conditions us, which envelops and sustains and supports us and all things. Hence it is more real, rather than less real, than any particular entity. Thus it is also called *tathata*, "suchness," "is-ness."

Inasmuch as *sunyata* eludes every name or concept which we form of it, it is clearly something we cannot "grasp." What is needed is a way to lay hands on it which does not "seize" it, a "grasping" which is also a "no grasping," a "thinking" which is also not a thinking. This spiritual state of mind is called by Hui-neng "no mind" or "no thought" (*wu-nien*). "No mind" means to be detached from all thoughts and images, to be free of all affection and cravings, to be unaffected by all objects (Suz., 192-3). It means not to be "tainted" by the objective world even while remaining in the midst of it. In other words, "no mind" is a clearing away of all thoughts and desires in order to "let" the unconscious base of our existence exert itself through us—just as Herrigel let "It" shoot the arrow.

Sunyata is clearly not "achieved," for it is not the result of a striving on our part, but only of the complete surrender of all striving. This is the role of the famous "*koans*" employed by the Zen masters ("what is the sound of one hand clapping?"): to bring every conscious and rational effort to its knees. When consciousness gives up, "the task is accomplished by itself" (Suz., 202). We recall Herrigel's final disconsolate efforts at releasing the bowstring correctly. Suzuki records a delightful dialogue between a Zen master and a young monk seeking to "attain Buddhahood" (unity with the Void), which illustrates vividly how *sunyata* is nothing to be "accomplished" by us. The master tells the monk: there is no mind with which we can attain Buddhahood; there are no teachings of Buddha (i.e., no "thoughts" which "grasp" *sunyata*); there is no Buddhahood (it is the Void); no attaining it (it comes about of itself), and even no Emptiness (it is not a thing) (Suz., 200-6). When asked what then Buddhahood could possibly amount to, the master answered: "When hungry, I eat and when cold I put on more clothes." By this the master meant to say that it is not a matter of leaving the world but of learning to find Buddhahood within the world of commonplace things. The Void is not "out there." It is within us; we already possess *sunyata*, and the suggestion that we have to "attain" it is testimony to our alienation from our truest nature. The more we take up teleological activity—acting for the sake of external ends—the less we find Buddhahood. For Buddha is within us. We need only stop asking for the "why" of this and the "how" of that, Suzuki says (Suz., 211), and the Buddha-nature will reveal itself to us before our very eyes (Suz., 211).

When the Buddha-nature is revealed, then Zen speaks of attaining "*satori*," enlightenment, an experience of surpassing peace and freedom. Here is the ultimate solution to the problem of *dukkha* which Buddha first pondered centuries before Hui-neng. There is no pain or pleasure, no birth or death, no health or illness: "from the first nothing is." Those who have experienced *satori* have transcended the sphere of all such relativities and particularities.

Now this account of *sunyata, wu-nien,* and *satori* is laced with Eckhartian and Heideggerian themes. Let us begin with Meister Eckhart first. Eckhart's concept of *Abgeschiedenheit* bears a striking resemblance to *sunyata* and *wu-nien.* For Eckhart too determined the absolute as a "pure nothing," that which is totally detached from all particularity (every this or that), absolutely "pure," a "mind" which is not "tainted" with creatures (the "nothingness" of the "intellect" in the *Parisian Questions*), a "naked" Being, a "desert." Eckhart's "Godhead" (*Gottheit*), like *sunyata*, eludes every name and form and determination we can give to it.[28] And as in Zen, God is not only pure Nothingness but also, inasmuch as He is more real than any creature, pure Being (*isticheit, puritas essendi*), which corresponds to the Zen notion of *tathata*.[29] So too Eckhart calls for the soul itself to be detached from every creature, "empty" of every "this or that," to have in Hui-neng's

211

words, "no mind" (*wu-nien*), no thought or desire for anything created. The soul must be "empty of creatures" in order to be "full of God."

Having detached itself from everything created the soul enters into its innermost hidden "ground." In Zen, this is the Buddha-nature or self-nature which is concealed within each man. And in this inner "emptiness" there occurs, according to Eckhart, not "*satori*" but its Christian analogue, the eternal Birth of the Son, by which the soul enters into an eternal now and becomes one with the Godhead. The soul leads a life of peace and freedom, for it lives "without why," without the troubled strivings of a teleological consciousness, with all its yearnings and longings and cravings.[30] The soul need find no rationale for its actions, for it acts in unison with God within it, so that all its actions are divinized.

Shizutera Ueda has argued that Angelus Silesius's saying "The Rose Is Without Why" is appropriate to both Zen and Eckhart.[31] In a famous *mondo* (conversation), a Zen master is asked "Why did the Patriarch (Bodhidharma) come from the West (India)? To this he responds: "The cypress tree in the garden." The master means that the essence of Zen —its origin in Bodhidharma—is to find the divine in everyday experience —e.g., the cypress tree in the garden—and that it has nothing to do with abstract formulae. Ueda argues that a similar question and answer (*mondo*) can be found for Eckhart: Why did the Son become man (*cur deus homo*)? To this Eckhart could respond: the rose is without why—or simply: the rose. By this Eckhart would mean that the innermost meaning of the Incarnation transcends any rational attempt to explain it and can be experienced only in the heart of one who has become like the rose, without why. It would furthermore mean that the soul which is without why would be able to see God's life in all things, even the most commonplace. Thus the rose which we see here with our outer eye is, as Angelus Silesius said, seen by the detached heart as it blossoms for all eternity in God's mind. Thus the cypress tree in Zen and the rose of Angelus Silesius are each resplendent with the divine—for those who have learned to find God in all things.

If there can be no doubt about the proximity of Eckhart and Zen, as I think there is not, there is similarly no doubt about the proximity of Heidegger and Zen. For to the Zen teaching of *sunyata* we can relate Heidegger's notion of "the Nothing" (*das Nichts*). For Heidegger, Being is that which is wholly "other than the being" (WM, 51/360), that which is not any particular being, any particular entity. As such it is the "not," the differentiating in the difference between Being and beings. Thus in *Unterwegs zur Sprache* the following dialogue takes place:[32]

Inquirer: That emptiness then is the same as nothingness, that essential being which we attempt to add in our thinking, as the other, to all that is present and absent.

Japanese: Surely. For this reason we in Japan understood at once your lecture "What is Metaphysics?" when it became available to us in 1930 through a translation which a Japanese student, then attending your lectures, had ventured. (US, 108/19)

Now the Nothing, Heidegger tells us, is not to be construed nihilistically, as Suzuki continually insists about *sunyata*. For the Nothing, as that which withdraws behind beings and is *not* any being, is no less than Being itself. The being as such emerges in the ground of this Nothing which, as Being, is the sustaining ground of the being. Even so in Zen, *sunyata* is also *tathata*, suchness, is-ness. Thus the Japanese in *Unterwegs zur Sprache* continues:

We marvel to this day how the Europeans could lapse into interpreting as nihilistic the nothingness of which you speak in that lecture [WM]. To us, emptiness is the loftiest name for what you mean to say with the word "Being." . . . (US, 108-9/19)

One difference I should point out between Heidegger and Eckhart on the one hand, and Zen on the other, is that neither Heidegger nor Eckhart wishes to destroy or weaken the real distinction between beings, to reduce "particularity" to an epiphenomenon, as is done in Zen. Heidegger does not want to say that the death of the individual is ultimately unreal, nor would Eckhart want to deny that each soul is a unique creation of God. Both are, on this point at least, very Western. Zen, on the other hand, teaches that "from the first nothing is," that the "being" (*ein Seiendes*) is an epiphenomenon.

Moreover, just as the Zen master tells us that *sunyata* can only be "grasped" by a thought which is "no thought" (*wu-nien*), Heidegger tells us that in order to think upon Being we must take up a thinking which is wholly unlike everything that "thinking" has previously meant. We must adopt a "thinking" which does not "represent," which does not "calculate" or "reason." To the scientist and man of reason, this thinking is indistinguishable from "not thinking" at all. Indeed, Heidegger describes it in terms which are very similar to those of the Zen masters. Where Hui-neng teaches the doctrine of "letting go of yourself" Heidegger teaches "letting-be" (*Gelassenheit*). Again, Heidegger speaks of "meditative" (*besinnlich*) thinking, and we know that "Zen" as a term is the counterpart to the Chinese "*ch'an*" which itself translates the Sanskrit "*dhyana*," meaning "meditation." "No-thought" is

213

"meditative," even as "releasement" is "meditative thought". In each case, then, to "think" means to have cleared away all concepts and representations and every trace of willing in order to be open to what is truly thought-worthy. And in each case this "thinking" is attained only by a "leap" from rational to meditative thought. As Heidegger speaks of the "leap of thought," Hui-neng champions the "abrupt" school among the ancient Chinese masters (Suz., 185).

We have also seen that *sunyata* is not an "achievement" or "accomplishment" on the part of the ego. Herrigel, we recall, deserved no credit for his accomplishments. So too in the *Discourse on Thinking* Heidegger writes:

> *Teacher:* If only I possessed the right releasement, then I would soon be freed of that task of weaning.
> *Scholar:* So far as we can wean ourselves from willing, we contribute to the awakening of releasement.
> *Teacher:* Say rather, to keeping awake for releasement.
> *Scholar:* Why not, to the awakening?
> *Teacher:* Because on our own we do not awaken releasement in ourselves.
> *Scientist:* Then releasement is effected from somewhere else.
> *Teacher:* Not effected, but let in.

(G, 34/60-1)

Moreover, in the same way that Herrigel was told that "letting go of yourself" was a matter of "waiting" for the tension to build up so as to release the bowstring at the right time, the teacher in *Gelassenheit* tells us that true releasement consists in "waiting" for thought.

In Zen, when the self has become entirely ego-less and will-less, it is admitted into "*satori.*" In Heidegger, Dasein is admitted into the truth of Being, the "event of appropriation". Thus to *satori*, the state of "enlightenment," we relate the "lighting" (*lichten*) process of the "clearing" (*Lichtung*) which is made in Dasein for the event of truth. In and through this "event," Dasein enters into its ownmost essential being (*Wesen*), even as the soul enters into its innermost ground (*Seelengrund*), and the self in Zen is awakened to its "Buddha-nature" or "self-nature." Both Zen (*satori*) and Eckhart (Birth of the Son) describe this experience as one of "peace" and "consolation," a kind of heavenly bliss on earth. But for Heidegger, while there is a certain "tranquillity" in Dasein's "openness to the Mystery," there is also the element of surrender to an "ominous" power. Once again, when we find *Gelassenheit* in its religious context, even in a religion such as Zen Buddhism where there is no doctrine of a loving heavenly Father, we find it is an act of trust. In Heidegger, on the other hand, it is a "high and dangerous game."

There is one final, and important, point of comparison. When the young monk asked what is the meaning of Bodhidharma's coming from the West, the master said: the cypress in the garden. Ueda has shown that Eckhart can answer the question, "what is the meaning of Christ's coming to the soul?" by responding, "the rose." Now what if a novice in "thinking" should ask: what is the essence of Being as the un-concealed? Surely, Heidegger can answer: "the jug," or "the bridge at Heidelberg," or even "the rose"—for he has made Angelus Silesius's rose his own. What I am suggesting is this. In Zen, Heidegger and Eckhart there is a very comparable letting-go of all rational, calculative, and teleological thinking. For all these thinkers the questions "why?" and "how?" are to be overcome (Suz., 221) for they serve to close us off from "*sunyata*," from the "divine God," from the "truth of Being." Each can make his own the saying of Angelus Silesius: "The rose is without why; it blooms because it blooms." Each counsels the same selflessness and egolessness of the second line: "It cares not for itself; it asks not if it's seen." Heidegger, Eckhart, and Zen all ask the self to live without why, to be "free" of the calculative mentality which never accepts a thing for what it is, but always seeks to "explain" (*erklären*) it by "founding" (*er-gründen*) it on something else—its cause or purpose. To the detached man the elemental mystery of things is allowed to shine through even the most commonplace things. Things become "things" in Heidegger's sense of this term. They become resplendent with their source and ground and for the first time stand forth as what they are. In Zen, in Eckhart, and in Heidegger there is a "letting lie forth" (*Vor-liegenlassen*) which lets the cypress tree, the rose, and the jug "be" the "thing" that it is.

A Zen master once said that before a man studies Zen mountains are mountains; when he has advanced a little way, mountains are no longer mountains; but when he experiences *satori*, he recognizes that mountains are once more mountains (Suz., 14). So, too, in Heidegger, when Dasein has fully opened itself to Being, then it has released the "thing" in its essential being; it allows the thing to truly be what it is. Thus the jug—or the bridge at Heidelberg—becomes transparent in its Being, resplendent, refulgent with Being (*Be-dingnis*). The truth of Being demands as a precondition that we adopt a new attitude towards things which lets them lie forth as the things which they are. Nowhere, I think, can one find a better idea of what the "truth" of Being is for Heidegger than in his account of the "thing" as the intersection of the Fourfold. Without this account, without an *experience* of the "thing," "Being in its truth" is forever an empty formula. Thus if a student in an undergraduate course on Heidegger asks "but what, sir, *does* Heidegger mean by the truth of Being which is concealed from metaphysics?", perhaps we need only place a jug upon the lectern and point to it knowingly!

I should like to conclude this section by noting two important differences between Heidegger and Zen.[33] When Bodhidharma came from the West he brought this message:

> A special transmission outside the Scriptures;
> No dependence upon words and letters;
> Direct pointing to the soul of man;
> Seeing into one's nature and the attainment of Buddhahood.
>
> (Suz., 61)

Zen is not dependent upon any "sacred scriptures" which contain its essential teachings. The "essential being" (*Wesen*) of Zen is an experience which is translated directly, from mind to mind, from master to disciple. Language for Zen is like a finger pointing to the moon; it must be disregarded in favor of a "direct pointing" without fingers, or words—lest we see the finger instead of the moon. That is why when a disciple asks a question about the essence of Zen, he is frequently met with stone silence and he sometimes is even slapped in the face or struck with the master's stick. But where Bodhidharma says, "No dependence upon words and letters," Heidegger says that language is the house of Being: "Where words give out no thing may be." It is interesting to observe that Meister Eckhart occupies something of a half-way house with respect to these two positions. With the Zen masters, he agrees that the divine Godhead is understood only in absolute silence and so, on this point, is nearer to Zen than to Heidegger. But, like Heidegger, he is considerably interested in language and is himself a master of the German vernacular; as a Christian he is deeply interested in the Sacred Scriptures and, most importantly, in the doctrine of the "divine Word."[34] Thus, like Heidegger, he is interested in a language which is more than human.

The second difference between Zen and Heidegger is that, like Meister Eckhart, Zen is more interested in eternity than time. For "time" belongs to the world of relativity and opposites. Like Meister Eckhart, Zen

216

wants to find an eternal "now" wherein the soul never grows old—for this is its solution to the problem of birth and death, illness and old age (*dukkha*). But for Heidegger it is only when man awakens to the essentially historical character of Being (*das Seinsgeschick*) and of his own mortality and temporality that his forgetfulness of Being is overcome. On this point Heidegger is radically Western and "worldly," and parts company with the mystics of both the East and West.

CHAPTER FIVE

MYSTICISM AND THOUGHT

THE extensive preparation which we insisted was necessary in order to deal with the problem of the mystical element in Heidegger's thought is now complete. We have analyzed Heidegger's critique of metaphysics and discussed the alliance which Heidegger makes with the mystic by means of his step back out of metaphysics. The existence of a mystical element in Heidegger's thought, the profound analogy of Heidegger with the mystic, can no longer be doubted. The task that now remains is to assess the significance of this analogy, to determine what relationship Heidegger's thinking bears to mysticism and what implications this relationship has for our understanding of Heidegger.

We have articulated the problem of the mystical element in Heidegger's thought in the form of six questions. (1) Is Heidegger a self-styled mystic whose overtures to a mystical relationship to Being are pretentious and arrogant? (2) Is Heidegger a genuine mystic and his "thinking" a "mysticism"? (3) Is the mystical element in Heidegger's thought a clear proof of the anti-humanistic character of "thought"? (4) Has the path of "releasement" (*Gelassenheit*) in Heidegger become dangerous and ominous, having cut itself off from the "divine consolation" found in the religious mystic Meister Eckhart? (5) What is the significance of "thinking" for ethics? (6) Finally, what interest can a thinking which is allied to mysticism hold for philosophy? We will take up each of these questions in turn in the course of this chapter. Then, in a concluding section, we will offer some final remarks aimed at developing a critical appreciation of Heidegger's achievement.

1. The "False Eckhart"?

Hühnerfeld has contended that the mystical overtones we so clearly detect in Heidegger's later writings are an arrogant disguise intentionally created by Heidegger himself. Hühnerfeld has two reasons for charging Heidegger with "masquerading" as a modern-day Eckhart. (1) Unlike Eckhart, Heidegger harbors a disdain for the world and regards the social community as a contemptible "they." The Christian Eckhart, on the other hand, regards the world as God's creation and other men as sons of God. (2) There is no "God" in Heidegger's self-styled mysticism, but that is the one thing which true mysticism cannot lack. Eckhart abandons himself to the loving arms of God, Heidegger to the abyss of "Nothingness" (Hühn., 125).

As to the first point, Hühnerfeld is simply mistaken. As the preceding analysis has brought out, Eckhart and Heidegger—and even, as a matter of fact, Zen Buddhism—are all in agreement that it is not things and places and people which hinder us but our attitude towards them. Eckhart and Zen do not tell us that we must leave the world and enter a monastery to find God, nor does Heidegger tell us that we must re-create a pre-technological society such as the early Greeks had in order to experience Being. In each case it is a matter of learning to break the shell of creatures in order to find God within, of learning to see that the *Tao* is our everyday experience, of learning to find a new "rootedness" (*Bodenständigkeit*) in the technical world. Moreover, there is in the case of Eckhart, Heidegger—and Zen—as we have seen, a similar doctrine of letting-lie-forth (*Vorliegenlassen*), of letting the rose, the cypress tree, and the jug be the things which they are. Had Hühnerfeld taken the trouble to compare carefully what Eckhart and Heidegger actually say about the "world" and "things," he would have found as much. He was instead content to lay it down *a priori* that there can be no true likeness between the Christian Eckhart and the "post-Christian" Heidegger (as Löwith calls him).

But let us add here our familiar word of caution. In Heidegger, learning to say "yes" and "no" to technology, learning to acquire a new relationship to technical things (G, 24-5/53-4), does not suffice

219

of itself to bring about a new dawn. It is at best a precondition which Being requires of thought. For Heidegger is not talking about a personal conversion by which a man learns to approach the world with a new attitude. He has in mind more deeply the movements of Being itself, of the *Ereignis*, and this is a matter of the course that world-history will follow, which is something over which no individual, be he converted or not, has mastery. The best that man can do in this regard is to think, but thinking does not produce effects (*Wirkungen*: Sp. 212/279) in world history.

Nor does Heidegger regard the social world as a "they" which is always to be avoided. In *Being and Time*, for example, there are at least two interesting texts in which Heidegger discusses authentic being-with (SZ, § 26, 122/159; § 60, 298/344-5). His intention in *Being and Time* is not to say that all being-with takes the form of being subjugated to the quiet dictatorship of the they, but that such subjection is what being-with tends to become insofar as Dasein is fallen. Authentically resolved Dasein, on the other hand, not only acquires an authentic relationship to its own innermost potentiality for Being, it also acquires a comparable relationship to that of others. So too in the later writings Heidegger occasionally refers to thinking as a "conversation." Thus in "The Thinker as Poet" Heidegger devotes one section to the "companionable reflection" which takes place in a genuine "conversation" (*Gespräch*). By this he means a dialogue which does not represent the matching of wits of two contestants who wish to show one another what they know, but a thoughtful dialogue which occurs because thought descends upon the participants in the dialogue like a ray of sun over the meadows (AED, 10-1/6). This is not the place to enter into a full-scale debate about the place of the social in Heidegger's thought, for this is a problem which would distract us from the central thesis of this book. We simply wish to show that there is hardly grounds for trying to dismiss the analogy between Heidegger and Meister Eckhart on this basis.

The second reason Hühnerfeld advances for the "pretentiousness" of Heidegger's mysticism is the fact that there is no God in this modern-day Eckhart, that Dasein is released not to God but to Being. This is an equally shaky argument. For it is hardly clear in what sense there is a God in the various species of Buddhism, and there is certainly no monotheistic creator-God in any of them. Yet Buddhism, and particularly Zen, is one of the most time-honored forms of Eastern "mysticism." Moreover, Hühnerfeld's choice of Plotinus as a paradigm mystic is a further refutation of what he himself contends. For Plotinus is no Christian, his "one" is no loving Father, and Plotinus surely taught no doctrine of creation. The fact is that Hühnerfeld is describing only Western Christian mysticism. He has not shown that Heidegger is not a mystic, but that he is not Meister Eckhart, that his thought differs from Meister Eckhart's, which of course it does. But it remains entirely possible that Heidegger's is a mysticism of a different sort.

When all is said and done, Hühnerfeld is suggesting that Heidegger is some kind of pretender to an experience which he has never had. Heidegger parades his later thought about in the costuming of traditional mysticism in order to conceal its own bankruptcy. Heidegger does not speak "out of the experience of thought"; rather he is cribbing from his unacknowledged mystical sources. At this point, it seems to me, Hühnerfeld has painted himself into the corner. For the best response one can make to the question he is raising, of whether Heidegger speaks out of a genuine experience of Being, is that there is no way to tell. That is not only true of Heidegger, but of every thinker, Meister Eckhart included, who claims to speak from experience. It is a commonplace in epistemology that we do not have experience of other people's experiences. Now historians of Western religion have generally agreed, e.g., that Meister Eckhart was one of the great Western mystics, but that Angelus Silesius, on the other hand, was an anthologizer of mystical ideas who did not speak from experience—although he was indeed a very gifted poet. There is no way to tell if this is so. One simply reads Angelus Silesius and finds ideas and images which others have already expressed. But when one reads Meister Eckhart one gets the "sense" of freshness, of a writer who is speaking first-hand, who has "been somewhere," "seen something" —none of which, however, proves anything about Meister Eckhart. One cannot even be certain that Meister Eckhart was not a false Eckhart.

The best one can do in approaching Heidegger's thought—as also with Meister Eckhart—is to see if one gets a sense of a fresh and original first-hand experience. And if that is the criterion by which one judges Heidegger's thought, then a very strong case indeed can be made on behalf of the authenticity of Heidegger's "experience." For Heidegger's path of thought began in the method of "first-hand seeing," of the direct intuiting of essences—and it later culminated in the call to undergo an "experience" of the subject matter of thinking. Being for him is the *Sache* of thought, which is something that can only be *experienced.* That is why he contends that he always remained faithful to the most basic meaning and orientation of phenomenology, which is the first-hand experience of the *Sache* itself (SD, 87/79).[1]

221

Heidegger's entire thought can be aptly characterized by the title which he gave to the poetic utterances which he composed in 1947: *Out of the Experience of Thought*. In this short work he says:

Few are experienced enough in the difference between an object of scholarship and a matter of thought.   (AED, 9/5)

One does not follow along Heidegger's path by learning a doctrine or by doing research on a body of writings. In this respect he is very close to Kierkegaard, to Zen—and to Meister Eckhart. Instead, one must have an experience of the matter of thought, of Being. His essays on language illustrate this well. The aim of these essays is "to prepare to undergo an experience with language" (*mit der Sprache eine Erfahrung zu machen*: US, 159/57). To undergo an experience of something means that something "befalls us, strikes us, comes over us, overwhelms and transforms us" (US, 159/57). To experience language is to have one's relationship to language transformed. For analytic philosophy, for linguistics, metalinguistics, psycholinguistics, and the rest, language is an "object" of scholarship and calculative thought, not the source of an experience. In the experience of language, we discover that we are in the grips of language, that if the appropriate word is missing or found, it is because language itself withholds or bestows itself (US, 161-2/59); we learn that it is not we who play with words, but language itself which plays with us (WHD, 83/118). We discover in this experience that words let things be (appear). Our very relationship to language is thereby transformed, for we come to realize that it is not we who speak but language which speaks through us.

If such a view of language is presented to the linguistic analyst, e.g., he would want to know what "proofs" we have for Heidegger's "thesis." But none of what Heidegger says takes place in the realm of "assertions" "about" language. Heidegger's thoughtful experience of language occurs outside the sphere of influence of the Principle of Ground (SG, 72). It can be understood only by those who have had the experience, who can shut off concepts and representations and listen to what language is really saying.

Speaking for myself, I find Heidegger's talk of an "experience" of Being, or of language, or of the essence of *Technik*, to be expressed with an impressive virtuosity and richness, to be subtly detailed and finely nuanced, to be sensitive at every turn to the intrusions of calculative, objectivistic thought. I find everything to suggest, therefore, that Heidegger's thought does indeed arise from a penetrating and genuine experience, and nothing to suggest that it is a masquerade draped out in the vocabulary of Meister Eckhart; I find nothing to suggest that it is a second-hand record of someone else's insight. This is, I might add, as Biemel also points out,[2] something one cannot say of a good deal of the Heidegger literature, the "secondary" literature, which is often pretentious. The sense one gets from reading Heidegger's later writings is very like the sense one has in reading Meister Eckhart, who also seems to speak from "first-hand seeing." Heidegger's thought has always been dominated by a keen and sharpened sensitivity to the meaning of Being as Being. In his early writings he thought that such an insight could be contained within the confines of an ontology, albeit of a more radical sort. He even sought in those days to find a new "concept" of Being (SZ, § 2, 6/26). But as that experience developed and deepened, he came to hold that every "concept" and every "assertion" spoke from the outside, spoke "about" Being, and that to be faithful to the chosen path—the question of Being—he had to learn a new way of speaking—from the "inside," from "*out of* the experience" of Being itself.

2. *Mysticism and Thought*

But while I believe that Heidegger speaks to us out of an experience of Being, I do not mean to suggest that his experience is *mystical*. I believe that Heidegger is right to insist, as he sometimes does, that his thinking is *not a mysticism*. In the minutes of the seminar which Heidegger gave on "Time and Being," there occurs the observation that this "experiencing is nothing mystical, not an act of illumination, but rather the entry into dwelling in appropriation" (SD, 57/53). And in "The End of Philosophy and the Task of Thought," he asks rhetorically whether thought is to be treated as a "groundless mysticism" which is here equated with "irrationalism" (SD, 79/71). We thus find ourselves with a state of affairs quite the opposite of that described by Hühnerfeld. For while there is everything to suggest that Heidegger has undergone a unique and special experience of Being, we find on the other hand that Heidegger himself denies that it is a mystical experience. Thinking is not mysticism, although mysticism might be added to the list of the three dangers to thought—along with poetry, philosophy, and thought itself (AED, 14-5/8). For there is, as we have well seen in these pages, something mystic-like in Heidegger, some kind of a "mystical element" with which we are tempted to identify "thought" itself.

There is in "thinking," as also in mysticism, an extraordinary sensitivity to an encompassing presence, a presence which we cannot seize with concepts, but to which we must open ourselves in letting-be. But it would be in the end very misleading to call Heidegger's later thought a modern-day mysticism, for that would suggest the existence of certain elements in Heidegger which are not to be found there, and it would preclude the existence of other elements which are found there. To speak of "Heidegger's mysticism" tends to disfigure the total significance of his work, to throw his reader and potential reader off. There are, I will now show, six essential elements in Heidegger's thought which put him at odds with traditional "mysticism," and these constitute six reasons why, in my judgment, thought is not to be identified with mysticism.

(1)   The first of these has to do with the fact that Heidegger's experience is an experience with *language*. Our analysis in the preceding chapter of Heidegger's relationship to Eckhart—and indeed to Zen—on the question of language unearthed an important disanalogy between Heidegger and the mystic. For while Eckhart spoke of a primal "word" (*verbum*, *Wort*), he wanted to say that the truest language of all was absolutely silent, and is spoken in eternity. Human words are for Eckhart only "images" of the eternal Word. But in Heidegger the "metaphysical" distinction between an eternal and silent word and words spoken in time does not appear. Indeed, what Heidegger pursues is the very *opposite* of Meister Eckhart: a renewal of language itself. If Wittgenstein is right in identifying the mystical with that which cannot be put into words (*Tractatus Logico-Philosophicus*, 6.522), then it is in Eckhart alone, and not in Heidegger, that we find mysticism. Eckhart writes:

> The most beautiful thing which man can express about God is found in the fact that, out of the wisdom of inner treasures, he is able to keep silent about God.   (Q, 353,21-3/ Ev., 246)

But contrary to this, Heidegger's intent is to bring Being into language, to find the words to bring language itself into language (*die Sprache als Sprache zur Sprache zu bringen*: US, 242/112).

For Heidegger, silence is the condition for authentic language, inasmuch as it is only in silence that one hears what is to be said. Silence is also an attribute of authentic language, inasmuch as one must never say too much. Finally, silence is even a very important mode of authentic language—there can, e.g., be a "pregnant silence," or a "silent look" which says more than any words. But such silences as these can occur only within the framework and boundaries of language, as a caesura *within* language. What never happens for Heidegger is that silence altogether *replaces* language, as it does in Meister Eckhart, and even more so in Zen—in which the young initiate is told to stop using bad language when he utters the name "Buddha," or is even thrashed with a stick for speaking at all. Heidegger does not want to cut off all language for the sake of "inner silence." He wishes instead to curb the pretensions of the rational, technical language of philosophy and the sciences in favor of a richer and more supple language, a language which is found both in his own very unusual style in the later writings (*die Sprache spricht, die Welt weltet*, etc.) and in the language of the poets.[3] Heidegger does not want to replace ordinary and technical language with silence but with a new and transformed language. Eckhart was a representative of the *theologia negativa*, and he stood for mystical silence. Heidegger's thought did not take a *mystical* but a *linguistic* turn. Like the poet George, Heidegger "renounces" the mystical, for he renounces the hope of having an experience with Being—or with language—which takes place outside the limits of language.[4]

(2) The second element in Heidegger's experience which is misrepresented by calling it "mystical" is that Heidegger's experience of Being is an experience with *time* and the *historical*. Eckhart was very much under the influence of Augustine and the neo-Platonic tradition. He emphasized that God was an eternal, timeless one, far removed from change, multiplicity, and number. Accordingly, the goal he set for the soul was to enter into the same timeless "now" in which God Himself lives:

> . . . God is in this power [the ground of the soul] as in the eternal Now. If the spirit [the soul] were always united with God in this power, man would never grow old—for the Now in which God created the first man, and the Now in which the last man perishes, and the Now in which I speak are the same Now and are nothing but *one* Now. Now, look, this man dwells in one light with God; consequently, there is in him neither suffering nor the sequence of time, but one eternity which remains the same. From this man in truth all wonder has been taken away, and all things stand in their essence in him. Consequently, he receives nothing new from future things nor from any "chance" event, since he dwells in *one* Now, always new, without intermission. (Q, 162,2-13/Serm., 136)

In detaching itself from everything created, the soul is detached from time itself. In the passage just cited, Eckhart refers to one of the most

225

characteristic teachings of Christian Neoplatonism, viz., the theory of the Divine Ideas. He says that in the ground of the soul "all things stand in their essence." The detached heart becomes one with God, and so with the Divine "Mind" in which is contained the eternal ideas or exemplars which precede the existence of things in space and time. Indeed, by detachment, a man becomes one with his *own* exemplar and so "most like the image of what he was when there was no difference between him and God, before God had created the world" (DW, V, 539/Cl., 160). This same desire to enter into a timeless now, free from all change and suffering, we might add, is also characteristic of Buddhism. The Zen masters even speak of seeing one's face before one's birth—i.e., of becoming one with the source from which one's being in time originates—even as does Eckhart.

Eckhart's attitude toward time is in keeping with traditional mysticism; he wishes to see God in all things so that one "day"—in eternity—he may see all things in God. But for Heidegger such "mysticism" is "metaphysical" because it moves within the distinction between time and eternity. Like Plato, Plotinus, and Augustine, Eckhart makes time an image of eternity—despite the fact that Käte Oltmanns was able to find in his idea of time Heidegger's "authentic temporality" (Olt., 153-4). He defines time in terms of the primacy of the now; eternity is the permanent now (*nunc stans*); time is the moving now (*nunc movens*). And the aim of the soul is to transcend the flowing time in which the outer man is caught up in order to enter into the eternal now in the ground of the soul. Eckhart's whole theory of time rests on the basis of a conception of Being as permanent "presence" (*Anwesen*) and stands in the shadows of Greek metaphysics. This is the restriction which must be put on our earlier comparison of Being as *physis* in Heidegger and Being as a welling up and overflowing (*ebullitio*) in Meister Eckhart.

Heidegger's "concern" (*Sache*), on the other hand, is not with eternity but with time. While Eckhart wants to transcend time for eternity, Heidegger remains a thinker for a *time* of need. The Principle of Sufficient Ground is by no means for Heidegger an "eternal" truth, as for the Platonic-Rationalist tradition, but a profoundly "historical" principle. It is historical not because it "has a history" but because it is by its essence historical. As it is understood by Heidegger the Principle of Sufficient Ground is a response to a call which has addressed Western philosophers from Plato to the atomic age. It does not "have a history" but rather it determines the historical fate of the West and even today holds us under its sway. Now it is precisely this "historical fate of the West" which really interests Heidegger. It is all along this historical reference—this reference to the needs of the time—which gives to Heidegger's work from *Being and Time* to "Time and Being" its great interest, and which gives to his "question of Being" its great urgency:

> The attempt to think Being without beings becomes necessary because otherwise, it seems to me, there is no longer any possibility of explicitly bringing into view the Being of what *is* today all around the globe (*Erdball*), let alone of adequately determining the relation of man to what has been called "Being" up to now. (SD, 2/2)

There is in Heidegger—in contrast to Meister Eckhart's Christian Neoplatonism—a profoundly "secular" character, despite all of Heidegger's talk of the "gods" and the "holy." Secular means having to do with the *saeculum*, the ages, the times. But the "times" are to be understood, for Heidegger, in terms of the mission (*Geschick*) of Being, and the mission of Being in terms of the Event of Appropriation (*Ereignis*). The secular character of Heidegger's thought consists in his unwavering concern with the history of the West, with its "epochal transformations," with the "future" of the West which is, for him, bound up with and hidden in its first beginnings in the Greeks. This could not be the case for Eckhart. While Eckhart is, to be sure, a man of his times, while he addresses himself to the needs of his contemporaries, while he is "historically important," nonetheless, time, history, the ages, are not the final and ultimate concern of his thought. What is at *issue* for Eckhart, what genuinely concerns him—the real "*Sache*" for Eckhart—is God in His eternity—not the history of the West. But the *Sache* of Heidegger's thought lies precisely in the Event from which the successive ages of Western history issue.

Once again it is evident that Heidegger does not make the typically mystical move. It is profoundly *un*characteristic of the mystic to be concerned with the historical; it is profoundly characteristic of him to identify his experience as an experience of a timeless now. Heidegger's concern is secular and worldly. His question is not a religious question, about sin and alienation from God—but a secular one, a "world-question" (*Weltfrage*: SG, 211), about the history of the West.

We should point out that there is one further complication concerning the problem of time and eternity in Heidegger's thought. As we have seen in our first chapter, Löwith has argued that Heidegger's expressions in his later writings often gravitate away from time and the historical and towards something like eternity (Löw., 33-6). He singles out in particular Heidegger's references to the "abiding" (*das Bleibende*) and

227

to "eternity" in *Erläuterungen zu Hölderlins Dichtung* (HD, 71) and to the "indestructible" in the "Postscript" to *What is Metaphysics?* (WM, 50/359), all of which are for Heidegger descriptions of Being. In this "permanent" origin of beings, Heidegger seems to say, man finds rest from the succession of ages, from the sequence of epochal transformations. To the extent that Heidegger does move in this direction, his thought does indeed come closer to mysticism and begin to lose its "secular" character. For this attempt to escape from the fluctuations of time and to find "rest" in something "permanent" is distinctly typical of the mystics.

This problem is faced in the "Seminar" on "Time and Being." In the lecture itself Heidegger claimed that the "It" (*das Es*) which "gives" (*Es gibt*) is not time—for time is also "given" (*Es gibt Zeit*)—but the Event (*Ereignis*) itself. The Event, therefore, to the extent that it is the source of time, is itself beyond time. In the seminar it is pointed out that Heidegger here seems to think upon something "missionless" (*Geschicklos*) and so "unhistorical" (SD, 44-5/40-2). But it is argued in the Seminar that there is a motion proper to the Event. What this means is perhaps clarified by a remark in *On the Way to Language* where Heidegger is discussing "rest":

> As the stilling of stillness, rest, conceived strictly, is always more in motion than all motion and always more restlessly active than any agitation.
> (US, 29/206-7)

For a rest is not the absence of motion, he says in SG, but the "assembling together of all motions" (SG, 144). While every part is in motion—like Heraclitus's river—the whole is at rest within its boundaries. But since the whole which remains at rest is greater than any moving part, the whole is more in motion than any of its parts. Thus the Event, as the abiding source of the succession of metaphysical epochs, is more in motion than the historical movement to which it gives rise. I am not convinced that this explanation answers Heidegger's critics,[5] but I do not think that Heidegger is therefore aligning himself with a mystical "flight from time." For while the Event as the *source* of history is prior to time, still it is the source of *history*. Heidegger's concern is still plainly the "world," the globe (*Erdball*), the history of the West. The primal "It" which sends "Being" in its various historical forms is introduced in the wake of an experience with the *history* of Being. It is something deeper "within" history; it is not "beyond" history in eternity (Eckhart), nor does it make history an epiphenomenon (Zen). It is something which lies at the base of this "world"; it is not to be found in "another" world. Thus I think that Löwith—and others—have pointed out a serious difficulty with Heidegger's thought on time—one which does indeed typify a certain "mystical tendency" in Heidegger's later work. But I do not believe that this difficulty undermines the "secular" character of Heidegger's work, for it in no way suggests that Heidegger's ultimate concern is *not* with the history and fate of the West, as the very title of Löwith's book testifies.[6]

(3)   Our discussion of the first two disanalogies between mysticism and thought allows us to formulate a third one, one which is in a sense but a generalization of the first two. Although I believe that mysticism, certainly the mysticism of Meister Eckhart, effects the step back out of metaphysics, I believe too that there is in mysticism a certain residual presence of metaphysics. This can be explained as follows. The mystic has certainly stepped back out of metaphysics in a number of clear and indisputable ways. The God of the mystics is not the God of onto-theo-logic, not a first cause, not a metaphysical creator. Man is not for the mystic the rational animal. Thinking for him is not conceiving but letting-be. So too the sphere of the will is overcome for will-lessness. But still there remains in a mystic like Meister Eckhart a tendency to move within certain metaphysical distinctions. We have already addressed ourselves to two of these, viz., the distinction between speech and silence, and between time and eternity. We have also noted in Chapter Three, in discussing the ground of the soul, that Eckhart liked to speak in terms of the "outer man" and the "inner man," again a distinction which is appropriate to Christian Neoplatonism but not to "thought."

We might generalize this tendency of Eckhart's mysticism by saying that it tends to move within the distinction between sensible and super-sensible being, which is of course a distinction implied by the literal meaning of the word "metaphysics." As a scholastic *magister* Eckhart subscribed to a unique blend of ideas inherited from Augustine and Plotinus, Aquinas and Albert the Great, and very skillfully and originally synthesized by himself. The predominant impression one has in reading the Latin writings is of a thinker whom one would classify among the Christian Neoplatonists. One need only mention the central role played in Eckhart's thought by the doctrine of the pre-existence of all things in the divine mind as eternal exemplars, or the centrality of the doctrine of God as the One who is beyond being itself. There is thus a set of metaphysical oppositions in Eckhart which try to make their way from the Latin to the German writings. All these oppositions

229

turn on the distinction between the sphere of unchanging eternal super-sensible being, on the one hand, and changing temporal being, on the other, between the inner sphere which is one and the outer sphere which is the home of multiplicity.

Of course, if these metaphysical oppositions played a predominant role in his German writings too, then the analogy we have drawn between Eckhart and Heidegger would collapse. But this is not the case. On the contrary, one of the most significant impressions one gets from the German writings is Eckhart's interest in overcoming these oppositions. "God" and "creatures" are different only to those who have not entered into the ground of the soul and discovered there the God who is neither "God" nor creator and the creature as it was before it was created. Eternity and time are different only to the man who has not found the eternal now which lies silently at the core of his soul. Action and contemplation are opposites only to those who have not read the story of Mary and Martha and understood its mystical sense. The "world" is a place of Godlessness from which we should take flight only to those who do not know how to break the shell of creatures and find God within. Eckhart was a precursor of the Reformation precisely because he never saw the need to leave the world in order to find God. In other words to the extent that Eckhart's writings are mystical they are bent on overcoming the contrarieties he has inherited from metaphysics. Nietzsche wrote:[7]

> This mode of judgment constitutes the typical prejudice by which meta-physicians of all ages can be recognized; . . . The fundamental faith of the metaphysicians is *the faith in antithetical values.*

If Nietzsche is right, and Nietzsche does indeed appear to be the source of this element in Heidegger's idea of metaphysics, one can say that in his mystical, German writings Eckhart attempts to overcome these antitheses and to throw this faith into doubt. Still the residue is there.

(4) We are now in a position to formulate a fourth distinction between Heidegger and the mystic, one which is closely related to the preceding distinctions. We said in the previous discussion that there is a certain residual streak of metaphysics detectable in Eckhart's mysticism. We insisted too, however, that Eckhart's mystical writings broke through this metaphysical mold and entered a new sphere, the sphere of letting-be and of the truly divine God. However there is a sense in which, from a Heideggerian perspective, Eckhart still remains part of the "tradition," even if Eckhart has effected a breakthrough beyond

metaphysics. There is a sense in which both mysticism and metaphysics belong to a larger "tradition," for both mysticism and metaphysics belong to the "history" of the West, an historical tradition indeed which it is the purpose of Heidegger's thought to meditate and so to overcome.

In other words, Heidegger's thought is from this point of view more radical than Eckhart's insofar as his thought is radically historical. If Meister Eckhart has moved beyond metaphysics this has been effected by moving from one alternative within the Western tradition, the metaphysical one, into another, the mystico-religious alternative. His metaphysical side is rooted in his Aristotelian scholasticism; his mysticism is inspired by Plotinus and St. Augustine. Heidegger on the other hand wants to think that from which the entire tradition springs. Heidegger does not want to be identified with either alternative within the Western tradition, but rather to think the primal "It" which "gives" both mysticism and metaphysics, which gives both Augustinianism and Aristotelianism.

Hence insofar as we have undertaken to interpret Heidegger from the standpoint of Eckhart, we may give the mistaken impression that we want to locate Heidegger *within* the tradition, that "thinking" is a part of the tradition, albeit a different part than metaphysics. This is, however, not the case. For insofar as thinking thinks in terms of the mission of Being (*Seinsgeschickliches Denken*) thinking cannot assume a place within the tradition, even a non-metaphysical place. It must, if it is true to itself, assume a place not "outside" that tradition but at the heart and origin (*Ursprung*) of it, at the very place, namely, from which the tradition springs up, from which the various dispensations (*Geschicke*) originate. Therefore, Heidegger's thought is not mysticism insofar as mysticism belongs to the history of the West and thinking is bent on overcoming that history. This applies not only to Western Christian mysticism, which can, as we shall see, be integrated into the development of the Western tradition as the historical alternative to metaphysics. But it also applies to Eastern mysticism where what we in the West tend to call "mystical" thought is not an alternative but rather is (or has been up until now) the predominant and guiding tradition. Presumably, were thinking to take place in the setting of the Eastern world, thinking would have the task of finding the "It" which gives the Eastern tradition.

This seems to me an important part of the disanalogy in the analogy between Heidegger and Meister Eckhart. I would therefore like to develop this idea somewhat more fully. To do this let us look briefly at an essay by Paul Tillich entitled "The Two Types of the Philosophy of Religion."[8] For in this essay Tillich makes an interesting distinction between two approaches to God or the "unconditioned" which allows us to situate mysticism and Eckhart *within* the Western tradition. Having done this one can then view Heidegger's thought as an attempt to make the step back out of that tradition. We will in this way be able to form a sharper idea of the difference between Heidegger and Eckhart, and we will be able to see the limitations of approaching Heidegger from the standpoint of the mystic. For our strategy in this book, let us remind the reader, is not to say that Heidegger is a new Eckhart and his thinking a modern mysticism. It is rather to find an avenue of approach to Heidegger's own distinctive path of thought; it is to find an access to Heidegger by way of a thinker who has, I am convinced, exerted an influence on Heidegger and to whom Heidegger bears an analogy. This approach, however, should in no way be construed as an attempt to reduce Heidegger to Eckhart, that is, to reabsorb thinking into mysticism. If anything it helps to underline and highlight what is uniquely his own about Heidegger's path, what we might call the "*Jemeinigkeit*" of Heidegger's path. Every "approach" to Heidegger is necessarily limited; every approach comes at him from but one perspective. And the best that any author can do who takes an "approach," after having exploited the advantages afforded by his vantage point, is to point out the limitations of the perspective he has adopted. That is the task in which we are currently engaged.

Tillich distinguishes the "ontological" and the "cosmological" approach to God or what is better called the "unconditioned." The ontological approach regards God as a possession of the soul, an *a priori*; the discovery of God is the discovery of oneself, one's own truest being. But the cosmological approach regards God as something other than the self, something transcendent which one must "prove" by argument or "assent to" by faith. In the cosmological argument there is no immediate contact with God, no direct awareness; rather God must in some way be "established." Hence in the cosmological tradition we meet proofs for God's existence and the whole enterprise which Heidegger calls "onto-theo-logic." The cosmological approach is "positivistic," for God is something other, a particular being albeit of the highest sort, which we "posit" either from faith or by reason. But in the ontological approach God is not a being but Being itself; He is not posited but is the *a priori* which precedes every proposition. He is the light in whose light other things are seen; He is the truth by which other truths are possible. He cannot be denied because He is the condition under which all questions are asked. We are always certain of His presence even if we do not know His name or know how to speak of Him. Atheism is possible only in the cosmological approach, where we are free to posit or not to posit Him. But in the ontological approach, we live and move and have our being in God. Tillich is fond of citing Augustine's remark that God is closer to the soul than the soul is to itself. But of course what is ontically closest can be ontologically farthest. We do not necessarily understand our preontological possessions.

The prototype and paradigm of the ontological approach is found in St. Augustine. Augustine is a profoundly "religious" man. The theological tradition which interested Tillich strongly was the Franciscan tradition in the thirteenth century because it carried out the theology of St. Augustine. The prototype of the cosmological approach to God is Thomas Aquinas who draws his inspiration from Aristotle. The difference between Augustine and Thomas is the difference between wisdom (*sapientia*) and science (*scientia*). Aquinas insisted that man draws his knowledge from the senses and the sensible world and that he must rise from there up to knowledge of God through the principle of causality. Augustine and the Franciscans claimed that man already possesses God from within and from the start and that the world is but the occasion for discovering that truth, God, lies within, in the interior man. Aquinas "cut the nerve" of the ontological argument when he adopted his theory of knowledge, for he rejected the presence within the mind of the divine light, of God himself. The significance of the ontological approach is that it takes God as a prepossession and a presupposition of all discourse. Indeed once the ontological "argument" was formulated as a "proof" for the existence of a being called God, it already degenerated and deserved the refutation it received at the hands of Aquinas and Kant. The ontological approach is meant not as a kind of argument but as a form of sensitivity to oneself and to what takes place in the inner man. It is an awareness that one has been touched by God in the depths of one's soul.

Now it is clear that mysticism belongs to the ontological approach. And Meister Eckhart himself stands quite directly in the tradition of Augustinian mysticism. He too—like Tillich—likes to quote St. Augustine's remark that God is closer to the soul than the soul is to itself (Q, 201, 15-6/Serm., 198). We have also seen his own formulation of the same motif: the soul is in its ground more closely united to God than it is to its own faculties (Q, 315, 25-7/Ev., 153). That is no doubt why Tillich himself quotes Eckhart in this very essay we are now considering. Eckhart is a splendid example of the "religious" author, the man who does not see God as something other, who finds God "at home," who takes God not to be a being but rather Being itself and who, in his mystical sermons, has not the least desire to prove God's existence to his hearers' but to awaken within them a sense of the treasures they already possess in the ground of their soul.

Tillich sees these two approaches as forming a complementarity and a dialogue throughout the Western tradition. He does not envisage the eradication of the cosmological approach in favor of the ontological but merely its subordination to the latter. For each has a certain legitimacy and a certain point of view which merits consideration. Indeed the quarrel between these two approaches is age-old and a constant in Western culture. Originally it was the quarrel between Plato and Aristotle; then it took the form of the quarrel between the Augustinians and the Thomists; then between the rationalists and the empiricists. Whatever particular historical shape it may take, the dialogue itself is an animating spirit within the Western tradition, and the various epochs of Christian thought are what they are on the basis of the particular resolution which they give to this conflict. The ontological approach, for example, is not to be identified with Augustine, or Meister Eckhart, or with any particular historical figure; these figures are but historical concretizations of the more fundamental moment in Western history which they embody.

One can see very nicely on the basis of Tillich's analysis how Meister Eckhart has a place within the history of the West, how his speculative mysticism belongs within a tradition which is itself but one of two complementary albeit antagonistic moments in the larger Western tradition. But it is hardly possible, at least it should not be possible, to make a comparable claim about Martin Heidegger. His thought does not aim at assuming its rightful place within the tradition but at bringing the whole tradition itself into question. "Thinking" is not—or ought not—to have a locus within the tradition as something which takes its place alongside philosophy, science, or religion. Rather the task of thought is to think the whole tradition through, back to its origins in the primal thinkers who preceded the Western tradition of reason and philosophy, back to the primal "It" which gives itself to be thought and which, in doing so, gives birth to the various historical epochs. One cannot assimilate Heidegger to Meister Eckhart because Eckhart's mysticism takes its rightful place within the Western tradition, whereas Heidegger's thought is meant to confront that tradition in its entirety, mystical and metaphysical. Heidegger does not by that fact attempt to stand above the ages but rather to step back into the simple presencing which makes its presence felt in every age. Thus the attempt to liken him to a single figure who belongs to a particular age within that tradition must in principle fall short.

(5) The fifth element in Heidegger's experience of Being which is misrepresented if this experience is called "mystical" is its "poetic" quality. What Being "means"—what Being is in its "truth"—can be learned best of all by listening to the poets who have the eyes to see and the ears to hear the genuine essence of things. The "thinker" dwells in the closest proximity to the "poet" who, like the thinker, escapes the disfiguring effect of calculative reason and lets things be what they are. Thus, one ought not to assume that because "thinking" is neither science nor philosophy it is therefore mysticism—for this overlooks the possibility that it has become instead a "poetic thought."

After all, Heidegger never did write his promised work on Meister Eckhart, but he did indeed write numerous commentaries on the poets. Indeed, he has even composed and published some verse—such as "*Abendgang auf der Reichenau*" and more recently a collection of poems called "Thoughts" (*Gedachtes*).[9] And what are we to say of *Aus der Erfahrung des Denkens*? The format of this piece is that of a verse, and the sentences which compose it are quite poetic in tone. In this very work, Heidegger says:

> The poetic character of thought is still concealed. When it shows itself, it is likened for a long time to the utopia of a half-poetic understanding.
>
> (AED, 23/12)

When thinking is truly recognized for what it is, its poetic character will be acknowledged. The great poets think, the great thinkers think poetically. That is what Heidegger means by his reference to "thoughtful poetizing" (*das denkende Dichten*) in the next sentence of the text just cited.

Poetry (*Dichtung*) and poetizing (*Dichten*) are not for Heidegger a matter of composing verse, although he does consider poetry in the narrow sense (*Poesie*) the highest form of art (*Kunst*) (Cf. Hw, 61/74). Rather poetry is the instituting of a world, the uncovering of the matrix of meaning in which an historical age lives and dwells. The great poet, the poet who achieves the stature of a Hölderlin, is not a "literary" figure, and his significance cannot be assessed by the representational thought of literary criticism (Sp. 214/281). A poet such as Hölderlin, like the thinker and the mystic, has made the step back out of metaphysics. He poetizes out of an experience of the truth of Being, of the genuine dwelling place of mortals. His step back out of metaphysics

235

differs from that of the thinker in terms of the form in which it is given expression, viz., the work of art (the poem, painting, musical composition, etc.). But his poetizing must be thoughtful, even as the meditation of the thinker must be poetic. The thoughtfulness of the poet and the poetry of thought consist in their common world-disclosiveness, their common power to illuminate the place of human dwelling, to disclose our mortality and world-liness. Thus Heidegger criticizes contemporary art just as much as contemporary metaphysics; for art today does not know its "place." It does not disclose a new world for us, and we cannot look to it for light (Sp., 219/283-4; Hw, 65/78).

Heidegger considers the kinship between thought and poetry to be considerably stronger than that between thought and mysticism. The reason for this lies at least in part I think in the residue of metaphysics that tends to cling to mysticism of which we spoke above. For the poet is considerably less likely to be ensnared by the distinction between the sensible and the supersensible. He is so much a being of the senses and the sensible world that he is dispositionally disinclined to treat the world as appearance and epiphenomenon. He is less likely to see a distinction between God and the world, between time and eternity. This is not to say that this is what Eckhart's mysticism amounted to, as we have by now repeatedly shown, nor is it to say that the poet necessarily escapes metaphysics, as is clear from Heidegger's own interpretations of Rilke.

But on the whole thought moves in a greater proximity to poetry than to mysticism, a proximity of course separated by an abyss. The poet sings the song of the world; he responds to the needs of the time. Hence, while the step back out of metaphysics is a step in the direction of the mystic, it is much more a step in the direction of poetry. Thinking is more exposed to the "good and wholesome danger" (AED, 15/8) of the poet than to the mystic.[10] Still I think we have learned in these pages to recognize that mysticism represents at least the "fourth danger."

(6)   The final disanalogy of Heidegger's experience with mystical experience lies in the fact that Heidegger has thoroughly purged his thought of any ethical or moral dimension. Unlike Eckhart and most mystics, Heidegger is not calling for a moral renewal of the self. He is not asking us to overcome our inclination towards self-love, or to become more just, more temperate, or more charitable towards others. He does not see "technology" (*Technik*) as the source of moral evil but as a darkening in the Truth of Being. His thought is neither ethical, unethical, nor meta-ethical. It simply takes place in a sphere which has left all metaphysics and metaphysical ethics behind.

236

I should add at this point that I do not mean to suggest that *"Gelassenheit"* in Meister Eckhart is an ethical category, for I have already argued that it is not. We have seen that Eckhart contrasts those who have detachment not with bad people but with good ones (Q, 304, 4-20/ Bl., 228). But I do believe that it is fairly clear that in Eckhart the mystical sphere *presupposes* the ethical as a *precondition*. It is evident, for example, that the birth of the Son does not occur in those who are sinful (Q, 427, 27-32/Bl., 105). And the whole argument of the treatise *On Detachment*, which we examined in the first chapter, is to show that detachment is the highest of the virtues, that is, that detachment is the state of perfection towards which the ethico-moral tends. Detachment is the fulfillment, the *pleroma*, of the virtues. To be sure, detachment and letting-be belong outside the sphere of willing in a state of will-lessness and are therefore of an essentially different order from the virtues. But they presuppose in the sphere of willing itself a certain purity of will. Thus those who have a bad will are the worst, Eckhart says, for they are the most steeped in their own self-will. But those who bend their own will to God's will are better, for they are to that extent purified of self-love. But the highest of all are those who are will-less (Q, 183, 10-30/Serm., 186). One can see an ascent here, a gradual self-purification process which is crowned in mystical detachment. It could hardly be more obvious that the crown of union with the Son is not bestowed upon those whose wills are turned away from God. Eckhart's model is Martha, for she is at once inwardly one with the Godhead in the ground of her soul and at the same time outwardly the practitioner of a life time of good works and virtue. It is no wonder that Eckhart often called the one who possessed a detached and will-less heart a "just man." For such a man is like Martha inwardly justified by Justice itself, born again in Justice in the ground of the soul, and outwardly a man of just works.

But there is nothing comparable to this to be found in Heidegger. We have found an analogy between self-love in the mystic and the perverted self-importance of the subject in what Heidegger calls modern subjectism. But one of the precise points of disanalogy in this analogy is that in Heidegger modern metaphysics is not some kind of human fault, and certainly not a moral fault. However much one criticizes Descartes's *Meditations*, still we do not want to say that Descartes is morally culpable for writing this treatise. However much modern technology has darkened the truth of Being, Heidegger does not accuse scientists of moral evil. Nor does he regard moral self-purification as a precondition for entering into thought. If it is inconceivable that the

Father would bear His Son in the heart of a sinful man, it is no commentary at all on the moral character of Hölderlin to say that his is a poetry which has overcome metaphysics. *Gelassenheit* is not an ethical-moral category in either Eckhart or in Heidegger. But in Eckhart "*Gelassenheit*" is the crown jewel of a life of moral perfection, and it subsists in unity with a virtuous life, as is so splendidly symbolized by Eckhart's Martha. But in Heidegger releasement is simply a non-ethical category altogether. It neither signifies the repudiation of ethics nor presupposes any ethical demands at all upon the thinker. Thinking is not ethics at all except in the sense in which Heidegger speaks of an "original ethics" in *A Letter on Humanism*; but this is an ethic which has nothing to do with human culpability. We shall, however, discuss Heidegger's "original ethics" at somewhat greater length below.

The fact is that we cannot assimilate Heidegger into any fixed and traditional category—such as "poet," "mystic," or even "mystical poet." For Heidegger has staked out a path of his own, as he himself says every thinker must. His work is best described as neither "philosophy" nor "mysticism" nor "poetry." It takes place, to be sure, in the "neighborhood" of mysticism and poetry, but it is not reducible to either of them. For Hühnerfeld there is no such "neighborhood." Heidegger's thought, he says, takes place in an imagined sphere of his own devising. But that is so much rhetoric. Whether there is such a sphere is discovered by attempting to think along with Heidegger and trying to enter into the experience from which, as he claims, his thinking issues. And that is something each of us must attempt for himself.

The best thing we can do with Heidegger's thought is to leave it uncategorized, to "let it be," and to call it, if one must call it anything, what Heidegger himself calls it—"thought," "thinking" (*Denken*)—without trying to reduce it further. If we call it "mysticism," or a "mysticism of Being," we are misrepresenting the quality of Heidegger's experience, and we are, in the end, being more misleading than helpful. For not only is there no God in this "mystic," there is no eternity and no call for mystical silence, and while this is a plea for "detachment," it does not presuppose moral purification. There is instead a thinking for a time of a need—the age of the atom—a thinking which thinks in harmony with the poets.

We must be careful not to be misled by Heidegger. We must not forget the need we are under, according to Heidegger, to "play along with" the play of language in which we are caught up. Part of Heidegger's "language game," it seems to me, is to be found in the way in which he makes use of the language of the religious tradition. In the same way that the early Heidegger was able to harness the language of the Kierkegaardian-Lutheran tradition—guilt, conscience, fallenness, resoluteness—to the needs of the "analytic of Dasein"—so the later Heidegger appropriates the language of the mystical tradition—releasement, poverty, sacrifice, etc.—for the purpose of explicating "thought." But Heidegger remains throughout his own man. He appropriates religious language but for his own purposes.

In Eckhart, Heidegger found a language formed by one of the creators of the German tongue, a language which was capable of breaking through metaphysics. In Eckhart, too, Heidegger found not only a language but an entire "structure" or "relationship" (of the soul to God) which would be of the greateat service in articulating his own meditation on the relationship of Dasein and Being. In the mystic, Heidegger recognized a kin and an ally—"the most extreme sharpness and depth of thought belongs to genuine and great mysticism" (SG, 71)—who says a great deal of what he himself wished to say: there is a realm outside the sphere of influence of the laws of "reason"; there is a language which is more than "human" and which belongs together with silence; in *Gelassenheit* things are allowed to appear for what they are, etc. So Heidegger freely takes over and appropriates what he finds of service in the mystic. But Heidegger remains his own man; he follows his own path.

Rather than speaking of "Heidegger's mysticism," it seems to me a fairer description of what is happening in Heidegger's later writings to speak of the "mystical element in Heidegger's thought." What the misleading expression "Heidegger's mysticism" amounts to in the end is this very "mystical element." What, then, can we say is the mystical element in Heidegger's thought? It consists in this: that Heidegger has appropriated the structural relationship between the soul and God which is found in Meister Eckhart's mysticism in order to articulate the relationship in his own work between thought and Being. Put in another way, the mystical element in Heidegger's thought means that one way to understand Heidegger is to examine his thought on an analogy with a mystic like Meister Eckhart—by whom he has been historically influenced and with whom his thought is structurally akin. Mysticism, then, is one of the "models" (SD, 54/50) for "thinking," but thinking is not a species of mysticism. Thinking belongs in the "proximity" of mysticism, but thinking does not dwell within the walls of mysticism.

We might add one concluding note to this entire discussion. We have, without explicitly raising the question, laid to rest the problem of Hei-

239

degger's "originality." We recall from Chapter One Versényi's charge that Heidegger has indeed overcome metaphysics but only to say something which many non-metaphysicians before him have already said. In the light of the discussion we have just concluded, that objection is manifestly false. For while Heidegger's thought bears an extensive analogy to Meister Eckhart, it can in no way be made to coincide with Eckhartian mysticism. Indeed, we have not yet even touched upon the most important difference of all between Heidegger and Meister Eckhart—a difference which, as we shall see below, must be discussed in terms of the "danger" of Heidegger's path.

3. *The Problem of Humanism*

Heidegger's later writings have inevitably provoked the charge that they are "anti-humanistic." For it is a characteristic of the "mystic," or so it is thought, to allow man to be consumed in the mystical union, to "disappear" in a surrender to the divine being. Mysticism, Nietzsche said, is a "narcotic state of disgust with oneself," "voluptuous enjoyment of eternal emptiness."[11] Thus Versényi argued, as we recall from Chapter One, that in the third and final—and for him the "mystical"—stage of Heidegger's writings, Heidegger moved into "an all too empty and formal, though often emotionally charged and mystical-religious, thinking of absolute unity" (Vers., 168). Heidegger's search for Being had become, in this interpretation, a search for an immediate experience of the "ab-solute," i.e., "pure" Being, dissolved and loosened from beings. But this absolute, Versényi contended, is something that man can neither attain nor endure.

Versényi is, I believe, seriously misrepresenting Heidegger's views. It is true that in contrast to his earlier writings, in which Being is always considered to be the Being of beings (WG, 26-7), Heidegger tends in the later works to speak of "the attempt to think Being without beings" (SD, 2/2). But in the "Seminar" on "Time and Being" this expression is explained as "the abbreviated formulation of 'to think Being without regard to a foundation of Being in terms of beings' " (SD, 35/33). The expression does not imply that "the relationship to being is inessential to Being," but that one is "not to think Being in the manner of metaphysics" (SD, 36/33). Thus, by this expression, Heidegger means to rule out: (1) the attempt to explain Being in terms of a highest being or first cause; (2) the attempt to reduce Being to a common property of beings: matter, energy, will, consciousness, etc. Being, Heidegger is saying, is nothing "entitative," i.e., having to do with entities—a cause, e.g., or a common property.

Heidegger is in no way suggesting that the experience of Being is the experience of something absolutely detached from beings, something which takes place apart from beings. This is a point which has already become clear from our discussion of the significance of the "thing" in Heidegger's thought. The truth of Being, the "essential nature" (*Wesen*) of Being, lies in the coming to pass of the "world" and the "thing":

> That the world comes to pass as the world, that the thing comes to be a thing, this is the distant arrival of the essential nature of Being.
>
> (K, 42/10)

The truth of Being comes about in the "thing" in which the "four" play together. In the thing, the disfiguration of the world, which is rooted in modern technology, gives way to the genuine configuration of earth and sky, mortal and god. Moreover, not only is this true of Heidegger, who "keeps company" with the mystics, but something like it is also true of Meister Eckhart and of Zen Buddhism as well. For, as we saw above, there is a comparable doctrine of the "thing"—the rose, the cypress tree in the garden, and the jug—in all three positions, Heidegger, Eckhart, and Zen. Versényi's criticism applies to neither Heidegger nor the mystics. His critique is based on a caricature of "mysticism" which plays off the popular connotation of the word. The experience of Being—or of God, or of *sunyata*—takes place in a being—the "thing"—which has been freed for and released into its function of revealing the four together.

Versényi accuses Heidegger of having fallen into a "transcendental illusion," viz., of having transgressed beyond the limits of the experience which is possible to a man (beings) into an "immediate" experience of pure Being—which is impossible. But a transcendental illusion consists in seeking "unconditional" knowledge, knowledge which is in fact impossible because, as Kant says, all the "conditions" which make knowledge possible have been removed (KRV, A592-3 = B620-1). Now that is precisely what the account of the "world" in the later writings succeeds in avoiding. As early as 1915, Heidegger was making use of the following quotation from Novalis:

> We everywhere seek the unconditioned (*Unbedingte*) and ever find only things (*Dinge*). (FS, 541)

Thirty-five years later, in the lecture entitled "The Thing," Heidegger says in his own name:

> We are—in the strict sense of the word—conditioned (*Be-Dingten*). We have left the presumption of everything unconditioned behind. (VA, 179/181)

Man's approach to Being, he says in the clearest possible terms, is never "immediate"; it is always mediated by the "thing," in which and through which Being is allowed to appear. Any attempt to think Being without the help of things (beings) has been "left behind."

Heidegger by no means wishes to say, therefore, that we must leave the sphere of beings to take up residence in the uninhabitable region of "pure Being." On the contrary, if man releases the "thing" in its essence as a thing, then he enters for the first time into the most inhabitable region of all, the region where a genuinely human "dwelling" (*habitare, Wohnen*: cf. SZ, §12, 54/81-2; VA, 145 ff./145 ff.) takes place, the authentic "world." Man's relationship to Being is not an unendurable exposure to the "pure light" of Being; it is not an "anti-human" because "in-human" attempt to think upon an unconditioned and totally transcendent Being. Heidegger's thought is, on the contrary, thoroughly "conditioned" (*Be-dingte*), "worldly," and humane.

Since this is a point of some importance, let us develop further the extent to which the "world" of the fourfold is a place of authentic human dwelling. The fourfold, we recall, signifies that the "heavens" are the measure of the day, that the "earth" is the source of our sustenance, the "gods" are messengers of the divine, and that we men are "mortals." In this enigmatic, perhaps even semi-mythological, account of the "four," Heidegger has captured something profoundly humane. For to be "human" (*humanus*) is to be composed of "earth" (*humus*). It is to be brought forth and sustained by the earth, on the one hand, and to be destined to return to the earth, on the other. It is a differentiated, developmental process, with a beginning, a middle, and an end. One is born, one grows and matures, one's powers begin to subside, one dies. To be human is to be at once earth-ly, mortal, and temporal. Heidegger has, it seems to me, captured the essence of the "human chronology," the "arc" which takes its origin from the earth and returns to the earth, while passing through the days and seasons of its years.

The analysis of the fourfold thus recalls us to the passage of human time, to the rhythm of human life, within which each one can reach an understanding of his own life. It is this natural rhythm of life which is destroyed by the fast pace of technology. Technology destroys the "world" and flattens out the arc of human time. It holds up, e.g., the ideal of a youthful, ageless life in which the old must appear to look young and in which the generations are all but physically indistinguishable—or aim to be. By means of the mass media, technology indoctrinates us in the necessity to restore the original color of our hair, to maintain the habits and interests and even the complexion of those in their youth. With its artificial lighting and central heating and air-conditioning, technology even begins to erode the difference between day and night, and among the four seasons. It is as if technology has the ideal of a globe which is always lighted, kept at a uniform temperature, and constantly "running." The hurried pace of technology is for Heidegger the rapid and monotonous succession of "now's" which stand at the extreme opposite of his own conception of human "temporalization" (*Zeitigung*) and of a "world" in which a genuinely "human" life can be led.

The analysis of the fourfold is a protest against the dehumanization of the earth, against rendering it inhumane and unlivable. There is all the difference, Heidegger says, between the Rhine River as it is exploited as a source of power for our generators and the "Rhine" in Hölderlin's poetry. There is a chasm between the "heavens" which are studied by aeronautical engineering and the heavens which give the measure of the day. The earth, for Heidegger, must become a place in which we can dwell; the "thing" must become resplendent with Being. In this splendor (*Scheinen*) is its beauty (*Schöne*). Just as for the Zen master, mountains must become mountains again—not obstacles or challenges to human cleverness. Suzuki says somewhere that when Western man climbed Mount Everest, he said he "conquered" it; a Japanese would have said he "befriended" it. That is the import of Heidegger's account of the world: to overcome the Western-technological—and metaphysical—preconception that nature is something to be conquered, that it must submit to our will. For Heidegger—as for Zen—nature is something to be befriended, i.e., to be freed to be the thing that it is. To befriend nature is to "dwell" with it, to let it be, and to find in it a hidden address of Being.

Versényi's critique of Heidegger's final and—for him—"mystical" stage holds true neither for Heidegger nor for the genuine mystic—at least not for the mysticism which we have examined in this study. For Meister Eckhart has said:

> If [the soul] could know God without the world, the world would never have been created for its [the soul's] sake. (Q, 295,14-5/Bl. 161)

243

And Suzuki says of Zen:[12]

> Zen is the ocean, Zen is the air, Zen is the mountains, Zen is thunder and
> lightning, the spring flower, the summer heat, and winter snow. With the
> development of Zen, mysticism has ceased to be mystical.

It has ceased to be "mystical," we should add, in Versényi's sense of
the word, which suggests "self-annihilation" and "contempt of the
world" and "unhappy consciousness" (as Hegel portrays late medieval
mysticism in *The Phenomenology of Spirit*). For there is something profoundly human in the ideal which Heidegger and the mystics suggest
to us, something which has nothing to do with the loss of self or "alienation." They propose a life in which man is freed from acquisitiveness
and tyranny over things. Rather than attempting to possess and manipulate things, they propose to us a kind of piety towards things which
detects in them a deeper presence. In this selflessness towards things
there is no self-annihilation and destruction of man. There is, on the
contrary, for the first time, a genuine recovery of the human essence.

It is therefore no accident that both Heidegger and Eckhart stress
that when man has become truly "released," when he has opened himself up to what is truly present in things, man for the first time comes
into his "own" (*eigen*). We must always, Eckhart says, act "on our
own," "out of our own grounds" (*wir aus unserm eignen wirken*). But in
releasement, God has become our own, so that in being moved by God
we are moved "from within on our own":

> If we then live in Him or through Him, then He must be our own and we
> must work on our own.   (Q, 176 13-5/Serm., 235)

So too in Heidegger one of the main thrusts of his use of the word "*Ereignis*" is to emphasize that by it Being comes into its "own" (*eigen*),
that the "thing" is released into its ownmost Being, and that man enters
into his ownmost essential nature. In the Event (*Er-eignis*), man is "appropriated" (*ver-eignet*) or brought forth into his ownmost "proper"
being, for his ownmost being is to provide the place of disclosure for the
revelation of Being. This is, as with Eckhart, the extreme opposite of
"loss of self" and "alienation." In this selflessness there is genuine self-
possession (*Eigentlichkeit*).

That is why Heidegger can defend a "higher humanism" in his discussion of this subject in *A Letter on Humanism*:

"Humanism" now means, in the event that we determine to hold on to this word: the essence of man is essential to the Truth of Being.

(HB, 94/212)

Humanism means to bring man into his essence and to provide for the real "worth" (HB, 75/203) of man, a worth which all metaphysical humanisms are unable to grasp:

Metaphysics is closed off to the simple and essential certitude that man "is" (*west*) only in his essence (*Wesen*), in which he is addressed by Being. Only in this address has he found that wherein his essence dwells.

(HB, 66/199)

The essence of man lies in his openness to the address of Being. In this openness man releases the "thing" to be what it is. This openness to the address of Being is therefore the "letting-lie-forth" (*vorliegenlassen*) by which the thing is left to rest on its own grounds. By means of this openness, which belongs to his very essence, man is admitted into a new region, the region in which "reasons" are neither demanded nor supplied, in which things stand forth and emerge out of their own grounds, free from the categories of metaphysical thought—like the rose of which Angelus Silesius speaks. Such a "world" can hardly be called "inhumane" or "antihumanistic." It seems to me in the deepest sense a place of "dwelling" and of "being human."

4. *The Danger of Heidegger's Path*

If man is open to the address of Being then Being may "turn" towards man and renew the earth. But there are no assurances about that, for the ways of Being are inscrutable and without measure. The possibility of a new world is "dark" and its coming is "uncertain" (SD, 66/60). In this darkness and uncertainty lies one of the largest difficulties with Heidegger's work. For what becomes of *Gelassenheit* once it is detached from its religious matrix? Hühnerfeld puts the difficulty this presents sharply when he writes:

Meister Eckhart would never have taken the mystical step if he had believed that he was leaping into Nothingness instead of into the arms of God. (Hühn., 125)

245

Is "releasement" then still possible, or even desirable, if we are asked to be released, not into the arms of a loving Father, but into the "inscrutable play of Being"?

In order to bring this difficulty into focus as sharply as possible, let us go back to Meister Eckhart and sketch some of the important features of *Gelassenheit* as it is found in its original religious setting. The pivotal idea of the birth of God in Eckhart's writings has its source in the words of St. John, the "beloved" disciple:

> Think of the love that the Father has lavished on us, by letting us be called God's children; and that is what we are. (1 John 3:1)

John is the apostle of love:

> My dear people, let us love one another, since love comes from God and everyone who loves is begotten by God and knows God. Anyone who fails to love can never have known God, because God is love. (1 John 4:7-8)

The primary relationship of the soul to God in Meister Eckhart is not one of "fear" of offending the "law" of a supreme lawgiver, but loving trust in a father who would spare nothing for his children's welfare. Thus the fruit of *Gelassenheit* is peace:

> To the extent that you are in God, to that extent will you have peace, and to the extent that you are outside God, you will be outside of peace. If only something is in God, it will have peace. As much in God, so much in peace. By this test you will know how much you are in God: by whether you have peace or lack peace. For where you lack peace, you *must* necessarily lack peace, for the lack of peace comes from the creature, and not from God. Everything that is in God is only to be loved; there is nothing in God which should be feared. (Q, 100,15-22/Cl., 108)

One of Eckhart's most celebrated works is entitled *The Book of Divine Consolation*, a title which is modeled after Boethius's *De consolatione philosophiae*. In it Eckhart shows how the soul which has "released" itself to God's loving care attains a divine and not merely philosophical peace, for that is the fruit of *Gelassenheit*. "Love cannot distrust," he says, "it trustfully awaits only good" (Q, 75, 3-4/Cl., 83). That is how it is between a father and a son.

There is nothing of a Kierkegaardian leap into a paradox in Eckhart's *Gelassenheit*, for God is a plenum of Being, goodness, and intelligibility. But one finds a radically different situation when one turns to

246

Heidegger. Heidegger's Being is by no means "fatherly" or "loving" or "benevolent." Nor is Heidegger's Being a plenum of "intelligibility," as Werner Marx has shown so masterfully.[13] For inasmuch as it is a process of *a-letheia*, Being is necessarily a process of emerging out of a primal and ineradicable core of concealment (*lethe*). Thus there can be no analogue to *The Book of Divine Consolation* in Heidegger's writings, and that is the critical point of difference in the analogy between Heidegger and Meister Eckhart. "Composure" (*Gelassenheit*) in Heidegger goes hand in hand with "anxiety" (*Angst*). This strange admixture of anxiety in composure is captured by Heidegger's notion of "awe" (*Scheu*):

> For awe dwells close by to essential anxiety as the terror of the Abyss.
> (WM, 47/355)

In awe there is a kind of calm before something overwhelming, mixed with an uneasiness in the face of something fearsome. Awe, anxiety, releasement stand before the "terror of the abyss" (*Schreck des Abgrundes*). What is the abyss? The answer is found in SG:

> Being and Ground: the same. Being as grounding has no ground but, as the Abyss (*Abgrund*), plays that game which, as mission (*Geschick*), plays up to us Being and Ground. (SG, 88)

Heidegger's Being is the groundless play of Being. Far from being a plenum of intelligibility, it is equiprimordially unintelligible. Far from being a loving father, Being is the inscrutable play of a child: "The mission of Being: a child who plays" (SG, 188).

Heidegger's Being is a ground without ground, as Meister Eckhart's God is a *"principium sine principio"* (LW, III, 16, n. 1/Cl., 239). But for Eckhart this means that God is the fullness of being (*plenitudo esse*), a principle of perfect goodness and intelligibility, a "final explanation" which itself stands in need of no further justification. For Heidegger, on the other hand, Being is a ground which does not *admit* of explanation. Being comes to pass as it does. There is nothing more anyone can say:

> What does there remain to say? Only this: the Event of Appropriation comes to pass (*das Ereignis ereignet*). (SD, 24/24)

There is no determining "why" the Event comes to pass as it does, why it has thrown us into the darkness of the technological world, why or

247

how it will "turn" away from the "*Gestell*" towards a new world. If to live "without why" for Meister Eckhart means to live with a disinterested and loving trust in God's fatherly care, in Heidegger it means to acknowledge the inscrutability of the play of Being:

> Because is swallowed up in the play. It plays because it plays. There remains only play: the highest and the deepest. (SG, 188)

That is why, where the author of *The Book of Divine Consolation* can speak of peace, Heidegger speaks of a "venture," a "wager" on the outcome of a portentous game:

> We must venture out into the play of language upon which our being is staked. (WHD, 87/128)

Again, man must confront:

> . . . the high and dangerous play upon which the being of language has staked us. (WHD, 84/119)

The essence of technology (*Technik*) is the "danger" (*Gefahr*) for Heidegger. It is a concealment of the Truth of Being. It distorts the meaning of nature, of dwelling in the world, of thinking, and of man himself. It is a danger which man did not bring upon himself but which Being itself has perpetrated. Being itself has withdrawn in its truth and has advanced in the form of an untruth. The illusions of the age of technology are mistakes for which no man is responsible.

Heidegger asks: will the illusions of the age of technology pass away (ID, 71/72)? Will the "West," which Heidegger takes to be a true "evening-land" (*Abendland*), become the eve of a new day? Will man ever get beyond the conception of himself as the "rational animal" (SG, 210-11)? These are only questions; no one knows the answers. The best Heidegger can do is to speak of a "hope" that Being will turn a new face, that the "danger" will give way to the "saving" element within it (VA, 41; cf. WHD, 13/31-2). But Heidegger has virtually undermined all possibility of hope. For there can be no "rational basis" for hope, as in Hegel, for whom the history of Being is a rational, law-governed becoming. Nor can there be the hope which is founded on love, of which authors like Gabriel Marcel speak. For Marcel, true hope is a loving trust in a being (God) about whom we can have an absolute assurance that He will allow us to suffer no ultimate harm.[14] But Heidegger's "Being"

248

cannot be determined personalistically. It is no accident that there is *no* talk of "father," "son," or "giving birth" in Heidegger's account of the relationship between Being and Dasein, whereas these are important expressions in Eckhart's Christian, indeed Johannine, mysticism. And in my view this must be counted as the most decisive difference of all between Eckhart and Heidegger. Heidegger uses many words to explain the relationship of Being and Dasein—giving, using, thanking, playing, saying, etc.—but never "giving birth" as a "father" generates his "son." The reason for this is not that the relationship of father and son is an "ontic" relation between beings, because that is also true of giving and playing and all the rest. The point is that some ontic relations are capable of being reworked and transformed so as to become possible ways of speaking—in a "non-objective" way—about Being and Dasein, while others are not.[15] The relation of father and son is not susceptible of such a reworking because it is a radically personal relationship, and as such involves such dispositions as love and trust. And it is as plainly non-sensical to describe Being in these categories as it would be to describe it in terms of the categories of Hegel's *Logic*.

One does not "trust" in the outcome of the Event. The best one can do is wait (G, 37/62); the "serenity" (*Gelassenheit*) one has comes from knowing there is nothing more one can do. Dasein may prepare for the possibility of a "new beginning"; it may open itself to it. But Dasein can neither effect it nor trust in its coming to pass. Eckhart so trusted that God would return love with love that he said we could "force" God to come to us (Théry, 218-19/Bl., 286-7). Eckhart said that although there are unknown depths in God, and the Godhead is an "abyss" of which nothing can be spoken, still there is nothing to fear in God; everything in God should only be loved (Q, 100,21-2/Cl., 108). But there is nothing in Heidegger's "*Ereignis*" to love and much to fear. The releasement of which Heidegger speaks has taken on a more ominous aspect than Eckhart's, for it has been detached from its religious matrix. It is no longer releasement to a loving God, but releasement to a truth which is equiprimordially un-truth.[16]

It is true that Heidegger speaks of the Event as "giving" and of Dasein as "thanking," which does endow the Event with something of a benevolent aspect (WM, 49/358; WHD, 91 ff./139 ff.). Such personalistic language is close to Eckhart's, for the Father gives the "gift" (*gratia*) of the Son and the soul is indeed grateful. However, Heidegger is adopting here but another "model" for thinking out the relationship of Being and Dasein. The Event does not "give" Being and truth to us in the same sense as the Father gives us to be His Son. Heidegger does not at all mean to suggest anything like the Johannine motif that God "so loved the world that He sent His only begotten Son to us." What Heidegger does mean by the model of "thanking" is that the revelation of Being is nothing that Dasein can bring about—e.g., through its "questioning," as *Being and Time* supposed. Only Being itself can effect it. Consequently, if Being is revealed to Dasein it comes "gratuitously," as it were, as a "gift" (or "favor"). Dasein however cannot and will not receive the gift if it is not disposed towards the giver as a recipient should be, viz., with "gratitude." The correct disposition of Dasein towards the self-revelation of Being is "openness," which is "thinking" (*Seinsdenken*). Hence Dasein's "gratitude" is "thinking"; its "thinking" (*Denken*) is "thanking" (*Danken*). The whole notion of "thanking" therefore rests not on any personalistic overtones of the Event but the kinship—etymological or otherwise—of "*Denken*" and "*Danken*." Indeed the whole notion of "giving" arises out of a sentence in *Being and Time* which Heidegger would like to reinterpret and which uses the phrase "*es gibt*" (SZ, §43, p. 212).

Heidegger is not talking about any sort of personal relationship, but about "manifestness." He does not conceive of the coming to pass of manifestness in terms of the loving care of a father but, on the contrary, in terms of a "world-play" (*Weltspiel*).

It may be rejoined that Heidegger often argues that "thinking" is a higher kind of "acting" and so that it is "efficacious"—i.e., capable of effecting the new beginning—in a "higher" way. The trouble with us, Heidegger says, is that we have not understood "acting" deeply enough (HB, 53-5/192-4). But Heidegger has also said that thinking is not an achievement of man, that it is something which is achieved in man by Being. Thinking is not an act of man but an event of Being (WM, 47/356). Thus whether thinking will ever be brought to completion, whether it will ever be in its own higher sense "effectual," is beyond man's control. It depends upon the movements of Being and Being is a groundless play. The situation is quite different for Meister Eckhart; for if the soul opens itself up to God's presence, God will "rush in" upon the soul. We can "compel" God to come to us:

> For this reason, a soul which loves God overpowers God so that He must give Himself to it wholly.
> (Q, 274,27-8; cf. Q, 219,9-12/Serm., 238; 259,10-8/Serm., 215)

This is not an "ontological" compulsion—Meister Eckhart is a scholastic *magister*, after all. It is the necessity of the law of love. A lover must return love with love. Thus, in Christian monasticism, the prayer of the contemplative is efficacious because it is addressed to a being who responds to love with love. In the monastic tradition, contemplative monks pray for the "conversion of the world"; and that is, given their presuppositions about the nature of God and of prayer, perfectly intelligible. But no comparable or analogous efficaciousness can be attributed to Heidegger's "thinking." Thinking can only open itself to Being—and wait.

What emerges from this comparison of the way of Meister Eckhart and of Heidegger is that there is no "absolute" or "unconditioned" hope in the advent of Being, even as there is no absolute or unconditioned Being. Being for Heidegger is always conditioned (be-dingt), finite, and permeated with negativity. There can be—if anything—only a "finite hope" in Heidegger, a hope which is never insulated from despair, a waiting which acknowledges the possibility of a final disappointment. Because Heidegger does not conduct his thinking in the same sphere as the religious mystic, there is a world of difference between his hope in the advent of Being and the absolute hope of the religious man. This comparison with a religious thinker such as Meister Eckhart thus underlines something distinctive about Heidegger's thought, the danger in Heidegger's thought.

In Heidegger's view, Western man is subject to an error which he did not commit. The history of the West rests upon the mission of Being, and the mission of Being has left man in a state of darkness and has subjected him to the danger of technology. Like the classic Greek tragic hero, Western man is victimized by a "fate" (Geschick) he cannot control. Heidegger tells us that, if given free rein, human reason will perpetuate the illusion of technology and continue the kingdom of darkness. Hence he bids us lay aside metaphysics and undertake "thinking," for by thinking we will help to open up the possibility of a new dispensation of Being. But this possibility is in his own words dark and uncertain.

Heidegger's thought exposes us to the fatefulness of the world-play. He tells us that we dwell within the sphere of influence of a principle and power which it is not within our power to break. He holds that by thought we may awaken the possibility that the world-play will play in our favor and so, he says, we are not left "defenseless" before it (G, 23/52-3). Yet Heidegger's thought seems to me to move close to the edge of despair. For he makes us dependent upon the outcome of a "game" upon which our very essence is staked, a game in which thinking may

251

lend a hand but in which it has no final say. There is an almost Nietzschean tone in Heidegger. I mean by this not that he wants us to resign ourselves to the eternal recurrence of the same, but that he insists upon our dependence upon the succession of the epochs, upon the play of Being. Like Nietzsche, Heidegger submits us to a world-play, not in the sense that we must be "taken in" by the illusions of the epochs of metaphysics, but in the sense that we are powerless to alter them. Thus Heidegger too can make his own these words from *Beyond Good and Evil*:[17]

> . . . he who, like us, has recognized the tremendous fortuitousness which has hitherto played its game with the future of man—a game in which no hand, not even a "finger of God" took any part . . . he suffers from a feeling of anxiety with which no other can be compared.

Thinking is aptly called by Heidegger a "sacrifice" (WM, 49/359), for it is a sacrifice of man's ability to take charge of his own affairs, and it allows man only to assist in, to prepare for, to lend a hand to, a new beginning whose coming to pass he is incapable of bringing about.

This is not to contradict the "higher humanism" of which we spoke in the previous section of this chapter. I do not mean to suggest by these remarks that Heidegger's vision is anti-humanistic, but only that his new dawn has been put almost out of reach. The advent of the fourfold, the coming of the "thing," gaining a new rootedness in the technical world, have all become matters of such extreme contingency as to float like a dream beyond our grasp. The new beginning of which Heidegger speaks is nothing inhumane; it is the expression of hope for a renewed dwelling. But it is a possibility we have little confidence will be reached and every fear will be withheld from us. The difficulty with Heidegger is not that he is a mystic, but that he is *not*. His thought is so radically worldly and secular and drained of absolute and divine assurances that it can at best assist in a world-play; for the kingdom is in the hands of a child.

This is a serious difficulty with Heidegger's work, and on this point I am in agreement with the critical studies of Heidegger which I examined in the opening chapter of this work. The way of *Gelassenheit*, once it has been detached from its religious matrix, has become awesome and austere and comfortless, quite in contrast with Eckhart's way of divine consolation. It does not seem to me that many of Heidegger's excited and enthusiastic followers, who speak like Heidegger, as though they have experienced what Heidegger experienced, have recognized the austerity of Heidegger's path or acknowledged the danger which lies along this path. Yet this danger is something that can be easily seen once the confrontation of Heidegger with Meister Eckhart is undertaken.

We are none of us in a position to say whether Meister Eckhart or Heidegger is "right." We cannot say that Meister Eckhart's call to give ourselves over to God's loving care is correct, or that Heidegger's call to release ourselves to an inscrutable world-play is not. We can neither prove nor disprove what Eckhart and Heidegger have said, because they are not proposing theses which are to be substantiated or rebutted. That there is a way of divine consolation in Meister Eckhart does not prove anything. Nietzsche has already pointed out that the ability of an idea to comfort us is no criterion of its truth.[18]

> Happiness and virtue are no arguments. . . . Something might be true although at the same time harmful and dangerous in the highest degree; indeed, it could pertain to the fundamental nature of existence that a complete knowledge of it would destroy one—so that the strength of a spirit could be measured by how much 'truth' it could take, more clearly, to what degree it *needed* it attenuated, veiled, sweetened, blunted, and falsified.

It might well be that the most forbidding path of all, the one which only the hardest can endure, is the most honest, the most free from illusion and "concealment." That is why we have likened Heidegger to Nietzsche in this discussion. For like Nietzsche, he asks us to face up to a great fortuitousness, a great world-play, to say "yes" to it by releasing ourselves to it, without demanding that it conform to our wishes or submit to our will.

Nietzsche's view, of course, is "deterministic"; the wheel of history is relentless. The movement of the mission of Being in Heidegger, on the other hand, is not fixed into a definite pattern. The future is open. But the difficulty is that in Heidegger man can but assist in and tend to a world-historical process over which he has no ultimate say. He can prepare for a new beginning, and without this preparation the renewal will not take place, but whether and how Being will turn towards man in its truth is something we cannot control.

In his *Der Spiegel* interview Heidegger said:

> . . . philosophy will not be able to effect an immediate transformation of the present condition of the world. That is not only true of philosophy, but of all merely human thought and endeavor. Only a god can save us.
>
> (Sp., 209/277)

By "a god" here Heidegger means a power greater than man, a more than human force, in short, a new clearing in Being itself. But the difficulty with Heidegger is that at this precise point in his thought he must say "a god" (*ein Gott*), a dispensation of Being (*Seinsgeschick*), and not "God Himself." He has transposed the originally mystical-religious relationship between God and the soul expressed in the word "*Gelassenheit*" into a non-religious setting where we are divested of God. I do not mean that there is no place for God in the later Heidegger,[19] but that Heidegger's God is not the lord of history. He does not govern the missions of Being with loving care. Rather His own appearance in history is subject to the movements of the world-play. For God can appear only if the mission of Being prepares a clearing for Him in which he can make an appearance (HB, 85-6/208). It may well be that only God Himself can save us, but all that Heidegger offers us is a world-play.

5. *Thinking and Ethics*

In discussing the differences between thinking and mysticism we touched upon the point that in Eckhart's mysticism there is a collaboration, although to be sure no identity, between the realm of the mystical and that of ethics. For in Eckhart, as we have seen, the life of virtue provides a precondition for mystical union. So too mystical union represents the crowning glory towards which the ethico-moral life strives. Moral discipline is a preliminary, elementary kind of self-purification which belongs, as the Christian spiritual masters said, to the "purgative stage." The principle of evil is love of the self, of the ego. The moral man is one who bends his will to the commandments of God. This is on a lower level a form of self-purification of which mystical union itself is the perfected and crowning form. The mystical life itself has left all willing and striving behind. It has broken through the sphere of ethics altogether in order to enter a new realm. But it has done so by passing *through* ethics in order to realize that for which the ethical is but a preparation, viz., union with the Son.

One observes, incidentally, a comparable proximity of mysticism and ethical virtue in Zen Buddhism. For in Zen, once one has achieved *satori*, the result is a great "compassion." Having overcome all "particularity"—"from the first not a thing is"—we likewise break down the artificial barriers that divide individual men from one another. When the "ego" is destroyed, the way towards universal brotherhood is opened up. *Satori* brings an intense realization and experience of the belonging together of all men. Its effect, then, is an unselfish love of others.

But in Heidegger, as we have seen, there is no such proximity of thought with ethics. Thinking, we said, has left all metaphysics and all metaphysics of morals behind, and it does not require moral purity as a precondition. Now this separation of thought and ethics has been the source of no little criticism of the later Heidegger. We have seen that Versényi argues that not only does Heidegger fail to supply us with criteria for determining what is and what is not to be done (Vers., 176 ff.), but that also in the final "mystical" stage of his writings, all human action—good or evil—has been so devalued that the question of ethics cannot even arise (Vers., 186-7).

But Versényi's position turns out to be rather peculiar. For he argues that it is because Heidegger is a mystic that all human behavior and ethical action has become something negligible. He writes:

> In *Being and Time* Heidegger counseled facing death as a way of salvation for man. But in his later writings he goes a great deal further and advocates death pure and simple. . . . This is of course not a new solution. Mysticism, ecstatic and transendent (not transcendental) philosophy have traditionally offered the same advice. (Vers., 193)

But that is a very strange position. For if Heidegger *were* a mystic then the numerous problems that are constantly arising about the relationship of thinking to ethics would never come up, no more than they do with Meister Eckhart. For it is quite typical of the mystic to see the life of moral action as a preparatory, purgative stage which must be passed through on the way to mystical union.[20] The whole argument of *On Detachment* is that in detachment all the virtues reach their fulfillment. The whole point of the story of Mary and Martha for Eckhart is to insist upon the compatibility of mystical union with the exercise of moral virtue.

Quite to the contrary of Versényi, it seems to me that the problem with Heidegger's thought on this point is that he is *not* a mystic and that he therefore is under no compulsion whatsoever to address himself to the ethical or moral sphere.

Is there, then, any relationship at all between what Heidegger calls "thinking" and "ethics"? Heidegger answers:

> If the name ethics, according to the fundamental meaning of the word *ethos*, means that it thinks the abode of man, then that thinking which

255

thinks the truth of Being as the primordial element of ek-sistent man is in itself original ethics. (HB, 109/219)

By "original ethics" (*ursprüngliche Ethik*) Heidegger means that "thinking" which is directed at man's mode of "dwelling" (*Wohnen*) in the "world." *Ethos* means for Heidegger man's abode, man's mode of being-in-the-world. Original ethics therefore does not have to do with conduct which is measured by a rule—which would be for him a derivative, "metaphysical" sense of the word ethics. Now man's mode of dwelling is ultimately determined by his relationship to Being, which is itself based upon whether we are "thinking" or not.

Thus, Heidegger's "ethics"—in the sense of "original ethics"—is to be found in his account of the Fourfold. For it is in this more pristine relationship to "things" that man's true mode of "dwelling" is to be found. Heidegger wants to deal with the "human condition," not on the level of determinate ethical problems, but on what is for him the "deeper" level of the "truth of Being." The withdrawal of Being is always more basic for him than any determinate ethical question.

In the light of this, it is simply wrong-headed to criticize *Being and Time* or the later works because there are no determinate ethical principles and directives to be found there. For Heidegger's attempt has all along been to deal with the "ontological" rather than the "ontic," to use the language of *Being and Time*. His concern has been with the essence or Being (*Wesen*) of man, rather than with man's ontic activities. In *Being and Time*, e.g., he was concerned with the structure of resoluteness itself, as belonging to the existential-ontological make-up of Dasein, rather than with what determinate (existential-ontic) activities Dasein should or should not resolve upon. In the later works, he is concerned with the essence of our technological age rather than with the numerous specific moral problems—such as fertilization *in vitro*—to which technology gives rise. And it is perfectly plausible to me to maintain that the essence of our relationship to technology precedes, and provides the framework for, any discussion of the concrete problems—moral or otherwise—which technology presents.

I do not mean to suggest, however, that Heidegger's position on ethics leaves nothing to be desired. I only mean to say that Heidegger's position should not be criticized for failing to be what it was never intended to be—viz., metaphysical ethics—which is, it seems to me, what is usually done.[21] The difficulty which I have with Heidegger's views on this matter is that I do not see how there is any way *back*, if we may say so, from original ethics to ethics in the usual sense. I feel somewhat stranded when reading Heidegger on this point. For there are in this time of need numerous ethical problems which have been generated precisely because of the technological mission of Being, problems surrounding the use of technical equipment in dealing with human life and the human body, the use of life-sustaining equipment, the artificial production of human life, etc. Now I do not see where one is to turn in Heidegger's view for light on these problems. For the thinker, on the one hand, must not be expected to give concrete directives:

> *Der Spiegel*: We politicians, semi-politicians, citizens, journalists, etc., we constantly have to make decisions of one kind or another. . . . We expect help from the philosopher, if only indirect help, help in a roundabout way. And now we hear: I cannot help you.
> *Heidegger*: And I cannot. (Sp.,209/279-80)

But philosophy on the other hand has degenerated into the particular sciences and cybernetics:

> *Heidegger*: . . . Philosophy dissolves into the individual sciences: psychology, logic and political science.
> *Der Spiegel*: And now what or who takes the place of philosophy?
> *Heidegger*: Cybernetics.
> *Der Spiegel*: Or the pious one who keeps himself open?
> *Heidegger*: But that is no longer philosophy. (Sp.,209/278)

Ethical problem-solving, philosophical reflection on fundamental ethical questions, has evaporated—sublimated on the one side into original ethics and degenerated on the other side into cybernetics and what Skinner calls the technology of behavior.

This position seems to me to leave the rest of us to face the worst, for it leaves us with a choice between the piety of thought and cybernetics, neither of which clearly is suited to deal with ethical problems. Eckhart's position in this matter seems to me the better one. For he insists upon the unity of the mystical life with the concrete life of virtue. His Martha sermon is a ringing tribute to the insight of this reformer before the Reformation who saw the harmony of the world of practical ethical action with the stillness of the ground of the soul. I do not see such a harmony in Heidegger. I do not see where we are to turn in Heidegger's view for help in dealing with questions which are neither the questions of thought, on the one hand, nor purely technical questions on the other hand.[22]

6. *Heidegger and the Philosophers*

The final question which demands resolution in dealing with the problem of Heidegger's affinity to the mystics is this: what interest can philosophy have in a thinker who thinks at the end of philosophy, who has moved beyond the sphere of influence of philosophical principles into the neighborhood of mystics and poets? By philosophy, of course, I should remind the reader, I mean philosophy in the traditional sense, philosophy as an affair of reason, as a forum for ideas whose worth must be tested against rival points of view. Heidegger has left that tradition behind for a "philosophy" which is no longer philosophy but "thought," to think a "Being" which is no longer Being but the Event (*Ereignis*). Most of us, including those of us who write "about" Heidegger's thought, are philosophers in the usual sense, trained in Plato and Aristotle, Descartes and Kant, logic and the theory of knowledge. We have all learned to stay within the realm of the Principle of Sufficient Ground, whereas Heidegger has in truth found a way beyond this sphere. The question I now raise then is, what interest can we philosophers have in a thinker who has so thoroughly left behind the methods and procedures of philosophy?[23] I should like in this section to offer two explanations of the great interest Heidegger holds for philosophers.

The first of these has to do with the lineage or derivation of thought from philosophy. I do not mean to suggest of course that thought is a derivative *of* philosophy, but that it takes its point of departure *from* philosophy.[24] The step back is a step back out of philosophy; the leap of thought is a leap beyond philosophy; the transformation of thought is a transformation from philosophy into thought. In every case, philosophy is the *terminus a quo* for thought. The history of metaphysics provides Heidegger with his "texts"—like the Principle of Sufficient Ground. Heidegger develops an *expositio* or *commentarium* upon these texts which penetrates behind these texts by means of a "leap" which tries to get at what Heidegger thinks are their still unthought presuppositions. Now this is an undertaking which is of the utmost interest to philosophers and metaphysicians.

Let us illustrate this point. From Parmenides's philosophical poem on the ways of being and non-being, Heidegger "retrieves" the saying that "being" and "thinking" are the "same," i.e., that they belong together. In a poem which philosophers take to be a critique of becoming, and one of the first and most powerful applications of deductive logic in the West, Heidegger finds an appeal elicited to man by Being to "think." From Aristotle's question about the being as such and about its "manifold sense," which is the question of "first philosophy," Heidegger un-covers the question about Being as such, about the "truth of Being." Where philosophers find a "science" about "being as being," Heidegger sees a "thinking" which "thinks Being without beings." In Leibniz's Principle of Sufficient Ground, "nothing is without ground," Heidegger discovers the possibility of another intonation, one in which we will hear the ringing together of "Being" and "ground," the ringing of Being as the groundless ground. The "Principle of Sufficient Ground" (*Satz vom Grund*) is transformed into a leap (*Satz*) away from beings into Being itself. In Nietzsche's critique of the history of Christian-Platonic metaphysics as a history of nihilism, Heidegger finds the history of metaphysics as the oblivion of Being, which is the true nihilism. And where Nietzsche calls for an overcoming of the slave morality of Christian-Platonism, Heidegger calls for overcoming Western metaphysics. From the idea of truth as the "correspondence" (*adequatio*) of mind and thing, Heidegger moves back into the more fundamental conception of truth as the unconcealment of Being itself, which is the original meaning of the Greek *aletheia*. In Husserl's appeal to return to the things themselves (*zu den Sachen selbst*), Heidegger hears the call of the matter of thought (*zur Sache des Denkens*).

Metaphysics has long been the medium in which Heidegger has learned what he has to say. And his thinking has to a large extent consisted in finding another way of saying what he has learned. He says what metaphysics would say, were it able, viz., the truth of Being (N II, 353-4, 397). The history of metaphysics is the "hiding place" of Being and Heidegger's thought has been an attempt to flush it out, to uncover the wealth which is hidden in and by that tradition. The question "what is metaphysics?" remained essential to Heidegger (WM, 43/349) even after he had given up the attempt to develop a "metaphysics of metaphysics." For the question "what is metaphysics?" is an inquiry into the "essence" of metaphysics which, in Heidegger's view, is hidden from metaphysics itself. The question of the essence of metaphysics is fundamentally an attempt to overcome metaphysics. For Heidegger, metaphysics contains the truth of Being—in a concealed way—rather the way that Christianity contained the "absolute truth" for Hegel in a "pictorial way." And just as for Hegel (and later for Feuerbach) the "essence" of Christianity is concealed from Christian theology itself, so for Heidegger the essence of metaphysics is hidden from metaphysics.

Heidegger's thought has, to a large extent, consisted in a dialogue with the history of metaphysics in the hope of uncovering what metaphysics has kept concealed. He claims to have laid bare the essence of metaphysics. And what philosopher or metaphysician would not be interested in such a task? Indeed, it is quite doubtful that anyone could understand Heidegger who does not understand the history of Western metaphysics. Thus despite all his attempts to leave metaphysics behind, Heidegger inevitably finds the metaphysicians attracted to him. For they are captivated by Heidegger's concerns—Being, truth, history, art, man—which are the concerns of metaphysics.[25]

The second source of interest of philosophy in Heidegger is that, in "overcoming" philosophy, Heidegger has in fact made an interpretation of the limits of philosophy. Now the question of the limits of philosophy is a serious and proper philosophical problem, one which has occupied such great philosophers as Kant and Wittgenstein. The difference, however, between Heidegger, on the one hand, and Kant and Wittgenstein, on the other hand, is that, instead of merely talking about the limits of philosophy, Heidegger has in fact attempted to *traverse* these limits. He has not merely described certain limits on philosophical discourse; he has indeed undertaken to create and speak a non-philosophical, or post-philosophical, language, a language which borrows much from the poets, mystics, and mystic-poets. Heidegger does not, like Wittgenstein, tell us that beyond the limits of philosophical discourse lies the "mystical," and bid us to be silent about it. He does not, like Wittgenstein, remain on "this side" of the limits of philosophical language and attempt to show forth its limits by delineating everything that can be said clearly (*Tractatus Logico-Philosophicus*, No. 4.114-5). Rather he takes the "leap" beyond philosophical discourse into the language of thinking. In sentences like "*das Ding be-dingt*" and "*die Sprache spricht*," in semi-poetic essays like *Aus der Erfahrung des Denkens*, he attempts to create a post-metaphysical language.

But what are the limits of philosophical discourse as Heidegger sees them? To begin with, philosophy for Heidegger operates within a "correspondence" theory of truth, which locates truth in the "proposition" and which holds that by these propositions "reality" (Objectivity, *Gegenständlichkeit*) and "consciousness" (Subjectivity, *Subjectivität*) must be brought into agreement. Hence philosophy is cut off from a primordial "experience" of Being, and must always be content with "propositions" which talk "about" what is. Moreover, because it is propositional, philosophy is subject to the jurisdiction of "fundamental propositions" (*Grundsätze*), like the Principle of Identity and, especially, the Principle of Sufficient Ground. Thus it is bound to "render reasons" and to look for causes of beings. It never lets the being "lie forth" and rest in its Being. Driven on by the search for a cause, metaphysics misses Being altogether and is satisfied with the "highest being," the first cause, which is God. The God of philosophy is not the "divine God" (ID, 71/72; cf. Q, 60,26/Cl., 70), to whom one can bend one's knee, but the *causa prima*. Of all these beings, caused and uncaused (God), metaphysics further attempts to determine their "common ground," i.e., the common properties of beings (*ens in communi*), which Heidegger calls the "beingness" (*Seiendheit*) of beings. Philosophy even understands man philosophically, in terms of philosophical reason; hence for philosophy man is always the "rational animal." Finally, philosophy has by an innate dynamism led to a proliferation of the sciences in the Twentieth Century. These sciences, both humanistic and natural, do not represent the dissolution of philosophy but its completion and full actualization. Western philosophy—a redundant expression for Heidegger—is Western rationality. Philosophy is not the opposite of technology; it is the source of it. Ontology gives birth to technology, for the *logos* ("-logy") is the same: *ratio*, *Grund*. So long as thinking means only philosophy, so long as *logos* means *ratio*, the West will remain an "evening-land" and the oblivion of Being will persist.

All of this cannot fail to be of concern to the philosopher. Heidegger has made an important and challenging critique of philosophy which cannot—or should not—leave his philosophical reader untouched. One must come to grips with Heidegger's critique; one must make a decision about the legitimacy of Heidegger's judgment of metaphysical, i.e., philosophical, rationality. Heidegger leads us into (*intro-ducere*) asking the question about philosophy: what is philosophy?

7. Conclusion: Towards an Appreciation of Heidegger

Our investigation into the mystical element in Heidegger's thought provides us with a way of access to Heidegger. The confrontation of Heidegger with Meister Eckhart not only discloses the mystical element in Heidegger's thought; it also uncovers the distinctively Heideggerian, non-mystical element as well. It shows us clearly how Heidegger has remained throughout faithful to his own path of thought, how he has remained his own man. For each thinker has his own appointed path to travel. The confrontation with Eckhart shows us how Heidegger has overcome metaphysics without thereby becoming mystical, even as he overcomes metaphysics without becoming a poet. A complementary study to the present one would differentiate the way that thinking over-

261

comes metaphysics from the poet's way. In the topology of Being, all three—mysticism, poetry, and thought (so long as they are "genuine and great," SG, 71)—lie outside the sphere of influence of Leibniz's principle of great power. A complete topology of Being would undertake to survey the entire region which lies outside of Leibniz's principle. The perspective offered by the present study makes a contribution in that direction.

The confrontation of Heidegger and Eckhart opens up for us the region in which Heidegger's later thought takes place. It discloses for us the stature of Heidegger and the dimensions of his achievement. It shows us in a convincing way that Heidegger belongs to a long tradition of "deep thinkers," and that he can rightly take his place alongside such "old masters" as Meister Eckhart. Heidegger is the great thinker of this century, and this philosophical age will likely bear his name. Heidegger "thinks"—deeply, penetratingly, and with astonishing originality. He does not repeat opinions or defend party lines. He is constantly on guard against the trivialization and standardization of meaning that inevitably creeps into our language and into our traditional Western habits of thought. He unearths a deeper and richer level of meaning lying beneath the surface, sometimes far beneath the surface, of Western philosophy.

His call for the leap of thought is no invitation to irrationalism. Rather it is a call which is made to each of us to suspend the noisy chatter of everyday existence, to suspend the machinery of our incessant rationalization, in order to "listen" to the "essence" of things. That is a call which few of us apart from Heidegger and his like can take up in a sustained way:

> *Der Spiegel*: Approximately two years ago, in a conversation with a Buddhist monk, you spoke of "a completely new way of thinking" and you said that "only a few people are capable of" this new way of thought. Did you want to say that only a very few people can have the insights which in your view are possible and necessary?
> *Heidegger*: To "have" them in the utterly primordial sense, so that they can, in a certain way, "say" them. (Sp., 212/279)

One of the discomforting things about reading Heidegger's later writings is precisely the realization that the sort of thing that Heidegger does, which invites comparison with the likes of Meister Eckhart, is fully possible only to a few people, people who like Heidegger and Eckhart have the delicate sensitivities and penetrating powers of thought which it requires. In the mystical tradition one usually speaks of "mystical gifts," for it is realized that one cannot acquire the sensibility of the mystic the way one can acquire a Master's degree or seniority in a firm. It is an endowment, a gift of a higher order, a blessing.

But still we are all to some extent, some to a greater extent, others to a lesser extent, capable of entering into this experience. We are all in some way able to be at least partly touched by the grace of thought:

> Yet anyone can follow the path of meditative thinking in his own manner and within his own limits. Why? Because man is a *thinking*, that is, a *meditating* being. Thus meditative thinking need by no means be "highflown." It is enough if we dwell on what lies close and meditate on what is closest; upon that which concerns us, each one of us, here and now; here on this patch of home ground; now, in the present hour of history.
>
> (G, 15-6/47)

Each of us can within our own limits and in our own way respond to the call of thought. Each of us is in our deepest essence, in the "ground" of our being, a being who thinks, and thinking is only on the surface a matter of reason. Thinking is in its deepest dimension what Heidegger calls meditating, reflecting, releasing, letting-be. Each of us is surrounded by what is closest to him or to her. And so we can each take up our own meditation upon the depths that lie hidden beneath the surface of the commonplaces of our own lives.

Heidegger's call, it seems to me, is ultimately a call to retrieve our humanity by understanding the attunement of man with what he calls the "world." The world is not a spatio-temporal-causal system, not the "nature" of the "natural sciences." The world is on the contrary the matrix of meaning within which a man lives his life. The world is daylight and night time, oceans and mountains, water and soil. It is the theatre of all giving birth and dying, growing ill and growing well, sleeping and waking, succeeding and failing, maturing and aging. From the world issue meanings in which a man experiences his mortality and his humanity, his grandeur and his misery, his powers and impotencies. I believe that the central thrust of his later writings consists in calling us back *to* this forgotten and withdrawn world, calling us back *out* of the technological world in which we are systematically divested of our humanity and robbed of our worth. The technical world threatens to consume us, and Heidegger's writings are a summons to find a new possibility in the midst of an all too present and suffocating actuality. Indeed on no point has Heidegger been more unjustly criticized than on the question of his alleged anti-humanism. To my knowledge there is no more eloquent, powerful, and penetrating defense of the humanity of man in the twentieth century than is to be found in Heidegger's later writings.

This is not to say that I am in every way satisfied by Heidegger's writings. I have already discussed in this chapter certain elements of his work which I find unsettling and in which I think that he compares unfavorably with Meister Eckhart. I am thinking in particular of what we called the problem of the "danger" of Heidegger's path of thought and also of the relation of thinking to ethics. I should like to conclude these pages by offering a criticism of Heidegger's work of a more generalized nature, a criticism, I hasten to add, which is made in the interest of furthering the matter to be thought, and which is not meant in any way to detract from the enormity of Heidegger's achievement, for which I have an abiding respect.

There are, according to Heidegger, two kinds of thought, meditative and calculative (G, 15/46). The first is what we, in accordance with Heidegger's own practice, have simply been calling throughout this work "thought" itself, somewhat in the way that Hegel referred to his own philosophical system as "science" itself. Meditative thought deals with Being itself. It makes no use of concepts and representations or deductive argumentation, but speaks from out of a direct experience of Being. It speaks moreover in an extraordinary kind of language which strives to be liberated from the traditional grammatical categories of subject and predicate and the metaphysics this grammar implies. Calculative thinking, on the other hand, is directed at beings. It employs representations (*Vorstellungen*) and makes use of the laws of logic, both inductive and deductive. It speaks as mathematically precise a language as is possible and in strict accordance with traditional grammar. In its sharpest and most prominent form, representational thought takes the form of the mathematical sciences.

Now Heidegger's purpose in making this distinction is to formulate the possibility of breaking the grip which representational thought has upon us all. We are rapidly coming to believe that the only form of truth is the truth which the mathematical sciences establish, and that such science is the only legitimate kind of thinking. It is not Heidegger's intention to do away with the sciences, or to denounce them as spurious. Both calculative thought and meditative thought are each "justified and needed in its own way" (G, 15/46). His intent is simply to restrict the claim of the sciences, of calculative thought, to exclusive validity, to "curb the pretensions of reason" as Kant said, in order to make way not for faith, as was Kant's intention, but for what he calls the "other thinking" (Sp., 212/279), that is, the thought of Being. And in all of this we can only applaud and endorse Heidegger's program.

The difficulty I see with Heidegger's undertaking begins to emerge when we consider the place of philosophy in Heidegger's scheme of things. By "philosophy," I hasten to add, I mean that tradition which begins most clearly in Plato and Aristotle, and which stretches on up to Husserl and even to *Being and Time* itself and to Heidegger's other writings in the 'twenties. Now philosophy for Heidegger is science (*Wissenschaft*); hence it falls on the side of calculative, not meditative thought.

Now there surely ought not to be anything unsettling about that. Did not Plato, Aristotle, Aquinas, Descartes, Leibniz, Kant, Fichte, Hegel, and Husserl all think themselves to be doing scientific thinking, not to be sure in the sense of the mathematical sciences, but in the sense of a strict, tightly argued, logical thinking? To be sure. But Heidegger's distinction does not differentiate the sort of "science" which we find in a Kant or Husserl, say, from that of the mathematical sciences. In fact it actually collapses this distinction. For Heidegger believes that there is an inherent drift, a fundamental tendency in Western philosophy to pass into the particular sciences. There is an inherent dynamism in metaphysical psychology to give birth to the empirical science of psychology, and in political philosophy to become political science, in philosophical cosmology to become mathematical-natural science. Such too is the story of the birth of sociology, logistics, semantics, economics, and all the rest (SD, 63/57). Nor is this development from philosophy to the particular sciences anything illegitimate for Heidegger. It is not a usurpation but the perfectly logical outcome of the inherent tendency of philosophy itself. "The development of philosophy into the independent sciences . . . is the legitimate completion of philosophy" (SD, 64/58). In other words, what philosophy is in the West is a rational, calculative thinking which finds its complete expression in the mathematical sciences and which therefore fulfills itself when it completely dissolves into such sciences. Philosophy is rationality, and rationality takes its most fully developed form in the mathematical sciences.

Heidegger's distinction between meditative and calculative thought compresses philosophy from both sides. Heidegger sees the philosophical tradition as disintegrating in two directions. On the one side there is the thinker who goes back to philosophy and retrieves its ownmost essence, its innermost life, its animating spirit, viz., the question of Being which brought philosophy into existence to begin with. Such a question cannot be genuinely asked in philosophy, even though the whole philosophical tradition has always been obscurely grappling with this question and in fact drawing its life's breath from it. The thought of Being is a possibility which cannot be actualized by philosophy but which the thinker can retrieve from philosophy and take up anew. That is the task of thought at the end of philosophy, which is the title of one of Heidegger's most important essays, and the one which we discussed at the beginning of this study. On the other side philosophy dissolves into scientific rationality; it breaks down into the particular sciences. Thus what the West has always called philosophy, the tradition from Plato to Husserl, loses its life; its soul is wrested from it by "thought," and its body is consumed by the particular sciences. If one is interested in philosophy one must make a decision and find where one's heart lies. If one is truly interested in philosophy, in philosophy's deepest concern (*Sache*), then one must be prepared to overcome philosophy and take up the task of thought. Or if this task seems to be so much mysticism or mythology to the philosopher, then his only alternative is to become rational with a vengeance and to give oneself over to the physical and social sciences.

In other words, Heidegger rejects the possibility of philosophy as a *tertium quid*, that is, as a thinking which is neither will-less, non-representational "meditation" (*Besinnung*) nor a calculative, mathematical science. Such a third thing is for him an unstable stuff which must either be repossessed by thought or decompose into the particular sciences. And this is the precise point in Heidegger's philosophy to which I take exception. For I believe that it leaves us men today holding the bag. It leaves us with a whole host of problems for which I do not see that there would be, in Heidegger's view, any place to turn in order to find a solution. I believe that there is a whole network of difficulties which are not merely technical problems and with which the methods of the technological sciences are simply unsuited to deal. Nor are they questions from which we can expect an answer from the thinker. It is interesting to read the *Der Spiegel* interview and to observe the increasing frustration of the interviewers with Heidegger's insistence that the thinker cannot offer advice, even of a general and indirect sort, to men of practical concerns:

> *Der Spiegel*: We expect help from the philosopher, if only indirect help, help in a roundabout way. And now we hear: I cannot help you.
> *Heidegger*: And I cannot.

Der Spiegel: That surely discourages the non-philosopher. . . . You do not number yourself among those who could show a way if people would only listen to them? (Sp., 212/280)

And a bit later in the same interview *Der Spiegel* adds, "But if no one has it and the philosopher cannot give it to anyone . . ." (Sp., 214/ 281).

The *Der Spiegel* interview brings out rather clearly, I think, the point I am trying to make. The renewal of the earth of which Heidegger speaks can come about only if two conditions are met. The first, and this is a precondition, is that men begin to think, that they open themselves up to the presencing in that which is present. But this of itself is not enough; it is a necessary, not a sufficient, condition. The second thing, and the essential thing, which is necessary, is that Being itself turn towards us again. Then, and only then, will the "frame" (*Gestell*) give way to the "world"; then alone will the evening-land become the land of a new dawn. But in the meantime we live in a time of need, a time in which Being is draped out in the costume of technology and in which the human essence is exposed to the "danger" of uprootedness. Now my question is this, what if we men do take up the task of thought, and Being still withholds itself? What if we keep ourselves open, and the night of the evening land persists? What if men are thinking, but the essence of technology does not loosen its grip? What if we prepare a readiness, and Being does not arrive? What if we "wait on" (*warten auf*) Being, not in the sense of sitting back on our haunches dreaming of a new day, but in the sense of "tending to," "waiting on" Being in its truth, but Being still refuses our service, spurns our overtures?

The first answer to this question, of course, is that we must persist in thinking, persist in preparing a readiness for Being's coming. Thinking demands patience (*Langmut*) and courage (*Mut*) (AED, 17/9). And in the meantime, in the time of waiting, the darkness will persist and perhaps even spread. Now what are we to do about the encroachment upon the human essence which will continue to take place in this technological world *in the meantime*? What are we to do about the vast sea of problems and difficulties which will assault us during this time of preparation in the age of the *Gestell*? Some men, for example, during this time will want to arrange our affairs for us with a technology of behavior. They will want to educate our children according to specific pedagogical techniques which are modeled after the methods of the physical sciences and which understand the essence of man in terms of an organism which responds to its environment. They will want to

267

arrange political affairs according to the same principles. Other men will want to alter our genetic endowment, now in one direction, now in another, depending upon the needs of the day. Still other men will counsel us to abort the unborn, and perhaps to take the life of the newborn and of the aged and infirm. Some will experiment with non-natural methods of fertilizing the female ovum. Debates will rage about the legitimate use of life-sustaining equipment, drugs which alter consciousness. Vast mass media, empowered by increasingly so-phisticated technological equipment, will exert greater and greater influence on the minds of our children and the opinions of our adults. And so on. One could fill pages just enumerating the problems which beset men in the technological world, the age of the *Gestell.*

Now granted that we are thinking, but that the withdrawal of Being persists, where does Heidegger hold that we should turn for help in dealing with these problems? Whose advice do we seek? What principles do we invoke? Where does the light originate which is to be shed on these problems? We cannot go to the thinker; we must not expect the thinker to render such judgments. That is fair enough. But where then? To the calculative sciences (for there are only two alternatives)? Who is left other than the scientists for guidance in these matters? Not just the natural scientist, of course, but also the social scientist, the psychologist, the sociologist, the political scientist, etc., all of whom belong to what Heidegger calls collectively "cybernetics."

But Heidegger himself said in *Being and Time,* and he was on this point a good student of Husserl, that all such sciences are themselves in need of direction by a "productive logic" which runs ahead of such sciences and lays down their basic framework and clarifies their fundamental concepts. Without such a productive logic all science and all ontology "remains blind and perverted from its ownmost aim" (SZ, §3, 11/31). But the later Heidegger leaves us between the devil and the deep blue sea. To adapt the language of the *Der Spiegel* interview: thought cannot give it and the sciences do not have it. We can hardly expect the thinker to render judgments of this sort, and the particular sciences cannot do so unless they are guided in their fundamental concepts by their various regional ontologies, by what has been called since the time of Plato and Aristotle "philosophy." What sort of advice will we get about the human situation from psychology if psychology is perverted from its own aims? What advice will we get from the psychology of Skinner, say, which is so badly lacking in proper foundations about the nature of man? What help could be forthcoming from sciences which by their very meaning are swept up in the *Gestell* and the kind of thinking which holds sway in the *Gestell?* Where are such sciences to receive guidance?

The simple truth of the matter is that in this time of need, (and even, I suspect, afterwards in the new beginning) we have need of the *tertium quid*, of philosophical insight, of a thinking which, while it does not attain the simplicity of thought, is not swept up by the techniques of the mathematical sciences. We need philosophers who will provide guidelines to the medical scientists. We need philosophical anthropologists who can throw light on the practice and the principles of psychologists. We need political philosophers to offer direction to political scientists.

In *Being and Time* there were clear lines of communication established between the question of Being itself (Fundamental Ontology) and the various regional ontologies, and then again between the regional ontologies and the particular sciences. At least that was the very Husserlian inspired program of §3 of *Being and Time*. But in the later writings there is a bifurcation, a bifurcation which originates in the decay of philosophy. For philosophy is overcome from above by the thinker who takes up in a higher way its essential task. And it dissolves from below into the particular sciences which are its natural completion. That leaves us, for example, with original ethics on the one hand and the "technology of behavior" on the other. The first cannot give it, and the second does not have it. Where then are we to turn in the time of need? I do not see how the very thing which is now necessary is possible. We need another alternative to the piety of thought and cybernetics, a third thing, a *scientia media*, a cognition which is neither held captive by the cave of mathematical science nor released into the upper world of thought. We need philosophical reflection, a reason which, while it does not match the simplicity of thought, still does not degenerate into technological calculation. We need ethics, philosophical anthropology, philosophical psychology, political philosophy, and all the other regional ontologies, and we need them now in the age of the *Gestell*, even as we also need thought. But for Heidegger such an intermediate knowledge is impossible; for philosophical reason is at an end, deteriorated into the particular sciences on the one hand and sublimated into thought on the other hand. Then that is so much the worse for us. Perhaps we will not need philosophy when the new day dawns. That is hard to say for we are not engaging in prophecy. But it does seem to me that, so long as the dark night of the evening land persists, Heidegger would leave us unnecessarily exposed to its hazards, some of which could hardly be more dangerous.

My purpose in making these remarks is not to detract from Heidegger's accomplishments. I have neither the skill nor the desire for such an undertaking. I believe, as I have said, that Heidegger is the great thinker of our age, and I mean by these remarks not to attack his work

269

but to carry it further. I raise these difficulties not with the desire to "parade polemical opinions" but with the hope of avoiding "complaisant agreement" (AED, 11/6). Like his mentor at Freiburg, Heidegger is interested in the matter to be thought, not in philosophers and their philosophies (cf. SD, 69/62). He wants us to be able to tell the difference between an object of scholarship (*ein gelehrter Gegenstand*) and the matter of thought (*eine gedachte Sache*) (AED, 9/5). He wants us not merely to expound his texts, though that is a matter of importance, but to take up the task of thought. His work is not furthered by epigones who talk as Heidegger talks, and who repeat what Heidegger has written, and who tiresomely charge that every criticism is a misunderstanding. His work is experienced properly only if we are led thereby to think it through and to take on ourselves and within our own limits the questions he raises.

And on this point he shares something in common with Meister Eckhart. Eckhart's sermons were not meant to inform his hearers of the latest developments in Christian theology, but to transform their lives. I can think of no more fitting way to bring this study of the mystical element in Heidegger's thought to a close than with a quotation from Meister Eckhart which, *mutatis mutandis*, Heidegger too can make his own. It is drawn from the sermon on mystical poverty, and Eckhart tells his hearers how they must *be* in their own lives if they want to *understand* what he is saying:

> Now I ask you to be so poor that you may understand this discourse. For I say to you by the eternal truth: if you do not make yourselves like to this truth of which we are now speaking, then you will not be able to understand me.   (Q, 303,17-20/Bl., 227)

In the same way Heidegger's writings must be for us not a body of texts to be subjected to a learned exegesis, but a voice which calls us to set our own reflection into motion.

And whose voice is it which calls to us from these texts? Is it only the voice of Martin Heidegger of Messkirch?

ENDNOTES

NOTES TO CHAPTER ONE

1. Friedrich Nietzsche, *Beyond Good and Evil*, trans. R. J. Hollindale (Baltimore: Penguin Books, 1973), No. 20, p. 31.

2. Werner Marx, "Heidegger's New Conception of Philosophy," *Social Research*, XXII (1955), 451-74.

3. Richard Wisser (ed.), *Martin Heidegger im Gespräch* (München: Karl Alber Verlag, 1970), p. 77. Engl. Trans. "Martin Heidegger: An Interview," *Listening*, VI (1973), p. 40.

4. The Middle High German text of this work is to be found in DW, V, 400 ff. and Quint's modernized German in DW, V, 539 ff. An English translation of the Pfeiffer text, which differs considerably from Quint's critical edition, is found in Bl., 82 ff. A good English translation of Eduard Schaeffer's edition of *Von Abgeschiedenheit*, which is very close to Quint's, is provided in Cl., 160 ff., to which I will provide cross-references.

5. In Quint's edition of the Middle High German: "*ein vernunftic bilde oder etwaz vernunftiges ane bilde*" (DW, V, 421, 1). In Quint's modernization: "*eine erkenntnismässige Bildvorstellung oder etwas bildlos Erkenntnismässiges*" (DW, V, 544). For Quint's justification of his version, see DW, V, 452, n. 68. Compare Bl., 87 and Cl., 166 for the translations of variant readings.

6. Thomas Aquinas, *Quaestiones disputatae de veritate*, Q. XIII, a. 2, ad 9m.

7. Norman Malcolm, *Ludwig Wittgenstein: A Memoir* (London: Oxford University Press, 1962), p. 70, n. 1.

8. According to Max Müller, Heidegger was going to distinguish the "theological difference" between God and creatures from the "ontological difference" between Being and beings in the never published Division III ("Time and Be-

ing") of *Being and Time.* See Max Müller, *Existenzphilosophie im geistigen Leben der Gegenwart,* 3. Aufl. (Heidelberg: F. H. Kerle, 1964), pp. 66-7.

9. We will see below (Chapter IV, section 8), in our discussion of Käte Olt-manns's *Meister Eckhart,* the limitations which are imposed on any attempt to relate Heidegger to Eckhart on the basis of the early Heidegger alone.

10. Müller, p. 61. See also WHD, 159/146, where Heidegger speaks of the "detachment" (*Abgeschiedenheit*) of what is most "thought-provoking." Cf. also US, 52-76/172-93.

11. For full bibliographical information on these titles, as well as on the abbreviations which we will hereafter use to refer to these works, we refer the reader to the "List of Abbreviations" which appears at the beginning of this

12. Alfred Rosenberg, *Der Mythus des 20. Jahrhunderts,* 12. Aufl. (München, 1933).

13. Walter Biemel, "Poetry and Language in Heidegger" in *On Heidegger and Language,* ed. J. Kockelmans, Northwestern University Studies in Phenomenology and Existential Philosophy (Evanston, 1972), p. 66.

14. *Op. cit.,* p. 68.

NOTES TO CHAPTER TWO

1. For the sake of convenience I will hereafter refer to *Der Satz vom Grund* as "SG," not only in the notes but also in the text itself. For commentary on SG in English see Rudolph Allers, "Heidegger on the Principle of Sufficient Reason," *Philosophy and Phenomenological Research,* XX (1959-60), 365-73. Also, see Jean Beaufret's "Preface" to the French translation of SG: *Le Principe de raison,* trad. André Préau (Paris: Gallimard, 1962), as well as the occasional notes to this translation. See also the various reviews of SG which are listed in our bibliography and which appear in Hans-Martin Sass, *Heidegger-Bibliographie* (Meisenheim am Glan: Hain, 1968) under the following entry numbers: 1.1324, 1.1358, 1.1380, 1.1414, 1.1417, 1.1426, 1.1434, 1.1768, 1.1826, 1.1890.

2. *Kierkegaard's Concluding Unscientific Postscript,* trans. David Swenson and Walter Lowrie (Princeton: at the University Press, 1941), pp. 99-107.

3. Ever since he broke away from his teacher Heinrich Rickert, Heidegger has made a similar critique of ethical values. For more on Heidegger and ethics see Chapter V, sections 2, 5, and 7 below.

4. One can see the entire "reversal" orchestrated in Heidegger's self-criticism of WG in SG. See the "Appendix" to the present chapter.

5. *Hegel: Texts and Commentary,* trans. and ed. W. Kaufmann (Garden City: Doubleday Anchor Books, 1966), p. 42.

6. Heidegger's discussion of *logos* in SG is very compacted. For a better understanding of his interpretation of *logos* see EM, 94 ff./104 ff. and VA, 207 ff./59 ff.

7. Cf. Kathleen Freemantle, *Ancilla to the Presocratic Philosophers* (Oxford: Basil Blackwell, 1962), p. 28.

8. For more on the play of Being in Heidegger see John Caputo, "Being, Ground and Play in Heidegger," *Man and World* 3, No. 1 (February, 1970), 26-48; Eugen Fink, *Spiel als Weltsymbol* (Stuttgart: Kohlhammer, 1960); Eugen Fink, "The Ontology of Play," *Philosophy Today*, 18 (Summer, 1974), 147-61; David Krell, "Towards an Ontology of Play: Eugen Fink's Notion of *Spiel*," *Research in Phenomenology* II (1972), 62-93; Ingeborg Heidemann, *Der Begriff des Spieles* (Berlin: Walter de Gruyter, 1968), pp. 278-372.

9. *Ancilla*, p. 28. Heidegger seems to have drawn some inspiration in his interpretation of this fragment of Heraclitus from Nietzsche's *Philosophy in the Tragic Age of the Greeks*. For G. S. Kirk, however, *aion* does not refer to a world-time at all, but to a human lifetime. See his *Heraclitus: The Cosmic Fragments* (Cambridge, at the University Press, 1962), p. xiii.

10. See James Demske, *Being, Man and Death* (Lexington: University of Kentucky Press, 1970), Ch. 6, "Death in the Game of Being," pp. 147 ff.

11. Otto Pöggeler, *Der Denkweg Martin Heideggers* (Pfullingen: Verlag G. Neske, 1963), pp. 36 ff.

NOTES TO CHAPTER THREE

1. The account that follows of Angelus Silesius is based upon Jeffrey L. Sammons, *Angelus Silesius*, Twayne's World Authors Series (New York: Twayne Publishers, 1967) and Horst Althaus, *Johann Schefflers "Cherubinischer Wandersmann": Mystik und Dichtung* (Giessen: Schmitz Verlag, 1956). Since we are not interested here in an analysis of the poetic quality of Scheffler's work we have tended to translate his verse in a more literal style. To give the reader a sense of its poetic quality perhaps it would be useful to quote some of the texts we make use of in a recently published and very beautiful volume entitled *The Book of Angelus Silesius. With Observations by the Ancient Zen Masters*, trans. Frederick Franck (New York: Knopf, 1976). CW, I, 108: "The rose that / with mortal eye I see / flowers in God / through all eternity" (p. 42). CW, II, 198: "It is as if God played a game / immersed in contemplation; / and from this game / all worlds arose / in endless variation" (p. 55). CW, I, 289: "She blooms because she blooms, / the rose . . . / Does not ask why, / nor does she preen herself / to catch my eye" (p. 66). CW, III, 87: "My heart could receive God / if only it chose / to turn toward the Light / as does the rose" (p. 119). The verse from Angelus Silesius cited at the beginning of the book is from Franck's book. For more on Angelus Silesius, see Franck's "Introduction," pp. 3-38.

2. See E. B. Koenker, "Potentiality in God: Jacob Boehme," *Philosophy Today*, XV (Spring, 1971), 44 ff.; William Kluback and Jean Wilde, "Preface" in SF, 9.

3. For full bibliographical information on *Meister Eckhart: Deutsche Predigten und Traktate*, hereafter referred to as "Q," see the "List of Abbreviations" at the beginning of this book. Since the Evans translation (Ev.) follows the Pfeiffer edition, and since Blakney (Bl.) did not have Quint's critical edition fully available to him, the reader will often discover a disparity between them and Quint. Clark's excellent translations (Cl., Serm.), however, follow Quint's critical edition of the sermons.

4. The best general introduction to Meister Eckhart in English is by James Clark in his "Introduction" in Serm., 3-121. See also Quint's superb *"Einleitung"* in Q, 9-50.

5. H. S. Denifle, "Meister Eckharts lateinische Schriften und die Grundanschauung seiner Lehre," *Archiv für Litteratur- und Kirchengeschichte des Mittelalters*, II (1886), 417-615.

6. On the history of Eckhartian scholarship, see Ingeborg Degenhardt, *Studien zum Wandel des Eckhartbildes* (Leiden: Brill, 1967). For Schopenhauer's reference to the Pfeiffer edition, see Arthur Schopenhauer, *The World as Will and Idea*, trans. R. B. Haldane and J. Kemp (London: Routledge and Kegan Paul, 1957), vol. I, p. 492.

7. See Ernst Benz, "Die Mystik in der Philosophie des deutschen Idealismus," *Euphorion*, 40 (1952), 280-300; Ernst Benz, *Les sources mystiques de la philosophie romantique allemande* (Paris: J. Vrin, 1968); Degenhardt, 110 ff.; Ernst von Bracken, *Meister Eckhart und Fichte* (Würzburg, 1943); G. Ralfs, "Lebensformen des Geistes: Meister Eckhart und Hegel," *Kant-Studien*, Erg.-Heft Nr. 86, Köln, 1964.

8. His fellow Dominican Aquinas defended the primacy of the intellect over the will, but not, as does Eckhart, over *esse* itself. See my "The Nothingness of the Intellect in Meister Eckhart's *Parisian Questions*," *The Thomist*, XXXIX, No. 1 (January, 1975), 85-115.

9. John Loeschen, "The God Who Becomes: Eckhart on Divine Relativity," *The Thomist*, XXXV (July, 1971), 405-22.

10. There is something to be said for the opinion that Eckhart here anticipates an essential tenet of the Reformation, that a man is not sanctified by his works. Cf. Alois Dempf, *Meister Eckhart*, Herder Bücherei Band 71 (Freiburg: Herder, 1960), pp. 55 ff.

11. Thomas Aquinas, *Summa Theologica*, I, Q. 37, a. 6, c.

12. Martin Grabmann, *Der Einfluss Alberts des Grossen auf das mittelalterliche Geistesleben: Das deutsche Element in der mittelalterlichen Scholastik und Mystik* (München, 1926-36), Vol. II, pp. 324-72; cf. Étienne Gilson, *A History of Christian Philosophy in the Middle Ages* (New York: Random House, 1955), pp. 451-56.

13. For an account of the "birth of the Son" in English see Karl G. Kertz, "Meister Eckhart's Teaching on the Birth of the Divine Word in the Soul," *Traditio*, XV (1959), 327-63.

14. All Scriptural citations are from *The Jerusalem Bible* (Garden City, N. Y.: Doubleday, 1966).

15. For reasons which were not Eckhart's, the Idealists too insisted that the Incarnation was not restricted to the empirical individual Jesus of Nazareth. Both Fichte, in his *Lectures on the Blessed Life* (1. vii), and Hegel, in *The Spirit of Christianity*, e.g., argued that the Incarnation signified a spiritual event that affected all men. Nonetheless there is somewhat of a tendency in Eckhart to emphasize the second person of the Trinity, the eternal Son, over the historical Christ.

16. Hugo Rahner, "Die Gottesgeburt," *Zeitschrift für katholische Theologie*, 59 (1933), p. 352; *loc. cit.*, n. 17.

17. Rahner, p. 411.

18. Dempf, *Meister Eckhart*, pp. 107-8.

19. Soren Kierkegaard, *Fear and Trembling* in *Fear and Trembling and The Sickness Unto Death*, trans. W. Lowrie (Garden City, N.Y.: Doubleday Anchor Books, 1954), p. 49.

20. Shizutera Ueda, *Die Gottesgeburt in der Seele und der Durchbruch zur Gottheit* (Gütersloh: Mohn, 1965), pp. 140-5.

21. Cf. Thomas Aquinas, *Summa Theologica*, IIa-IIae, Q. 182. See also Quint's fine "*Einleitung*" on this sermon (Q, 36-7, 44-8).

NOTES TO CHAPTER FOUR

1. James Robinson, "The German Discussion" in *The Later Heidegger and Theology*, eds. James M. Robinson and John B. Cobb, Jr. (New York: Harper & Row, 1963), pp. 42-3.

2. For an account of a Thomistic theory of analogy inspired by Cardinal Cajetan, see James Anderson, *Reflections on the Analogy of Being* (The Hague: Martinus Nijhoff, 1967).

3. For a full length study of the *Habilitationsschrift* which was part of the research which led up to the present book, see my "Phenomenology, Mysticism and the *Grammatica Speculativa*: A Study of Heidegger's *Habilitationsschrift*," *Journal of the British Society for Phenomenology*, Vol. 5 (May, 1974), 101-17.

4. Martin Grabmann, *Mittelalterliches Geistesleben* (München: Huebar Verlag, 1926), Band I. See Grabmann's reference to Heidegger on pp. 145-46.

5. Edmund Husserl, *Logical Investigations*, trans. J. N. Findlay (New York: Humanities Press, 1970), Vol. II, p. 493. Cf. FS, 269-70.

6. For a discussion of the tension between the existential-historical side of the youthful Heidegger and his abstract-logical side, see my review of Heidegger's *Frühe Schriften* in *Research in Phenomenology* III (1973), 147-55.

7. William Richardson, *Heidegger: Through Phenomenology to Thought*, Phaenomenologica, No. 13 (The Hague: Nijhoff, 1963), p. 663.

8. Heidegger's reference to Eckhart in FW, 4/35 as "the old master of life and books" is a reference to a legend recorded by Pfeiffer, a translation of which is to be found in Bl., 236.

9. Zygmunt Adamszewski, "On the Way to Being," in *Heidegger and the Path of Thinking*, ed. John Sallis (Pittsburgh: Duquesne University Press, 1970), pp. 13-8.

10. In assigning such importance to the poet, we might add, Heidegger is anticipated by Schelling, not Eckhart.

11. See Reiner Schürmann, "Heidegger and Meister Eckhart on Releasement," *Research in Phenomenology* III (1973), 95-119.

12. Peter Kreeft, "Zen in Heidegger's *Gelassenheit*," *International Philosophical Quarterly*, XI (December, 1971), 530-32.

13. Müller, *Existenzphilosophie*, pp. 45-6. See also Richardson, pp. 563-65. Note that the English translation (p. 354) follows the older version.

14. For full bibliographical information on this title—hereafter referred to as "Olt."—see the "List of Abbreviations" at the beginning of this book.

15. Martin Heidegger, *Phaenomenologie und Theologie* (Frankfurt: V. Klostermann, 1970), pp. 13-33. Eng. Trans. in Martin Heidegger, *The Piety of Thinking*, trans. with notes and commentary by J. Hart and J. Maraldo (Bloomington: Indiana Univ. Press, 1976), pp. 5-21.

16. Otto Karrer, "Von Meister Eckhart und seiner Nachwirkung," *Schweizer Rundschau* (1935-36), p. 406.

17. Otto Pöggeler, *Der Denkweg Martin Heideggers*, pp. 303-4, n. 20.

18. Ernst Benz, "Zur neuesten Forschung über Meister Eckhart," *Zeitschrift für Kirchengeschichte*, 57 (1938), p. 581.

19. For full bibliographical information on this title—hereafter referred to as "Schür."—see the "List of Abbreviations" at the beginning of this book.

20. Benz, "Zur neuesten Forschung," p. 581.

21. See Heidegger's letter to Albert Borgmann in *Philosophy East and West*, XX (July, 1970), p. 221. This entire issue is devoted to the papers given at this meeting.

22. Hans-Martin Sass, *Heidegger-Bibliographie* (Meisenheim am Glan: Verlag Anton Hain, 1968), p. 25. One of Heidegger's Japanese translators is a Prof. Tezuka (Tokyo), with whom the "Dialogue on Language" is held (US, 85/1 ff.).

23. For full bibliographical information on this title—hereafter referred to as "Suz."—see the "List of Abbreviations" at the beginning of this book.

24. D. T. Suzuki, *Mysticism: Christian and Buddhist* (New York: Macmillan, 1969); Shizuteru Ueda, *Die Gottesgeburt in der Seele und der Durchbruch zur Gottheit: Die Mystische Anthropologie Meister Eckharts und ihre Konfrontation mit der Mystik des Zen-Buddhismus* (Gütersloh: G. Mohn, 1965). And of course the relationship between Eckhart and Zen is indirectly established through the relationship of Angelus Silesius and Zen. Not only does Ueda make use of Silesius's verse on the rose, but one can also point to Franck's book, *The Book of Angelus Silesius. With Observations by the Ancient Zen Masters*, which is a most successful juxtaposing of verse from *The Cherubinic Wanderer* and passages from Hui-neng and other Zen masters.

25. Huston Smith, *The Religions of Man* (New York: Harper Colophon Books, 1958), p. 125.

26. For full bibliographical information on this title—hereafter referred to as "Herr."—see the "List of Abbreviations" at the beginning of this book.

27. Smith, *Religions*, p. 181.

28. Suzuki, *Mysticism: Christian and Buddhist*, pp. 18-21, 70; Ueda, *Gottesgeburt*, 149-50, 163-64. See Ueda, pp. 165-66 for the difference between the Nothing in Eckhart and Zen.

29. Suzuki, *Mysticism: Christian and Buddhist*, pp. 13-4.

30. See D. T. Suzuki, *An Introduction to Zen Buddhism* (New York: Grove Press, 1964), p. 13 for a description of a deed done "without recompense" in Zen; compare this with Eckhart's notion of *"ohne Warum."*

31. Ueda, *Gottesgeburt*, pp. 153 ff.

32. It is clear that one of the best places to begin comparing Eckhart and Heidegger—*What is Metaphysics?* (cf. Chapter I, secs. 2-3, *supra*)—is also one of the best places to begin comparing Heidegger and Zen. Another good place, as Peter Kreeft has shown so well, is *Gelassenheit*. See Peter Kreeft, "Zen in Heidegger's *Gelassenheit*," *International Philosophical Quarterly* XI (December, 1971), 521-45.

33. On the difference between Heidegger and the East see Joan Stambaugh, "Commentary," *Philosophy East and West*, XX (July, 1970), 285-86, and J. L. Mehta, "Heidegger and the Comparison of Indian and Western Philosophy," *Philosophy East and West*, XX (July, 1970), 303-17.

34. On the difference between Eckhart and Zen on language, see Ueda, pp. 150, 167-68.

NOTES TO CHAPTER FIVE

1. Richardson, pp. xiv-xv.

2. Biemel, in Kockelmans, *On Heidegger and Language*, pp. 66-7.

3. To the extent that Eckhart developed a similarly original and poetic and—to the logician—paradoxical style of discourse in his sermons, Eckhart too was himself a practitioner of a similar relationship to language. But the point is that the content of these sermons proposed the ideal of silence. The situation is not unlike Plato's highly poetic critique of poetry in the *Republic*.

4. See Pöggeler's comments on Heidegger's "sigetics" in Kockelmans, *On Heidegger and Language*, pp. 114-15, 145.

5. See my "Time and Being in Heidegger," *The Modern Schoolman*, L (May, 1973), 325-49.

6. See also Werner Marx, *Heidegger and the Tradition*, trans. T. Kisiel and M. Greene, Northwestern University Studies in Phenomenology and Existential Philosophy (Evanston, 1971), p. 254; see also Marx's comments in Kockelmans, *On Heidegger and Language*, pp. 255-56; cf. op. cit., p. 253, n. 60.

7. Nietzsche, *Beyond Good and Evil*, No. 2, p. 16.

8. For what follows on the ontological and the cosmological approach to God see Paul Tillich, "Two Types of Philosophy of Religion" in *Theology of Culture*, ed. R. C. Kimball (New York: Oxford University Press, 1964), pp. 10-29. See also Tillich's account of medieval theology in *A History of Christian Thought*, ed. C. Braaten (New York: Harper & Row, 1968) where he refers to the "ontological" point of view as "mystical" (p. 141). For an account of this distinction and its relations to the Augustinian tradition see John P. Dourley, *Paul Tillich and Bonaventure: An Evaluation of Tillich's Claim to Stand in the Augustinian-Franciscan Tradition* (Leiden: Brill, 1975), pp. 1-49.

9. Richardson, p. 1; cf. p. 3, n. 1. "*Gedachtes*/Thoughts," trans. K. Hoeller, *Philosophy Today* XX, No. 4 (Winter, 1976), pp. 286-90. See also the poem "*Sprache*" on p. 291 of this same issue.

10. See Reuben Guilead, *Être et Liberté: une étude sur le dernier Heidegger*

(Louvain: Éditions Nauwelaerts, 1965), pp. 142-46, for a comparison of Heidegger's *Gelassenheit* and "aesthetic disinterest" in Kant. Guilead concludes: "Kant is replaced with Eckhart." That is, the mystical sense of *Gelassenheit* predominates over its aesthetic sense. Cf. also pp. 172-73. Heidegger's thought, Guilead says, is "mystical in the broad sense" (173).

11.   Friedrich Nietzsche, *The Will to Power*, trans. W. Kaufmann and R. J. Hollingdale (New York: Vintage Books, 1967), No. 29, p. 20.

12.   Suzuki, *Introduction to Zen Buddhism*, p. 45.

13.   Marx, *Tradition*, pp. 145-52 and *passim*.

14.   Gabriel Marcel, *Homo Viator*, trans. E. Craufurd (New York: Harper Torchbooks, 1962), p. 65.

15.   Heidegger, *Phaenomenologie und Theologie*, pp. 37 ff. *Piety*, pp. 22-31.

16.   Löw., 16-7, 43; cf. Guilead, pp. 177-78.

17.   Nietzsche, *Beyond Good and Evil*, No. 203, pp. 108-9.

18.   *Op. cit.*, No. 39, p. 50.

19.   On the place of God in Heidegger's thought see James L. Perotti, *Heidegger on the Divine* (Athens: Ohio University Press, 1974); Henri Birault, "De L'Être, du divin et des dieux chez Heidegger," in *L'existence de dieu*, Cahiers de l'actualité religieuse, 16 (Paris: Casterman, 1963), pp. 49-76.

20.   See W. T. Stace's interesting discussion of the ethical implications of mysticism in *Mysticism and Philosophy* (London: Macmillan & Co., 1961), pp. 323-41.

21.   See my "Heidegger's Original Ethics," *The New Scholasticism* XLV (Winter, 1971), 127-38.

22.   It would be interesting to compare Heidegger's critique of ethics with Karl Barth, who writes ". . . man is not in a position to solve the ethical problem with his thought." Karl Barth, *The Word of God and the Word of Man*, trans. D. Horton (n.p.: The Pilgrim Press, 1928), p. 177. For Barth, a merely human ethic must necessarily be a failure.

23.   For a recent and quite interesting attempt by a philosopher from the Anglo-American tradition to address himself to this very question, and with rather different results than the present study, see Richard Rorty, "Overcoming the Tradition: Heidegger and Dewey," *Review of Metaphysics* XXX, No. 2 (December, 1976), 280-305.

24.   Originally, of course, the opposite was the case: philosophy took its origin, by way of a certain withdrawal of Being, from thought. Thus, by taking his point of departure from philosophy and taking the step back into thought, Heidegger is in fact retracing the steps of the Western tradition itself.

25.   Richard Rorty writes "The whole force of Heidegger's thought lies in his account of the history of philosophy." See "Overcoming the Tradition: Heidegger and Dewey," p. 303.

BIBLIOGRAPHY

Note: The following bibliography does not contain those titles which have already been mentioned on the "List of Abbreviations." It does, however, include works of Heidegger not mentioned on that list, as well as other titles containing works of Meister Eckhart. In the case of the secondary literature, which is quite extensive with respect to both Heidegger and Eckhart, we have included only very important books and articles on Heidegger and Eckhart, or those which have a direct bearing on this study. For as complete a bibliography as possible on Heidegger there is no substitute for: Hans-Martin Sass, *Heidegger-Bibliographie* (Meisenheim a/Glan: Hain, 1968) and also his *Materialien zur Heidegger-Bibliographie 1917–1972* (Meisenheim a/Glan: Hain, 1975).

I. *Heidegger*

A. Primary Sources

Heidegger, Martin. "Anmerkungen zu Karl Jaspers' *Psychologie der Weltanschauungen.*" In: *Karl Jaspers in der Discussion.* München: Piper Verlag, 1973. Pp. 70-100.

———. "Antrittsrede," *Jahresheft der Heidelberger Akademie der Wissenschaften* (1957–58). Heidelberg: Winter, 1959. Pp. 20-1.

———. "*Gedachtes*/Thoughts," *Philosophy Today*, XX, No. 4 (Winter, 1976), 286-90.

———. *Die Grundprobleme der Phänomenologie. Gesamtausgabe*, B. 24. Frankfurt: Klostermann, 1975.

———. "Grundsätze des Denkens," *Jahrbuch für Psychologie und Psychotherapie* (1958), 33-41.

————. *Hebel der Hausfreund.* 3. Auflage. Pfullingen: Verlag Günther Neske, 1965.

————. "Hegel und die Griechen." In: *Die Gegenwart der Griechen im neueren Denken.* Tübingen: Mohr, 1960. Pp. 43-57.

————. und Fink, Eugen. *Heraklit.* Frankfurt: Vittorio Klostermann, 1970.

————. "Hölderlins Himmel und Erde," *Hölderlin Jahrbuch.* Tübingen, 1960. Pp. 17-39.

————. *Identität und Differenz.* 3. Auflage. Pfullingen: Verlag Günther Neske, 1957.

————. *Kants These über das Sein.* Frankfurt: Vittorio Klostermann, 1963.

————. *Logik: Die Frage nach der Wahrheit. Gesamtausgabe,* B. 21. Frankfurt: Klostermann, 1976.

————. *Phänomenologie und Theologie.* Frankfurt: Vittorio Klostermann, 1970.

————. *Die Selbstbehauptung der deutschen Universität.* Breslau: Korn, 1933.

————. *Schellings Abhandlung über das Wesen der menschlichen Freiheit (1809).* Tübingen: Max Niemeyer, 1971.

————. *Vom Wesen des Grundes.* 5. Auflage. Frankfurt: Vittorio Klostermann, 1965.

————. *Was ist das—die Philosophie?.* Pfullingen: Verlag Günther Neske, 1956.

————. *Wegmarken. Gesamtausgabe,* B. 9. Frankfurt: Klostermann, 1976.

————. *Zu einem Vers vom Mörike.* Zürich: Atlantis, 1951.

————. *Zur Seinsfrage.* Frankfurt: Klostermann, 1956.

Martin Heidegger im Gespräch. Ed. Richard Wisser. Freiburg: Karl Alber Verlag, 1970.

Martin Heidegger: Zum 80. Geburtstag: Von seiner Heimatstadt Messkirch. Frankfurt: Klostermann, 1969.

B.   Translations

Bibliography of: "Heidegger Bibliography of English Translations," Compiled by Keith Hoeller. *Journal of the British Society for Phenomenology,* 6, No. 3 (October, 1975), 206-8.

Heidegger, Martin. "Art and Space," Trans. C. H. Seibert. *Man and World,* VI (1973), 3-8.

————. "Kant's Thesis About Being," Trans. T. E. Klein and W. E. Pohl. *Southwestern Journal of Philosophy,* IV (1973), 7-33.

————. "Martin Heidegger: An Interview," Trans. V. Guagliardo and R. Pambrun. *Listening,* IV (1971), 34-40.

————. *The Piety of Thinking.* Trans. J. G. Hart and J. Maraldo. With notes and commentary. Bloomington: Indiana University Press, 1976.

————. *Le principe de raison.* Trans. André Préau. Preface de Jean Beaufret. Paris: Gallimard, 1962. (French Translation of SG).

Seigfried, Hans. "Martin Heidegger: A Recollection," *Man and World,* 3 (February, 1971), 3-4. (Translation of Heidelberg "Antrittsrede".)

¿ Qué es Metafísica? Versión española de Xavier Zubiri y *Sermón del Maestro Eckehart.* Version española de Eugenio Imaz. Madrid: Cruz del Sur, 1963. (Spanish translations of *Was ist Metaphysik?* and Eckhart's treatise *"Von Abgeschiedenheit."*)

C. Secondary Sources: Books

Biemel, Walter. *Martin Heidegger in Selbstzeugnissen und Bilddokumenten.* Hamburg: Rowohlt, 1973.

Demske, James. *Being, Man and Death.* Lexington: University of Kentucky Press, 1970.

Feick, Hildegaard. *Index zu Heideggers "Sein und Zeit."* Tübingen: Max Niemeyer Verlag, 1961.

Guildead, Reuben. *Être et liberté: une étude sur le dernier Heidegger.* Louvain: Éditions Nauwelaerts, 1965.

Gray, J. Glenn. *On Understanding Violence Philosophically.* New York: Harper & Row, 1970.

Heidegger: Perspektiven zur Deutung seines Werks. Hrsg. v. Otto Pöggeler. Koln: Kiepenheuer & Witsch, 1969.

Heidegger and the Path of Thinking. Ed. John Sallis. Pittsburgh: Duquesne University Press, 1970.

Heidemann, Ingeborg. *Der Begriff des Spieles.* Berlin: W. de Gruyter, 1968.

Koza, Ingeborg. *Das Problem des Grundes in Heideggers Auseinandersetzung mit Kant.* Ratingen: Henn, 1966.

Kockelmans, Joseph. (Ed.) *On Heidegger and Language.* Northwestern University Studies in Phenomenology and Existential Philosophy. Evanston, 1972.

Levinas, Emmanuel. *Totality and Infinity: An Essay on Exteriority.* Trans. A. Linguis. Pittsburgh: Duquesne University Press, 1969.

Löwith, Karl. *Nature, History and Existentialism.* Ed. and trans. A. Levinson. Northwestern University Studies in Phenomenology and Existential Philosophy. Evanston, 1966.

Macquarrie, John. *An Existentialist Theology: A Comparison of Heidegger and Bultmann.* New York: Harper & Row, 1965.

Martin Heidegger in Europe and America. Eds. Edward Ballard and Charles Scott. The Hague: Martinus Nijhoff, 1973.

Marx, Werner. *Heidegger and the Tradition.* Trans. T. Kisiel and M. Greene. Northwestern University Studies in Phenomenology and Existential Philosophy. Evanston, 1971.

Mehta, J. L. *Martin Heidegger: The Way and the Vision.* Honolulu: University Press of Hawaii, 1976.

Müller, Max. *Existenzphilosophie im geistigen Leben der Gegenwart.* 3. Auflage. Heidelberg: F. H. Kerle, 1964.

New Frontiers in Theology. Vol. I. *The Later Heidegger and Theology.* Ed. James Robinson and John Cobbs, Jr. New York: Harper & Row, 1963.

281

Palmier, Jean-Michel. *Les écrits politiques de Heidegger.* Paris: L'Herne, 1968.

Perotti, James L. *Heidegger on the Divine.* Athens: Ohio University Press, 1974.

Pöggeler, Otto. *Der Denkweg Martin Heideggers.* Pfullingen: Verlag Günther Neske, 1963.

―――. *Philosophie und Politik bei Heidegger.* Freiburg: Karl Alber, 1972.

Richardson, William. *Heidegger: Through Phenomenology to Thought.* With a Preface by Martin Heidegger. Phaenomenologica, No. 13. The Hague: Martinus Nijhoff, 1963.

Sass, Hans-Martin. *Heidegger-Bibliographie.* Meisenheim: Verlag Anton Hain, 1968.

Schmitt, Richard. *Martin Heidegger on Being Human.* New York: Random House, 1969.

Vycinas, Vincent. *Earth and Gods: An Introduction to the Philosophy of Martin Heidegger.* The Hague: Martinus Nijhoff, 1961.

D.   Secondary Sources: Articles

Allers, Rudolph. "Heidegger on the Principle of Sufficient Reason," *Philosophy and Phenomenological Research.* XX (1959-60), 365-73.

Birault, Henri. "De l'Être, du divin, et des dieux chez Heidegger," *L'Existence de dieu.* Paris: Casterman, 1963. Pp. 49-76.

―――. "Existence et verité d'apres Heidegger," *Revue de métaphysique et morale,* LVI (1950), 35-87.

Buchanan, James. "Heidegger and the Problem of Ground, "*Philosophy Today,* 17 (Fall, 1973), 232-45.

Brunner, A. "Rezension: Heidegger, *Der Satz vom Grund,*" *Stimmen der Zeit,* 163 (1958-59), 313.

Caputo, John D. "Being, Ground and Play in Heidegger," *Man and World* 3 (1971), 26-48.

―――. "Heidegger's Original Ethics," *The New Scholasticism,* XLV (1971), 127-38.

―――. "Language, Logic and Time: A Review of Heidegger's *Frühe Schriften,*" *Research in Phenomenology,* III (1973), 147-55.

―――. "Meister Eckhart and the Later Heidegger: The Mystical Element in Heidegger's Thought." In two parts. *The Journal of the History of Philosophy,* XII, No. 4 (October, 1974), 479-94 and XIII, No. 1 (January, 1975), 61-80.

―――. "Phenomenology, Mysticism and the *Grammatica Speculativa*: A Study of Heidegger's *Habilitationsschrift,*" *The Journal of the British Society for Phenomenology* 5 (May, 1974), 101-17.

―――. "The Principle of Sufficient Reason: A Study of a Heideggerian Self-Criticism," *The Southern Journal of Philosophy,* XIII, No. 4 (Winter, 1975), 419-26.

―――. "The Rose is without Why: An Interpretation of the Later Heidegger," *Philosophy Today,* 15 (1971), 3-15.

Guzzoni, Alfredo. "Rezension: Heidegger, *Der Satz vom Grund*," *Il Pensiero*, 3 (1958), 232.

École, J. "Review: Heidegger, *Le principe de raison*," *Les études philosophiques*, 17 (1962), 547-48.

Flaumbaum, I. "Meister Eckhart y Martin Heidegger," *Minerva*, i (Buenos Aires: 1944).

Fumet, Stanislas. "Heidegger et les mystiques," *La Table Ronde*, No. 182 (Paris: 1963), 82-9.

Garcia-Bacca, J. D. "El Sentido de la nada en la fundamentacion de la metafisica segun Heidegger y el sentido de la nada como fundamentacion de la experiencia mistica, segun San Juan de la Cruz," *Cuadernos* (Mexico), 18 (1944), 87-100.

Hansen-Löve, F. "Fundamentalontologie oder Seinsmystik? Zur jungsten Schrift Martin Heideggers," *Wort und Wahrheit*, 4 (1949), 219-23.

Ihde, Don. "Phenomenology and the Later Heidegger," *Philosophy Today*, 18 (Spring, 1974), 19-31.

Koenker, E. B. "Potentiality in God: Jacob Boehme," *Philosophy Today*, XV (Spring, 1971) 44 ff.

Lewalter, C. E. "Heidegger und die Mystik," *Die Zeit* 5, No. 21 (1950), 5.

Löwith, Karl. "Les implications politiques de la philosophie de l'existence chez Heidegger," *Gesammelte Abhandlungen: Zur Kritik des geschichtlicher Existenz*. Stuttgart: Kohlhammer, 1960.

Marquet, J. F. "Review: Heidegger, *Le principe de raison*," *Critique*, 19 (1963), 239-47.

Marx, Werner. "Heidegger's New Conception of Philosophy: The Second Phase of Existentialism," *Social Research*, XXII (1955), 451-74.

Mehta, J. L. "Heidegger and the Comparison of Indian and Western Philosophy," *Philosophy East and West*, XX (July, 1970), 303-17.

Philosophy East and West, XX (July, 1970). Topic: Heidegger and Eastern Thought.

Piguet, J. C. "Les oeuvres recentes de Martin Heidegger," *Revue de théologie et philosophie*, Series 2, Vol. 8 (1958), 283-90.

Pöggeler, Otto. "Sein als Ereignis," *Zeitschrift für philosophische Forschung*, XIII (1959), 597-632. Engl. Trans.: "Being as Appropriation," *Philosophy Today*, 19 (Summer, 1975), 152-78.

———. "Metaphysics and Topology of Being in Heidegger," *Man and World*, 8 (February, 1975), 3-27.

———. "Rezension: Heidegger, *Der Satz vom Grund*," *Philosophischer Literaturanzeiger*, 11 (1958), 241-51.

Przywara, Erich. "Rezension: Heidegger, *Der Satz vom Grund*," *Les études philosophiques*, 12 (1957), 408.

Rorty, Richard. "Overcoming the Tradition: Heidegger and Dewey," *Review of Metaphysics*, XXX, No. 2 (December, 1976), 280-305.

Schulz, Walter. "Über den philosophiegeschichtlichen Ort Martin Heideggers," *Philosophische Rundschau*, I (1954), 65-93, 211-32.

283

Schürmann, Reiner. "Heidegger and Meister Eckhart on Releasement," *Research in Phenomenology*, III (1973), 95-119.

———. "Trois penseurs de délaissement: Maître Eckhart, Heidegger, Suzuki." In two parts. *Journal of the History of Philosophy*, XII, No. 4 (October, 1974), 455-78 and XIII, No. 1 (January, 1975), 43-60.

Riverso, E. "Review: Heidegger, *Der Satz vom Grund*," *Rassegna di Scienze Filosofiche*, 15 (Naples, 1962), 100.

Wahl, Jean. "Sur des écrits recents de Heidegger et de Fink," *Revue de métaphysique et de morale*, 63 (1958), 474-82.

Welte, Bernhard. "La metaphysique de S. Thomas d'Aquin et la pensée de l'histoire de l'être chez Heidegger," *Revue des Sciences Philosophiques et Theologiques*, 50 (1966), 601-61.

Zimmerman, Michael. "Heidegger, Ethics and National Socialism," *Southwestern Journal of Philosophy*, 5 (Spring, 1974), 97-104.

II.   *Meister Eckhart*

A.   Primary Sources

Daniels, Augustinus. "Eine lateinische Rechtfertigungsschrift des Meister Eckhart," *Beitrage zur Geschichte der Philosophie und Theologie des Mittelalters*, XXIII, Heft 5 (1923).

Denifle, H. S. "Aktenstücke zu Meister Eckharts Process," *Zeitschrift für deutsches Altertum*, XXIX (1885), 259-66.

———. "Meister Eckharts lateinische Schriften und die Grundanschauung seiner Lehre," *Archiv für Litteratur- und Kirchengeschichte des Mitteralters*, II (1886), 417-615.

Grabmann, Martin. "Neuaufgefundene Pariser Questionen Meister Eckharts," *Abhandlungen der Bayerischen Akademie der Wissenschaften*, Philosophisch-philologische und historische Klasse, Vol. 32, B. 7. München, 1927.

Longpré, Ephrem."Questions inédites de Maître Eckhart, o.p. et de Gonzalve de Balboa, o.f.m." *Revue néocholastique de philosophie*, 26 (1927), 69-85.

Jostes, Franz. *Meister Eckhart und seine Jünger. Ungedruckte Text zur Geschichte der deutschen Mystik*. Freiburg (Switzerland), 1895.

Magistri Eckhardi opera latina auspiciis Instituti Sanctae Sabinae in Urbe ad codicem fidem edita. Eds. Raymond Klibansky et al. Leipzig: Felix Meiner, 1934-36.

Pffeifer, Franz. *Deutsche Mystiker des 14. Jahrhunderts*. Band II: *Meister Eckhart*. Leipzig, 1857. Reprinted Aalen, 1962.

Quint, Josef. Hrsg. *Meister Eckharts Buch der göttlichen Tröstung und Von dem edlen Menschen (Liber Benedictus) unter Benützung bisher unbekannter Handschriften*. Berlin, 1952.

———. *Die Überlieferung der deutschen Predigten Meister Eckharts*. Bonn, 1932.

———. *Deutsche Mystikertexte des Mittelalters*, I. Bonn, 1929.

Schaeffer, Eduard. *Meister Eckharts Traktat "Von Abgeschiedenheit".* Untersuchung und Textneuausgabe. Bonn, 1956.

Strauch, Philipp. *Paradisus anime intelligentis.* Deutsche Texte des Mittelalters, Band XXX. Berlin, 1919.

Büttner, Hermann. *Meister Eckhart: Schriften.* Aus dem Mittelhochdeutschen übertragen u. eingeleitet. Jena, 1934.

Leeson, N. *After Supper in the Refectory: Talks of Instruction.* London, 1917.

Meister Eckhart Speaks. Ed. with an introduction by Otto Karrer. Trans. E. Strakosch (New York: Philosophical Library, 1957).

Schulze-Maizier, Friedrich. *Meister Eckharts deutsche Predigten und Traktate.* 3. Auflage. Leipzig, 1938.

B. Secondary Sources: Books

Althaus, Horst. *Johann Schefflers "Cherubinische Wandersmann": Mystik und Dichtung.* Giessen: Schmitz Verlag, 1956.

Ancelot-Hustache, Jeanne. *Master Eckhart and the Rhineland Mystics.* Trans. H. Graef. Men of Wisdom Books. London: Longmans, Green and Co., 1957.

Benz, Ernst. *Les sources mystiques de la philosophie romantique allemande.* Paris: J. Vrin, 1968.

Bracken, Ernst von. *Meister Eckhart und Fichte.* Würzburg, 1943.

Brunner, Fernand. *Maître Eckhart.* Philosophes de tous les temps. N. 59. Paris: Seghers, 1969.

Cognet, Louis. *Introduction aux mystiques rhéno-flamands.* Paris: Desclée, 1968.

Degenhardt, Ingeborg. *Studien zum Wandel des Eckhartbildes.* Leiden: Brill, 1969.

Dempf, Alois. *Meister Eckhart.* Herder Bücherei B. 71. Freiburg: Herder, 1960.

Ebeling, Heinrich. *Meister Eckharts Mystik.* Stuttgart, 1941. Reprinted: Aalen: Scientia Verlag, 1966.

Fischer, H. *Meister Eckhart.* Freiburg im Breisgau, 1971.

Gilson, Étienne. *A History of Christian Philosophy in the Middle Ages.* New York: Random House, 1955.

Grabmann, Martin. *Mittelalterliches Geistesleben.* Band I. München: Huebar Verlag, 1926.

———. *Der Einfluss Alberts des Grossen auf das mittelalterliche Geistesleben: Das deutsche Element in der mittelalterlichen Scholastik und Mystik.* Munchen, 1926-36.

Henry, Michel. *L'Essence de la manifestation.* 2 Tomes. Paris: Presses Universitaires de France, 1963.

Hof, Hans. *Scintilla animae: Eine Studie zu einem Grundbegriff in Meister Eckharts Philosophie.* Lund and Bonn, 1952.

Karrer, Otto. *Meister Eckhart: Das System seiner religiosen Lehre und Lebensweisheit.* München, 1926.

285

Kopper, Joachim. *Die Metaphysik Meister Eckharts.* Saarbrücken: West-Ost Verlag, 1955.

Lossky, Vladimir. *Théologie negative et connaissance de Dieu chez Maître Eckhart.* Paris: Librarie philosophique J. Vrin, 1960.

Meister Eckhart der Predigter. Hrsg. U. Nix u. R. Oechslin. Freiburg: Herder, 1960.

Muller-Thyme, Bernard J. *The Establishment of the University of Being in the Doctrine of Meister Eckhart of Hochheim.* New York & London: Sheed & Ward, 1939.

La Mystique Rhénane. Colloque de Strasbourg, 1961. Paris: Presses Universitaires de France, 1963.

Otto, Rudolph. *Mysticism East and West.* Trans. B. Bracey and R. Payne. New York: The Macmillan Co., 1960.

Sammons, Jeffrey. *Angelus Silesius.* Twayne's World Authors Series. New York: Twayne Publishers, 1967.

Suzuki, D. T. *Mysticism: Christian and Buddhist.* New York: Macmillan, 1961.

Stace, W. T. *Mysticism and Philosophy.* London: Macmillan & Co., 1961.

Ueda, Shizutera. *Die Gottesgeburt in der Seele und der Durchbruch zur Gottheit: Die mystische Anthropologie Meister Eckharts und ihre Konfrontation mit der Mystik des Zen-Buddhismus.* Gütersloh: G. Mohn, 1965.

C. Secondary Sources: Articles

Benz, Ernst. "Die Mystik in der Philosophie des deutschen Idealismus," *Euphorion,* 40 (1952), 280-300.

Caputo, John D. "The Nothingness of the Intellect in Meister Eckhart's *Parisian Questions,*" *The Thomist,* XXXIX (January, 1975), 85-115.

———. "Review: Armand Maurer, *Master Eckhart's Parisian Questions and Prologues,*" *The Thomist,* XXXIX (July, 1975), 619-23.

Hodl, L. "Metaphysik und Mystik im Denken des Meister Eckhart," *Zeitschrift für katholische Theologie,* 82 (1960), Heft 3.

Karrer, Otto. "Von Meister Eckhart und seiner Nachwirkung," *Schweizer Rundschau* (1935-36), 403-16.

Kelly, Dom Placid. "Meister Eckhart's Doctrine of Divine Subjectivity," *The Downside Review,* 76 (1958), 65-103.

Kertz, Karl. G. "Meister Eckhart's Teaching on the Birth of the Soul," *Traditio,* XV (1959), 327-63.

Koch, Josef. "Zur Analogieslehre Meister Eckharts," *Mélanges offerts à Étienne Gilson.* Paris: Librarie philosophique J. Vrin, 1959. Pp. 327-50.

Loeschen, John. "The God Who Becomes: Eckhart on Divine Relativity," *The Thomist,* XXXV (July, 1971), 405-22.

Pahncke, Max. "Meister Eckharts Lehre von der Geburt Gottes im Gerechten," *Archiv für Religionswissenschaft,* XII (1925), 15-24, 252-64.

Quint, Josef. "Die Sprache Meister Eckharts als Ausdruck seiner mystischen Geisteswelt," *Deutsche Vierteljahresschrift für Literatur- und Geistesgeschichte,* 6 (1928), 671-701.

————. "Meister Eckhart" in Friedrich Uberwegs *Grundriss der Geschichte der Philosophie*, 2. Teil, 11. Auflage. Berlin, 1928.

————. "Mystik und Sprache," *Deutsche Vierteljahresschrift für Literatur- und Geistesgeschichte*, 27 (1953), 48-76.

Rahner, Hugo. "Die Gottesgeburt: Die Lehre der Kirchenvater von der Geburt Christ im Herzen Glaubigen," *Zeitschrift für katholische Theologie*, 59 (1933), 333-418.

Ralfs, G. "Lebensformen des Geistes: Meister Eckhart und Hegel," *Kant-Studien*, Er.-Heft Nr. 86. Köln, 1964.

Spann, Othmar. "Meister Eckharts mystische Erkenntnislehre," *Zeitschrift für philosophische Forschung*, III (1949), 339-55.

La Vie Spirituelle, LIII (January, 1971). (A special Meister Eckhart issue; guest editor: Reiner Schürmann.)

Weiss, Konrad. "Die Seelenmetaphysik des Meister Eckhart," *Zeitschrift für Kirchengeschichte*, LII (1933), 467-524.

III.   *Other Works Mentioned in the Endnotes*

Anderson, James F. *Reflections on the Analogy of Being*. The Hague: Martinus Nijhoff, 1967.

Aquinas, Thomas. *Questiones Disputatae de veritate*. Ed. R. Spiazzi. Editio VIII. Rome: Marietti, 1949.

————. *Summa Theologiae*. Cura et studio Instituti Studiorum Medievalium Ottaviensis. College Dominicain d'Ottawa, 1941.

Barth, Karl. *The Word of God and the Word of Man*. Trans. D. Horton. N.p.: The Pilgrim Press, 1928.

Bonaventure (St.). *The Mind's Road to God*. Trans. G. Boas. The Library of Liberal Arts. Indianapolis: Bobbs-Merrill Co., 1953.

Dourley, John P. *Paul Tillich and Bonaventure: An Evaluation of Tillich's Claim to Stand in the Augustinian-Franciscan Tradition*. Leiden: Brill, 1975.

Fink, Eugen. *Spiel als Weltsymbol*. Stuttgart: Kohlhammer, 1960.

————. "The Ontology of Play," *Philosophy Today*, 18 (Summer, 1974), 147-61.

Freemantle, Anne. *Ancilla to the Presocratic Philosophers*. Oxford: Basil Blackwell, 1962.

Hegel: Texts and Commentary. Trans. and ed. W. Kaufmann. Garden City N. Y.: Doubleday Anchor Books, 1966.

Husserl, Edmund. *Logical Investigations*. Trans. J. N. Findlay. New York: Humanities Press, 1970.

The Jerusalem Bible. Garden City, N. Y.: Doubleday, 1966.

Kierkegaard's Concluding Unscientific Postscript. Trans. D. Swenson and W. Lowrie. Princeton: at the University Press, 1941.

Kierkegaard's Fear and Trembling and The Sickness Unto Death. Trans. W. Lowrie. Garden City, N. Y.: Doubleday Anchor Books, 1954.

Kirk, G. S. *Heraclitus: The Cosmic Fragments.* Cambridge, at the University Press, 1962.

Krell, David. "Towards an Ontology of Play: Eugen Fink's Notion of *Spiel*," *Research in Phenomenology*, II (1972), 62-93.

Malcolm, Norman. *Ludwig Wittgenstein: A Memoir.* London: Oxford University Press, 1962.

Marcel, Gabriel. *Homo Viator: Introduction to a Metaphysic of Hope.* Trans. E. Craufurd. New York: Harper & Row, 1962.

————. *Tragic Wisdom and Beyond.* Trans. S. Jolin and P. McCormick. Northwestern University Studies in Phenomenology and Existential Philosophy. Evanston, 1973.

Maritain, Jacques. *Existence and the Existent.* Trans. L. Galantiere and G. Phelan. Garden City, N. Y.: Doubleday Image Books, 1956.

————. *A Preface to Metaphysics: Seven Lectures on Being.* New York: Mentor Omega Books, 1962.

Nietzsche, Friedrich. *Beyond Good and Evil.* Trans. R. J. Hollingdale. Baltimore: Penguin Books, 1973.

————. *The Will to Power.* Trans. W. Kaufmann and R. J. Hollingdale. New York: Vintage Books, 1967.

Rosenberg, Alfred. *Der Mythus des 20. Jahrhunderts.* 12. Auflage. München, 1933.

Schopenhauer, Arthur. *The World As Will and Idea.* Trans. R. B. Haldane and J. Kemp. 3 Vols. London: Routledge and Kegan Paul, 1957.

Smith, Huston. *The Religions of Man.* New York: Harper & Row, Colophon Books, 1958.

Suzuki, D. T. *An Introduction to Zen Buddhism.* New York: Grove Press, 1964.

Tillich, Paul. *A History of Christian Thought.* Ed. C. Braaten. New York: Harper & Row, 1968.

————. *The Theology of Culture.* Ed. R. C. Kimball. New York: Oxford University Press, 1964.

INDEX

Abgrund (Abyss), in Eckhart, 8, 106, 180, 190, 249; in Heidegger, 8, 24, 29, 40, 58, 69, 80, 81, 98, 247
Adamszewski, Z., 163, 275n9
Albertus Magnus, 101, 111, 229
Allers, R., 272n1
Althaus, H., 273n1
Ambrose, St., 115
analogy between Heidegger and Eckhart, meaning of term, 143-4, 232; limits of, 29-30, 144-5, 155, 161-2, 170-3, 183-5, 188-9, 202, 216-7, 219-20, 223-40, 245-51, 252-3, 254-5; see also "mystical element"
analogy, scholastic theory of, 148, 200
Angelus Silesius, vi, 9, 40, 48, 50, 60-6, 72, 79, 88, 89, 97-100, 102, 122, 123, 124, 126, 139, 140, 141, 142, 182, 188, 189, 190, 191, 192, 197, 212, 215, 221, 245, 273n1, 276n24
Anwesen (presencing), 78, 183, 226
anxiety, 21-3, 26, 247
Aquinas, St. Thomas, 15, 101, 103, 106, 111, 135, 137, 143, 200, 229, 233, 265, 271n6, 274n8, 274n11, 275n21
Aristotle, 1, 3, 10, 16, 29, 52, 79, 103, 107, 108, 110-1, 137, 143, 148, 151, 154, 200, 231, 258, 265, 268
Augustine, St., 37, 101, 113, 117, 126, 225, 226, 229, 231, 233, 234

axioms, 52-4

Baader, F. von, 102
Barrett, W., 204
Barth, K., 278n22
Beaufret, J., 272n1
Being, and ontological difference, 19-20, 43, 196; and play, 58, 80-9; as ground, 40, 64-5, 72, 189; epochs of, 76-7, 82-3; see also "*Ereignis*," "*Geschick*"
Benz, E., 198, 202, 204, 274n7, 276n17
Bernard of Clairvaux, St., 118
Biemel, W., 41-2, 44, 70, 223, 272n13, 277n2
Birault, H., 278n19
Bodenständigkeit, 57-8, 219
Bodhidarma, 204, 216
Boehme, J., 98, 102, 126
Boethius, 198, 246
Bonaventure, St., 6, 277n8
Buddha, 209

Cajetan, Cardinal, 143, 275n2
Cicero, 77
Clark, J., 274n4
Congar, Y., 199
Cyril of Alexandria, 115

Degenhardt, I., 274n6

289